T0355171

The Making of American Buddhism

The Making of American Buddhism

SCOTT A. MITCHELL

OXFORD
UNIVERSITY PRESS

OXFORD
UNIVERSITY PRESS

Oxford University Press is a department of the University of Oxford. It furthers
the University's objective of excellence in research, scholarship, and education
by publishing worldwide. Oxford is a registered trade mark of Oxford University
Press in the UK and certain other countries.

Published in the United States of America by Oxford University Press
198 Madison Avenue, New York, NY 10016, United States of America.

Library of Congress Cataloging-in-Publication Data
Names: Mitchell, Scott A., 1973– author.
Title: The making of American Buddhism / Scott A. Mitchell.
Description: 1. | New York : Oxford University Press, 2023. |
Includes bibliographical references and index.
Identifiers: LCCN 2022060514 (print) | LCCN 2022060515 (ebook) |
ISBN 9780197641569 (hardback) | ISBN 9780197641583 (epub)
Subjects: LCSH: Buddhism—United States—History.
Classification: LCC BQ732 .M578 2023 (print) | LCC BQ732 (ebook) |
DDC 294.30973—dc23/eng/20230119
LC record available at https://lccn.loc.gov/2022060514
LC ebook record available at https://lccn.loc.gov/2022060515

DOI: 10.1093/oso/9780197641569.001.0001

Printed by Sheridan Books, Inc., United States of America

For David Ryoe Matsumoto

Contents

Figures

Acknowledgments

This is a book about the possibility-making labor of often unseen and uncredited persons; therefore, it is appropriate that I begin these acknowledgments with Theo Caldera, Zara Cannon-Mohammed, Aimee Wright, and their teams at Oxford University Press. Without their unseen but deeply valued labor, there would be no book in your hands.

A deep bow and *gasshō* of gratitude is extended to the members of the Berkeley Buddhist Temple, past-present-future, without whom none of what follows would be possible. In particular, I wish to thank Rev. Kiyonobu Kuwahara, Lucy Hamai, Madeline Kubo, and Bradley Menda for making temple archives available, giving permission for images, and generally being patient with the questions of this insufferable scholar. Further thanks are owed to Hoshina Seki, Sei Shohara, Rick Stambul, Kenneth Tanaka, Mark Unno, Seigen Yamaoka, and the Imamura family, in particular Hiro Imamura David. どうもありがとうございます.

A great many people read early drafts and book proposals, engaged me in conversation over drinks or in passing on the sidewalk at conferences, challenged me in overly pedantic Twitter threads, or invited me to give talks where I further developed the ideas in this book. Thanks go to Courtney Bruntz, Michael Conway, Ralph Craig III, Mitsuya Dake, Daniel Friedrich, Ann Gleig, Lisa Grumbach, Chenxing Han, Arthur Holder, Jamie Hubbard, Jane Iwamura, Richard Jaffe, Daijaku Judith Kinst, Bryan Lowe, Jessica Main, Michael Masatsugu, Levi McLaughlin, David McMahan, Victoria Montrose, Eisho Nasu, Aaron Proffitt, Natalie Quli, Jeff Schroeder, Naomi Seidman, Caroline Starkey, Justin Stein, Jolyon Baraka Thomas, Duncan Ryûken Williams, Devin Zuber, and many others for their encouragement, support, and feedback. Special thanks to Jessica Main for hosting one of the more coherent public presentations I gave on this work; to Ann Gleig for taking on the alt-right; and to Aaron Proffitt for hosting an ongoing reading group on the *Kyōgyōshinshō* that kept me grounded. Everyone, including myself, is indebted to Brian Nagata. And thanks go to Paul Fuller for an unexpected and deeply appreciated tweet of support. Hope you like Chapter 1.

I am thankful for the advice from Justin Ritzinger and Richard Payne that brought me to Oxford University Press. I am doubly grateful to Richard both for being a supportive mentor for the entirety of my academic career and for having a copy of the *Śrīmālādevī Sutra* lying around his office, thus inspiring my discussion in Chapter 5.

As always, our students are our greatest teachers. I am particularly thankful for my comrades in HRHS-5526—CJ Sokugan Dunford, Aki Rogers, Landon Yamaoka, and Thomas Calobrisi. Thanks also go to Todd Tsuchiya and his excellent work on Buddhist taiko and generational trauma. I am also grateful for the kindness of former students and colleagues, in particular Ichido Kikukawa and Takashi Miyaji for their assistance with some of the Japanese material. As always, all errors in translation are my own.

Similarly, whereas all errors in my analysis of labor, gender, and religion are my own, I would not have been able to think through these issues were it not for the generosity and above all brilliance of Gwendolyn Gillson, Paulina Kolata, and Jessica Starling, who invited me to their reading group. Profound appreciation for your support and encouragement.

An apology and a word of thanks are due to Harry Gyokyo Bridge—apologies for forgetting him in the acknowledgments to my last book, and thanks for being over these many decades a true *kalyāṇamitra*. Thanks also go to Alyson Shively and Yvonne Leung for decades of unwavering friendship.

A special note of thanks to Jeff Wilson for being an early reviewer, for supplying me with his own notes and contacts, and for generally being an excellent conversation partner. It is often said in academia that we are interested in niche subjects that only a handful of people know anything or care at all about; I am grateful that someone as generous and kind as Jeff is one of the few people in the world who knows this history, can catch my mistakes, and cares so deeply for the subject. (Let's get to organizing that Shin Buddhism and *Star Trek* panel at AAR, shall we?)

Acknowledgment must be made of my brother, Eric, who passed away during the final editing of the manuscript. An early draft of the epilogue was written on my way to San Diego to be with him and support our family, an experience that brought home to me in an immediate and visceral way the fundamental truths of samsara, *duḥkha*, birth, sickness, and death. I'd have never become a scholar were it not for his optimistic belief that I was smarter than I believed. We had a good run, big brother. Thanks for teaching me all your best tricks. (Thanks, too, go to Julianna Vermeys for putting up with my random texts during this time and David Sciarretta for taking care of his girls.)

This book is dedicated to Rev. Dr. David Ryoe Matsumoto. Through various causes and conditions, we were thrust together as dean and president, destined to spend our days wading through institutional polices and budgets and far less interesting things than the subject of this book. But somehow we found the time to digress to matters of history (and sci-fi), and his unwavering support of this project was a constant guide, inspiration, and imperative to see it through to completion. My only hope is that the final product lives up to expectations.

And finally, as always, I am deeply grateful to my wife and daughter, Dana and Cleo, for their support and encouragement, for being patient while I spent hours, days, weeks lost in archives, communing more with the dead than the living. And especially to Dana, for valuable feedback on grant proposals and early drafts. As I said over dinner the night of the Albatross (you know the one), were it not for you, I would not be here. And I remain profoundly grateful.

Prologue: Kashiwagi's Narrative

The final piece of the 1956 volume of the *Berkeley Bussei* is "A Narrative" by Hiroshi Kashiwagi. He opens his informal essay with "As a child I had little or no religion," noting that the Buddhist temple was in another town and thus the family rarely went. Kashiwagi's father, who owned a fish market in Loomis, California, would occasionally deliver the best, most beautiful fish to the temple's minister, but after the minister was reassigned, his father stopped this practice. Kashiwagi continues:

> Perhaps father was a Buddhist who was not Christian, that is, disliking Japanese Christians he was a prouder Buddhist. He said that Christians were always shaking his hand and slapping him on the back and asking him, "How are you Mr. . . . ," in English. . . . Father said that Japanese Christians were trying not only to be Christian but white as well. I think that this is what bothered him most of all. From many bitter experiences in America he could only see himself as an outsider and he was always telling me that though I was born an American I could not forget my Japanese background. . . . In his way father was preparing me for what was to come.[1]

Hiroshi Kashiwagi was born in Sacramento in 1922 to Japanese immigrants, the eldest of three children. Early in his life, the family attempted to make ends meet on farms in California's Central Valley. By the early 1930s, they had settled in Loomis. Kashiwagi's father defied the local custom of closing shop on Sundays because his customers were mostly Japanese immigrants and their children, customers who labored on white-owned farms and had one day off a week to shop for the Japanese goods the Kashiwagi family sold. This defiance of local custom would later be recounted in Kashiwagi's memoir, *Swimming in the American*, when a local businessman came to the fish shop and demanded that they close on Sundays. The young Kashiwagi served as translator between his father and the white businessman. An argument ensued. The father demanded the white man leave his store, and afterward Kashiwagi recalled that he "was glad it was over. This was an adult problem, a fearful one, with all the tensions underlying it, and I felt caught in the middle."[2]

Such encounters between the Japanese and white population were, of course, not uncommon. In his "Narrative," Kashiwagi writes:

Slowly I was to learn what it meant to be a Nisei. There were the usual child-hood skirmishes and name calling was common practice. But a child has a short memory of unpleasant things. In high school it was a little different. There I learned about various places—places on the bus, places to eat lunch, places for them, and places for us.

Kashiwagi, the child of an immigrant family, was born an American cit-izen, a Nisei. The Nisei were often "caught in the middle," trapped between the expectations of their parents (which were colored by their experiences as perpetual outsiders) to be Japanese, on the one hand, and the expectation, the desire, to be fully American, on the other. The Japanese Christians derided by his father had chosen one response to this dilemma—conversion. And cer-tainly there were other young Nisei who chose to assimilate, who chose to associate more with their white friends than with other Nisei, as Kashiwagi implies when he writes: "Gradually I made friends, more Caucasians than Niseis. . . . By graduation I was firmly convinced that I was an American first, last, and always, and being a Nisei was just incidental. And what about Buddhism? That was my old man's religion. But then the war came and with it evacuation."

But then the war came. One narrative would posit that everything changed for America on December 7, 1941, when the Empire of Japan attacked Pearl Harbor. But for Japanese immigrants and their children living in the United States it was but another chapter in an ongoing narrative of anti-Japanese racism, discrim-ination, and betrayal, one that culminated in President Roosevelt's signing of Executive Order 9066 and the subsequent forced removal of the entire Japanese American population from the West Coast and into concentration camps for most of the war.

The Kashiwagi family was initially separated; the father was hospitalized with tuberculosis shortly before the outbreak of war. Kashiwagi, his mother, and siblings were sent first to Arboga Assembly Center and then, a few months later, to Tule Lake, on the remote northern border of California. He would stay there for the next four years. While some were allowed to leave this camp, usually transferred to other camps across the country, Tule Lake became the destina-tion for those who refused to answer the loyalty questionnaire.[3] Kashiwagi was among them, unwilling to volunteer for the armed services and bitter that he was asked to forswear allegiance to the Japanese Empire when he had been born here, in California—an American citizen.

"But the war ended and you came back," he writes in his 1956 "Narrative," abruptly shifting to the second person.

> Out of the wreckage you picked up the broken pieces and began to rebuild. It was slow and painful at first, yet quiet almost meditative. You began to see; for the first time in your life you began to see because a part of you stood aside and watched. There were no illusions this time, only truth. You were an American yes, but this did not mean being a poor copy of another American; it meant being what you were. You had an identity which was plain as the name and the face you bore. Why hide it? Why distort it? Why not live with it?[4]

What is elided in this passage is one consequence of Kashiwagi's camp experience: in 1943, he renounced his U.S. citizenship. Whatever efforts he had made in his youth to be an American, to embrace his American identity, were disrupted by the evacuation, a betrayal of his Americanness, and like nearly five thousand other American citizens, he faced the prospect of being deported to Japan. The decision to renounce his citizenship haunted him, and in the postwar years, with the support of a civil rights attorney, he sued the government to have it reinstated.[5] But this process was still ongoing in 1956 when "A Narrative" was written. Kashiwagi was still picking up the broken pieces, still rebuilding his identity, though this time not as a "poor copy" of an American but as a Japanese American. "Why hide it?"

"And what about Buddhism?" His old man's religion?

> Inexorably you were drawn by your senses to the culture of Japan—the language, the history, and the religion. You seemed to understand it, feel it. Then you realized that you were very much a part of it. The habits and manners were you; the music was you; the colors were you; the awe of nature was you; and the simplicity, the order, the spirit, the calm—all were you.[6]

* * *

The unlawful incarceration of Japanese and Japanese American citizens during World War II looms large in scholarly accounts of Japanese American history and American Buddhism. This event, for some, remains an open wound; for others, a scar, a reminder of the darkest days not only of personal or family histories but also of our collective history, of American history. Following decades of anti-Japanese sentiment, once Japanese Americans were rounded up and put on trains and buses to the hinterlands of the American West, Japanese-owned businesses, homes, and land were sold off or stolen. Buddhist temples were shuttered, many were vandalized, and religious objects were lost, buried, or burned to protect people from the frenzy of war.[7] After four years of incarceration, the internees were given twenty dollars and bus fare. Some returned to their prewar hometowns, others scattered across the country building new homes, new communities—and most tried to put the camps behind them, not wanting to dwell in this collective trauma.

What happened next? How did the community rebuild? And what role did Buddhism play in the process? Kashiwagi's narrative demonstrates the rupture pre- and postwar, the conflict of being Japanese and being American at midcentury. In some ways, his narrative suggests a healing process, a reconciliation of his Japanese and American selves; in others, it suggests something unfinished—why the switch to second person, the switch from "I" to "you"? On the one hand, perhaps we can read this as a work in progress, a subtle distancing of this process of reconciliation; he's just not quite there yet, not in 1956. On the other hand, perhaps the "you" is literal. Perhaps Kashiwagi is speaking directly to his audience, to his fellow Nisei Buddhists who are also struggling to reconcile their pre- and postwar selves, their Japanese and American identities, and pointing a way forward. It is not a personal or individual quest for reconciliation but a communal one.

And yet "A Narrative" was published in a philosophical and literary magazine, produced by the Berkeley Buddhist Temple, that in the 1950s was publishing not only the work of Nisei authors but that of white scholars, philosophers, and poets as well. Prior to the war, white Americans were responsible for the mass incarceration of the Japanese population in the United States, and Buddhism in that moment was branded as the religion of the enemy, something to be feared and rejected. By the late 1950s, Buddhism was becoming more and more acceptable as the religion of Beat poets, countercultural hippies, and avant-garde artists. How was this change made possible? How did the religion of the enemy so quickly turn into the religion of peace, an acceptable alternative religion for white America? And what role did Japanese Americans play in this transformation? If Kashiwagi's narrative was published alongside poems by Gary Snyder and essays by Alan Watts, are Snyder and Watts part of the collective "you" he is speaking to in his narrative?

In what follows, I explore these questions through an examination of an important midcentury Buddhist publication, the *Berkeley Bussei*. I hope to reconcile parts of American Buddhism's identity, betwixt and between its Asian, Asian American, and white American selves. In locating the origins of the late twentieth-century popularization of Buddhism in the midcentury activities of the Japanese American Buddhist community, I recenter their voices and their experiences, both before and after the camps. Inspired by Hiroshi Kashiwagi, I hope to find a direction, a way forward, for scholars and Buddhists alike to think through and narrate their collective history. Rather than foregrounding the trauma of the war or the activities of white converts, I think through a series of false choices, the rhetoric of rupture, and unhelpful binaries. I ask, *what if?* What might American Buddhist history look like had the events in the following chapters never happened? In this speculative space, I offer an alternative telling of American Buddhist history and, to paraphrase the conclusion of Kashiwagi's narrative, show how different the world seems, how full of wonder.

Introduction

Buddhism Rephrased

In March 1941, the California Young Buddhist League held its fifth annual convention, a four-day event that brought nearly a thousand young Japanese American Buddhists to Los Angeles's Little Tokyo neighborhood. Meetings and Buddhist services were held at the Nishi Honganji Los Angeles Temple and Betsuin. Conventioneers were treated to sightseeing tours of the Huntington Gardens and NBC Radio City and an elaborate banquet at the Deauville Beach Club in Santa Monica. In addition to business meetings and elections for league leaders, there were debates and ping-pong tournaments, seminars on home economics and agriculture, basketball games, and the Sayonara Ball, which closed the event. There was, to be sure, a good deal of drinking, smoking, and laughing interspersed with serious and spontaneous debate and conversation about a wide range of things, from Buddhism to politics to gossip. In this way, the convention was as much a social affair as a religious one. For some young attendees reflecting on their time at the convention while riding a rented bus home to the San Francisco Bay Area, what lingered were memories of the elaborate banquet, glimpses of Hollywood landmarks, and "the many new acquaintances made and the strengthening of former ties, that 'big stuff' feeling of tossing tips, and the general hectic life of a convention [that] will linger and bring back a pleasant smile or two for many years to come."[1] Indeed, these young Buddhists were just that—young—many still in college or even high school and free of their parents' oversight, having a good time, and connecting on multiple levels: personal, cultural, spiritual.

The convention's religious aims, of course, were not merely incidental; Buddhism was the primary reason for the gathering. Between ping-pong and Hollywood tours, banquets and dancing were dharma talks (sermons), classes and workshops about Buddhist thought and practice, leadership elections, and planning meetings about how to further develop Young Buddhist Associations and, ultimately, propagate the dharma (Buddhist teachings). The fact that this was the fifth annual meeting of the Young Buddhist League is telling; it signals the fact that by 1941, there were not only enough local young Buddhist associations across California to create a statewide league but enough young Buddhists to begin with. These young Buddhists were the children of Japanese immigrants

The Making of American Buddhism. Scott A. Mitchell, Oxford University Press. © Oxford University Press 2023.
DOI: 10.1093/oso/9780197641569.003.0001

who had begun to arrive in the continental United States in the 1890s. By the mid-1930s, not only were local associations, clubs, and organizations for young Buddhists being formed, but networks began linking them across the state and, eventually, the nation.

The convention included ample time for socializing and networking but also time for leadership training and religious teaching. There were numerous public presentations and talks about the nature of the "Buddhist movement in America." One speaker was the "head of the Buddhist Brotherhood of America," the Rev. Julius Goldwater.[2] He noted:

> During the Convention it became increasingly clear that the Bussei are willing to accept Japanese Buddhism, but for understanding purposes, for living purposes, they want intensely American Buddhism. What is American Buddhism?
>
> American Buddhism is the simple teachings to be found in Buddhism rephrased in American terminology to the extent that with every contact there is immediate vitality in association with the living today. How may this be accomplished? Will it be accomplished?
>
> When Buddhism entered Korea, China, Japan it had first to take on the consciousness of the country in order to appeal to, assist and prove helpful to the peoples of those countries; the same is true in this country. We will have an American Buddhism because the need is recognized to be as great as the want for it within us all. That now with the beginning, we should be ultra-careful to preserve the true values and allow the incidentals to fall by the way.[3]

Goldwater opens his remarks with reference to the "Bussei," a term generally understood to be an abbreviation of *bukkyō seinenkai*, or Young Buddhist Association (YBA), but here used more as a term of identity. The Bussei he is addressing were Nisei (second-generation) Japanese American Buddhists. His remarks were published in the spring 1941 edition of the *Berkeley Bussei*, published by the Berkeley YBA. By comparing the introduction of Buddhism to America to its past introductions to Korea, China, and Japan, Goldwater argues that Buddhism needs to be rephrased in local terms while preserving its true values and letting go "the incidentals." His observations in the 1940s echo sentiments expressed by American Buddhists a generation later—namely, the desire to strip away the "cultural baggage" of Buddhism-as-imported-religion and locate the essence of the teachings, the "heartwood," as something transcendent and ahistorical.[4] This rephrased Buddhism would then become American Buddhism. In his talk, Goldwater asks: What is American Buddhism? Contributors to the *Bussei* answered this question time and again in familiarly modernist terms. Buddhism is consistently presented as a rational religion, commensurate with modern science, inherently civilizing and pacific, and superior to other religions because of its lack of dogma and superstition. Across the print run of the *Bussei*, from its prewar origins in 1939 through the final 1960 volume, one finds repeated reference to this American Buddhism and an oft-expressed desire to make Buddhism relevant to America. Whereas from our present vantage point this characterization of Buddhism and its relevance might seem obvious, it is important to remember that in the 1930s and 1940s, for most Americans, Buddhism was the religion of the enemy.

Since the arrival of Chinese and Japanese immigrants to the United States in the late nineteenth century, Asian immigrants had been subjected to intense racial prejudice. This prejudice from the white Christian majority manifested in immigration restrictions, discriminative property ownership and housing laws, and the foreclosure of even the possibility of naturalization. For Japanese immigrating to Hawai'i and the West Coast mainland, this prejudice dovetailed with religious animosity against "Mikadoism," a conflation of "emperor worship" and Buddhism that was used as evidence of Japanese immigrants' inherent incompatibility with American cultural and civic life.[5] As the Empire of Japan expanded its influence across the Pacific in the early decades of the twentieth century, the situation only became worse. Japan was an economic threat, one that stood in the way of America's own dreams of empire. First-generation (Issei) Japanese immigrants looking to avoid suspicion in their adopted homeland impressed upon their children the necessity of being good citizens. Their Nisei children, of course, were well aware of the contradictions of American racial and religious politics, the promise and denial of equality. So for Nisei Buddhists to argue that Buddhism was modern, that it was American—indeed, that America *needed* Buddhism—was also an argument for their own status as Americans, as natural-born citizens of the United States. One must remember that for young Japanese American Buddhists at midcentury, their religious identity was always bound up with their identity as Nisei, as Asian Americans.[6] Thus, Nisei Buddhists' answer to Goldwater's question "What is American Buddhism?" would necessarily reflect their experiences as racial and religious others.

As the children of immigrants, Nisei were caught between two worlds. On the one hand, they needed to live up to the expectations of their parents and retain their Japanese culture, language, and religion. On the other, as American citizens, they desired the same opportunities and successes as their white friends and contemporaries. Throughout the 1940s and 1950s, within this intergenerational space, one finds the discourse of assimilation not just in the *Bussei* but in the Japanese American community writ large. Assimilation was necessary if the Japanese were to thrive in the United States. But how? To assimilate one needed to work hard, be a good citizen, and contribute something to society, rhetoric that plays well to the self-determination ethos of American culture. And for some Nisei, with assimilation came conversion.[7] America is a Christian nation; why stand out by retaining the religion of Japan? For others, this was naive. They knew too well that Nisei could pretend to be white but that they would always be marked as other. And for those Nisei committed to their Buddhist faith, the idea of conversion was a nonstarter. One finds in the pages of the *Bussei* ample assimilationist rhetoric whereby the Nisei are implored to work hard and contribute to American society, but this assimilation does not come at the cost of their religious faith. Indeed, Nisei claim that if they are to contribute something to America, they will contribute Buddhism.

Buddhism-as-contribution is directly related to Buddhism-as-modern. In arguing for assimilation as Buddhists, both before and after the camps, Nisei simultaneously "rephrase" Buddhism in modernist language and argue that this modern Buddhism is their contribution to America. Nisei position themselves as ideally suited for this contributive work. Because they are Japanese, Buddhism is their cultural inheritance; because they are American, they are perfectly positioned to offer and explain Buddhism to other Americans. Nisei thereby become bridges between East and West. In 1952, the resident minister of the Berkeley Temple expresses this sentiment succinctly when he writes that "it is on the shoulders of the Nisei and Sansei, the inheritors of both the Eastern and Western cultures, to bring the true Buddhism to the West and help enrich the American way of life."[8] The case for Buddhism's relevance is made in part through a critique of American and Western culture. Nisei claim that whereas Buddhism is compatible with science, science is limited and potentially dangerous, as evidenced by, among other things, nuclear weapons. In the Cold War, the *Bussei* argues, people are adrift and looking for meaning, a task for which dogmatic Christianity is ill-equipped; Buddhism has a proven history as a civilizing and cultural force, a wellspring of ancient wisdom. Because Nisei inherit Buddhism from their parents but have been raised in America, they rhetorically cast themselves as being in the best position to offer this modernist vision of Buddhism to America. To make this happen, however, they must prove themselves as American, must present themselves as moral, hardworking, and faithful persons. And in doing so, Buddhism will be seen as something of value, as that which will bring together the once enemies and now friends of Japan and the United States.

This bridge-building is not merely metaphorical. The literal bringing together of East and West can be read in three distinct ways inside and outside the pages of the *Bussei*. First, whereas this articulation of a modern American Buddhism functioned as part of a larger assimilationist rhetoric for Nisei Buddhists, they were not alone in this project, walled off in an "ethnic fortress."[9] White sympathizers and converts were involved in the process of rephrasing Buddhism in American terminology. Goldwater is far from the first or last white American contributor to the *Bussei*. The rephrasing of Buddhism as modern and American was as likely to be done by Hiroshi Kashiwagi and Jane Imamura as by Gary Snyder and Alan Watts. Indeed, by the early 1950s, the activities at the Berkeley Buddhist Temple were attracting the attention of West Coast countercultural artists and poets as well as budding intellectuals and scholars who contributed essays, translations, and poetry to the *Bussei*. Collectively, these white converts to Buddhism have been named responsible for ushering in the "Zen boom" in the later 1950s and 1960s.[10] The first way to understand this bridge-building is to understand how Nisei made bridges with white sympathizers in America, how they created multiethnic and pansectarian communities.[11] The second way one can read this bridge-building is to see it within Nisei themselves. When Goldwater writes that the Bussei (i.e., Nisei) accept a Japanese Buddhism but desire an American one, he is hinting at their own dual or internalized location between East and West, the chasm between the two bridged by this process of rephrasing Buddhism. In this way, to offer Buddhism to American society is to offer it to themselves, a sentiment Jane Imamura suggests when she writes in 1952 that Nisei prefer services in English, prefer Western-style music to the "Oriental tone" of Japanese Buddhism.[12] Finally, the bridging of East and West happened in the postwar period through physical travel. Either as tourists, by studying in Japanese universities, or as part of the Allied occupation of Japan, Nisei Buddhists traveled across the Pacific. Showing up in the *Bussei* as conference reports, letters home, and reflections on religion in Japan and America, these experiences tell the story of what Michael Masatsugu calls the pan-Pacific Buddhist world.[13] Some Nisei remark how out of place they feel in their ancestral homeland or how America provides much more fertile ground for the development of Buddhism. Apart from merely reading about their experiences, we can trace connections, networks, and the religious infrastructure that allows for the spread of religious ideas, discourses, and persons. In these dispatches from Japan, we can see the movement of D. T. Suzuki and other Japanese Buddhist scholars, postcolonial and anti-communist Buddhist political confraternities, and the emergence of academic Buddhist studies itself.

This, at last, is perhaps the greatest contribution Nisei Buddhists made to American society—not Buddhism per se, but the *possibility* of Buddhism. In making communities, in starting magazines and publication projects, in hosting scholars and conventions, in organizing translation and scholarly projects, Nisei Buddhists built religious infrastructure. Without this infrastructure, the Buddhist modernists, Beat poets, and white converts who are usually credited with popularizing Buddhism in the later twentieth century would not have had places to publish their ideas nor communities in which to learn Buddhist practice. Religious infrastructure is a necessary precondition for the spread and popularization of Buddhism, and in the case of the United States, this infrastructure was first built by immigrants and their children, by Japanese American Jōdo Shinshū Buddhists.

The Making of American Buddhism is a story about the intersection of race and religion in the United States before, during, and after World War II, when Nisei Buddhists reacted to the trauma of racial and religious discrimination by laying claim to an American identity inclusive of their religious identity. In the pages of temple-supported magazines such as the *Berkeley Bussei*, Nisei argued that Buddhism was both what made them good Americans and what they had to contribute to America, a rational and scientific religion of peace. And whereas this rhetorical work was often done in the *Bussei*, this study also explores the behind-the-scenes labor that made these rhetorical articulations possible. The *Bussei* was one among many publication projects that were part of educational and propagational programs embedded within Japanese American Buddhist communities and connected via national and transnational networks that shaped and allowed for the spread of modernist Buddhist ideas in the 1950s.

The *Berkeley Bussei* was a publication of the Berkeley Buddhist Temple's Young Buddhist Association. The Berkeley Buddhist Temple was established in 1911 by Japanese immigrants who practiced in the Pure Land Jōdo Shinshū Buddhist tradition. As the community matured and the second generation was born, two groups for young Buddhists were formed, one for men and one for women, which merged in 1934 into the Young Buddhist Association. Due to discriminatory housing practices in Berkeley at the time, Japanese American students studying at the University of California and other nearby colleges had difficulty finding housing. To address this problem, the Berkeley Temple opened a dormitory for Nisei college students, one for women and a separate one for men, named Jichiryo.[14] This influx of young Japanese Buddhists in the prewar years created a dynamic and creative community that precipitated the publication of the *Berkeley Bussei* and many related publications across the Bay Area and the West Coast.[15] Beginning as a biannual publication in 1939, the YBA produced the *Bussei* through early 1942, publishing its last edition on the eve of the forced evacuation of Japanese and Japanese Americans from the West Coast.[16] Following their release from the camps and resettlement, YBA activities resumed in Berkeley and so did the *Bussei*, now as an annual journal running from 1950 to 1960.[17] Most volumes were published and distributed early in the calendar year and reported on club events from the previous year. Early on, the *Bussei* not only published religious and philosophical essays but also published reports on the activities of and membership information about the YBA. Such reports and occasional gossip columns reveal the day-to-day lives of the young Buddhists, some still in high school but most in college or even graduate programs at the university, as well as their connections to other Buddhist groups across California and the Pacific. In the prewar volumes and through 1953, the *Bussei* included a Japanese-language section with articles written by many of the same contributors to the English section. Beginning in 1954, the *Bussei* became more and more exclusively a religious and literary magazine. YBA activity reports stop being published, as does the Japanese-language section. The amount of poetry increases, as does the overall print and production quality. Whereas the 1957 volume may represent the apex of the *Bussei*'s run, the final 1960 volume is the slimmest and is almost entirely poetry.[18] I use the *Bussei* and corresponding activities in Berkeley as a case study to discuss the intersection of religion and race in the making of American Buddhism. In addition to the *Bussei*, this study relies on contemporaneous Buddhist and Japanese American publications, including Japanese language newspapers and publications by other Young Buddhist Associations; official community histories compiled by the Buddhist Churches of America and the Berkeley Buddhist Temple; collections held at the Bancroft Library of the University of California, Berkeley, in particular the Japanese American Evacuation and Resettlement Records; memoirs and oral histories; and an uncatalogued collection of personal papers, letters, and other ephemera belonging to Kanmo and Jane Imamura.[19] Whereas this book is focused primarily on the Berkeley community and activities immediately before and after the war, I argue in part that Nisei Buddhists built on a foundation laid by their Issei parents and that their work had repercussions for Buddhism's reception well past midcentury. In this way, I draw a connection between the pre- and postwar periods, and the following chapters shift from the late 1800s to the early 1960s as our vision expands and contracts from a single temple in Berkeley to pan-Pacific networks.[20]

In the interest of full disclosure, it should be noted that the work of Nisei Buddhists at the Berkeley Buddhist Temple resulted in the establishment of a study center that, in the 1960s, incorporated as the Institute of Buddhist Studies— the institute at which I am currently employed. My connection to this community has given me substantial access to archives, persons, and histories not readily available to the general public or average academic researcher; from this point of view, my association with the community is of great value. From another point of view, this connection could be construed as a great liability. The reader may be right in asking if I have the proper critical distance from my subject. As I will discuss in Chapter 5 and in the conclusion, however, I believe this question is misguided; in a very real sense, the entire field of Buddhist studies is indebted to the Buddhist tradition, each of us having some connection to Buddhism and Buddhist practitioners regardless of our own religious commitments. I am also a student of one of my teachers, Duncan Ryūken Williams, who has advocated for "sympathetically understanding" Buddhism as a living tradition and being attentive to the multiple locations and contexts within which we do our work as scholars.[21] What I present in this book is supported and buoyed by a Buddhist community, but it is not an apologetic. Neither is the story that follows my own.

The primary focus of this book is Japanese American Jōdo Shinshū (or Shin) Buddhists who, I argue, are responsible for making American Buddhism possible.[22] In making this claim, I critique a series of false choices and reductive binaries that continue to haunt the study of American Buddhism. Such binaries as Asian/white, traditional/modern, sectarian/universal, and authentic/inauthentic are ill-equipped to account for the complexity of American Buddhist history. Rather than requiring my subjects to choose sides, rather than forcing them into arbitrary categories, I argue that they are fully and simultaneously Asian/American/modern/Shin/Buddhists whose experiences are shaped by their local context and connections to translocal networks. Such a perspective necessitates an interdisciplinary approach, one that draws on the insights of American Buddhism studies, Asian American studies, and transnational religious studies.

Converging Streams, Overlapping Disciplines

A cursory review of scholarship on American Buddhist history reveals a persistent meta-narrative, one that I call a "two-streams" approach to the story of how Buddhism arrived and developed in the United States.[23] This is the first binary, our first false choice. Do we follow the stream of intellectuals, Orientalists, and converts credited with making "American Buddhism"? Or do we tell the story of immigrants and their descendants, often referred to as "Buddhists in America"? In sum, the two-streams meta-narrative highlights mutual exclusivity at the cost of interrelated reciprocity and dubiously suggests a white Buddhist lineage over and against a mass of unrelated and inward-looking Asians.

Buddhism in America/American Buddhism

To begin. Many scholars, when telling the story of how Buddhism made its way West, will begin in colonial Asia. This is the story of how European and later white American colonial civil servants and Orientalists "discovered" Buddhism and began translating Buddhist texts. For example, in *The Buddhist Religion* Richard Robinson and Willard Johnson conclude their survey of Buddhist history and thought with a chapter titled "Buddhism Comes West." After charting centuries of precolonial contact between Asia and Europe, the authors eventually come to the eighteenth century and the "Europeans who . . . began the serious recovery of Buddhist texts and archaeological sites in Asia," a project motivated primarily by the colonial need to learn about the cultures and peoples under their power such "that they could design an enlightened form of colonial rule, one that would combine rational European principles with a sensitivity to local conditions."[24] This narrative, even when framed within a postcolonial or anti-racist scholarly project, invariably becomes a "great men" history, lifting up such figures as Brian Houghton Hodgson and his correspondence with Eugène Burnouf, who is credited with first translating the *Lotus Sutra*, which in turn was translated by Transcendentalists in New England (with Henry David Thoreau usually getting more credit than Elizabeth Peabody, who actually did the work).[25] This activity is often credited as giving inspiration to late nineteenth- and early twentieth-century Theosophists, spiritualists, and other occultists to embrace Buddhism and/or travel to Asia, as Henry Steel Olcott did, and become Buddhists. These figures, in turn, become the main actors in Chicago when Buddhism makes its debut at the World's Parliament of Religions in 1893, which "radically changed the entire landscape for Japanese Buddhism in America."[26] D. T. Suzuki's connection to this event vis-à-vis his teacher, Shaku Sōen, is often used as a bridge between 1893 and the later 1950s, when, seemingly out of nowhere, Buddhism becomes very attractive to a rising generation of young Americans, particularly the Beat poets and, over the next two decades, hippies and other disaffected and countercultural figures who convert to the tradition and are read as popularizing Buddhism into the last decades of the twentieth century.

This stream—a lineage of Orientalists, philosophers, and converts—is contrasted with the immigrant story. This story begins slightly later than the colonialist story with the arrival of Chinese laborers in California following the Gold Rush (which, incidentally, precludes the possibility of taking seriously a theory of pre-Columbian Chinese exploration of the Americas).[27] Owing to the overt and widespread racist discrimination against Chinese immigrants, their ability to establish and maintain Buddhist communities at this time was severely curtailed. By contrast, the slightly later Japanese immigrants—the majority of whom were Jōdo Shinshū Buddhists—were much more successful, establishing Buddhist communities in Hawai'i (before it was a U.S. territory) and the mainland, many of which survive to this day.[28] Their story has been told in great detail and to great effect, noting that even in the face of racial discrimination and illegal incarceration during World War II, they managed to survive and thrive. However, the post-1945 history of Japanese American Buddhism has received substantially less attention. Many studies, such as Michihiro Ama's excellent *Immigrants to the Pure Land*, only cover the prewar period of North American Jōdo Shinshū Buddhist history.[29] In Charles Prebish and Damien Keown's *Introducing Buddhism*, in their chapter devoted to Buddhism outside Asia, Jōdo Shinshū is only mentioned in reference to World War II concentration camps (despite the "radically changed landscape" for Japanese Buddhism ushered in by the World's Parliament of Religions). Whereas individual charismatic Japanese teachers such as Shunryu Suzuki have received their share of scholarly attention, Japanese American Buddhist communities more generally have not. Moreover, with the passage of the Hart-Celler Act in 1965, which reformed racist and restrictive immigration laws in the United States, this narrative stream shifts focus to the large influx of Asian immigrants and refugees, many from South and Southeast Asia, which dramatically increased the number and diversity of Buddhists in North America. No narrative connection is made between these later immigrant communities and those established before World War II; generally speaking, their story is told through the lens of assimilation, acculturation, and racial formation, focusing on the ways Asian American Buddhists either adapt to or resist white American norms.

This two-streams narrative (and it should be clear that it is related to the "two Buddhisms" trope) has several consequences for our understanding of American Buddhist history, obscuring as much as it reveals.[30] Namely, it suggests that white and Asian American Buddhists have had little to do with each other; it rhetorically constructs a white Buddhist lineage; and it strongly suggests that Japanese American Buddhist history generally and Jōdo Shinshū Buddhist history specifically effectively end in the camps.[31]

It is no doubt true that Buddhism arrived in the United States via two streams—more accurately, it could be said that Buddhism has arrived via multiple streams, rivers, tributaries, canals, and so on and so forth. To draw our attention to the multiple ways that Buddhism arrived is not, in itself, problematic and can reveal important and distinct histories. A thorough telling of the lives and activities of Hodgson, say, or Olcott is certainly a worthwhile project. To explore the unique history of Burmese Buddhist refugees in the late twentieth century and place their experiences in conversation with, say, the experiences of Chinese immigrants a century earlier can reveal the multiple and diverse ways Buddhism has spread, adapted, failed, and succeeded in the West. The problem arises when we paint in broad strokes a "history of American Buddhism" that reinforces the idea that these streams are not, in fact, tributaries of a larger river. As Michael Masatsugu writes, "During the 1950s and 1960s the boundaries dividing Japanese American and white convert Buddhists were more fluid than has been assumed and . . . ideas about the form and content of Buddhism in America were open to discussion and debate."[32] I would go further and note that this fluid exchange of ideas, interpretations, and adaptations of Buddhist practice and thought in the West is not limited to the postwar period. For example, when we segregate Olcott to the white Buddhist stream we overlook how he was invited in 1901 by Yemyō Imamura (father of Kanmo, who will figure prominently in this volume) to deliver lectures to the nascent Jōdo Shinshū Buddhist community in Hawai'i.[33] Thus, a white Buddhist convert was an active participant in the development of Japanese American Buddhism, and Japanese American Buddhists actively sought to include white converts within their communities well before and long after World War II.

This narrative of mutual exclusivity has the further consequence of allowing for the construction and maintenance of a white American Buddhist lineage. As mentioned above, the Orientalist narrative begins in colonial Asia with the translation of Buddhist texts. The main thrust of this narrative is that Europeans were primarily interested in locating the essence or "real" religion in the texts, divorced from the lived experiences of Asian Buddhists in situ. While we could pause here and take note of the problematic nature of this project—its concern for origins, its reliance on Orientalist assumptions about the Asian other, the quest for purity, and so forth[34]—many grand narratives of American Buddhist history instead (or in addition) link this project very explicitly to several prominent European and American thinkers (sometimes framed as the "founders" of academic Buddhist studies).[35] The subtext is always that their translation work is to be lauded, regardless of the problematic (colonial) contexts in which that work was done, because the text serves both as the primary mode of transmission and as the metaphorical thread holding the white American Buddhist lineage together.

Stephen Prothero is explicit about this lineage in his introduction to a collection of Beat Generation Buddhist writing, *Big Sky Mind*. He opens with an anecdote about how Jack Kerouac, in the "winter of 1953–54," was inspired by Henry David Thoreau's *Walden* to read Hindu scriptures. This inspiration led him to a San Jose, California, library where he discovered Dwight Goddard's *A Buddhist Bible*, which Prothero suggests set off his long interest in Buddhism and Asian thought. Prothero then goes on: "Other members of the Beat Generation also came to Buddhism by way of books. Philip Whalen may have been the first of the Beats to read about Buddhism."[36] The text is the method of transmission. And if it is unclear that this transmission is to be understood as a lineage, Prothero is explicit: "These literary encounters define a lineage of sorts in the transmission of Buddhism to America—from Thoreau . . . to Dwight Goddard . . . to Jack Kerouac, the Beats, and the writers of the San Francisco Literary Renaissance; to today's American Buddhists."[37] Whereas I do not know when, exactly, in the "winter of 1953–54" Kerouac was at the San Jose library, I do know that he was at the Berkeley Buddhist Temple during the same period. Kerouac—as well as Philip Whalen—published his poems in the *Berkeley Bussei*, evidence that his desire to learn about Buddhism may have initially been *inspired* by books but was not *limited* to books—it included being part of a living community of Buddhists.[38] In short, the rhetorical construction of a white Buddhist lineage depends entirely on transmission through text, and despite running directly through communities of practice in the United States, it conveniently ignores those communities. Moreover, despite there being no direct connection between many of these figures (Thoreau, Goddard, Kerouac, etc.), separated as they are by decades and oceans, their connections and thus their lineage is told and retold in stark contrast to the in-fact lineages and communities with documented histories in the United States dating to the late 1800s.

This is the first lacuna in the two-streams narrative—lineage gaps and the exclusion of Asian American Buddhists who often fill these gaps. The lineage of white Buddhist converts jumps from the World's Parliament of Religions in 1893 to the conversion of Beat poets in the 1950s. D. T. Suzuki (1870–1966) is a central figure here, connecting these two historical moments, but we would do well to recall that he was not actually in the United States for most of this period; apart from some limited engagements and speaking tours in the United States and Europe, for most of the first half of the twentieth century he was in Japan, teaching at Tokyo and Ōtani Universities. On the contrary, Zen, Pure Land, and Nichiren Buddhists were living and practicing in the United States for the entirety of this period, often deeply engaged in propagational activities, making attempts to spread the dharma to white Americans, ordaining white people as priests, and publishing widely in English.[39] If we want to go looking for lineage connections between the Beat Generation and nineteenth-century Buddhist Asia, we must pay attention to this first generation of Asian American Buddhists. A mutually exclusive two-streams narrative is ill-equipped to do this work, as it assumes that the immigrant story is somehow distinct from or disinterested in the white Buddhist narrative.

The second lacuna of this approach is the sidelining of Japanese American Buddhism—and specifically Jōdo Shinshū or Shin Buddhism—to the camps. Whereas the history of American Shin Buddhism has been well told up to the 1940s, very few sustained treatments or monographs of the community post-1945 have been published.[40] Several scholars, including Jane Iwamura, Tetsuden Kashima, Anne Spencer, Karma Lekshe Tsomo, Jeff Wilson, and others, have published journal articles on one aspect of the community or another, and Patricia Usuki's *Currents of Change* deftly examines the role of women within the community both historically and contemporarily.[41] The Buddhist Churches of America (the largest and oldest continually operating Buddhist organization in North America) is certainly given ample attention in book-length treatments of American Buddhism more generally, such as Richard Hughes Seager's *Buddhism in America*. However, Seager's framing of the community as "America's old-line Buddhists," when coupled with other scholars' repeated insistence that the community is dying off, leaves one with the impression that nothing much has happened in American Shin Buddhism since World War II, and, any minute now, the community is going to vanish before our eyes.[42] What I hope to demonstrate in the following chapters is that this narrative is both unfair and false. That is, this lack of scholarship on American Shin Buddhism after the camps is an indication of scholarly oversight, not inaction on the part of Shin Buddhists. In the immediate postwar years, American Shin Buddhism not only recovered from the camp experience but also saw substantial growth, growth that included such projects as the *Berkeley Bussei*, educational programs, and overt attempts to network and promote Buddhism outside the Japanese American community and support of new immigrant groups post-1965. And it was this infrastructure-building that was a necessary precondition for the spread and popularization of Buddhism in the decades to come.

Asian American Studies

The academic study of American Buddhism was made possible in no small part by the work of Charles Prebish. His decision to study Buddhism in the United States was, in the 1970s, a considerable risk. A trained Buddhologist, not only was Prebish's intellectual upbringing rooted in philology and Asia, but the field was not supportive of studies focused on contemporary religion, and the authenticity of American Buddhism was constantly in doubt.[43] In the forty-plus years since his first monograph on the subject, *American Buddhism*, the subfield has grown and matured while, thankfully, influencing the broader field of Buddhist studies to be more inclusive and accepting of a wider range of methodologies and field sites.

It is worth telling this origin story of the subfield of American Buddhism studies and noting its relation to the broader field of Buddhist studies to account for the intellectual commitments and interests of the scholars who have shaped it and policed its borders. Generally speaking, early scholarship on American Buddhism was conducted by scholars located in religious studies and Buddhist studies—that is, scholars well trained in philology and history. Historically, Buddhist studies has been concerned with Asia and textual studies and not particularly interested in Buddhist communities outside Asia, contemporary forms of Buddhism, or Asian American Buddhists. Consequently, some of the early studies of American Buddhism were done by Buddhist scholars well trained in textual studies (or by sociologists outside Buddhist studies). It was not until the 1990s that ethnographic studies began to be published and that Buddhist studies as a field began to take more seriously Buddhisms outside Asia. Arguably, then, the perspectives of Asian American studies did not figure prominently in the field until relatively recently.

Despite the clear and obvious connection between Buddhism and Asian America, scholars of American Buddhism have been slow to adopt the methods and orientations of Asian American studies, ethnic studies, or critical race theory despite an awareness of the varied and at times conflicting racial projects that have shaped the tradition. It was not until the turn of the twenty-first century that Buddhist studies scholars began to more seriously engage with questions or theories of race and racism in their work, with Joseph Cheah's *Race and Religion in American Buddhism* being a prime example.[44] Over the course of the 1990s and early 2000s, a bevy of scholarship was produced on American Buddhism; however, most studies treated white convert and Asian American communities in isolation from each other, reinforcing the two-streams narrative described here. And while scholars such as Jane Iwamura, Sharon Suh, and Duncan Ryûken Williams drew from the insights of Asian American studies, scholarship focused on the "pioneers" of American Buddhism (e.g., white converts to the tradition) seems almost unaware of the insights offered by Asian American religious studies.[45] Again, according to Masatsugu, these mutually exclusive approaches to American Buddhism reinforce the notion that white convert Buddhism is primarily a stream of textual transmission from Asia and, simultaneously, "the notion that Asian American religious practice operated in an ethnic vacuum. This approach supports the portrayal of Asian Americans as a 'model minority'—passive, silent, insular, and largely disengaged" from the broader culture.[46]

On the other hand, Asian American studies, at least as it initially developed, was not predisposed to asking questions about religion. Developing within the intellectual milieu of the civil rights era, early scholarship on Asian America saw an "emphasis on Marxist, postcolonial, postmodernist, and feminist theories . . . [which] neglected to examine Asian Americans' religious experiences, as David Yoo has pointed out, partly because of the scholars' bias against religion as an opiate of the masses and their postcolonial association of Asian Christianity with Western missionary activities."[47] Since the turn of the twenty-first century, the field has taken an increasing interest in Asian American religion, in no small part due to the work of the Asian Pacific American Religions Research Initiative and other scholarly projects.[48] Such work has shed light on how disciplinary boundaries are ill-equipped to capture the fullness of the lived experiences of Asian Americans. This is to say that the field of Asian American studies, drawing on sociological methods, economic data, and/or literary analysis, was predisposed to chart the history of assimilation or acculturation among Asian immigrant groups, say, or elucidate the complex of meanings and subjectivities within Asian American literature while either overlooking religion or deeming it something to be overcome. At the same time, religious studies tended to foreground religious and spiritual experiences, allowing the researcher to overlook how race, gender, and class necessarily shape these experiences, at best, or, at worst, to write hagiographies of "Zen missionaries" divorced from their experiences as racial and religious others in a foreign land. "Along with Asian American literature," Rudiger Busto writes, "Asian American and Pacific Islander religions refuse to be subsumed under the dominant methods and approaches of either Religious or Asian American studies as they have developed. This is why it is essential to acknowledge the constellation of relationships among colonialism, the plantation political economy, and the religious experiences" of Asian Americans and Pacific Islanders.[49]

What such studies reveal is the complex interplay of race and religion, categories that are, to put it mildly, contested. It would be beyond the scope of this or any one book to fully disclose the complex development of race and religion on both sides of the Pacific in the early twentieth century. Here, a few points should be noted, many of which we will return to in later chapters. First, we would do well to recall that when Japanese immigrants first arrived in Hawaiʻi and on the West Coast in the late nineteenth century, citizenship was available only to native-born whites and, due to the recently passed Fourteenth Amendment to the U.S. Constitution, formerly enslaved Black Americans. Over the ensuing decades, Congress and the courts determined who could become naturalized U.S. citizens. As Ian F. Haney López shows, in the late 1800s and early 1900s several "prerequisite cases" were brought before the U.S. Supreme Court as Asian immigrants argued for their rights to naturalize, a privilege only given to "free white persons" and European immigrants. Such cases, in essence, defined what exactly was a "white person" largely by determining who was not—Asians. By declaring nonwhites as ineligible for citizenship, the Supreme Court showed "that whites exist not just as the antonym of nonwhites but as the *superior* antonym."[50] By legal decree, Japanese and other Asian immigrants were both denied the rights of full citizenship and cast as racially inferior to white Americans. Importantly, as a result of the Fourteenth Amendment, their children were natural-born citizens. Whereas this status may have made Nisei experiences easier, being born Americans did little to assuage the trauma of racism, as we will see in Chapter 3, and their legal status was one among many points of distinction between their and their parents' experience in America.

Being marginalized as racial others was only further compounded by the marginalization of Buddhism. By the early twentieth century, "American religion" was well on its way to being defined exclusively in terms of its "Judeo-Christian" roots. Despite being "part of the American religious scene since the nineteenth century, Japanese American Buddhists discovered that the passage of time did little to remove the wide-spread suspicion that they could never really become part of the fabric of American life. Doubly marginalized by virtue of race and religion, Buddhists were cast as the 'Other,' masking how they were very much a part of their lager social-cultural contexts."[51] Particularly on the West Coast, we find the conditions ripe for the exclusion of Japanese generally from full political participation and for Buddhists specifically being deemed suspicious or enemies of the state.[52] Moreover, the categories of "Japanese" and "American" were being reconfigured in terms of nationality, race, and religion on both sides of the

Pacific in the years leading up to Pearl Harbor. As both Japan and the United States expanded their spheres of influence, nationalist and imperialist projects necessitated the expansion of national identities. As Takashi Fujitani puts it, the closer the two countries came to war, the more their respective racist discourses shifted "toward an inclusionary rather than exclusionary form, and thus away from 'vulgar racism,' and toward a more refined and, at least in appearance, often less overtly violent 'polite racism.'"[53] And as Jolyon Baraka Thomas points out, both before and after the war, religion and "religious freedom talk" were deployed legalistically to define "good religion" and differentiate it from "bad religion."[54] It was within these shifting contexts that American Buddhism was first "rephrased," first articulated, not by the "pioneers" so often cited in American Buddhism studies but by Japanese Americans navigating these unstable terrains of race and religion.

The Transnational

A focus on the shifting terrain of race and religion on both sides of the Pacific points to Japanese immigrants' and their children's transnational positionality in and between the United States and Japan. As Eiichiro Azuma states in his *Between Two Empires: Race, History, and Transnationalism in Japanese America*, Japanese immigrants were "wedged firmly between the established categories of Japan and the United States."[55] At the turn of the twentieth century, both nations were on their way to creating transnational empires abroad and (re)defining national identity (inflected with racial identities) at home. Writing on Japanese immigrants leaving Meiji-era Japan, Azuma states:

> Because they were always faced with the need to reconcile simultaneous national belongings as citizen-subjects of one state [Japan] and yet resident-members (denizens) of another [the United States], the Issei refused to make a unilateral choice, electing instead to take an eclectic approach to the presumed contradiction between things Japanese and American. . . . As such, their ideas and practices were situational, elastic, and even inconsistent at times, but always dualistic at the core.[56]

Whereas Azuma acknowledges the importance of transnational perspectives in studies of Japanese Americans, he argues instead that this perspective deterritorializes Issei who are rooted simultaneously in the nation-states of Japan and the United States, and for this reason he urges an "inter-National perspective." This is necessary to account for the fact that, despite their transnational movement from Japan to the United States, Japanese immigrants were physically in the latter. "While they were caught between the conflicting ideological and often repressive apparatuses of the two nation-states, their bodies were anchored in America, their interests rooted in its sociological structure, and their activities disciplined by its politicolegal system."[57] His study allows us to see how transnational agents were embodied in a specific locale, and how that locale's social and political context shaped their self-understandings and motivations. Such a perspective is invaluable for thinking through the experiences of Issei; however, these experiences are not directly comparable to the experiences of their Nisei children. Nisei were certainly rooted, embodied, in the same American politico-legal system as their parents, but they were disciplined by a different set of laws owing to their status as natural-born citizens. Moreover, their transnational crossings were not from the East to the West but from the West to the East, especially in the postwar period, when they participated in the creation of a pan-Pacific Buddhist world.

The postwar years saw the emergence of a transnational network of Buddhist modernists, revivalists, and nationalists, connecting, among other locales, Sri Lanka, Thailand, Japan, and the United States. During this period, various parts of Asia were being (sometimes slowly, sometimes swiftly) decolonized; as direct European control receded, Buddhism was often used discursively in the construction of nationalist identities. Such Buddhist nationalist projects, sometimes backed by clandestine U.S. intelligence operations, were deployed to counter concomitant communist projects across South and Southeast Asia. One notable project during this period was the World Fellowship of Buddhists, which sought to promote Buddhism globally and overcome sectarian differences between Buddhist traditions. Its inaugural conference was held in Sri Lanka in 1950, and the second conference took place in Tokyo in 1952, an event that was recounted in the *Bussei* the following year. Several Nisei Buddhists attended both conferences. In theorizing these projects, Masatsugu invokes Azuma's "inter-Nationalism" but ultimately prefers Arif Dirlik's concept of the "historical ecumene." He writes, "The concept of the historical ecumene is useful for thinking about the transnational religious networks in which Japanese Americans participated, and the particular contours and dynamics that shaped an emerging global Buddhist perspective shared by Japanese American and Asian Buddhists."[58] Such networks allowed for the movement, the flow, of particular Buddhist ideas and persons across the Pacific, uniting disparate parts of the pan-Pacific Buddhist world. The term "ecumene" is useful in this regard, as it points to both sameness and difference; local or regional articulations of Buddhist thought, practice, or culture nevertheless all participate in a translocal and inter-National pan-Pacific Buddhist world. This is to say that whereas Asian Buddhists were articulating a particular vision of modern Buddhism against the backdrop of receding colonization and/or rising communism, the Japanese

American Buddhist co-inhabitants of this pan-Pacific world deployed the same modernist vision, albeit in the context of postwar American victory over Japan and in the shadow of the camps. Thus, the concept of the historical ecumene, to paraphrase Dirlik, foregrounds "commonalities as well as differences" and recognizes a "multiplicity of spatialities within a common space marked not by firm boundaries but by the intensity and concentration of interactions."[59]

Azuma's and Masatsugu's work calls our attention to both the movement of Japanese American Buddhists across the Pacific and their rootedness to a specific place. *The Making of American Buddhism* focuses on Nisei Buddhist experiences on the American side of the Pacific while being attentive to their travels in and around the pan-Pacific Buddhist world. Here in the United States, as mentioned earlier, part of this experience was the project of articulating a specifically modern American Buddhism at a time before the line between "heritage" and "convert" Buddhist communities existed. Whereas Nisei may have come to this project with a different set of motivations than the Beats, come together they did, creating a community that would allow for the growth and eventual spread of Buddhism in the United States, turning what had been only a decade earlier the religion of the enemy into a religion of peace.

How do we theorize the complexity of this history? How do we make sense of intergenerational dynamics, transpacific crossings, pan-ethnic projects, the bridging of East and West, Buddhism as definitional to an American identity, an identity marked by racial trauma? Whereas I do not presume to answer these questions in their fullness, I submit that their answer necessitates multiple theoretical perspectives and voices, and in the following chapters I work (however tentatively) toward a theory of messiness.

The Messiness of Lived Religion

My use of the term "messy" is inspired by the work of Lisa Lowe. In her 1991 essay "Heterogeneity, Hybridity, Multiplicity: Marking Asian American Differences," she writes:

> Asian American discussions of ethnicity are far from uniform or consistent; rather, these discussions contain a wide spectrum of articulations that include, at one end, the desire for an identity represented by a fixed profile of ethnic traits, and at another, challenges to the very notions of identity and singularity which celebrate ethnicity as a fluctuating composition of differences, intersections, and incommensurabilities. These latter efforts attempt to define ethnicity in a manner that accounts not only for cultural inheritance, but for active cultural construction, as well. In other words, they suggest that the making

of Asian American culture may be a much "messier" process than unmediated vertical transmission from one generation to another, including practices that are partly inherited and partly modified, as well as partly invented.[60]

It would be somewhat straightforward to apply this approach to our present task: our focus, primarily, on the Japanese American contributions to the *Bussei* both before, but mostly after, the war. In reading the *Bussei* we find expressions, perspectives, and experiences of being Nisei Buddhist that are not consistent across time or across volumes—there are internal incommensurabilities. Nisei at turns inherit culture from their parents and actively create new culture in American idioms. But the situation is messier still. Lowe's essay is concerned most directly with intergenerational change—an important topic, to be sure— but it is not explicitly concerned with the transnational, the movement of persons between and among different imagined worlds. Nor is it concerned with religion.

A full accounting of our subject will need to consider intergenerational dynamics and cultural trauma. It will also need to foreground religion, Buddhism, and Jōdo Shinshū. The *Bussei* was a product of the Berkeley Buddhist Temple's Young Buddhist Association; its Nisei members were as concerned with being good Americans and with being good Japanese sons and daughters as they were with being good Buddhists. This is in marked departure from Azuma's work, focused as it is on their parents, the Issei, and that generation's interest in creating an inter-National cosmopolis. Here we may also invoke the work of Thomas Tweed and his charge that we "follow the flows" of culture, to be attentive to how cultural practices and discourses are forged in transnational processes and are often overtly and necessarily religious.[61] In this way, Masatsugu's invocation of Dirlik draws our attention to the historical ecumene of the postwar era, of the pan-Pacific *Buddhist* world.

In this formulation, the *Berkeley Bussei* becomes one node in the larger project of discursively constructing midcentury Buddhist modernism. More than a mere rhetorical construction, however, this pan-Pacific Buddhist world was an in-fact network, traversed by persons often located in contradictory and incommensurable spaces, negotiating power and meaning within and between the nation-states of Japan and the United States, within and between the complicated and contested realms of race and religion—to say nothing of the complicated space between generations. What emerges in this discourse is familiar: Buddhist modernism. But oft elided in our studies of Buddhist modernism are the specific voices of Japanese American Buddhists promoting modernity both for the sake of the dharma and for the sake of their inclusion in these contested categories. These voices, Japanese/American/Buddhist, evince a tripartite identity that is not easily summarized, cannot be contained within necessarily contested and porous categories, cannot be appreciated in their fullness by adherence to disciplinary purity. They are intertwined and interconnected by way of race, place, religion, and nationality. In short, it's messy. And our academic discomfort with messiness should not be used as an excuse to trap these voices in the amber of either/or dichotomies; let us allow them, instead, to be both/and.

This perspective is one of distinctive simultaneity. A full accounting of the *Bussei* must read it as a Japanese/American/Buddhist publication, in the fullness of those terms, each in its own distinct way, and all at once. That is, it is not that the *Bussei* is either Japanese or American or that it is Buddhist or American or even some hyphenated combination thereof; rather, it is all of the above, all at once. We can approach and appreciate the work as situated within the discourse of Japanese culture or Japanese transnational religion or Japanese transnationalism; we can appreciate it as fully and authentically American Buddhist; we can view it simply as an expression of American culture or Buddhist spirituality. The *Bussei* is both an expression of pansectarian cosmopolitanism *and* thoroughly Jōdo Shinshū. None of these perspectives negates or devalues the others. They operate in distinctive simultaneity. And to apprehend them all at once is to necessarily appreciate the complexity, the nuance, the messiness that is lived religion, that is, human behavior—of which academic accounts are always and only approximations.

Such multivalent sightings of the *Bussei* require us to interrogate and critique received academic tropes and structures of thought. Rather than viewing the material through binary lenses of traditional/modern, East/West, authentic/inauthentic, and so on, *The Making of American Buddhism* asks different questions, speculates on alternative histories, and reads its sources across disciplinary lines. In this, I am again inspired by Lowe and her suggestion that disciplines not only frame how we read and interpret texts but also determine which texts are to be read and which are to be overlooked.[62] These methodological and theoretical commitments are not merely abstract considerations but also determine this book's structure. Rather than telling a straightforward or linear historical narrative, we will move backward and forward through time and across geography as we follow the flows of Buddhist culture throughout the pan-Pacific Buddhist world. Rather than reading the *Bussei* through a single disciplinary lens, we will return to some pieces time and again and read them from different perspectives, revealing their multiple and simultaneous meanings. In my discussion of Alan Watts and other West Coast countercultural figures, for example, I read their works discursively in an attempt to understand the logics of their arguments or rhetorics; however, I also approach them in terms of genre and canonization, looking beyond the texts themselves to their larger contexts. How are these authors presented to their audience? In the process of media presentation, representation, and repetition, I argue, a genre is formed regardless of whether or not anyone agrees on the genre's definition. I extend the logic of this process, one akin to canonization, to the development of a genre of religion that has come to be known as American Buddhism—one indelibly linked to the Beat Generation and the post-1950s "Zen boom." Once firmly established as a genre, American Buddhism's origins in the Japanese American Jōdo Shinshū community are lost, their creative labor rendered invisible by its own success (Chapter 5).

Labor is often undertheorized in standard histories of American Buddhism; it is simply taken for granted that immigrants, missionaries, and converts *worked hard* to establish Buddhist communities. Religious labor is devalued or rendered invisible because of a series of false equivalencies and evaluative binaries. In the juxtaposition of the public sphere with the domestic, the public becomes both the domain of men and the domain of wage labor. Because wage or productive labor produces surplus value, it is valued above all else in a capitalist society. Religion in the West has been relegated to the domain of the private (not the domestic), and thus it sometimes operates on the margins of or even outside capitalist systems (though obviously the borders between religion and the public or between religion and capitalism are both porous and policed). In the case of Japanese Buddhism, however, a good deal of religious labor is done by women, in part because the Japanese Buddhist temple is also a home—Buddhist priests and their families typically live at the temple, as the Imamuras did in Berkeley in the 1950s. Women and the domestic, however, are devalued in patriarchal capitalist systems in part because they are juxtaposed with the public, with the realm of wage labor and surplus value. And while the affective, emotional, reproductive, and domestic labor—all of which in our case overlap with religious labor—that makes possible American Buddhism may be obscured and devalued, its import cannot be overstated. Without this labor, the work of more visible men does not happen. It is not just that D. T. Suzuki wrote books and articles that popularized a particular version of Japanese Buddhist modernism in midcentury America; he was also supported by a community who drove him to his appointments, paid his bills, and made him a home free from worry so that he was able to do this intellectual work. To see this labor, to value it, we must therefore move past the text and explore extra-canonical sources such as memoirs and personal or family histories that humanize the religious actors who did the labor that made possible American Buddhism (Chapters 3 and 4).

This is also the work of infrastructure-building. The California Young Buddhist League, which hosted the 1941 conference, is a type of horizontal network, a network connecting persons and communities within a specific religious community. But religions also create vertical networks, exploiting them for material support or working within political or legal systems. Collectively, these networks do the work of spreading religious ideas, persons, artifacts, and cultures around the transnational imaginaries of, for example, the pan-Pacific Buddhist world.

Rather than merely following the flows, however, I draw our attention to the structures that make such flows possible.[63] The making of American Buddhism would not have been possible without vast networks of exchange, some Buddhist (horizontal), others political or economic (vertical). And in particular, I call our attention to the work of Jōdo Shinshū missionaries not only working in support of an immigrant community but also actively working to spread the dharma beyond that community (Chapters 1 and 4). In doing so, I foreground the agency of immigrants and their children. That is, rather than suggesting that Japanese missionaries and their American children were passively reacting to an active West, I argue that they were engaged in a specific racial project. According to Michael Omi and Howard Winant, racial formation is a process that occurs through "a linkage between structure and signification. *Racial projects* do both the ideological and the practical 'work' of making these links and articulating the connection between them."[64] That is, whereas racial formation is the process whereby differences between human bodies are given social or cultural meaning, a racial project is the process by which these meanings are both explained and organized. This process of organization may take the form of legal structures or the distribution of economic, political, or cultural resources, and it serves to reinforce the racial meanings articulated in the process of racial formation. Racial projects are carried out both by dominant and subordinate groups and on a variety of scales, not just "at the macro-level of racial policy-making, state activity, and collective action, but also at the level of everyday experiences and personal interaction."[65] In the case of this book, I am concerned with the racial project of Nisei American Buddhists, a project that was, on the one hand, about defining themselves as Japanese American, arguing for their full inclusion in American society, and organizing resources to support their community and the simultaneous project of propagating the dharma. On the other hand, this project was *also* concerned with changing American society. First, Nisei Buddhists' claim to an American identity inclusive of both their ethnic and religious identity allows them to claim space within a multireligious and multicultural America; second, such a claim necessarily forces America to *become* multireligious and multicultural.[66] If Nisei Buddhists are accepted as American Buddhists, this necessarily changes what it means to be American; America can no longer be limited to a white Christian nation. So in claiming for themselves the identity of American Buddhist, Nisei simultaneously make America itself more Buddhist (Chapter 3).

It is worth noting here that the ideology of white supremacy is in itself a racial project, one that defines whiteness and white human bodies in opposition to the racialized other, the norm against which other bodies, other persons, other cultures are judged.[67] Based on this definition, the racial project of white supremacy then sets about organizing and distributing resources along racial lines, as per Omi and Winant's definition above. As part of this project, white supremacy centers itself as the active agent of history and thereby renders the other as passive and invisible. Within the study of American Buddhism, white converts have received far more scholarly attention, which reinforces and (re) centers these experiences, leaving untold the experiences of Asian American Buddhists. A central thesis of this book is that the Japanese American Shin Buddhists who published the *Bussei* created networks, built a community, opened their religious homes to white converts and sympathizers, and were then promptly forgotten. This book is in part an attempt to recover the origins of American Buddhism by tracing out the connection between communities heretofore presumed to be mutually exclusive.[68]

The *Bussei* is not shy about the failings of American society; however, these failings are often framed in terms of the broader failings of the modern world. In the shadow of the camps, in the aftermath of war, at the dawn of the atomic age, the *Bussei* declares that the world is on the brink of disaster. Buddhism is offered as a panacea, as an ancient, civilizing, and peaceful religion of reason and science. This rhetorical Buddhist exceptionalism is, of course, a standard modernist move, and a Buddhist modernism discourse permeates the *Bussei*. Rather than merely treating the *Bussei* as yet one more example (or one more type) of modernism, I call our attention, first, to how American Jōdo Shinshū has been ignored in the academic study of Buddhist modernism. As has been said, the traditional/modern binary works to authenticate some forms of Buddhism while delegitimating others. In studies of American Shin Buddhism, the community is often treated as little more than an immigrant group or ethnic enclave, and thus "traditional," while also nonsectarian, promoting a universal or even "Theravadaized" version of the religion. Such a move doubly erases Shin American contributions both to American Buddhism and to Buddhist modernism. However, what I call our attention to is how the study of Buddhist modernism is in fact the work of lineage construction; in constructing a lineage of Buddhist moderns that includes the usual suspects of Alan Watts, D. T. Suzuki, and others, but excludes the work of American Shin Buddhists who supported and promoted their work, scholars are also policing the boundaries of this lineage. In so doing, we are creating our own canon, our own genre, implicating ourselves as both observers and (co-)creators of modern Buddhism (Chapters 2 and 5).

Such binaries and their associated disciplinary boundaries are ill-equipped to deal with the complexity and messiness of lived religion. They create and reinforce habits of thought and blind spots. We assume that American Buddhism, that Buddhist modernism, will "look" a certain way, and we search for it in the writings of well-known modern popularizers and charismatic figures. Perhaps nowhere is this more evident than in the lack of serious engagement with American Jōdo Shinshū Buddhism. In *The Making of American Buddhism*

I am not only arguing that the *Bussei* was the product of Nisei or Japanese Americans and thus reflected their particular experiences as a racial and religious minority, not only arguing that they consistently deployed a rhetoric of Buddhist modernism in the pages of the magazine, not only arguing that they built religious infrastructure that supported their own community and generations of American Buddhists to come, but also arguing that all the while they were Jōdo Shinshū Buddhists. Galen Amstutz has argued that Pure Land generally and Shin Buddhism specifically have been grossly overlooked in Western Buddhist studies.[69] Over the past several decades, a growing body of scholarship has focused on Shin Buddhist modernizers in Japan; American Shin Buddhist modernism has not attracted the same level of attention.[70] Despite the fact that Issei missionaries were raised and educated in the same cultural and intellectual context as Kiyozawa Manshi, for example, their work as Shin modernists in the Americas has been largely overlooked on the assumption that they were more interested in promoting a universal and nonsectarian perspective. Ultimately, my concern is that scholarship has tended to foreground normative definitions of Pure Land Buddhism, predefined what Shin Buddhism *should* look like, and found the historical record lacking. I argue contrary to this view, noting, for example, that Yemyō Imamura's well-cited essay *Democracy According to the Buddhist Viewpoint* is best understood as a sophisticated Shin Buddhist apologetic (in addition to a defense of the Japanese immigrant community), provided one knows what to look for. For this reason, I begin this book with a short introduction to Jōdo Shinshū Buddhism (Chapter 1).

A Note on Terminology

In this book, Japanese names are listed in the Western format (first name followed by family name), following the primary source material. Generational terms are frequently invoked in the *Berkeley Bussei*—"Issei" for the first generation of Japanese immigrants; "Nisei" for their children, born as U.S. citizens; and, less commonly, "Sansei" for third-generation Japanese Americans. "Nisei" is generally used to describe a person who has at least one Issei parent, and this makes defining the specific dates for the Nisei generation somewhat difficult. The majority of Nisei were born before the attack on Pearl Harbor, and some of the Nisei in this book were already in their twenties when incarcerated; many other Nisei were still children at the time or even born in the camps. The Sansei generation overlaps more easily with the U.S. baby boom. Whereas the generational terms "Issei" and "Nisei" appear often in the *Bussei*, two other familiar terms are less common: "Nikkei" and "Kibei." "Nikkei" has generally come to be used as an umbrella term for Japanese living outside Japan, which would certainly include the subjects under study here. "Kibei" generally refers to Japanese persons born in the United States who were raised mostly or entirely in Japan before returning to America as adults. There are many Kibei contributors to the *Bussei*; however, this term is not frequently used. We might speculate as to what is meant by the absence of these terms in the *Bussei*, but this question is beyond the scope of the present volume. Similarly beyond this book's scope is the term used for post-1945 Japanese immigrants—"Shin Issei" or "new first-generation immigrant"—and the complexity and internal diversity of the Japanese American community from the 1950s to the present. Whereas this study seeks to recenter the experiences of Japanese Americans in the history of American Buddhism, I do not intend this book to be the final word on the postwar Japanese American Buddhist experience or the complex dynamics of race, immigration, geography, and history in the broader Japanese American community.[71]

The term "Bussei" also needs clarification. Tomoe Moriya notes that the term is an abbreviation of *bukkyō seinenkai*, or Young Buddhist Association.[72] However, contributors to the *Bussei* often refer to themselves and their contemporaries as "Bussei," suggesting that it is also used as a marker of identity—that is, not "I am a member of the YBA" but "I am a (young) Buddhist." Moreover, the term is often used in various phrasings of the "Buddhist/Bussei movement in America," which carries with it something larger, and perhaps more overtly political, than simply membership in a church group. At issue for many Nisei—especially in the postwar period—was the growing sense that they were coming of age and would be inheriting their Buddhist community, along with growing frustration that the Issei were not taking their concerns seriously.[73] For some, the "Bussei movement" may have been simultaneously a reference to their desire to spread the dharma as well as their desire to assume greater leadership roles within the community.[74]

Finally, as will be discussed frequently, the *Bussei* and related projects were not produced in ethnic vacuums but were collaborative projects between Nisei Buddhists and their white friends and co-religionists. I use the term "white" in this volume as a marker of racial ideology, not personal identity. The "white people" who show up on the pages of the *Bussei* certainly came from a diversity of Euro-American and religious backgrounds—from Kerouac's East Coast French Catholicism to Watts's British Anglicanism.[75] But these backgrounds and the differences between them become subsumed under the dominant ideology of white Christian supremacy in the American context, which had two impacts on the Nisei Buddhists under study here. First, owing to the conflation of "whiteness" and "Christianity" in the definition of what it meant to be "American," Japanese immigrants and their children were deemed suspicious enemies of the state, thus leading to their incarceration as a class during World War II. Second, and following from this logic, when Japanese sought to assimilate, it was to white Christianity as an ideal that they turned, such as in the "prerequisite cases" mentioned earlier whereby Asian immigrants sought to be "reclassified" as white—admitted into the white racial group, as it were. In this way, whiteness operates less as a marker of *individual* identity and more as a normative ideal that is detectable in the *Bussei*, as when Nisei write of being discriminated against or denied the same rights that their "Caucasian" friends take for granted. It is this complex of orientations and feelings around race, racial and religious categories, and inclusion and exclusion that is at the heart of this book and, I would add, the making of American Buddhism.

1

The Buddhist Movement in America

In a short piece for the 1952 *Berkeley Bussei*, an anonymous author discusses the Buddhist concept of nirvana. The essay begins with a discussion of the Buddha's own awakening, refutes the notion that nirvana is the cessation of life (as implied by its etymological roots), and instead claims that nirvana is actually about the cessation of suffering. It ends, however, with the following: "As Buddha explains to King Ajatasatru in a discourse on the advantages of the life of a recluse, every bit of ignorance removed, and passion conquered, brings about palpable benefit, such as purity, goodwill, self-possession, courage, unperplexed mind, unruffled temper."[1] The source for this discourse on the life of a recluse is not mentioned, and one could certainly read this short piece as relaying some general understandings of a core, even basic, Buddhist concept. However, the reference to Ajātaśatru is telling. In both the Indian and East Asian textual traditions, the story of Ajātaśatru, his attempted patricide of his father, King Bimbisāra, his relationship to the Buddha's cousin and rival, Devadatta, and various versions of the story that include his mother, Vaidehī, are well known—as they were to Shinran, the founder of the Jōdo Shinshū tradition of Pure Land Buddhism in Japan. In his principal work, the *Kyōgyōshinshō*, Shinran devotes significant time to a discussion of Ajātaśatru, and so even though this essay makes no mention of either Pure Land Buddhism generally or Shin Buddhism specifically, this reference to Ajātaśatru gives us a hint of the larger religious world within which American Buddhist missionaries and their children were immersed.

Generally speaking, scholars have approached the early phases of North American Shin Buddhism (and especially English-language material) by highlighting either its nonsectarian or "universal" nature, on the one hand, or the assimilationist strategies of Buddhists and the acculturation of Buddhist practices to the American context, on the other. In what follows, I argue that these are limiting frames and that they relegate Shin missionaries to the passive role of immigrants reacting to the forces of transnationalism and anti-Japanese racism rather than treating them as active participants in the creation of American Buddhism. As a corrective, I focus on the larger cultural currents on both sides of the Pacific, of which Shin missionaries were a part, to discuss the establishment of Jōdo Shinshū in America. Coming out of the Meiji-era intellectual milieu that was in conversation with nascent Western Buddhist studies scholarship, Shin missionaries were necessarily interested in promoting Buddhism from their

The Making of American Buddhism. Scott A. Mitchell, Oxford University Press. © Oxford University Press 2023.
DOI: 10.1093/oso/9780197641569.003.0002

specifically Japanese point of view while engaging with the eclectic and syncretic religious landscape of early twentieth-century America. The scholarly presumption that by promoting a universal or cosmopolitan Buddhism Issei missionaries were necessarily jettisoning their sectarian identity is the first unhelpful binary under critique in this book. Simply put, this binary assumes that one can never be simultaneously cosmopolitan and Shinshū but must choose between them. On the contrary, while figures such as Yemyō Imamura and his son Kanmo were explicit in promoting a cosmopolitan Buddhism and building inclusive and seemingly nonsectarian communities, a close read of their work reveals rather sophisticated Shin Buddhist apologetics.

In order to fully appreciate the "Shin-ness" of early North American Jōdo Shinshū, one needs to know where to look. As the reference to Ajātaśatru above attests, whereas this story is found across the Buddhist tradition, it has a particular relevance to the Shin tradition, one that may not be readily apparent to the untrained eye. Thus, this chapter begins with a short introduction to Shin Buddhism's history, core doctrines, and practices. This introduction draws from standard scholarly accounts of Pure Land Buddhism generally, but it also draws on selections from the *Berkeley Bussei*. I make this move for two reasons. First, contrary to the argument that North American Shin Buddhists have been primarily promoting a universal or nonsectarian Buddhism, I argue that a specifically Shin Buddhist perspective has been present since the beginning and through the postwar years. I can think of no better evidence for this claim than the *Bussei* itself. Second, I want to avoid a scholarly-prescriptivist read of the tradition. That is, whereas it is certainly worthwhile to know the orthodox claims of religious authorities, and it is certainly important to present a critical and unvarnished telling of religious history, these perspectives are limiting, forcing us to make assumptions about what Shin Buddhism is supposed to look like before we enter the world and engage with actual human beings. Lived religion is messy. Shin Buddhists practicing in the real world do not always behave or think or talk about themselves in ways that are in complete alignment with normative or scholarly expectations. And that is as it should be. Rather than evaluating whether or not the subjects of this book are properly Shin, I simply take for granted that they are and let them speak for themselves.

Jōdo Shinshū: A Brief Introduction

Jōdo Shinshū is a Japanese sect of Pure Land Buddhism, established by the descendants of the thirteenth-century monk Shinran (1173–1263). In its contemporary usage, Pure Land Buddhism generally refers to the range of texts, cosmologies, doctrinal interpretations, specific cultic practices, and, especially in Japan, sectarian lineages that focus on various buddharealms populated by buddhas other than the historical Buddha Śākyamuni. Embedded within normative Mahāyāna Buddhist cosmology, Pure Land Buddhism takes as a given that the cosmos contains an infinite number of other world-systems and other buddhas who may be petitioned for specific reasons or chosen as the object of devotion or visualization for specific ends. Within this pantheon of buddhas and buddhafields (*buddhakṣetra*), one specific buddha and his buddhafield became the subject of particular interest in East Asia, the Buddha of Infinite Light (and/or Life), Amitābha, and his blissful realm Sukhāvatī.[2]

In the *Sukhāvatīvyūhasūtra* (*Larger Sutra*), the Buddha Śākyamuni tells of the bodhisattva Dharmākara who lived in another world-system infinite eons ago. Dharmākara made a series of vows before the buddha of that age and realm declaring that when he attained full buddhahood, he would establish a buddhafield or pure land that would be free of the hardships and sufferings of our world. Most of the forty-eight vows enumerated in this sutra describe the pure realm in standard Mahāyāna fantastical language, replete with a perfectly flat earth, bejeweled trees, sexless human bodies emerging from lotus flowers at birth, and birds singing the dharma. The sutra goes on to state that Dharmākara did indeed attain full buddhahood, thus becoming Amitābha Buddha, and established his pure realm, thereby fulfilling all forty-eight vows. Several vows speak to how sentient beings may be born into his realm—namely, through bringing to mind (*buddhānusmṛti*) or reciting the name of Amitābha Buddha ten times. Once reborn in this realm, one will be in the presence of Amitābha as well as the bodhisattvas Avalokiteśvara and Mahāsthāmaprāpta, instantly attain the stage of non-retrogression (ensuring their awakening), and, indeed, attain full buddhahood.[3]

This seemingly straightforward path to awakening was, of course, endlessly varied as these practices made their way from India into Central and East Asia. For example, whereas *buddhānusmṛti* may be translated as "recollecting" or "recalling" the Buddha, in East Asian practice this has taken the specific form of reciting the Buddha's name (*nienfo*). But how should one recite the name? In what form? Whereas the *Sukhāvatīvyūhasūtra* says to recall the name ten times, does the state of mind of the practitioner matter? If saying the name ten times is karmically beneficial, is it quantifiably more beneficial to recite it one hundred times, one thousand times, endlessly? Does copying the name in printed form have the same benefit? In a related text, the *Guan wuliangshou jing* (*Visualization Sutra*), the Buddha Śākyamuni teaches a visualization practice wherein one can enter Sukhāvatī in this life, in this body, to hear Amitābha teach the dharma in the present. Should the practitioner engage in this practice or wait until the afterlife and hope for rebirth in Amitābha's pure realm? Does the state of mind of the practitioner at death determine a favorable rebirth? And, finally, is the pure land to be taken literally? Or, in line with various strands of "consciousness-only" thought, particularly in the Chinese context, is the pure land really a manifestation of the mind? That is, are we already in the pure realm but for a lack of pure perception unaware of it; and, once having purified our vision, will we realize our already awakened state?[4]

It is generally acknowledged that no discrete school or sect of Pure Land Buddhism existed in Central Asia or China; rather, Pure Land thought and practices were interwoven into the tradition more generally or taken as a given within the broader Mahāyāna Buddhist worldview.[5] That is, buddhaname recitation was a common practice in most of the major Chinese Buddhist schools; visualization practices focused specifically on Amitābha can be found in many esoteric traditions inside and outside Tibet; and deathbed rituals to ensure rebirth in Sukhāvatī can be found across East Asia. The single practice of buddhaname recitation became widespread among the laity, and several lay Buddhist movements were centered around the practice. And prominent Buddhist philosophers studied Pure Land thought and texts.[6]

The situation in Japan, however, was quite different. By the late Heian period (794–1185), the predominately esoteric schools of Shingon and especially Tendai had risen to ascendency with imperial or aristocratic patronage.[7] However, social upheaval and political instability created the conditions for the overthrow of the emperor and the rise of military rule during the subsequent Kamakura period (1185–1333). This was a period of instability for Buddhist institutions as well, and it was during this time that new ideas, new lineages, and wholly indigenous Japanese Buddhist schools were established, developments that would eventually lead to the Japanese Buddhist tendency toward sectarianism, a marked departure from mainland Asian Buddhism.[8]

One important figure during this period was the Tendai monk Hōnen (1133–1212). In 1175, after studying the work of Chinese Pure Land thinker Shandao, Hōnen left the Tendai establishment and began teaching a single-practice path to awakening—specifically, buddhaname recitation focused on Amitābha (Amida in Japanese). The Chinese practice of *nienfo* (*nenbutsu* in Japanese) was part of Tendai practice generally, but Hōnen taught that *nenbutsu* was all that was necessary for birth in Amida's pure land.[9] Hōnen began teaching the *nenbutsu*, in the form of reciting *namu-amida-butsu*, to the laity in and around the capital, and by the early 1200s he was well on his way to establishing a new school of Buddhism, the Jōdoshū. It was around this time that Shinran, a fellow Tendai monk, became one of Hōnen's disciples and similarly began to teach the single-practice path of the *nenbutsu*. Eventually the movement would be charged as heretical, and both Hōnen and Shinran were stripped of their monastic titles and exiled from the capital. Separated from his master, Shinran spent most of the rest of his life in the Kanto region, north of present-day Tokyo, where he taught the *nenbutsu* practice to the local laity and eventually wrote his magnum opus, the *Kyōgyōshinshō*. He never considered himself more than his master's student, but following Shinran's death his family and disciples enshrined his remains in a temple in Kyoto and, over the ensuing decades, a discrete lineage based on Shinran's teachings developed, the Jōdo Shinshū.

Shinran's thought, thus, diverged slightly from Hōnen's, and his unique understanding of both Pure Land and Mahāyāna Buddhism has been the subject of an immense amount of scholarship over the past seven centuries. For our present purposes, we need only focus on a few doctrinal and practical points that are both foundational to the tradition and expressed in the pages of the *Bussei*.

To begin, Amida Buddha is understood to be the central object of devotion; however, this does not mean that there is no place in the tradition for the historical Buddha. Indeed, Śākyamuni is understood as having appeared in the world specifically to teach the Pure Land path. Foundational Buddhist teachings, such as the four noble truths, are assumed to be skillful means (*upāya*) to lead sentient beings to the realization of the universal and nondiscriminative wisdom and compassion of Amida Buddha. Not only is this a fairly common "one vehicle" understanding of how the buddhadharma was originally taught by Śākyamuni, but it is a sentiment that can be inferred in the following passage from the *Bussei*:

> Lord Buddha, in His teaching taught us that the Path of the Buddhas which He trod is the Path also for us to tread. That even as He found the Eternal Buddhahood within Himself, so His Teaching is to show us the way to the same thing—to awaken our sleeping inner self to the realization of the Power of Amida Buddha.[10]

This piece, titled "What Did Lord Buddha Teach?," was written by "Rev. S. N. Pratt" and appeared in the fall 1939 volume of the *Bussei*. Rev. Pratt is Gladys Sunya Pratt (1898–1986), a white convert to Jōdo Shinshū. Pratt was ordained in 1936 and served the Tacoma Buddhist Church until her death fifty years later. As we will see later in this chapter and Chapter 4, in the early twentieth century American Shin Buddhists were engaged in a project of spreading the dharma beyond the Japanese immigrant community; the ordination of white converts was one consequence of this project.[11] According to Ama, many of these converts had varying levels of commitment to or even understanding of Shin Buddhism. In Pratt's case, Ama notes that her ordination ceremony included specifically Theravada elements and is thus evidence of a more general or "universal Buddhism" impulse in the community.[12] Nevertheless, despite the idiosyncratic language of "Lord Buddha" or "inner self," Pratt's essay here hints at a fairly normative Shin Buddhist idea that Śākyamuni Buddha appeared in this world specifically to direct us to Amida Buddha.

The logic of relying on Amida and the single-practice path of the *nenbutsu* can be understood in two interrelated ways. First, many of the "Kamakura reformers" (such as Hōnen, Shinran, Nichiren, and others) assumed that they were living in the age of *mappō*, or the age of the degenerate dharma.[13] *Mappō* is the idea that, over time, the dharma will decline in the world, individuals' ability to practice the dharma will weaken, fraudulent teachers will emerge teaching counterfeit practices, and eventually the dharma will disappear completely, making the conditions right for the appearance of the Buddha Maitreya in the far-distant future. Recent scholarship has suggested that *mappō* may not have been as central to the Kamakura thinkers as their spiritual descendants believed; nevertheless, the notion that we are living in an era where individuals are incapable of practicing the dharma was certainly part of Shinran's thought. Shinran regularly contrasts the Pure Land path of practice with the path of sages, that is, the monastic path of individual effort. According to Shinran, for those who are incapable of following the path of sages there is the possibility of awakening through reliance on Amida Buddha's compassion.

This reliance on the power of Amida to draw us toward the pure land is understood in terms of *tariki* or other-power (the pure land path), as opposed to *jiriki* or self-power (the path of sages). One of Shinran's central teachings is that sentient beings are incapable of successfully engaging in the arduous practices of the path of sages (possibly owing to the age of the degenerate dharma); yet, fortunately for us, an alternative path exists, one that grasps all beings regardless of their karmic burdens and failings. Whereas this may seem like fatalism—there is nothing we can do, just rely on a cosmic being with nothing but faith—Shinran's writings suggest that he is arguing for a radical denial of the self in keeping with the Buddhist concept of no-self or *anattā*. That is, the more we cling to self-power practices, the more we reify our belief in a separate self; the more we engage in a heroic quest to affect our own awakening, the deeper we dig ourselves into the hole of delusion. In fact, it is typically taught that it is not we, as limited and deluded beings (*bonbu*), who say the name, but Amida Buddha; we merely participate in the saying of the name, deconstructing any illusion of a distinction between self and other. Kimi Hisatsune writes in the *Bussei* that the "idea of jiriki (self-power) and tariki (other-power) has significance only in this relativistic world."[14] From the point of view the absolute, from the point of view of Amida, there is no distinction between self and other.

> There is a limit to the human intellect, and our passions and desires are difficult to subdue. It seems that all students will eventually arrive at a point beyond which they cannot go unless they cast away their logic, their intellectual cloak and any attempts at rationalization. . . . [I]f you are too concerned with your state of mind, the very mercy of Amida may prove to be a hindrance to the

growth of your faith. If you strive to grow in faith, thinking *this* must be accomplished for your salvation, the very effort will smother it.[15]

Hisatsune's use of the word "faith" here is likely a reference to the Shin Buddhist concept of *shinjin*, which, especially in the mid-twentieth century, was often translated as "faith." *Shinjin* is a notoriously difficult term to translate, so much so that more recent scholarly projects have decided to leave it untranslated.[16] To be clear, *shinjin* is not faith, at least not in the way faith is colloquially understood in modern English as a passive or uncritical belief in things that can be neither proven nor disproven. Rather, for Shinran, as is suggested in Hisatsune's writings, *shinjin* is not something one can aspire toward; it is an awareness of the interconnected nature of the world, an intuitive knowledge that one has already been embraced by the compassion of the Buddha, not in a dualistic or paternalistic sense but because one is already awakened, because of the deconstruction of the self/other dualism. "I" do not have *shinjin* so much as this limited being I foolishly think of as "my-self" participates in reality as it is (*tathatā* or suchness in the Mahāyāna sense of the term); once aware of this reality, one trusts that birth in the pure land (and, by extension, nirvana) is already ensured. Within this state, one utters the *nenbutsu* not out of a sense of blind faith and in the hope of some miraculous postmortem rebirth but out of gratitude for the already existing true nature of reality.

This sense of gratitude finds its expression in Shin Buddhism as the saying of the name, *namu-amida-butsu*, or *nenbutsu*. *Nenbutsu*, in turn, is related to *gasshō*, the Japanese transliteration of the *añjali mudrā*, wherein one places the palms together before the heart and bows slightly in a gesture of supplication, greeting, or gratitude. "When we rise in the morning, let our first thought be that of gratitude and veneration toward Amida," writes Pratt in the *Bussei*, "let it strike the keynote of the day, until at the close of evening our last thoughts are directed towards the Eternal Buddha."[17] In the Shin tradition, *gasshō* is almost always performed while saying the *nenbutsu* and is very often said ritualistically to open a service, meeting, or meal. As Manabu Fukuda writes in his 1940 *Bussei* piece, "I would like to stress also, the importance of gasshō at all our Bussei meetings, business or otherwise." He goes on to say:

> I have heard many who say that gasshō is merely a formality and there is no spiritual value in such an act. Perhaps that is true. However, we must recognize the importance of formalities.
>
> Gasshō is the outward expression of our gratitude towards our Lord Buddha. It is also an act of courtesy and respect toward Amida. If we say gasshō is useless, we must also assert that the customary act of bowing or handshaking is also unnecessary. If we must respect our elders and friends by such formalities, why should we not express our profound respect and courtesy towards Buddha.[18]

Owing to Shinran's rejection of the monastic practice model, and once exiled from the capital, he took a wife, had children, and began referring to himself as "neither monk nor lay." This rejection of monastic practice has had, in my view, two consequences for the tradition. First, Shin Buddhism, especially in the United States, has developed a rhetoric of being the Buddhist tradition of choice for ordinary persons in general and for families in particular.[19] We find in the fall 1939 *Bussei*, for example, an article titled "Buddhism in the Home," a summary of a Young Buddhist Association conference wherein home-centered practices were discussed, including a list of suggestions for the "creation of better Buddhist homes" such as setting up an altar (*obutsudan*) with offerings of flowers and rice, memorial services for deceased family members, and the observance of rites and Buddhist holidays.[20] Second, and related to this "neither monk nor lay" orientation, Shin Buddhism has valorized a particular religious character known as the *myōkōnin*. In Japan, *myōkōnin* were understood to be uneducated or untrained persons who nevertheless displayed deep wisdom and insight into the buddhadharma, and this is the subject of a 1954 *Bussei* essay by Taitetsu Unno (1929–2014). While a student at Berkeley, Unno was a frequent contributor to the *Bussei* as well as one of its regular editors; in the early 1950s he began studying for his doctorate at Tokyo University but continued to contribute essays to nearly every volume through the end of the decade. In "A Life of Naturalness," Unno recounts his experience traveling with an international contingent of priests and monks to the Second World Buddhist Conference in Japan.[21] Along the way, their train stopped in the small village of Tobari, where they were met by locals who were overcome with religious reverence and began bowing and saying the *nenbutsu*. Unno writes, "True religion does not live in the temple sanctuaries and academic halls, it lives with the simple believers like these inhabitants of Tobari. They are called Myokonin, men who are pure and beautiful like the lotus in the mire of society."[22]

Unno uses this experience to introduce the biography of a famous nineteenth-century *myōkōnin* named Genza, a biography told more or less in a series of vignettes attesting to the unconventional and antinomian nature of Genza's character. These vignettes are similar to stories of iconoclastic Zen monks or Nyönpa from the Tibetan tradition—narratives meant to disrupt one's attachment to the sacred/profane dichotomy. Unno concludes Genza's biography by writing:

> When one has attained the ultimate state of the Myokonin, his life is one of unrestrained naturalness. He performs goodness without being conscious of its goodness. He works for social improvements as spontaneously as though it was his work and play. His morality is a natural outflow of his goodness, not a sanction forced upon him by external powers. . . . To eat when hungry, to sleep when drowsy—this is the life of naturalness.[23]

Finally, a word must be said about Shōtoku Taishi (574–622). Prince Shōtoku, as he is popularly referred to, is considered to be largely responsible for Buddhism's dissemination in Japan following receipt of the *Lotus*, *Vimalakīrti*, and *Śrīmālādevī Sutras*, among other ritual objects, from Korean Buddhist emissaries. His establishment of a central government and promotion of Buddhism was an inspiration for later Buddhist thinkers including Shinran. According to standard biographies of Shinran, after leaving Mt. Hiei, he went to Rokkakudō temple in Kyoto which is said to have been established by Shōtoku. There, according to some accounts, Shinran had a vision of either Kannon (Avalokiteśvara) or Shōtoku, a vision that compelled him to seek out Hōnen and the Pure Land path.[24] In his later writings, Shinran refers to Shōtoku as a manifestation of Kannon, thus ensuring Shōtoku's central importance in the later Shin Buddhist tradition.

Following Shinran's death in 1263, his wife and daughter were entrusted with his shrine in Kyoto, and on that site the Honganji (Temple of the Original Vow) was established. Again, though he never considered himself more than his master's disciple, Shinran's heirs and spiritual descendants would eventually consider his movement a separate tradition. Over the intervening generations, Jōdo Shinshū would grow to become a dominant force in Japanese religion and politics. Of course, in the immediate years after Shinran's death, this rise to prominence was not at all a foregone conclusion. The new sect was small and struggling, and it eventually split into several different lineages, each with its own take on Shinran's thought and Pure Land practice, and often competing with other schools, including the much more powerful Tendai complex at Mt. Hiei. During the fifteenth century, the eighth head priest (*monshu*) of Honganji, Rennyo (1415–1499), became a defining figure for Jōdo Shinshū.[25] Early in his career, Rennyo traveled extensively and sought to bring the disparate groups of Shin followers under the banner of the Honganji. He was successful enough in this endeavor to pose a threat to Mt. Hiei, which attacked the Kyoto temple in the years before the outbreak of the Ōnin War in 1467. During this period, as Japan descended into civil war and the authorities were unable to contain Buddhist monastic armies, Rennyo was unable to return to Kyoto. Nevertheless, he continued traveling and shoring up support for the Shin movement until he was able to return in 1475, having turned Jōdo Shinshū into such a powerful force that it was no longer under threat from Mt. Hiei.

Importantly for our present purposes, in addition to organizing a large and disparate set of Pure Land movements into a major lineage, Rennyo was also responsible for systematizing Shin Buddhist practice. Many of his liturgies are still in use today, and his pastoral letters have become orthodox within the tradition.[26] For example, whereas Shinran seems to have been somewhat ambivalent in regard to whether or not one needed to recite the *nenbutsu*, Rennyo's position was clear; in short, yes, saying the name is essential to living a Shin Buddhist life. Or, as Tansai Terakawa wrote in the *Bussei* in 1939:

> Rennyo-Shonin once said, "You should display the Buddha's picture so constantly that it becomes torn, and read the sacred Books so repeatedly that it also becomes worn." Thus Rennyo-Shonin emphasized these twin practices . . . When he was once asked the question whether one should utter the nembutsu in gratitude for being already saved or do the same in expectation of being saved, he said both are correct in the sense that in the former case one utters the nembutsu of thanks for the assurance of becoming Buddha and in the latter one does the same in gratitude for being able to be born in the Pure Land after the completion of this Life.[27]

In the interests of space, here we will only briefly mention the three centuries or so following Rennyo. Having firmly established the Honganji as a dominant political and religious force in Japan, the sect was eventually split into the "Western" and "Eastern" branches (Nishi and Higashi Honganji, respectively), which, though not originally divided over doctrinal issues, nevertheless developed different views on Shinran's teaching over the years. At the same time, during the Edo Period (1600–1868), Japan went into a long period of isolationism, banned Christianity, and cut off international ties at the time of rising European colonialism on the Asian mainland. Following the arrival of U.S. Commodore Matthew Perry in the 1850s, and as we will discuss in greater detail in the next chapter, Japan began its rapid modernization period following the Meiji Restoration in 1868. Shin Buddhist thinkers and institutions played an important role in this modernization project, rethinking Buddhist doctrine and practice, creating new institutions, and engaging seriously with nascent Western Buddhist scholarship. And at it was at the dawn of the Meiji that Jōdo Shinshū missionaries began crossing the Pacific to the Americas.[28]

Shin Buddhist Missionaries to the West

Japanese immigrants first arrived in Hawai'i in 1868. At the time, Hawai'i was nominally an independent kingdom, though within a few decades the island nation would be annexed by the United States as a territory. This long and complicated history is deserving of far more attention than can be given here.[29] It is enough to point out that Buddhism's establishment on the islands predates the official U.S. presence, and as a result most Hawai'ian Japanese Buddhist organizations are run independently from their mainland counterparts. So while Shin Buddhism was formally established in Hawai'i in 1889, it was a decade later that Shin Buddhist priests were sent to the mainland. Mainland American Shin Buddhism begins in September 1899 when the Revs. Shūe Sonoda and Kakuryō Nishijima gave a series of lectures on the dharma at the Occidental Hotel in downtown San Francisco, a date now recognized as BCA Founding Day by the Buddhist Churches of America. Of course, Sonoda and Nishijima did not, technically, found anything that day. Rather, a few weeks later, they rented a building and posted a sign on the door that read "Hongwanji Branch Office," signaling their status as the official representatives of the Nishi Honganji organization in North America.[30] A year or so later, this organization was officially named the Hokubei Bukkyō Dan, rendered into English as the Buddhist Mission of North America (BMNA). During the wartime incarceration of Japanese Americans, the organization was officially renamed the Buddhist Churches of America. This community is generally considered to be the longest continually operating Buddhist organization in North America.

Sonoda and Nishijima's initial activity seems to have been supporting preexisting "young men's Buddhist associations" (*bukkyō seinenkai*) or establishing new ones up and down the West Coast, from Vancouver to San Diego. As mentioned previously, Shinran considered himself "neither monk nor lay," and the early Shin community in Japan was based not on a monastic model but on a "lay-based congregation," the *dōjō*, organized by fellow companions or believers in the dharma (*dōbo/dōgyō*).[31] This pattern of like-minded Shin followers congregating to share the teachings and establish a formal group represented the norm for how Shin Buddhism developed in the United States. A group of lay Shin Buddhists typically met in an individual's home or in a rented public space to engage in a range of Buddhist practices, from sutra study to ritual services. Once established, the group would petition Honganji—via Sonoda and Nishijima—for a priest to be assigned to oversee the group. Only after this assignment, and once the group reached some critical mass of members, would a formal temple be established. In the early decades of the twentieth century Sonoda and Nishijima oversaw this activity, and eventually the Buddhist Mission of North America became the umbrella organization that formally represented Nishi Honganji in both the United States and Canada as well as acting as a go-between for the local communities and the Kyoto headquarters.[32] As the number of local communities grew, so did the umbrella organization, and Sonoda was given the title of BMNA director, a position eventually renamed bishop (*sochō*).[33]

The Berkeley Buddhist Temple, at the heart of the present study, was established following this model. As early as 1901, a Shin Buddhist community had formed in Oakland. Following the 1906 San Francisco earthquake, the East Bay population grew considerably, and by the end of the decade, enough Issei Buddhists had relocated to Berkeley and surrounding areas to establish their own Buddhist group. The first meeting, held at the Independent Order of Odd

Fellows' Berkeley meeting hall in May 1911, is considered the official founding of the temple.[34] For nearly a decade, the nascent community was overseen by priests from San Francisco and met in members' homes or hotel conference rooms before being assigned a permanent resident minister, Kaisai Nagai. They then purchased a property, a classic "Berkeley brown-shingle" two-story home on Channing Street less than a mile from the University of California. The first floor of the building was converted into a worship hall (*hondō*) and the second floor became the resident minister's living quarters. Over the next decade, during what Kashima calls the "picture bride era" of North American Shinshū, the Berkeley community grew as more families moved to the area and, eventually, college-age Nisei began to arrive to study at local colleges and universities, setting the stage for the establishment of the Berkeley Young Buddhist Association in 1934 and the publication of the first *Berkeley Bussei* in 1939.[35]

We should take note here of the English terms used by the early North American Shin community—"bishop," "church," "minister," "mission," and so on. Whereas contemporary readers may simply equate a Young Men's Buddhist Association with a Young Men's Christian Association, arguably the YMBA is rightly *contrasted* with the temple rather than *compared* with the YMCA. That is, as mentioned earlier, the normal pattern of development for North American Shin Buddhist communities was first the establishment of a *bukkyō-kai* or Buddhist group by lay followers; only once a group reached a critical mass of members would an official temple be established. The *bukkyō-kai* thus may have resembled the *dōjō* of early Shin history in Japan. The choice to borrow Christian terminology when translating this term to English, and later adopting "church" for Shin Buddhist temples, is understandable given white Christian normativity at the dawn of the twentieth century. Naming one's minority religious community a "church" simply raises less suspicion. I draw our attention to this hypothetical connection between the *bukkyō-kai* and the *dōjō* simply in search of emic terms or concepts that foreground the agency of Issei Buddhists rather than portraying them as merely reacting to the forces of Christian normativity. Other terms, however, proved more complicated. Shin priests dispatched to North America held several different titles, the most important of which may have been *kaikyōshi*, a title conferring the authority for a priest to teach the dharma overseas.[36] Such terms also signal intent. Sonoda and Nishijima were responsible for establishing the Hokubei Bukkyō Dan, literally the American Buddhist Group but translated as "mission." This deliberate choice to name the organization a "mission" raises interesting questions about the motivations and intentions of its founders. In short, whom did they see as the *object* of their missionary activity?

Sonoda and Nishijima's arrival was noted by the San Francisco *Chronicle*, which reported on that initial meeting at the Occidental Hotel in 1899 with the headline "Two Representatives [of Buddhism] Are in San Francisco to Proselyte."[37]

The report claims that the two priests will attempt to convert not only Japanese immigrants but also Americans, teach that God is but a figment of the human imagination, and claim that Buddhism is morally superior to Christianity. The article's tone certainly conveys some anxiety; whereas American Christians may have been familiar and comfortable with their own missionary activity abroad in Asia, here were two Asians putatively in America to convert them. Of course, the American religious context in which Sonoda and Nishijima did their missionary activity was hardly Buddhism-free. The American fascination with and appropriation of Buddhism had begun well before the turn of the twentieth century. And for our present purposes, two issues are most deserving of our consideration: the Orientalist fascination with origins and the syncretic character of Buddhist modernism. During the Meiji Era (1868–1919) and the decades that followed, Japanese Buddhist intellectuals became increasingly aware of nascent Western scholarship on Buddhism, which was focused on the origins of the tradition in India and the historical person of Siddhartha Gautama. This modernist concern for the Indian origins of Buddhism is but one of the syncretic features of Buddhist modernism, a topic we will return to in Chapter 2. Here it is enough to mention how the confluence of Western cultural attitudes toward Buddhism, including this concern for origins as well as concomitant Romantic, spiritualist, occult, and emergent psychotherapeutic techniques, shaped the American religious landscape.

The Indian Turn and Spreading the Dharma

As discussed in the introduction, the colonial civil servants and Orientalists who "discovered" Buddhism in Asia did so primarily via texts and were concerned with locating the historical founder of the tradition in the human person of Siddhartha Gautama in ancient India. The Orientalist project of collecting and translating Buddhist texts and doing philological and historical studies of the tradition was the precursor to the modern academic discipline of Buddhist studies and established the proper focus of scholarly attention on "early Buddhism" or the Buddhism of the historical Buddha Śākyamuni. Such a focus favored the so-called Southern traditions of Buddhism, encouraged Pali-language study, and suggested that later developments (inclusive of Mahāyāna and East Asian Buddhism) were derivatives or divergences from the historical founder's true intent.

Beginning slightly before the Meiji Restoration and then continuing well into the early decades of the twentieth century, the Japanese were engaged in their own "Occidentalist project," so to speak. As part of the widespread project of creating the modern nation-state of Japan, Japanese intellectuals and political and cultural leaders spent considerable time abroad in Europe and the United States learning all they could about Western modes of governance and culture. Jōdo Shinshū Buddhists were engaged in this project as well, traveling across mainland Asia to collect Buddhist art and artifacts and studying in Western universities. In fact, among the first Japanese to study abroad was Nanjō Bunyū, who had been sent to England at the behest of the *monshu* of the Higashi Honganji. There Nanjō studied Sanskrit with Max Müller. Whereas Commodore Perry's "black ships" forced Japan into trade agreements with the West, this contact also exposed Japanese Buddhists to Western scholarship on their religion and the fascination with its origins in India. Nanjō, like many of his contemporaries, strongly desired to visit India. He was able to make the journey, and though he did not long stay in South Asia, it remained an important part of his scholarly career thereafter, and he contributed to a wave of Japanese travel and tourism to South and East Asia in the decades following. In constructing Japanese Buddhist modernism, not only did Japanese intellectuals embrace European and American modes of discourse around science, rationalism, nationalism, and empire, but they also embraced a fascination with India. As Richard Jaffe writes, "An indispensable aspect of forging Japanese Buddhist modernity in the late nineteenth and early twentieth centuries also entailed connecting Japanese Buddhism to South Asia, interpersonally, scholastically, spiritual, and artistically."[38] Orientalist scholarship, however, was a "two-edged sword," according to Lori Pierce. On the one hand, Western attention on Buddhism, the translation of Buddhist texts, and scholarship on the life of Śākyamuni Buddha made Buddhism comprehensible to Westerners; on the other, it "undermined the spiritual authority of Asian Buddhists and denigrated the philosophical underpinnings of the entire body of Mahayana philosophy that was perceived to be a later and therefore less authentic expression of 'true' Buddhism."[39]

It is within this context that Jōdo Shinshū priests and missionaries were educated and during this time that they were being dispatched to "Buddhist missions" in the West. As Victoria Montrose and others have documented, during the Meiji not only were modern universities built on European and American models, but so were sectarian Buddhist schools.[40] Students in these universities would have necessarily been exposed to new ideas and new scholarship on their traditions in addition to learning doctrinal orthodoxy and ritual orthopraxy. Virtually all of the first wave of ministers serving the BMNA in the early twentieth century were educated in sectarian universities established by the Nishi Honganji. Sonoda, for example, in addition to studying at Tokyo University and Berlin University, studied at Honganji Kangaki. Nishijima studied at the precursor to Ryukoku University, Bukkyo Daigaku.[41] They would have been exposed to Western scholarship on Buddhism, which was more concerned with India, at a time when Japanese Buddhist intellectuals were interested in asserting their position as authorities. This necessarily would have implications for how the tradition developed in the American context. In his discussion of the early history of the BMNA, Ama discusses the Dharma Sangha of Buddha, a group of white converts in San Francisco supported by the Shin community. In its founding documents, nowhere does one find reference to Shinran or Jōdo Shinshū, and Ama notes that Sonoda and Nishijima lectured on Śākyamuni to the white congregation but lectured on Shin Buddhism to Issei Buddhists.[42] This seems to suggest a type of "parallel congregation," and elsewhere Ama posits that early Shin missionaries were overtly promoting a nonsectarian, universal, or even "Theravadaized" Buddhism.[43] However, it is important to note that there were virtually no Jōdo Shinshū sources in English at this time; full translations of Shin texts were not widely available until much later in the twentieth century. So when teaching in Japanese, Shin missionaries would have been able to address Jōdo Shinshū thought or doctrine; when teaching in English, they simply would not have had the language to discuss Shin Buddhism and naturally would have focused on "general" or "early" Buddhism.[44] Rather than viewing this ministry to white converts as focused wholly on "early Buddhism" or a focus on Śākyamuni as evidence of a rejection of normative Shin doctrine, we must keep in mind what was available in English as well as the cultural currents of the day, including the generalized "Indian turn" among Japanese Buddhist intellectuals at the time. As George Tanabe comments, and as evidenced by Pratt's aforementioned *Bussei* article, Śākyamuni is after all the source of the Pure Land sutras.[45]

Religious Syncretism and Buddhist Periodicals

Buddhist modernism has been defined, in part, as a syncretic tradition, one that blends premodern Buddhist ideas with Western thought broadly defined. This heterogeneous blend of sources came together to present and represent Buddhism for curious white Americans in the late nineteenth and early twentieth centuries. This blend included the products of colonial-era Orientalists, late Enlightenment and Romantic-era thought, the occult, and the nascent field of psychotherapy. The English translation of Eugène Burnouf's French translation of the *Lotus Sutra* by Transcendentalists in New England, for example, demonstrates the movement of a Buddhist text via colonial networks being brought into conversation with nineteenth-century American Romanticism. It is within this milieu that Henry Steel Olcott and Helena Blavatsky championed the occult and spiritualism, founded the Theosophical Society, and were able to take Buddhist precepts in Sri Lanka. And it was this same collection of cultural trends and impulses that led to the production of Buddhist periodicals. Pierce charts out nearly twenty English-language Buddhist publications from the 1890s through the years leading up to the United States' involvement in World War II.[46] Some were published by white converts or sympathizers and "blended occult tendencies with more traditional Buddhist themes."[47] Others were produced by Asian Buddhist missionaries such as Sonoda and Nishijima. The *Berkeley Bussei*, published by the children of such missionaries, was part of a larger trend of English-language publications on Buddhism in the early twentieth century, publications that were directed at diverse audiences. This was a period of increasing exchange between North America and Asia generally, Japan specifically, and thus these publications reflected the complexities of pan-Pacific cultural exchanges, what Tweed has referred to as the Meiji-Victorian Pacific world.[48] Such publications reveal the complex religious landscape in which early North American Shinshū developed. And *The Buddhist Ray* provides us with one clear example of this complexity.

The Buddhist Ray, "the first English-language journal of Buddhism," was produced by Philangi Dasa from 1888 to 1895 and distributed from his home in the Santa Cruz Mountains in California.[49] Born Herman Vetterling in 1849, Dasa emigrated to the United States from Sweden in 1871 and became a naturalized citizen, homeopathic doctor, Swedenborgian minister, and Theosophist. By 1886 he was living with his wife in California, and around that time he published the expansive *Swedenborg the Buddhist or the Higher Swedenborgianism Its Secrets and Thibetan Origin*. This account of a series of conversations between Swedenborg and a host of religious figures and philosophers, conveyed to Dasa in his dreams, is similar in theme to such contemporaneous works as Blavatsky's *Isis Unveiled*, purporting to reveal the hidden meanings behind, in this case, Swedenborg's theology. "While Swedenborg claimed to reveal the hidden meanings of Hebrew and Christian scriptures, [Dasa] claimed to reveal the hidden meanings of Swedenborg."[50] That such meanings were Buddhist in origin and the common core of all religions was a familiar perennialist and theosophical refrain.[51] *The Buddhist Ray* was "quirky" and not as sophisticated as the journals and magazines that would follow it; nevertheless, it had a large distribution and wide influence in the late nineteenth-century Buddhist-occult-theosophical world. Subscribers could be found well beyond California and across Asia, and the work attracted the attention of Anagarika Dharmapala and D. T. Suzuki, who was introduced to Swedenborg's thought during his first visit to the United States in 1893. *The Buddhist Ray*—along with other such English-language publications, many of which were translated into Japanese[52]—"forms a node of communication in a complex web where syncretic adaptations of Buddhism fed and structured how Asian Buddhists regarded themselves, especially in a pancultural context."[53]

As Japanese culture, religions, and politics were being reframed and reimagined during and after the Meiji Restoration, a syncretic and eclectic blend of Asian and Western spiritual, religious, occult, and philosophical thought was converging in America, allowing for the publication and dissemination of Buddhist texts and Buddhist-influenced publications such as *The Buddhist Ray*. And, rather than viewing Jōdo Shinshū missionaries as simply attending to the needs of the Japanese immigrant community in a type of ethnic enclave, they were in fact a part of these cultural convergences. That is to say, Shin Buddhist missionaries were actively proselytizing to white converts and sympathizers and, in turn, white converts and sympathizers were a part of the nascent Shin community—though not always easy bedfellows, as in the curious case of Swami Mazziniananda.

While claiming to have attended the World's Parliament of Religions in 1893, Mazziniananda was almost certainly a patent medicine salesman who arrived in Pennsylvania from parts unknown in the 1890s before heading to California. In Los Angeles, he took on the role of Buddhist priest and began ordaining people as Buddhists in 1905. It wasn't long before the local press began a campaign to debunk his claims, his authority, and his psychic abilities. Despite the negative press, for several years he was able to easily navigate the nascent Buddhist scene in California, befriending Japanese missionaries and priests, and giving public lectures. In attendance at one such lecture was Shaku Sōen, Suzuki's teacher, who later wrote about the event. From 1908 until 1920, Mazziniananda lived mostly in Northern California, established several religious communities, ordained people constantly, wrote and published for journals such as Paul Carus's *Open Court*, and was a regular fixture at several BMNA-affiliated temples and churches. In fact, for a time he was apparently leading English-language services at several temples, including at the BMNA headquarters in San Francisco. Such services were eclectic to be sure, blending features of Buddhist, Hindu, occult, and wholly made-up costumes, rituals, and rites.[54] Figures such as Mazziniananda, Dasa, and even Olcott are all of a kind: white converts or sympathizers with an idiosyncratic blend of beliefs, practices, and understandings of Buddhism, all of whom traveled in many of the same circles, coming into contact with various Buddhist modernists such as Dharmapala or Sōen, and often claiming an explicit Buddhist identity (and, just as often, additional simultaneous religious identities or affiliations). Whereas what little we know about Mazziniananda suggests that he was not much more than a con man in stolen robes, there is evidence that he created liturgies or services that would be either influential in or explicitly used by North American Shin Buddhists.[55] Finally, such history attests to the fluid nature of religious belonging and the permeable boundaries between Buddhist identities in the early twentieth century.

As the twentieth century wore on, anti-Japanese and anti-Buddhist sentiment and discriminatory legislation increased. The overt racism directed at the community and the community's awareness of the need to not draw any unnecessary attention to itself almost certainly played a part in the eventual expulsion of Mazziniananda from any official role within the BMNA or affiliated communities.[56] At the same time, however, we must guard against the impulse to view this early stage of North American Shin Buddhist history exclusively in terms of immigration, racism, and ethnic exclusion. Indeed, the very presence of Mazziniananda and other white converts and sympathizers attests to the multiethnic character of the community almost from its very inception. English-language publications similarly attest to the desire on the part of Shin Buddhist leaders to reach out to non-Japanese Americans, to spread the dharma beyond the confines of the immigrant community. And *Light of Dharma*, published by Sonoda and Nishijima, is but one example of this impulse.

Light of Dharma was published from 1901 to 1907 and, like *The Buddhist Ray*, had a surprisingly large circulation across North America and the Pacific world. It was produced almost entirely by Sonoda and Nishijima, who, we should recall, had only just arrived in the United States and were responsible for a rapidly growing organization that oversaw Buddhist communities across both the United States and Canada. Pierce, in wondering why the pair would undertake such a project, rightly points out that in addition to attending to the needs of the Japanese immigrant population, Sonoda and Nishijima were missionaries: "Why *wouldn't* Buddhist missionaries attempt to make converts in addition to caring for their countrymen and women?"[57] Of course, whereas the Dharma Sangha of Buddha and *Light of Dharma* were proselytization projects, they were also more than this. Pierce argues convincingly that the publication of *Light of Dharma* was "part of the larger project of including Japanese Buddhism in the scholarly, intellectual, and religious discourses about Buddhism in the modern world."[58] However, she also notes that *Light of Dharma* presented "its audiences an idealized Buddhist universalism" rather than a specifically Jōdo Shinshū perspective. Like other publications of the time, the magazine was more likely to present a generalized Buddhism, one that was pansectarian, foregrounded Śākyamuni over Amida, and was focused on "early Buddhism" rather than later developments. Scholars have argued that this universalism is evidence that the BMNA and early North American Shin Buddhist community were explicitly distancing themselves from a sectarian Shin identity, especially when proselytizing to white converts. Ryan Anningson, for examples, argues that even for Nisei, American Shin Buddhists argued for a return to "original Buddhism" and that "most English language Buddhist publications at this time were about Theravāda."[59]

This inclination toward a universal Buddhism is, perhaps, not surprising. On the one hand, as Shin Buddhists were in effect introducing Buddhism to a general audience, starting with "the basics" makes sense from a purely pedagogical point of view. Moreover, given the general impulse toward universalism or perennialism, especially among white converts and sympathizers, framing Buddhism in such a way would not be out of step with larger intellectual currents of the day. However, it seems to me that scholars are overstating the idea that North American Shin Buddhists were wholly invested in a nonsectarian universal Buddhism or that any inclusion of Śākyamuni is evidence of a rejection of Amida. Indeed, the fact that Amida is the central object of devotion in normative Jōdo Shinshū does not mean that Śākyamuni is and always has been absent; rather, Śākyamuni plays an important role in normative Shinshū, as discussed earlier—namely, to teach the Pure Land path of practice. As we have seen in our earlier discussion of Jōdo Shinshū, direct references to Shin Buddhism can be found throughout the *Berkeley Bussei*, voiced by both Japanese American Buddhists and white converts. How do we reconcile these explicit sectarian references with this scholarly argument that North American Shin Buddhists were promoting a "universal Buddhism"? The answer, it seems to me, is simple: they were doing both. *In addition* to presenting a universal Buddhism, one that countered or was in dialogue with current Western intellectual trends, early North American Shin Buddhists were *also* promoting Jōdo Shinshū. I make this argument by noting that the first generation of Shin missionaries to Hawai'i and the mainland were educated primarily in sectarian Shin Buddhist universities; they would have been well versed in current Japanese Buddhist intellectual trends and historical scholarship as well as sectarian perspectives on their tradition. It is unlikely they would have simply abandoned a sectarian viewpoint upon arrival in America. Evidence for this can be found in the numerous references to Jōdo Shinshū in the *Bussei* by white converts. Moreover, I simply take for granted that Shin Buddhist missionaries were, in fact, Shin Buddhists. That is, it seems to me that there is an unexamined assumption being made about what constitutes proper Shin Buddhism—namely, the absence of the historical Buddha, references to the founder or specific texts, and so on—and once these elements are found lacking, the tradition is rendered not properly Shin. I take a different approach. Rather than asking *whether or not* the early North American Shin community is Shin, I ask *in what way* they express Shin Buddhism.

Modern Shin Buddhist Apologetics

To see in what way North American Shin Buddhists expressed a sectarian Jōdo Shinshū and how this perspective is elided in the scholarship on American Buddhism, here we will examine two pieces of writing by two Imamuras: *Democracy According to the Buddhist Viewpoint* by Yemyō Imamura and "Oneness" by his son Kanmo.

Yemyō Imamura (1867–1932) was born into a Nishi Honganji–affiliated Buddhist family in Fukui Prefecture. Educated at Keiō University in Tokyo, Imamura arrived in Honolulu in 1899 and, a year later, became the superintendent of the Honpa Honganji Mission of Hawai'i, a position he held until his death thirty years later. Given his long tenure at the start of Buddhism's establishment in Hawai'i, Imamura has received much scholarly attention, focused on his openness and cosmopolitan attitude toward the promotion of Buddhism outside Japan.[60] Additionally, scholars have noted his role as a community leader and involvement in the Japanese-language school controversies. Imamura opened the Honganji mission in Honolulu as a shelter for Japanese immigrant workers participating in labor strikes as well as during the 1918 influenza pandemic.[61] The Japanese-language school issue was particularly contentious on the islands. Whereas some immigrants simply wanted a way to ensure their Nisei children had access to the language and culture of their ancestors, others vehemently believed the schools were an obstacle to assimilation. Such a critique was as likely to come from white Americans as from Japanese Christians. Imamura wrote prolifically in English during this time, arguing that Buddhism was compatible with American ideals of freedom and democracy. It was within this context that he wrote the 1918 essay *Democracy According to the Buddhist Viewpoint*— which, I would argue, is more accurately titled *Democracy According to the Shin Buddhist Viewpoint*.

According to Jolyon Baraka Thomas, whereas this essay made claims about Buddhism that were "patently false" (as we will see below), "Imamura's immediate purpose was to forestall critique of Buddhism as antidemocratic and un-American."[62] During this period, Japanese Buddhist leaders were aware of the contradictions between the ideals of American liberal democracy, which claimed to afford equal rights to all persons, and the realities of racial discrimination and exclusion rendered both racially and religiously. "In other words," writes Tomoe Moriya, "he was questioning the exclusionary attitudes of those who were propagating 'democracy,' which ended up treating unfairly the Japanese immigrants who were regarded as 'aliens ineligible to citizenship.' "[63] There is little to dispute here, especially when reading Imamura's essay, wherein he writes:

Those who are not very well acquainted with the teachings and history of Buddhism are apt to regard it as advocating autocracy or absolutism. This is far from the truth. For the ethical, philosophical, and religious ideals of Buddhism, as manifesting themselves in the history of those nations where it has been most prospering, directly contradict the criticism, and are in perfect harmony with the principles of democracy.[64]

This is familiar modernist ground, an explicit attempt to bring the Buddhist tradition in line with modernist ideas of, in this case, democracy and the nation-state. At the same time, *Democracy According to the Buddhist Viewpoint* is *also* a Shin Buddhist apologetic.

Over the course of the first eight or nine pages of the essay Imamura discusses the many ways in which Buddhism and democracy are in accord. His argument rests on an idiosyncratic understanding of both Buddhism and democracy, namely, an emphasis on "oneness" and "egalitarianism." That is, according to Imamura, Buddhism's core philosophy is "absolute monism" and, based on such concepts as "suchness" (*tathātā*), rejects the idea of a duality between a creator god and human beings. This orientation lends itself to a sense of "universal brotherhood" and institutions such as the monastic sangha, "a perfect model of democracy" where the "principle of equality was carried out to its logical conclusion."[65] In linking this ideal of democracy and equality so closely, Imamura seems to be suggesting that the latter more or less defines the former. I think we can set aside our judgments as to the soundness of this argument (for example, the monastic sangha is simply not democratic) and recognize that it is of a time, as it were.[66] What I would like to call our attention to here is that for two-thirds of this essay Imamura does not discuss a general Buddhism at all but presents a rather sophisticated Shin Buddhist apologetic.

Imamura turns his attention to Shin Buddhism with a discussion of the sect's founding in Japan by Shinran. He mentions the pattern of early Shin communities being organized as *dōjō*, meeting places for *dōgyō*, as discussed earlier in this chapter. He links the Shin *dōjō* directly to the ideal of universal brotherhood, equality, and democracy. The basis for this social organization is linked to the tradition's core mythos, the ideal of the Pure Land and Amida's compassion, which embraces all sentient beings: "Love and Mercy. Love is infinite, faith is absolute, and this is where all sentient beings meet on terms of equality."[67] This core belief of Shin Buddhism is further explicated over several pages, leading Imamura to claim that Jōdo Shinshū's "pacific, liberal, and democratic influence is perceivable wherever the Shinshū Sect has found its way."[68] The next section of the essay is more challenging. On the one hand, Imamura discusses further what he believes democracy to be and criticizes those who claim but fail to live up to the ideal; he almost seems to be suggesting that democracy is doomed to failure. He goes on to make a distinction between "philosophical" and "religious" Buddhism. In philosophical Buddhism, one intellectually understands the nonduality of buddhanature; yet humans assert their individuality as a result of circumstance, heredity, environment, and education. This level of individuality draws some to democracy, others to autocracy, and this inevitability of what can only be described as karmic causes and conditions evokes a passage from the Shin classic *Tannishō*.[69] From the religious perspective, however, "the ideal of the Shinshū is the realization of the Pure Land in one's own life."[70] This is where the contradictions between the ideal of buddhanature and individual human difference are reconciled. From this point of view, democracy and autocracy are merely extremes on a continuum of viewpoints that stand in contradistinction with the ultimate reality of buddhanature, suchness, the Pure Land, and Amitābha. It is only once this realization is truly internalized that peace may prevail. "We do not advocate democracy, nor do we rejoice over autocracy. They are both fragmentary views of life; for whatever our individual and national differences, are we not living in the unity of the Dharma, in the great of Ocean of Love and Mercy of Amitābha Buddha?"[71]

Whereas this essay is rightly understood as part of a larger genre of English-language Buddhist writing attempting to defend Buddhism against anti-Japanese and anti-Buddhist sentiment, it is also clearly a Shin Buddhist exegetical work. Imamura's distinction between "philosophy" and "religion" evokes the classical Buddhist idea of the two truths, the truth of ultimate reality and the truth of conventional reality. His analysis also seems to draw on the specifically Shin Buddhist version of two truths—namely, a distinction between "Buddhist law" (i.e., the dharma) and imperial law.[72] As the early Shinshū community was often derided as both heretical and immoral, Shin thinkers promulgated the belief that one could be inwardly devoted to Amida while outwardly following the norms and customs of society.[73] In 1871, during the early Meiji period, Nishi Honganji's *monshu* Kōnyo wrote a pastoral letter to the community wherein he invoked this two-truths doctrine and made a "powerful case for Shinshū as a sect that [would] support the Meiji state and its projects."[74] Certainly, this is a sentiment that Imamura would have been familiar with as a Nishi Honganji priest and a product of late Meiji education. And yet we need to caution against a simplistic or reductionist read of Imamura's piece; that is, he is not simply arguing for an orthodox interpretation of Shin Buddhism. As Moriya reminds us, this is an antiwar message, "written *during* World War I."[75] His opening refrain, after all, is: "How long are we yet to be groaning in agony under the terrible pressure of the world-war?"[76] Like many at the time, Imamura was undoubtedly war weary and expressed this sentiment using the religious language most readily at hand.

Let us return to the beginning of the essay, when Imamura first brings our attention to Shin Buddhism:

> [Jōdo Shinshū] has the largest number of influential followers and is the most representative Buddhist sect in the East. The Shinshū Sect is really the rational culmination of the Buddhist teachings as they have gradually unfolded themselves in history. If Buddhism were to thrive among us as a living faith, it could not but be the Shinshū in which all the philosophy and religion of Buddhism finds its permanent solution.[77]

As we will see in Chapter 2, the modernist project in Japan created the conditions whereby Buddhist intellectuals did not merely define religion but defined Buddhism as essential to a Japanese spirit, one that would, over time, be used as justification for Japan's imperial and colonial projects across the Pacific. As a modern religion, Buddhism must be rendered in universal terms; at the same time, as a defining feature of Japanese nationalist culture, it must also be uniquely Japanese. Robert Sharf has explored this contradictory stance, especially in the work of D. T. Suzuki, in his well-known essay "The Zen of Japanese Nationalism." According to Sharf, for Suzuki, "while Zen experience is the universal ground of religious truth, it is nonetheless an expression of a uniquely *Japanese* spirituality."[78] Of course, Suzuki knew that Zen is originally from China, but he argues that "the Zen life of the Japanese came to full flower in Japanese spirituality." Sharf continues that for Suzuki "Japanese Zen constitutes not only the essence of Buddhism, but also the essence of the Japanese spirit. It is the key to everything authentic, sacred, and culturally superior in Japan."[79] We can see echoes of this rhetoric in Imamura's essay. There is a family resemblance between Suzuki's notion of Zen's full flowering and Imamura's claim that Shinshū is the rational culmination of Buddhist thought.

Let us now turn our attention to the *Berkeley Bussei* and Kanmo Imamura (1904–1986). Yemyō's eldest son, Kanmo, was born in Honolulu but was sent to Japan when he was four years old on the assumption that he would inherit the family temple, Sentokuji in Fukui Prefecture. Kanmo spent most of his youth in Japan, studied at Keiō University like his father, and then returned to Hawai'i to help his mother after the elder Imamura's death. It was during this time that he began a correspondence with the Matsuura family, who were living in Guadalupe, California. By the end of the decade, Imamura had started graduate work at the University of California, Berkeley, and immediately after Pearl Harbor, he and the Matsuuras' eldest daughter, Jane, were married.[80] As we will see over the course of this book, their partnership and time in Berkeley would prove invaluable for the development of American Buddhism, and the *Berkeley Bussei* played a crucial role. Like his father, the younger Imamura was open-minded and argued for a universal or cosmopolitan Buddhism; however, also like his father, this impulse did not come at the expense of Jōdo Shinshū.

In his discussion of the *Bussei*, Anningson observes that "article after article is written on [the historical Buddha], Nikāya study guides, and instructions for meditation, none of which are traditionally a part of Shin Buddhist practice."[81] He uses this observation to argue that Nisei Buddhists were more interested in a universal Buddhism or the historical Buddha than Jōdo Shinshū. This may have been the cause of conflict within the community: "[Kanmo] Imamura describes the disagreements within the Bussei groups over whether Amida or Śākyamuni should be the basis of faith, and writes that a 'battle' broke over some young people replacing Amida with Śākyamuni on the church altar."[82] In a 1951 *Bussei* article, "Oneness," Imamura makes reference to this conflict:

> The issue brought out at every gathering in the Buddhist circles now seem to be the controversial "Should we have Amida or Shakyamuni as our basis of faith?" I have even heard of occasions where young people considered replacing the picture of Amida with that of Shakyamuni. "Only Shin Buddhism!" one cries; "Original Buddhism" the other cries, ... until it is heard almost like a battle cry.[83]

First, it is clear that Imamura is not describing an actual "battle"; rather, the phrase "a battle cry" is used metaphorically to discuss ongoing debates within the community. As mentioned earlier, there was a dearth of English-language materials on Shinshū at this time, and as they were raised in a primarily English-speaking context, Nisei Buddhists would have had the unique experience of being raised in the world of Jōdo Shinshū culture and practice while having very little exposure to Shin doctrine. For figures such as Kanmo Imamura, bridging this divide would have presented significant challenges. Moreover, as someone with a demonstrated interest in spreading the dharma beyond the Japanese American community, it is probably not surprising, as Ama notes, that Imamura "kept Amidist faith to himself, but he remained open-minded" to other forms of Buddhist practice.[84] But did he, in fact, keep his Shin faith to himself? A close read of "Oneness" reveals other possibilities. Imamura opens this essay by claiming that if someone were to ask you to choose who was your "true parent"—your mother or your father—you would think they were delusional. He not only implies that making this choice between Amida and Śākyamuni is equally foolish but goes on to suggest that even debating the issue is a sign of immaturity and an impediment to Buddhism's success in this country. Evoking once again the notion of relativistic and absolute truth, he states "that as long as we are what we are, and must deal with relative terms, we must have a symbol for our faith." And, finally, it "is important that we understand what the symbol stands for, whether Amida or Shakyamuni, for are they not our Father and Mother, and ultimately the same and One?"[85] Whereas Imamura is gesturing toward some larger doctrinal debate among Nisei Buddhists, he seems to be dismissing it all at once. His argument, as we will see in the following chapter, relies on a fairly recognizable modernist trope of reinterpreting Buddhist doctrine in symbolic terms. But we would do well to keep in mind that Amida is not left out of this conversation, and regardless of the severity of the debate between those arguing for or against Amida or Śākyamuni, an Amida statue stands on the Berkeley Buddhist Temple's altar.

Whereas we are right to read both Imamuras as advocating for a universalistic or cosmopolitan (Shin) Buddhism, and whereas there were points of tension within the community regarding the "basis of faith" (either the historical Buddha or Amida), this point of tension should not be read as a rejection of a specifically Shin Buddhist perspective. Moreover, such scholarly interpretations of midcentury North American Shinshū should be read within the context of a general scholarly disinterest in Pure Land Buddhism. As Galen Amstutz wrote in his seminal work *Interpreting Amida*:

> What accounts for the fact that Japan's richest, most powerful, and most distinctive early modern Buddhist institution is little known outside Japan? . . . In religious studies, why have monastic, Zen, or gurucentric conceptions of Buddhism dominated Western thinking since the nineteenth century? Why, in historical studies, if Shin played such a vital role in East Asian and Japanese cultural history (even reflecting political values relatively friendly to Western political values), has it been excluded from the standard narrative of that history?[86]

One answer may simply be intellectual chauvinism, the idea that Pure Land generally is not as philosophically sophisticated or as interesting as other forms of Buddhism. As Aaron Proffitt writes: "Early Western scholars were highly dismissive of Pure Land Buddhism in general and Shin Buddhism in particular; they saw it as a deviant, otherworldly East Asian tradition. Indeed, Shin Buddhism is an East Asian Mahayana tradition focused on the transhistorical Amitābha Buddha, not the historical Śākyamuni Buddha, and it does not valorize meditation or secret gnosis."[87] Arguably, Amstutz's body of scholarship has been directed at overcoming these scholarly deficiencies, demonstrating the philosophic sophistication of Shin Buddhist thought, and (as in *Interpreting Amida*) exploring larger political discourses that have sought to "control world conceptions of Japanese culture."[88]

A further reason the Shin aspects of midcentury North American Shin Buddhism seem curiously absent from the scholarship may simply be that we are asking the wrong questions. In her study of *Light of Dharma*, Pierce notes that nowhere in the publication do the authors talk about specific Shin ideas. "The tension between the Japanese Buddhist devotion to Shinran and the virtual silence in *Light of Dharma* about anything pertaining to Shinran or the *Lotus Sutra* is both heartbreaking and puzzling."[89] Similarly, in discussing the ordination of Sunya Pratt, Ama points out how in her essay on why she became a Buddhist, nowhere does she mention Shin Buddhism explicitly, and he uses this as evidence of a generalized trend toward "Universal Buddhism" in the late nineteenth- and early twentieth-century Shin Buddhist community.[90] This Universal Buddhism, a theme Ama picks up in his *Immigrants to the Pure Land*, is defined in part by an emphasis on Śākyamuni Buddha to the exclusion of Amida. As a result, Shin Buddhism is defined in certain terms or characteristics (specific texts, Amida,

Shinran); scholars look for these markers in the material and are unable to find them; therefore, such materials are judged "not really Shinshū." This rejection of Shinshū is made despite the fact that—regardless of how idiosyncratic Pratt (or other white converts at the time) may appear, regardless of whether or not Imamura kept his "Amidist faith" hidden—these figures were all employed by a Shin Buddhist organization. They were active members of a Shin community.[91] Here I ask, *what if?* What if, instead of predetermining what Shin Buddhism is *supposed* to look like, we simply take for granted the idea that these figures are Shin Buddhists and that this is what Shin Buddhism looks like for them?

Here I am drawing on the work of Talal Asad, who defines Islam as a discursive tradition "that includes and relates itself to the founding texts of the Qur'an and the Hadith."[92] He rejects the essentialist and reductionist notions of Islam as either tribal or universal and argues, instead, that it is a tradition. "A tradition consists essentially of discourses that seek to instruct practitioners regarding the correct form and purpose of a given practice that, precisely because it is established, has a history."[93] Similarly, Shin Buddhism is a tradition, one that may be defined as a discourse seeking to instruct practitioners on the correct form and modes of practice within the tradition. This discourse takes the form of a dialogue, as it were, between various sources of authority, both internal and external to the community—canonical sources, commentaries, the works of the founder, teachers and priests both past and present, the "internal" orthodoxy set by the Honganji, the "external" orthodoxy set by the secular Buddhist studies academy. This discourse defines the tradition, and it may take the form not just of the "expected" (Shinran, Amida) but also of the "unexpected"—an emphasis on Śākyamuni. And, of course, references to Śākyamuni should not be unexpected. Not only does the historical Buddha play a role in normative Shin doctrine, but there was a generalized interest in Indian or "early Buddhism" in both Western and Japanese scholarship in the early twentieth century. This interest may have manifested as certain "incongruities," such as Yemyō Imamura's decision to build the Hawaiʻian Honganji mission in a style resembling an Indian stupa.[94] This decision, however, should be taken not as evidence of a lack of interest in Shin Buddhism but rather as reflecting a time, specifically his time, and the then-common "Indian turn" within Japanese Buddhism. So when we ask, "What does Shin Buddhism look like for them?," this question might be literal, a reference to material religion, architecture, art, ritual, and practice. That is, what does religion *look like*, as opposed to what do religious persons *believe or think*? We can read the *Bussei* for evidence of Shin Buddhist ideas, doctrine, or philosophy; we can also read it for evidence of Shin Buddhist practice (e.g., the practice of *gasshō* mentioned earlier in this chapter). And we can comb the pages of the *Bussei* for Shin Buddhist art, poetry, and literature.

This expanded view of what Shin Buddhism is (or could be) is as inclusive of written records as it is other forms of religious expression, including the architectural motifs in Hawai'i and artistic expressions we find in the *Bussei*. Take, for example, the cover of the fall 1940 *Bussei* (Figure 1.1). The image is a line drawing of the Statue of Liberty, slightly in silhouette, with rays of light emanating from the statue's torch. Keeping in mind our perspective of distinctive simultaneity, it is perfectly reasonable to read this drawing within the context of a Japanese American ethnic organization (the Young Buddhist Association) in the years leading up to World War II, a time when the young person responsible for this drawing would have been wrestling with questions of identity and belonging, would have been facing discrimination both overt and subtle as the child of immigrants, as a non-Christian, and yet was a native-born American citizen. To draw an image of the quintessential American symbol of freedom and equality—especially for immigrants—on the cover of this magazine was a bold choice, to be sure, but also not surprising. It is a claim to an American identity often denied. And yet, it is *also* a Buddhist image. Compare the *Bussei* cover to a fairly normative image of Amida Buddha, one that would not have been surprising to see on the main altar of any Shin Buddhist temple at the time (Figure 1.2). The standing Amida has his hands in a mudra, representing that wisdom is accessible to even the lowest of beings and that his compassion is directed to those who cannot save themselves.[95] And he is emanating light. Rays of light burst forth from his aureole. It is not hard to imagine that when the artist sat down to draw an image of the Statue of Liberty, they thought, "How does one draw light?" And the answer was obvious. *This*. This is how one draws light.

I freely admit that this is speculative on my part, that other explanations and other readings of this *Bussei* cover are possible.[96] This is simply a thought experiment: if an artist were to be immersed in a particular religious context, how might they see and then represent the world? Once removed from that context, would we recognize those religious influences? Some may be obvious, may be similar to those of our own time and place; others may be less so. My intention here is not to make a strong argument about the interior motivations of this unknown artist. Rather, I want to draw our attention to a more fundamental question: what *counts* as Buddhist art—indeed, *who* counts as a Buddhist, as an American, as worthy of consideration and of humanity? These questions will occupy our time in the following chapters, in particular Chapter 5, where such subtle images and orientations toward Shin Buddhism will be instrumental to Buddhism's coming popularity in the latter half of the century. For now, I want us to bear in mind that rather than prejudging what counts as Shin Buddhist, and then finding our subjects lacking, let us instead ask *how* our subjects are articulating a Shin

Figure 1.1 Cover of the fall 1940 issue of the *Berkeley Bussei.*

Buddhist perspective and how this was necessarily a reflection of their time and place: early to mid-twentieth-century America. This time and place saw the emergence of syncretic modernist ideas that would influence generations of American Buddhists, including the young Buddhists under study here, the authors of the *Bussei*. And just as Shin Buddhist discourse is deemphasized in

Figure 1.2 Amida Buddha, ritual image. Used by permission of the Berkeley Buddhist Temple.

studies of early American Shin Buddhist history, Shin Buddhism is often elided or excluded altogether in scholarship on Buddhist modernism, a point to which we turn in the following chapter.

2

A Rational Teaching

It would indeed be a sad day for Buddhism when intellectual pursuit becomes a detriment to Buddhist progress, for Buddha himself, if the scriptures be true, was an advocate of the true scientific spirit. He did not say "Accept my teachings on faith alone." Rather, he advised that nothing must be taken on trust of an authority. Only by a test of reason and experience are we finally to accept any belief or theory.[1]

This short passage is the opening salvo of an essay by Kimi Hisatsune (née Yonemura, 1923–2012) from the *Berkeley Bussei*. Hisatsune was an active member of the Berkeley YBA, resident of the girls' dorm, and composer of many Shin Buddhist songs. Later in her life, she would serve on the BCA Centennial History Project Committee and help compile the official record of Jōdo Shinshū's first century in the United States. Her claim here in 1953 that "nothing must be taken on trust of an authority" resonates strongly with the common modernist assumption that the Buddhist tradition is one of reason and free inquiry. In just this one short passage, we can immediately see the modernist tendencies within the *Bussei*, and indeed in what follows we will see several more. But are the *Bussei* and the work of the Young Buddhist Association so easily reducible to the tropes of Buddhist modernism? What might modernism have meant for them as they staked a claim for their American Buddhist identities before and after the camps? How did a modern Buddhism function at the intersection of race and religion at midcentury? And just what is Buddhist modernism anyway?

In this chapter, I begin with an answer to that final question and locate the origins of Buddhist modernism in colonial Asia. Fundamentally, scholars have deployed the trope of Buddhist modernism to explain the complex of reactions by Buddhists and rearticulations of Buddhism in the face of colonialism and modernization from the late nineteenth century through most of the twentieth. It was within these contexts that, according to David McMahan, several overlapping "cultural processes" emerged and subsequently (re)shaped Buddhism into a rational and scientific religion—in short, the making of Buddhist modernism.[2] These processes, however, were not uniform across Asia, and one needs to be attentive to the various ways in which such discourses overlapped with specific nationalist projects on both sides of the Pacific. Regardless, such tendencies are on full display in the *Bussei*, wherein we are repeatedly reminded that Buddhism is

The Making of American Buddhism. Scott A. Mitchell, Oxford University Press. © Oxford University Press 2023.
DOI: 10.1093/oso/9780197641569.003.0003

a peaceful and civilizing religion, consonant with modern science, and superior to other putatively superstitious religions and faiths. This type of exceptionalism is an important feature of any modernist project wherein the lacks and failings of the contemporary world are said to be corrected by Buddhist practice. However, as I argue here, we need to be attentive to the specific context of these Nisei Shin Buddhist modernists and how this project was deployed before, during, and after the camps. As will be discussed in greater detail in Chapter 3, Nisei Buddhists were staking a claim for themselves as fully and authentically American and in so doing called attention to the specific failings of America's multicultural and religious ideals. Buddhism as corrective to modernism's lack, then, has a particular valence here that cannot be separated from midcentury racial politics.

Finally, in claiming a space for Nisei Buddhists within the category of Buddhist modernism, I call our attention to the limits of this constructed scholarly category. On the one hand, I interrogate the unhelpful binary of traditional/modern by noting that American Shin Buddhists are often excluded from the category of Buddhist modernism despite their thoroughly modernist tendencies. However, and drawing on the work of McLaughlin, Payne, and Quli, I note that the inclusion of Asian American Buddhists in the category only serves to highlight one of the key weaknesses of the Buddhist modernism frame: it is totalizing. At the end of the day, virtually everyone becomes modern. So, rather than arguing for mere inclusion, I discuss the ways in which scholars have collected, authenticated, and codified a lineage of Buddhist moderns, one that necessarily excludes Asian Americans despite their active participation in the making of Buddhist modernism. Ultimately, this exclusion mirrors the exclusion of Asian Americans generally from American Buddhist history.

Defining Buddhist Modernism

For several decades now, scholars of Buddhism generally and of American Buddhism in particular have been seemingly preoccupied with one question— what happened? Specifically, what happened to the Buddhist tradition as it both entered the "modern period" and interacted with European culture? As discussed in the introduction, when tracing the movement of Buddhism to the West scholars occasionally present a *longue durée* historical sketch, stretching back to Gandhara, Alexander the Great, Barlaam and Josaphat, and so on, as Robinson and Johnson do in *The Buddhist Religion*.[3] Stephen Batchelor similarly takes the long view in his *Awakening of the West*, charting all manner of ways in which Buddhism interacted with various European cultures over the course of two millennia.[4] Such studies are, of course, interesting, but from a certain point of view they are meaningless and anachronistic. The way in which we conceptualize the world as divided into "the West" and "the Orient" would have been unknown to persons living in, say, the Mongolian steppes as they took their cultic practices with them into what is now part of the greater Russian Federation. Not only would people not have divided the world into these broad and ill-conceived categories, but they would not have had subjective identities linked to geopolitical modern nation-states, nor would they have thought about their cultic practices as being a "religion" at all, and certainly not as one religion among many that one could choose as various options in the religious marketplace. Europe itself was barely an idea. And so this question—what happened to Buddhism as it came into contact with European culture?—is not about the long view; it is about colonialism.

The answer to the question of how Buddhists responded to, and thus how Buddhism was affected and changed by, the violence of colonialism is complicated, as it should be, given the historically and geographically uneven and specific ways that colonial rule was deployed across Asia over several centuries. It is worth noting, however, that there are some general trends we can point to that marked a distinct change in the Buddhist world, trends that are usually blamed on colonial or European influence; further, this European influence arguably tells us more about the academic study of Buddhism than about Buddhism itself. To the first point, scholars have generally shown that Buddhist responses to colonialism and colonial control often involved the laicization of the sangha and decreasing monastic authority (often due to the colonial disestablishment of the sangha); the rise in secular meditation practices; the deployment of scientific rhetoric in Buddhist apologetics in response to Christian missionary efforts; and the use of Western philosophy and political ideologies in the interpretation of "traditional" Buddhist doctrines. This bundle of orientations, to borrow from Natalie Quli, has been collected into a generalized "paradigm of Buddhist modernism" and applied to different parts of Buddhist Asia in the colonial and postcolonial periods.[5]

What, exactly, is Buddhist modernism? Regardless of whether or not scholars describe Buddhist modernism as singular or multiple, as a narrative or a discourse, the vaguely specific (or specifically vague) term "modernism" has a set of broadly defined characteristics, which Quli helpfully summarizes in a thirteen-point bulleted list in her article "Multiple Buddhist Modernisms."[6] This list includes such features as the "extolling of reason and rationality," the rejection of ritual, social engagement, "the tendency to define Buddhism as a philosophy rather than as a religion," and "a belief in the compatibility of Buddhism and modern science," among other traits. In his seminal work on the subject, *The Making of Buddhist Modernism*, David McMahan details three "cultural processes" that have allowed for the emergence of various strands of Buddhist modernism: detraditionalization, demythologization, and psychologization.

Collectively, these processes reimagine Buddhist cosmologies and mythologies as symbolic, as metaphorical, or as representing states of mind rather than physical or literal realities. And in part as a consequence of the reliance on textual authority, Buddhist modernists shift religious authority from traditional religious experts (monastics and priests) to the authority of personal experience. As we will see in what follows, Buddhist texts such as the *Kālāma Sutta* are viewed by Buddhist moderns as evidence of Buddhism's compatibility with scientific rationalism, "exemplifying an empiricist spirit of free inquiry and self-determination."[7] Or, in Hisatsune's words quoted at the opening of this chapter, "nothing must be taken on trust of an authority."[8]

Whereas Buddhist modernism is inextricably bound up with the colonial and therefore suggestive of a specific era, it is important to keep in mind that modernism is as much, if not more, a marker of the *relationship* between past and present. The rhetoric of modernism is about the rupture between the two. That is, as Marylin Ivy writes, the ancient Romans thought of themselves as modern precisely because they looked to the past and judged themselves superior. It is not that the modern signals a specific era or epoch; rather, it concerns the discursive self-reflective turn whereby persons in the present evaluate their situation relative to the past. Each "modern" turn will necessarily be infused with the particulars of time and place. "While we can muse on the wonder of ancient Romans calling themselves modern," Ivy writes, "we should resist the seduction of unmediated identification with them or imagine that their notion of the modern is the same" as ours.[9] In other words, it is not the case that any people at any time may think of themselves as modern, thus rendering the term useless. The point is to notice the particular contours of the modern turn and the judgments that follow. Indeed, in declaring "We are modern," the moderns evaluate their position relative to the past, and the judgment that ensues—whether or not the past is better or worse—is not predetermined. Often it is contested. For contemporary moderns, while some may embrace the benefits of modern conveniences or the certainty of modern science, others will find these lacking, convinced that in our rush forward we have lost something, that we have disconnected ourselves from some idyllic or traditional premodern culture of purity and connection with the natural world. McMahan highlights this phenomenon when he writes of the double-edged sword of rational empiricism. While modern science provides answers about the workings of the natural world, it runs the risk of being pure materialism with no space for spiritual realities.[10] An essential feature of modernism—and especially Buddhist modernism—is *disconnection*. Disconnection may manifest in a Romantic's return to nature or the Victorian return to morals; more recently, it manifests in the ongoing deployment of what Jeff Wilson has called "Buddhist jeremiads," whereby Buddhist apologists detail all that is wrong with modern American culture and offer mindfulness as the cure.[11] This, it should be noted, is a type of "Buddhist exceptionalism" that rests on the uncritically accepted notion that the dharma is a necessarily ahistorical and transcultural fact (often explicitly linked to science, e.g., equating karma with Newtonian physics) rather than a religion. Rendered in this way, Buddhism may be offered as the cure to the failings of modernity.

As mentioned, European colonialism's impact across Asia was varied and un-even. Japan, as has oft been remarked, was never directly colonized, though the influence of Western imperialism cannot be denied. The history of Japanese and Japanese Buddhist modernism has direct relevance to American Buddhism, as this was the cultural and intellectual milieu from which the first generation of Japanese Buddhists emigrated to the Americas. Narratives of Japanese moder-nity almost always begin with the "opening of Japan," when U.S. Commodore Matthew Perry sailed his black ships to the island nation in the 1850s and demanded, at gunpoint, that they begin formal relations with the West. Such an origin story carries with it the rhetoric of rupture and belies the fact that al-though the Tokugawa government had a long-standing isolationist policy, Japan was well aware of European colonialist projects on the Asian mainland and had been visited by Jesuit missionaries centuries before Perry's arrival.[12] By the time trade agreements with the Americans had wrecked the Japanese economy and paved the way for the Meiji Restoration in 1868, Japan was primed to begin a modernization project that would turn the isolationist country into the major power in the Pacific within a generation. This modernization project had a pro-found impact on religion in Japan, and it goes without saying that the study of Japanese Buddhist modernism is a subject that has received ample scholarly attention—far more than we can do justice to here. Of concern for our present purpose is the fact that religion (and Buddhism) was defined in concert with "the Shinto secular," an ideology "formulated in terms of a nation-state ... distin-guished from religion, and intended to produce a unified Japanese subjectivity."[13] That is, Buddhism came to be defined not only as a religion but also within a broader context of defining Japanese national identity, and it was this complex of orientations and discourses that Japanese immigrants brought with them when they began arriving in Hawai'i and on the U.S. mainland in the late 1800s.

For a time during the early Meiji, Buddhism was an object of persecution as a putatively "foreign" religion.[14] This persecution was short-lived, as Japanese Buddhist leaders and intellectuals quickly began to reposition themselves and argue for their relevancy in the new modern Japanese nation-state. Buddhist thinkers sought to "claim some territory for themselves, with Shinto having seized the position of national tradition and Christianity claiming for itself the position of universal religion."[15] To claim this territory, some drew on preexisting doctrine to argue that one could follow the rule of secular law outwardly but Buddhist doctrine inwardly, as we saw in the previous chapter in our discussion of Yemyō Imamura's *Democracy According to the Buddhist Viewpoint* and the Shin Buddhist interpretation of the "two truths." According to Melissa Anne-Marie Curley, such a move ceded the national tradition territory to so-called state Shinto; however, it left Buddhism open to a challenge from Christians, who had recently been allowed to practice in Japan following the Tokugawa-era persecution. Buddhist thinkers began to argue that Buddhism was a better fit for the country because, though it was a "foreign" religion like Christianity, it "had long had a place in the hearts of Japanese people."[16] To make this two-pronged argument—that Buddhism is both an essential part of Japanese history/culture and a universal religion—meant necessarily to define Buddhism in relation to Christianity. Or, put another way, such arguments were part of the modernist zeitgeist and rearticulation of Buddhism and Buddhist doctrine in conversation with Western philosophy. The work of Enryō Inoue perhaps best exemplifies this mood. In brief, Inoue sought to define religion in contradistinction with both the secular and the superstitious, included Śākyamuni in a pantheon of philosophical sages alongside Confucius and Kant, and "asserted that Buddhism was a 'religion' and that, as such, it was an essential part of 'civilization' and could be beneficial for the nation."[17] Inoue, like many of his late nineteenth-century contemporaries, was both a Jōdo Shinshū priest and involved in the establishment of modern Japanese universities, both secular and Buddhist.[18] And many of the early missionaries to the Americas were students at these universities, immersed in the intellectual climate of late Meiji-era Buddhist modernism. Thus, as Shin Buddhist laborers were emigrating to Hawai'i and the U.S. mainland, the Buddhist priests and missionaries who followed them were being educated within the context of a developing modernist discourse about Buddhism and its role on the global stage.

This discourse overlapped with what has come to be known as *nihonjinron*: "a popular discursive enterprise devoted to the delineation and explication of the unique qualities of the Japanese, which invariably touts the cultural homogeneity as well as the moral and spiritual superiority of the Japanese vis-à-vis other peoples."[19] Of course, one should not presume that the *nihonjinron* project was itself "homogeneous"; how this chauvinistic understanding of Japanese culture and the Japanese people was deployed and developed over the course of the Meiji and through the Taishō and early Shōwa eras varied considerably. For example, whereas a general sense of Japanese superiority was clearly at work as the Japanese Empire waged war in and colonized parts of mainland Asia at the turn of the twentieth century, by the 1930s and 1940s this sense of superiority was increasingly intertwined with a samurai-inflected militarism, on the one hand, and a desire to include other ethnic groups in a nationalist identity, on the other. This turn is described by Takashi Fujitani as the move from a "violent racism" to a "polite racism," wherein people who were once deemed inferior and incapable of being included in the body politic are brought into the fold, so to speak, in circumscribed and managed ways largely for the benefit of the ruling power, a point to which we will return in Chapter 4.[20] Such impulses toward cultural superiority are certainly evident in what Azuma calls the "Issei pioneer thesis," the notion that Japanese immigrants "heroically" settled in the Americas as part of an expansionist impulse essential to the "racial blood" of the Japanese.[21] Religion, however, complicates things. While some Issei "pioneers" may have understood themselves as taking part in Japanese colonial projects here in the United States, others deployed rhetorics of "cosmopolitism," arguing merely for Japanese intellectual and cultural perspectives to be included on the modern global stage. This "Japanese spirit" (*Nippon seishin*) became part of a child-rearing strategy among Issei parents worried about their children's assimilation into American culture. And for Buddhists, Japanese-language schools in Hawai'i and on the West Coast were as much sites for learning about Buddhism as they were for learning the language. In this context, as will be discussed in Chapter 3, alongside a "Japanese spirit" one finds an explicitly *Buddhist* spirit among the Nisei.

Returning to our opening questions—what happened as the Buddhist tradition came into contact with European culture, and how was Buddhism impacted by colonialism and Western imperialism?—we see that one answer is the development of Buddhist modernism, the rearticulation of Buddhist ideas and practices, and the emergence of a particular type of Buddhist exceptionalism. The rhetoric of exceptionalism is a response to the modernist assumption that something has been lost in the transition from the past to the present, that there has been a rupture in that turn from the traditional to the modern. And in calling our attention to this rhetoric of rupture, we now return to the second point mentioned earlier—namely, that the history of colonialism and European influence on the development of modern Buddhism tells us more about the academic study of Buddhism than about Buddhism itself. That is, Buddhist modernism begins at the same moment as Buddhist studies as an academic field. This is not a coincidence.

The academic study of Buddhism took an important self-critical turn with the 1995 edited collection of essays *Curators of the Buddha*. In the introduction, Donald Lopez lists a number of persistent and recurring stereotypes about Asian culture and/or Buddhism and states that the following essays will "detail the historical conditions that led to the formation of these enduring ideas"—and inarguably these "historical conditions" are colonialism, which gave birth simultaneously to Buddhist modernism and to academic Buddhist studies. "Taken together, [the essays in *Curators of the Buddha*] offer new insights into the processes that have led to the construction of Buddhist Studies as an academic discipline by excavating the contested grounds upon which it was built."[22] *Curators* began what has been nearly three decades now of thoughtful and necessary self-reflective criticism within the academic field of Buddhist studies that accounts for the field's birth under colonialism. This is to say that the terms "Buddhism" and "religion" were articulated within colonial contexts that shaped not only how Buddhism-as-religion was *practiced* (the strategies Buddhists employed to counter European hegemony) but also how it was *studied* as the object of intellectual and academic fascination. As has been expertly detailed by Philip Almond, Richard King, Tomoko Masuzawa, and others, it was European colonialists and Orientalists who, in the late nineteenth century, "discovered" that "the resemblances, links, and genealogical relations among some extremely varied and seemingly discrete instances of cult practice observed" across a broad swath of Asia all had their origins in a historical figure named Siddhartha Gautama.[23] The fact that Buddhism had seemingly died out in India led to one version of the "what happened" question—specifically, what happened to Buddhism in the land of its birth, and how can we (scholars), in the modern period, recover what was lost? The answer to that second question, of course, was to locate and translate the sacred texts of the Buddhist tradition studied in isolation from the persons practicing the tradition in colonial Asia. Based largely on textual studies infused with the ideologies of colonialism and Orientalism, a distinction was drawn between "pure" or "original" Buddhism and "whatever the locals are doing nowadays," creating a hierarchy of value between Buddhism as lived tradition and Buddhism as one among many "world religions." Again, this discovery and creation of Buddhism is also regularly cited as the origin story of academic Buddhist studies itself. That is, the very category of "Buddhism-as-religion" was conceived by European Orientalists and colonial civil servants, and these same actors would later go on to become, as Charles Prebish and other have shown, the forebears of Buddhist studies.[24] Or, in Lopez's words, "the emergence of the academic study of Buddhism in Europe and America [happened] within the context of the ideologies of empire."[25]

And so, when seeking an answer to the question of "what happened," scholars necessarily come to face themselves as creators and curators of Buddhist modernism. Or, as Payne notes, "Buddhist modernism is an ideological framework. . . . [T]here are no leaders proclaiming Buddhist modernism, only scholars using the term to identify a complex of mutually supportive ideas and to describe the changes in Buddhist institutions and teachings over the last century and a half."[26] Drawing on the work of Talal Asad and Renato Rosaldo, among others, Quli critiques the use of the Buddhist modernism paradigm and the traditional/modern dichotomy and rightly names scholarship on Buddhist modernism as a type of "imperialist nostalgia."[27] Implicit within the "what happened" question is the assumption that, whatever it was that happened, it was bad. Again, this is the logic of modernism; when modernity is viewed not merely as temporal but also as an idea, we see how it is a discursive relationship between present and past whereby the moderns judge the past as either lacking or idyllic. Richard Payne describes this as the rhetoric of rupture, "a fundamentally religious formulation," by which the past is cut off from the future by the appearance of the prophet or whatever millennial or cataclysmic event is at hand. "Like all good rhetorics," Payne writes, "it is so deeply rooted in our literary culture as to flow from an author's fingers almost entirely unthinkingly and to pass before a reader's eyes almost entirely unnoticed."[28] In the specific case of the rupture between premodern and modern Buddhism, in the scholarly gaze it is the premodern that remains pure and pristine, unsullied by "the West" and the modern (often uncritically conflated) and, once placed into Masuzawa's hierarchy of values, is of more value, more real and more authentic, than whatever Buddhists may be doing today.[29] In Quli's formulation:

> The discourse concerning Buddhist modernism has carried with it a subtle claim that so-called "modern" Buddhists . . . are not "really" Buddhist at all; they are tainted by Western culture, philosophy, and religion, and as such are peripheral to the study of the "authentic" Buddhism that resides in a more "traditional" Asia. When mapped onto an essentialized Self/Other or West/East complex, Western Buddhists (of both the convert and so-called "ethnic" varieties), as well as Asian Buddhists of all stripes, are reduced to stereotypes of "traditional" and "modern" that fail to capture the multifaceted nature of their religious traditions, beliefs, and practices. It further produces "good savages" and "bad savages," condemning those who fail to live up to the standard of a non-Westernized "traditional Buddhism" that we have created as a mirror to the modern West.[30]

Moreover, because the proper field site for Buddhist studies is either the text or "those people over there," American Buddhism studies remains the unloved stepchild of Buddhist studies,[31] and Asian American Buddhists are dismissed as simultaneously practicing a bastardized version of Buddhism (corrupted either by modernity generally or America specifically) and doing so outside Buddhism's proper context (Asia).[32]

In the following section, we will see how Japanese Americans disrupt this binary formulation by deploying a fairly typical Buddhist modernist discourse despite being rendered "bad savages" by the scholarly modernist trope. In the pages of the *Bussei* one finds repeated references to Buddhism's compatibility with science, its pacifying and civilizing impulses, and a specific variety of Buddhist exceptionalism. This exceptionalism, I argue, is directly related to the fact that this version of Buddhist modernism is being articulated by a racially and religiously marginalized group in the midcentury American context. Their inclusion in the broader category of Buddhist modernism draws into question its utility and continued relevance.

American Buddhist Exceptionalism

In 1955, the Cambodian Theravada monk Vira Dharmawara was invited to the United States to attend a conference on education. During his time in California, he toured several Buddhist communities, including the Berkeley Buddhist Temple. The following year, his essay "Discourse on the Dharma" appeared in the *Bussei*. The "Discourse" is concerned primarily with *duḥkha*, or suffering, and begins with a refutation of the once common stereotype of Buddhism as essentially pessimistic. Dharmawara argues that one would not accuse a physician of being pessimistic for simply diagnosing an illness. He then provides the following gloss of the *Kālāma Sutta*:

> On one occasion the Buddha told Kalama: "Kalama, do not believe or accept anything simply because it has been said by your teacher or merely because it has been written in your sacred book, or merely because it has been believed by many, or merely because it has been handed down to you by your ancestors. Accept and live only that truth which you see face to face." With these words Buddha gave man the greatest freedom of thought and action, such as it is difficult to find anywhere throughout the long history of mankind.[33]

Dharmawara does not mention the *Kālāma Sutta* as such and has clearly conflated the villagers in Kalama with a specific person named Kalama. Leaving that aside, however, his essay makes direct links between the Buddha's teachings and the ability to overcome hate and prejudice, and it provides a paradigmatic modernist interpretation in his gloss of what McMahan has called "that most central of *suttas* in the modernist canon, in which the Buddha encourages a group of seekers to test teachings for themselves rather than accept them on faith."[34] This spirit of free inquiry is repeated elsewhere in the *Bussei*, such as by Hisatsune (as we mentioned at the opening of this chapter) as well as in the uncredited introduction to the "religious section" of the 1951 volume, which states: "True faith, we believe, must come from a careful consideration of the tenets expounded by the church. Nothing should be too sacred in our search for truth. The spirit of inquiry must be hampered neither by tradition nor authority. Such a quest is the Buddhist way."[35] This passage suggests not only a spirit of freedom of thought but also, in arguing that not even "tradition nor authority" should be immune from critique, that the authority of personal experience is to be valued above that of religious authority figures. This is what McMahan calls the process of "detraditionalization," which "embodies the modernist tendency to elevate reason, experience, and intuition over tradition and to assert the freedom to reject, adopt, or reinterpret traditional beliefs and practices on the basis of individual evaluation."[36]

In his discussion of the *Kālāma Sutta* within the context of scientific rationalism, McMahan argues that scientific rationalism and naturalism, a "general ... orientation endemic to modernity," has two features relevant to Buddhist modernism. First is the assumption that the world is "made up of predictable phenomena governed by natural laws that are discernible through systemic and detached observation, experimentation, and rational analysis." Second, and following from the first, is the possibility of nihilism. In short, if the world is reducible to natural phenomena, there is no space left for spiritual realities, leaving the world and persons without any intrinsic value or meaning. This is often cited as the cause of the modern malady of *disconnection*, the sense that there is something lacking in a purely materialist or scientific understanding of the world. Consequently, "Buddhist apologists ... began to articulate Buddhism in ways that would address both these features."[37]

This tension between rational empiricism and nihilism is apparent in the *Bussei* as well; there is a tacit assumption that Buddhism is rational and that this rationalism either leads to or is subservient to religious truths. Sei Shohara, for example, is to the point in his 1955 contribution when he writes: "It has been said many times in the past that Buddhism is a science, or that it is a scientific religion. The validity of this statement, of course, depends a great deal upon the definition that is placed on the word 'science.'" He goes on to show how the parallels between Buddhism and science are often superficial, easy conflations of karma with a generic, scientific cause-and-effect theory, for example. But when science is defined as "a branch of knowledge concerned with the systematic study of facts or principles," Shohara notes, these "facts and principles" are concerned only with the "physical and material world." Because "science is limited to the material world" it has "no place in the socio-humanistic world [and] any 'proof' of Buddhistic principles that Science is able to offer is merely another manifestation of the Truth of Buddhism"; therefore, the "appeal of Buddhism is not in the fact that it agrees with Science, but that Science today agrees with Buddhist Principles laid down centuries ago."[38] In other words, Buddhism is and has been true for over two millennia; modern science is simply playing catch-up.[39]

Like Buddhist modernists before them, contributors to the *Bussei* presented Buddhism as a rational and scientific religion while also placing Buddhism in a higher position than mere scientific rationalism. A short essay in 1956, for example, makes the claim that "Buddhism has a deep philosophical background. It holds nothing that contradicts natural science, yet is not merely cold logic."[40] The implication here is that Buddhist teachings are in accord with scientific

naturalism but that there is more to the dharma than a mere logical explanation of the world. The point of religion is to live "an enlightened life." A visiting
scholar of Tibetan Buddhism from Japan, Tokan Tada, echoes the logic of the
Kālāma Sutta in his 1953 piece with an emphasis on the concept of doubt. Noting
a conversation he had with Kanmo Imamura, Tada observes that Americans
"are taught to approach everything with inquiring mind," which results in scientific progress but can also lead one to doubt truth claims. This might seem like
a problem for Buddhism, but Tada suggests the opposite. An inquiring mind is
an important part of the Buddhist path. "When one is first entering Buddhism,
he should not doubt, but if he has such doubts, he should not deny it. If there is
a doubt, we should raise it, and when it is answered, there opens a new truth."[41]
From this point of view, doubt and the raising of questions lead naturally to a
confirmation of Buddhist truths.

The Buddhist truths to which one is led are, of course, exceptional. According
to *Bussei* contributors, Buddhism's spirit of free inquiry is unique when compared
to other religions and, simultaneously, makes possible the conditions for civilization and peace. In a 1941 essay we will return to in Chapter 3, "Buddhist and
Why," Tad Tani argues that it was Buddhism's essential character that allowed
for Japanese civilization to develop, and he links this directly to Shōtoku Taishi.
"Japanese historians," Tani writes, "do not overrate Shōtoku when they call him
the father of their country's civilization."[42] He is clear that Buddhism is responsible for Shōtoku's ability to bring civilization to Japan and replace "the darkness of semi-barbarism," in part due to the Buddhist establishment serving
as "schools, hospitals, dispensaries, orphanages, refuge for old age; and the
monks were school-masters, nurses, doctors, engineers, cultivators of land, and
explorers of the wilderness."[43] The language Tani uses in this piece is, to be clear,
problematic. He makes reference to the Ainu people of Hokkaido with deeply
troubling language, describing them as "primitive" with "no native literature, no
art" and comparing them physically to animals. "This may be a picture of the
Japanese before Buddhism," he writes, which not only reinforces an ethnic hierarchy between Ainu and Japanese but also glosses over the forced assimilation
of the former by the latter. In this way, Tani's essay replicates the tone of contemporaneous *nihonjinron* rhetoric or the "Issei pioneer thesis." And yet, while
acknowledging the problematic aspects of this discourse, we can simultaneously
note the nuances of Tani's argument. He claims that as "an American Buddhist,"
he and his fellow Nisei "are capable of understanding Japanese philosophy and
Bushido." Lest we mistake this reference to *bushido* (the so-called way of the warrior) as an affirmation of Japanese identity, Azuma reminds us that Issei parents
at this time generally desired that their Nisei children would embrace their
American identities. In this context, *bushido* values were advanced to support
this Americanization process. In short, a samurai must serve one master, and

the Nisei's master was the country of their birth, the United States.[44] Moreover, Tani here is claiming not that he is a samurai warrior but that he is an "American Buddhist." And as we will see in the following chapter, Buddhism is what he has to contribute to American society. In "Buddhist and Why" Tani is not merely claiming that Japanese culture is superior but also claiming that Buddhism is superior; as a peaceful and civilizing force, Buddhism acts as cure for the failings of the modern world.

That this argument is being made on the eve of Pearl Harbor is not incidental. Other Nisei writers make similar claims, seemingly in rejection of the very idea of a Japanese spirit, as Kanmo Imamura does in a Japanese article from 1941. The "Japanese spirit," Imamura claims, is limiting, nothing more than patriotism and bravado, and will surely be despised around the world. Not only that, it stands in the way of both democracy and the propagation of the dharma. On the contrary, Imamura argues for a "Buddhist spirit," one that will be of benefit to the world and help promote a "Buddhist democracy." He denounces Japanese nationalism and states plainly that "Buddhists are cosmopolitans who seek the improvement of humanity under truth without prejudice."[45]

Over a decade later, Hajime Nakamura continues this thread of wrestling with the complex character of Japanese culture while ultimately claiming the civilizing nature of Buddhism. In his 1955 essay "The Humanitarian Tendency of the Japanese," Nakamura states that "one of the most prominent features of traditional Japanese ways of thinking [is] the emphasis on the love of human beings."[46] This long and dense essay then traces the development of "humanitarian" thinking across Asian Buddhist cultures before arriving in Japan, where Buddhism's "spirit of benevolence" was emphasized by Shōtoku and later Japanese Buddhist teachers. Whereas the essay seems to suggest that there was an inherent or natural humanitarian spirit in the Japanese that was brought to perfection by Buddhism (much like Suzuki and other modernists who claimed that Zen was brought to perfection in Japan),[47] Nakamura demurs at the end: "A general impression is that the spirit of benevolence was introduced into Japan probably with the advent of Buddhism and exerted a renovating influence upon the mental attitude of the Japanese prior to it."[48] The message is clear: Buddhism engenders humanity's better impulses; it is a peaceful and civilizing influence. When Buddhism fully enters a culture, "all the departments of life are beautified and sanctified. Social intercourse is enriched; art, science, and philosophy are encouraged and the refinements of civilization are brought to perfection by that beneficent influence."[49]

It is important to pause here to reflect on this triumphalist presentation of Buddhism and remind ourselves that this presentation is being made in the years leading up to and immediately after World War II. As will be discussed in the next chapter, this is a period of intense racial and religious discrimination against the Japanese American population generally, Buddhists specifically. The pressures placed on this community to assimilate to white Christian American norms were immense and constant. And with them came the constant treatment of Buddhism as the religion of the enemy, as an impediment to Americanization. Japanese immigrants, their children, and their religion were cast as possible fifth-column saboteurs of American democracy. Public hearings and trials were held about the legality of their citizenship, their right to worship, or even their right to learn the language of their parents. And yet, within this context, we find Nisei Buddhists (and their supporters) arguing vigorously for the inherently civilizing and pacifistic nature of their religion and of Japanese culture more broadly. We might read this as part of a strategy of an oppressed class utilizing the discourse of the dominant power against it.[50] But for the moment, we might also simply appreciate the courage it took for these midcentury Buddhists to claim a religious identity despite persecution.

This rhetoric of Buddhism's civilizing influence and its superiority is perhaps clearest when authors contrast Buddhism to "other religions," specifically Christianity. In his contribution, "A Rational Teaching," YBA member C. F. Wakefield makes a series of declarative statements about Buddhism, such as "The Buddha's Dharma does not attempt to explain the unknowable"; "Buddhists do not call those of another religion 'heathens'"; and "No worship of a Creator-God."[51] The implication is clear: Buddhism is a rational teaching, especially when compared to theistic religions. In "A Layman's Viewpoint" from 1952, Shohara is more direct:

> I feel that other religions are experiencing difficulty in making their doctrines compatible with modern society and modern science because of the very nature of their doctrines. It is apparent from available statistics that the number of those who do not profess any belief are increasing, a situation of grave concern to church leaders in this country. Up to the twentieth century, the Church has been able to hold its following by the power of a supernatural, generally referred to as God. But people have slowly begun to "rebel" . . . In every instance, power in any form that denies the free exercise of mind and thought has been overthrown and cast aside. . . .
>
> In contrast, Buddhism recognizes no higher being who, by its power, decides the course of mankind, but it does recognize a higher state of mind which is the ultimate. In this way I feel that Buddhism has more to offer.[52]

Shohara's Buddhist apologetic contrasts Buddhism with "other religions," but given the context (1950s America) and reference to "a supernatural . . . God," he is clearly contrasting Buddhism with Christianity and finding the latter lacking. According to Shohara, to maintain power over people, the Christian church requires its followers to have "absolute faith" in the Gospels and disallows the "free exercise of mind." Such freedom of thought is presumably allowed in the Buddhist religion, which recognizes no higher supernatural deity but, instead, "a higher state of mind." Shohara thus makes a direct reference to an inferior Christianity as part of a larger argument justifying his faith in Buddhism. Christianity is set up as something of a straw man, an inferior choice for modern persons because it roots itself in unverifiable truth claims. In short, it is not a rational teaching.

Again, Shohara is writing from the shadow of the camps. World War II incarceration was a defining moment for these young Buddhists, and we would be wrong to assume that, once released, they were easily assimilated into mainstream white American culture. Indeed, the immediate post-camp years were extremely challenging for many Japanese Americans who faced resistance on the part of white Americans to their resettlement.[53] Evidence of ongoing anti-Japanese, and in this case anti-Buddhist, sentiment can be found in the *Bussei*. One finds in the 1952 volume "Father Murphy's Appeal to the Niseis" introduced with an editorial note:

> The following is a reproduction in its entirety of a pamphlet recently received in our possession from a "Father Murphy." The title of this "masterpiece" is "Father Murphy's Appeal to the Niseis." In case any of our readers wish to write to the "author" after reading this, [his address follows].[54]

Reproduced in full, over the course of three and a half pages, is Father Murphy's appeal for, in short, Nisei to convert to Christianity. His rationale is condescending, chauvinistic, and racist. He begins by lauding the accomplishments of Japanese in America, making such claims as "The late war established the fact that a more efficiently loyal group of young men does not exist than the Nisei boys of America." But Father Murphy quickly changes his tone, lamenting the fact that Issei have "[saddled] Buddhism on the American-born" Nisei, which "constitutes the greatest mistake the Japanese old folks have made in this nation. What happened during this last war proved that." He goes on to claim that in those parts of the world that have not accepted Christ one finds higher rates of illiteracy, and that now the world looks to presumably more civilized nations like the United States for leadership. Nisei would have an easier time in America as Christians, he argues, citing how easy it is for Japanese American Christians to find "friends among other Americans," and that Buddhist soldiers who fought in the U.S. Army in World War II did not have chaplains to support them. "How can the Niseis become an integral, active part" of the modern world? he asks. "There is but one way, young folks, and that is by true repentance and faith—faith in Him who is the author and finisher of our salvation."[55]

The editors of the 1952 *Bussei* offer a rebuttal, "in reply to the sound and fury," of Father Murphy's appeal, beginning with specific counterarguments to his points.[56] In response to the claim that there were no Buddhist chaplains, they write:

> An eyewitness account: The U.S. Army was ready to approve a Buddhist chaplain for the 100th and the 442nd, but it had to withdraw its approval under pressure from Nisei ministers of other faiths.[57]

This "eyewitness account" was undoubtedly from any one of the several members of the Berkeley Temple's Young Buddhist Association who served in the U.S. armed forces. Duncan Ryûken Williams writes that in 1943 the U.S. Army began recruiting Buddhist chaplains from within the incarceration camps. But that effort was ultimately overruled by the Army's Chief of Chaplains, William Richard Arnold, and several Japanese American Christians, including the Episcopalian priest John Yamazaki, who opposed appointing a Buddhist chaplain to these segregated units on the grounds that Buddhism was an impediment to Americanization.[58]

The *Bussei* rebuttal to Father Murphy continues, citing academic sources to the effect that Japan (and other Asian nations) in fact have higher literacy rates than Western nations, and that whereas the world may be looking to the West for economic or military leadership in the postwar years, no one is looking to the West for spiritual leadership. "Greater leaders of the West are realizing that technological advancement in itself is not a sign of civilization." In conclusion, the editors write:

> It is evident that Father Murphy has little to offer but one-sided accusations, characterized by vague generalities and completely devoid of evidence. It is a great pity indeed that a religious leader is defeating the very purpose of religion. . . . Now is the time for religious leaders to cooperate in spiritual harmony to promote brotherhood and good-will; it is not time for indiscriminate mudslinging. Father Murphy would do humanity a good turn if, instead of casting [a]spersions on something he knows so little about, he would teach the principles of Christianity *as it should be taught.*[59]

It is likely that Father Murphy's appeal was not the only such pamphlet received by Nisei Buddhists in the 1950s. It is also likely that they were on the receiving end of far worse prejudice in their daily lives. And it is because of these realities that we must understand how the Buddhist modernism expressed by Nisei Buddhists was infused with the specific experiences of a racial and religious minority. Whereas Nisei may have drawn upon the language of Japanese cultural superiority in their articulation of a specifically American Buddhist modernism, they were deploying this language to a different end. As we will see in the next chapter, Nisei Buddhists articulated a vision of Jōdo Shinshū Buddhism as an integral part of their identity as Americans. Nisei argued that they were able to be good Americans and good Buddhists simultaneously precisely because Buddhism was a modern religion, a modern religion that was good for America and would compensate for the lacks and disconnects engendered by modernity itself. With its spirit of free inquiry, progressive values, and peaceful and civilizing influences, Buddhism would be what Nisei had to offer to America *as* Americans. At the same time, we can also take note that the *Bussei*'s modernism was not limited to the experiences of Nisei. The essays under study so far have included Japanese Americans, Japanese scholars and religious thinkers, and white converts. This is to say that whereas Nisei Buddhists were articulating the specific ways in which Buddhism made them good Americans, they were not doing this in a vacuum, detached from larger social or cultural trends, and were in community with non-Japanese Buddhists. And, finally, just as the *Bussei*'s Buddhist modernism should not be seen as a generic modernism, it was also not a generic Buddhism; it was often specifically Jōdo Shinshū.

In her 1955 contribution "Shinshu in Changing World," Kimi Hisatsune reflects on the "orthodox view of Shinshu," focusing mainly on the story of Amida's bodhisattva practice, his establishment of a pure land, and how the faithful can be reborn in his land. She makes it clear that while this story is "beautiful" and represents the Buddha's unlimited compassion for humanity, it is nevertheless "simple" and not necessarily "in accord with the original teachings of Sakyamuni." However: "So long as people are happy with such a belief, so long as it helps them to maintain a well-balanced life, no problem arises. . . . In recent years, we have been witnessing an increasing undercurrent of unrest and dissatisfaction . . . [and] we must face the fact that a new interpretation is needed to replace the old if we wish to see Shinshu become a vital part of America." In the remainder of her essay she attempts to do just this, focusing on, first, the idea of the pure land and, second, the distinction between self-power and other-power. Rather than take the idea of birth in the pure land literally, she states:

> "To be reborn in Jodo" has only symbolic meaning because there is no entity to be reborn. Buddhism is not for escapists. It teaches us to face life's realities while transcending them spiritually. Buddhist Nirvana, or Jodo, is thus a state of mind, not a place.[60]

In some ways we might think of this essay as the "real-time" modernization of Shin teachings. Not content with literal understandings of Buddhist narratives and cosmologies and in response to the changing needs of her contemporaries,

Hisatsune reinterprets them symbolically, anticipating McMahan's modernist process of demythologization, "the process of attempting to extract—or more accurately, to reconstruct—meanings that will be viable within the context of modern worldviews from teachings embedded in ancient worldviews."[61] On the one hand, Hisatsune reframes the pure land as merely symbolic; on the other, she claims that nirvana is a state of mind similar to the psychological reimagining of other Buddhist moderns.[62] However, note that Hisatsune also explicitly conflates nirvana and the pure land, which subtly suggests that Shin teachings are not a deviation from the teachings of the historical Buddha but are merely of a kind. And, finally, like most Buddhist moderns, she places the emphasis not on the afterlife but on this world, "life's realities," suggesting that even a tradition such as Pure Land Buddhism—concerned as it is with a postmortem Buddhist paradise—is primarily of this world.

Shin Buddhism was rendered modern by Nisei and non-Japanese *Bussei* contributors alike. As early as the fall 1940 volume, Gene Wood begins his "Buddhism and Modern Life" with the standard modernist exhortation that the "principles of Buddhism have never been disturbed by modern philosophy and are in perfect accord with the discoveries of science." He also echoes the concerns about modernity's failings when he writes that people's faith in Buddhism "has either been shaken or destroyed by the skeptical atmosphere of modern life." But, rather than simply appealing to a generic Buddhist modernism, Wood pivots toward the end of his essay to Shin Buddhism when he writes:

> Surrender yourself to the Eternal Arms of Amida, and your suffering will be dissolved in limitless joy. . . . Filled with joy and delight, Our hearts awaken to the Law! Namu Amida Butsu! Reverence to all the Buddhas and Bodhisattvas whose Dharmakayas are omnipresent in all the quarters of the chiliocosmos![63]

While arguing for Buddhism's "freedom from creeds and dogmas," Wood simultaneously stresses what may be considered a rather more traditional form of Shin Buddhist devotionalism.

Over a decade later, Robert Jackson will make a slightly more nuanced argument for the compatibility of Shin Buddhism and the modern world—and the importance of such a project. His "A New Outlook" begins with a discussion of *mappō*, which he describes not so much as a prophecy as a challenge. Jackson argues that Śākyamuni, "knowing human nature—how slothful and neglectful we become," taught *mappō* to challenge us to take up Buddhist practice with earnestness. He goes on to say that "if statesmen could gain the perspective on life Buddhism offers, we would be in no danger of atomic warfare," suggesting not only that Buddhism is peaceful but also that if more people accepted Buddhist teachings, we could avoid nuclear war, certainly a concern for many in the early 1950s. For Jackson, this is the importance of Buddhism, the necessity of practicing and sharing the dharma. "It is due to the compassion of the Buddha that the law was proclaimed in the first place. Amida's compassion causes him to remain among sentient creatures outside Nirvana until all are saved. . . . Can we not hasten the enlightenment of humanity in respect and gratitude for Amida's selfless vow?"[64] Here we see the import of Buddhism, how it may function to engender not only individuals' enlightenment but indeed world peace, and how this concern is expressed within a specifically Jōdo Shinshū terminology not merely by Japanese American Buddhists raised in the tradition but by white converts as well.

A Lineage of Buddhist Moderns

The *Bussei* presents us with a specifically American Jōdo Shinshū Buddhist modernism, one that has particular meanings for Nisei Buddhists. Drawing on our previous discussion of Buddhism fulfilling a perceived lack in modernity, here I will discuss two issues within the study of Buddhist modernism. First, I will discuss what Buddhist modernism may have meant specifically for Japanese American contributors who deployed the rhetoric within the context of their larger racial project of claiming space in the American body politic. Second, I will draw our attention to how their inclusion in the standard histories of Buddhist modernism indelibly changes such studies.

Jane Imamura (1920–2011) contributed the essay "Gathas in the West" to the 1952 *Bussei* (Figure 2.1). As I have written elsewhere, in the American Shin context *gāthās* are, essentially, Buddhist hymns that have played an important role in the community almost since its beginning in the early twentieth century.[65] Whereas some *gāthās* are appropriated Christian hymns or were written by white converts, there is a long history of singing songs set to Western-style music that goes back to at least Meiji-era Japan. In the United States, and especially after the camps, Nisei women such as Imamura and Hisatsune were responsible for composing and popularizing a large body of Buddhist songs, and many of their songs are sung to this day.[66] Imamura was a natural musician with perfect pitch. Her parents encouraged her musical talents by purchasing a piano when she was child, no small gift given the family's limited financial means. While her dreams of a music career were derailed by the war and incarceration, she was responsible for organizing and developing a robust music program at the Berkeley Buddhist Temple in the postwar years, encouraging a generation of young Buddhist musicians.[67] In her 1952 piece she writes, "From time immemorial, religion has never existed without music. The primitive natives idolized the beating of the

GATHAS in the west

J. Imamura

From time immemorial, religion has never existed without music. The primitive natives idolized their gods with the beating of the drums. The Vedic scriptures were chanted in unison by the followers even before written language was created by men.

Religion is the expression of Truth.. Truth is beauty in the highest sense.... and music is the universal expression of beauty. In the West, sacred music has developed to such an extent in this age, from simple rhythm and melody to a grand intricate form, that it has become a great asset to the churches. Many people gain spiritual satisfaction by just listening to the great sacred music by such masters as Handel and Bach. The deep resounding vibration of the organ and the ethereal harmony of the choir has become a part of the church.

A problem was created for the Buddhist churches which came across the Pacific to America. In Japan, Buddhism is cloaked in a most Oriental atmosphere, with low chanting and oriental flutes, blocks and gongs. This is in line with the Japanese culture and habits where people live a subtle, quiet and meditative life. When Buddhists were confronted by the aggressive wide open customs of the West, they saw at once the acute differences that they had to overcome in order to become "one" with the American soil.

Fortunately, one of the noticeable advantages of Buddhism throughout history has been its lack of dogmas and, thus, its adaptability to the cultures and habits of the people. The principle, the basic essence, has never changed, but the outer surface, has changed according to the environment and habits of the people.

This flexibility is evident in the services we hold in this country. Many churches have bought electric organs to replace rusty pianos; choirs have been established; English is used wherever possible, and an attempt to create religious atmospheres which appeal to the Nisei has taken over. As for material much excellent choral and organ music was written recently in Japan, in a beautiful oriental mode. In the West too, we are not completely lacking in music with Buddhist temperament, for Wagner, who carried opera to the ultimate height, was a student of Buddhism. Somewhere there exists a manuscript of his unfinished last work, a vast opera on the life of Buddha.

Music in the Buddhist Churches of the West has a wide open field. It has a great future. However, the present situation is appalling at times. Even with the large number of followers, it is not infrequent to behold the inadequacy of a service where the gathas must be led by the cue of "1 2 3 hai" by the Reverend with no accompanists at hand to play an organ. We need individuals with adequate command of Buddhism to do research on the music already written and to transfer the teaching through expressions of music by composing new ones. We also need more persons to sing and play them.

"A PROGRAM" waits
(Cont'd from page 19)
2. That, after this period of training, they form a number of small evening classes (divided into age-groups) in every temple, meeting at least once a week, for a systematic study and discussion of Buddhist principles, using the following texts:
High School Group: Carus' Gospel of Buddha.
College Group: Christmas Humphreys' Buddhism.
Young Adults' Group: B. L. Suzuki's Mahayana Buddhism, or Humphreys' Buddhism.
Older Adults' Group: (Nisei) B.L. Suzuki's Mahayana Buddhism.
(Issei) At the discretion of the priest in charge of the temple.
The books suggested are the best available. They are not ideal for the pur-
(Cont'd on page 21)

20

Figure 2.1 Jane Imamura's article "Gathas in the West" from the 1952 *Berkeley Bussei*.

drums. The Vedic scriptures were chanted in unison by the followers even before written language was created by man."[68]

Leaving aside her outmoded use of language (e.g., "primitives" and their beating of drums), Imamura's piece is at base an argument for how music can serve the processes of cultural adaptation and keep Buddhism relevant for Americans and younger generations.

In Japan, Buddhism is cloaked in a most Oriental tone of dark horizontal atmosphere, with low chanting and oriental flutes, blocks and gongs. This is in
line with the Japanese culture and habits where people live a subtle, quiet and
meditative life. When Buddhists were confronted by the aggressive wide open
customs of the West, they saw at once the acute differences that they had to
overcome in order to become "one" with the American soil.

Fortunately, one of the noticeable advantages of Buddhism throughout history has been its lack of dogmas and, thus, its adaptability to the culture and
habits of the people. The principle, the basic essence, has never changed, but
the outer surface, has changed according to the environment and habits of the
people.[69]

We see here again the modernist assumption that Buddhism is dogma-free,
and here this is a positive trait by which the religion can adapt and change as necessary and remain relevant to different persons in different times and cultures. In
Imamura's reckoning, Japanese Buddhism is imbued with "Oriental" characteristics, presumably suitable to Japanese persons who live a "quiet and meditative
life." This will not do here in the American context, a more "aggressive" culture.
It would be more than appropriate here to pause and unpack this juxtaposition
between a "passive East" and "active West." However, let us be clear about who, in
Imamura's estimation, fits in the categories of East and West. She goes on:

[Buddhism's] flexibility is evident in the services we hold in this country. Many
churches have bought electric organs to replace rusty pianos; choirs have been
established; English is used wherever possible, and *an attempt to create religious atmospheres which appeal to the Nisei has taken over*. As for material much
excellent choral and organ music was written recently in Japan, in a beautiful
oriental mode. In the West, too, we are not completely lacking in music with
Buddhist temperament, for Wagner, who carried opera to the ultimate height,
was a student of Buddhism.[70]

Note that she does not say that many churches have purchased organs, started
choirs, or begun holding services in English for the benefit of white Americans;
rather, they have done so to *appeal to the Nisei*. When juxtaposing the Oriental
modes of music-making in Japan and the aggressive nature of Western culture,
Nisei are clearly on the American side of this binary, in the same category as
Wagner. This modernist view of Buddhism not only is being voiced *by* Nisei
but is *for* Nisei as well, and Nisei are understood as included in the category of
Westerners, of Americans.

Further, as we saw in the previous section, Hisatsune's 1955 "Shinshu in
a Changing World" argued for a symbolic reinterpretation of Shin doctrine.

She linked this interpretation specifically to its value for the Buddhist community: "The appeal of Buddhism lies in its emphasis on universal compassion... through which the Church can bring hope to the many questioning youths in this age."[71] It is almost certain here that the "questioning youths" Hisatsune had in mind were her own young Buddhist co-religionists, questioning and still living with the reality of racial and religious discrimination, as evidenced by the response to Father Murphy discussed earlier. But let us return once more to Hisatsune's 1953 piece, with which we began this chapter.

While the essay opens with the standard modernist aside—believe what you can prove through your own experience—the essay, titled "The Problem of Faith," is actually a reflection on academic study. Almost immediately after claiming that one should use reason and logic to accept religious truth claims, she goes on to say:

> *Faith* is a good word. To have faith in something finer, something greater than ourselves seems the only way to real peace and happiness. But blind faith leads only to mere superstition, and what is worse, narrow-minded fanaticism and bigotry.[72]

So far, we remain on stable modernist ground, with the modernist making a distinction between "good faith" and "bad (blind) faith." We are still being led to see the obvious truth of Buddhism. But Hisatsune goes on to seemingly critique the very same spirit of academic free inquiry (or at least the academics themselves) that she celebrated in the essay's opening paragraph when she writes:

> So far, the academic side has been upheld (for the good of Buddhist philosophy, the most profound the world has ever known). However, these neophyte academicians smugly settle back and continue their heated arguments on, for instance, "What is Karma?" or "What constitutes Nirvana?" at their periodic discussion group meetings.... Knowledge alone of Buddhism is not enough for the development of Buddhist leadership. A man who is ignorant but who has a compassionate heart is far better than a man of high intellects whose heart is as cold as the frigid North. Compassion and the intellect must be combined, however, in order to maintain the desired balance in this world of duality.[73]

Relying on the work of J. B. Pratt and William James, Hisatsune then argues that intellectual study can only take one so far. What is needed to maintain this "balance in the world of duality," what is needed to wed the intellectual or academic side with the experiential and compassionate side, is faith itself. And, in particular, faith in the teachings of Shin Buddhism. "How to acquire a new manner of life, a *transformation of character*, should be the important goal in the study of Buddhism—not a superficial and useless accumulation of Buddhist theories."[74] The study and practice of Buddhism is not an end in itself but is linked to the development of one's character. Hisatsune and other Nisei modernists are claiming that they can be good Americans, that they can contribute to American society, specifically by being good (Shin) Buddhists. And being a good Buddhist means being a good *modern* Buddhist.

In the *Bussei* modern Buddhism is presented as a balm to America—better than Christianity, civilizing, peaceful, a potential bulwark against atomic war, and so forth. It is also a means by which Nisei may better *themselves* and solve the "Nisei problem," as will be discussed in the following chapter. By claiming that they can contribute to American society and better themselves and their community, they are not simply making an assimilationist move whereby the immigrant group abandons their cultural heritage on the threshold. (In the words of Hiroshi Kashiwagi's father, if they did so, not only would they be acting Christian, but they would be acting white.)[75] On the contrary, Nisei are arguing for being included in the category of "American" *as Buddhists*. While not being a complete assimilation into white Christian American norms, this move is also not a complete rejection or retreat into some sort of walled ethnic fortress, keeping the Gene Woodses or Sunya Pratts at bay. No, in fact, they are included within the community, allowed to express their own views and ideas on what makes Buddhism modern and American, and, yes, even Shin. This articulation by Nisei of modern Buddhism is an invitation, a gift, and an act of self-recovery all at once.

This multifaceted Japanese/American/Shin/Buddhist modernism complicates our understanding of Buddhist modernism more generally in several ways. On the one hand, it may simply be nothing more than an example of "multiple modernities." As McMahan, Quli, and others have discussed, modernity should not be understood in hegemonic terms or as interchangeable with "the West." McMahan writes that

> while in the early phases of the Buddhist engagement with modernity—the late nineteenth and early twentieth centuries—reformist Buddhists vigor- ously attempted to translate Buddhism into the discourses of Western moder- nity ... more recently there are more complex intertwinings of Buddhism and modernity that require a more pluralistic conception of modernity.[76]

To further reinforce the idea of multiple modernisms and the decoupling of the equation of modernity with the West, Quli suggests that there may be mul- tiple modernisms that exist within one country. Specifically, she highlights the various and diverse ways Buddhists understand meditation practices within just one community in the United States.[77] Surely, then, a Japanese/American/

Shin/Buddhist modernism may simply coexist with other varieties of American Buddhist modernism. On the other hand, and lingering a bit on McMahan's reference to the "early phases" of Buddhist modernism, perhaps another way to approach the *Bussei* is to complicate our periodization of modernity itself. As mentioned earlier, modernity is perhaps best understood as an idea rather than as referring to a specific period of history. This hasn't stopped some from trying to trap modernity in time, of course. In compiling *A Modern Buddhist Bible*, for example, Donald Lopez chose to assign precise dates at which Buddhist modernism begins and ends—1873 to 1980. The 1873 has some logic to it; it is connected to a specific event, the debates between Sinhala reformists and Christian missionaries in colonial Sri Lanka. Lopez admits, however, that 1980 is "arbitrary, chosen in large part to provide a vague line of demarcation between the modern and contemporary."[78] Given that this "modern period" spans over a century, including the tail end of the long nineteenth century, one wonders if multiple modernisms could not be assigned to different historical periods, thus making a demarcation between McMahan's "early phase" of the late nineteenth and early twentieth centuries and later developments in midcentury Buddhist modernism. In other words, in addition to the specificity of the *Bussei*'s modernity as linked to its Japanese American and Shin Buddhist identities, does it also speak to a specifically midcentury modernism, one that is related to but distinct from the modernity of, say, the "Protestant Buddhism" of nineteenth-century Sri Lanka, or the *shin bukkyō* of Meiji-era Japan?[79] Perhaps. But in raising this question one must simultaneously raise the question of what value we get from layering an ever-increasing level of detail and specificity on an academic category. At what point do the modifiers become so lengthy as to render the final noun meaningless?

Two final concerns with the Buddhist modernism frame are raised by this study of the *Berkeley Bussei*: first, the uncritical grafting of the traditional/modern binary to the ethnic/convert binary in American Buddhism studies more generally; and, second, the scholarly project of lineage construction.

To the first point, as has been well argued by Quli and others, the terms "traditional" and "modern" often do the same rhetorical work as the terms "ethnic" and "convert" in the study of Buddhism outside Asia.[80] Martin Baumann's contribution to the edited volume *Westward Dharma* provides a useful example of how this connection is made, even if unintentionally. Concerned with the limitations of the terms "ethnic" and "convert," Baumann suggests instead that scholars use the terms "traditional," "modern," and "global" to describe different types of Buddhist communities. The problem, however, lies in the way in which the first two terms seem to simply replace "ethnic" and "convert." For Baumann, "traditional" Theravada communities in the United States would be those that focus on devotional practices and rituals, community-building, and so forth (and happen to be populated mostly by Asian immigrants and their children); "modern" Theravada communities would be those that focus more on meditation practices such as insight or mindfulness (and happen to be populated by mostly white converts and their children).[81] The basic structure of the binary remains even though the labels have been replaced, a point Victor Sōgen Hori draws our attention to when he notes that the "categories of Asian/ethnic and Western/convert unfortunately import value judgements into the analysis of our data."[82] Moreover, "ethnicity presupposes a self/other distinction. Ethnics are the others. . . . [E]thnicity is the majority population's way of labelling minorities' identities."[83]

Here I am not interested so much in debating the "two Buddhisms" typologies as I am in identifying habits of thought and the uncritical repetition of tropes that rely on unhelpful binaries—in Hori's terms, the way in which these patterns reinforce the self/other distinction. By framing contemporary Buddhisms in the context of the traditional/modern binary, scholars necessarily need to place different traditions or communities into one or the other of these categories. The uncritical deployment of the binary functions much in the same way as the binary between ethnic/convert as well as terms such as "Western Buddhism," terms that feel familiar despite their vague and imprecise uses. Again, Hori writes: "There is no denying that the dichotomy between Asian/ethnic and Western/convert Buddhist is very handy; I use it all the time since, for people in Canada, the distinction is immediately understood. I suggest however, that the very fact that the distinction is so immediately understood is a clue to what is wrong with the distinction."[84] He goes on to point out that the distinction divides the world into "us" and "them," with white Westerners as "us" over and against the "them" of Asian ethnics. Again, here I want to draw our attention to the "handy" aspect of these binaries, the fact that they are "immediately understood." This sense of immediacy is the pattern of thought that we need to untangle. We need to critically engage terms such as "Western" and "modern" that are too often taken as given.

A recent example of this can be seen in an excerpt from *Rebirth: A Guide to Mind, Karma, and the Cosmos in the Buddhist World* published in *Tricycle* magazine. In his discussion of rebirth, Roger Jackson helpfully divides Buddhists' approaches to the subject into four categories: literalist, neotraditionalist, modernist, and secularist. Though acknowledging that these "must be taken with many grains of salt," the excerpt makes several rhetorical moves worth noting. First, consider the opening paragraph:

> Although most Buddhists in premodern Buddhist cultures accepted, and
> sometimes defended, the traditional Buddhist karmic eschatology, it is evident
> that since Asian Buddhists began to take account of modernity and Western
> Buddhists to take account of Asian traditions, those Buddhists that have

bothered to talk about rebirth at all (and many have not), have typically done so by adopting one or the other of the four possible approaches to rebirth.[85]

This way of framing the discussion as between "traditional" Buddhists (in Asia) and "Western Buddhists" subtly ensconces the conversation firmly within the binaries of Asian/Western, traditional/modern. Further, in detailing the four approaches, the examples Jackson provides of Buddhists who take these positions are all associated either with Asia or are identified with "the West." The binaries established in the opening paragraph are reinforced by locating persons such as the Dalai Lama and "traditionally trained Theravada monks" in the categories of literalists and neotraditionalists with the likes of Alan Watts and Robert Wright in the categories of modernists and secularists.[86] The term "Western" is not defined, but by association with specific persons who inhabit particular places within this fourfold typology, certain connections are implied. And because the opening frame juxtaposes "Western" and "modernity" with "Asian" and "traditional," the terms' meanings are, in Hori's sense, "immediately known." To be clear, this is undoubtedly not Jackson's intent, nor is it even particularly relevant to his otherwise solid scholarship on the issue of rebirth and karma. Rather, this way of viewing the Buddhist world as easily categorized into a series of binaries (Asian/Western, traditional/modern) is merely a pattern of thought, one that, once it is brought to your attention, cannot be unseen.

This is a point already well made by Quli when she writes that replacing ethnic/convert with traditional/modern only serves to reinforce the "understanding of Asian Americans as 'traditional' and white Americans as 'modern' [and] simply reiterates the outdated Orientalist notion that the West is active and the East passive, or that Asian Americans are 'conservative' while white Americans are 'innovative.'"[87] The *Bussei* complicates these binaries. Consider, for example, how in his discussion of the debates and conversations between white converts and Nisei Buddhists, Ama claims that "because of the Euro-American Buddhist converts' criticism of Shin Buddhism, Japanese American Shin Buddhists emphasized Shakyamuni Buddha's teachings more than Shinran's teaching in *Berkeley Bussei*."[88] This subtly reinforces the agency of white converts and suggests that Nisei Buddhists were simply reacting to outside criticism. Compare this with Jane Imamura's essay discussed earlier wherein she clearly states that it is the Nisei who advocated for American (or Western) styles of music and services, thus locating the agency of cultural change in the Nisei. A close read of the *Bussei* draws our attention to how the "immediately known" aspect of the self/other, ethnic/convert, traditional/modern binaries is not so immediately known after all.

Once Nisei are understood as active agents in the making of Buddhist modernism, we can now return to scholarly treatments of the phenomenon and to my second concern: the scholarly project of lineage construction. The habit of thought that divides the world into either traditional or modern Buddhists results in scholarship that presupposes that certain Buddhists will "naturally" fall into one category or the other, and thus the lion's share of research on Buddhist modernism has focused on the work of archetypical figures—charismatic Asian Buddhists and their white interlocutors. One important exception is Jeff Wilson's *Dixie Dharma*, a study of the Ekoji Buddhist Sangha in Richmond, Virginia, originally founded by Takashi Kenryu Tsuji (1919–2004). Tsuji was born in British Columbia, studied at Ryukoku University in Kyoto, and was ordained as a Shin priest; he returned to Canada months before the Japanese attack on Pearl Harbor. He quickly became a leader in the Canadian Shin community during their incarceration and would later serve as the bishop of the Buddhist Churches of America for over a decade. Following his time as bishop, he settled in Washington, D.C., with the explicit purpose of spreading Jōdo Shinshū, an impulse that led to the establishment of the Ekoji sangha. Wilson notes that Tsuji was, like many of his contemporaries, a "modernist Shin Buddhist priest." He reinterpreted Shin doctrine in much the same way as others covered in this chapter, as a modern and scientific religion. For example, in discussing the concepts of rebirth and past lives, Tsuji declares that the realms of rebirth are "mental and spiritual states, created by men's thoughts, actions and words. In other words, they are psychological states."[89] (If we apply Jackson's four-fold typology, Tsuji fits neatly into the modernist approach.)

Wilson's work is, again, an exception to the general norm of scholarship that focuses on a limited set of charismatic figures. McMahan's *The Making of Buddhist Modernism*, for example, examines the work of, among others, Anagarika Dharmapala, the Rhys Davidses, both D. T. and Shunryu Suzuki, Paul Carus, Alan Watts and Allen Ginsberg, and the Fourteenth Dalai Lama. Lopez's *A Modern Buddhist Bible* "presents selections from the works of thirty-one figures—monks and laymen, nuns and laywomen, poets and missionaries, meditation masters and social revolutionaries—who have figured in the formation of modern Buddhism."[90] If we were to draw a Venn diagram for the selections in Lopez's *Bible* and the subjects under study in McMahan's *Making*, we would have two very nearly overlapping circles in which we would find D. T. Suzuki, Gary Snyder, and Alan Watts, among others. These figures are the "usual suspects," the persons on whom praise or blame is laid for making Buddhism modern, for either ruining or rescuing Buddhism, and/or for bringing it to "the West." I draw our attention to these studies of modern Buddhist makers not to critique either Lopez or McMahan; rather, I want to suggest that these usual suspects have become canonized. Through repetition, they have become associated with Buddhist modernism and hence "immediately known," in Hori's sense. I identify this work as a lineage construction project because Lopez, for example, is quite explicit about it. In the introduction to his *Bible*, he writes: "What is remarkable about the lives of these figures is the degree of their interconnection. There is not a single author here who was not acquainted with at least one other, thus *creating a lineage so essential to modern Buddhism*."[91] I would add that what is remarkable about the lives of these individuals is their interconnection with Asian American Buddhists. Returning to our Venn diagram, left out of the nearly overlapping circles are Kimi Hisatsune, the Imamuras, Hiroshi Kashiwagi, and Taitetsu Unno—despite the fact that all of them had direct connection with and so were "acquainted with" Alan Watts, Gary Snyder, D. T. Suzuki, and many others listed in the table of contents to *A Modern Buddhist Bible*. They are, in a very real sense, left off and excluded from this lineage, so essential to modern Buddhism.

Why might this be? The short answer, of course, is racism.[92] Simply put, the logics of the Buddhist modernism paradigm do not allow for the presence of "bad savages" within the lineage of Buddhist moderns. This methodological blind spot allows for scholars to simply overlook parts of the contemporary Buddhist world. Ironically, this exclusion mirrors the exclusion—both literal and metaphorical—Japanese American Shin Buddhists experienced during World War II, a point to which we will now turn.

3

All This and Discrimination

The early decades of the Japanese immigrant community in the United States were complicated. As a result of the 1907 Gentlemen's Agreement that effectively limited immigration to spouses and family members of Japanese already in the country, the community entered what Kashima calls the "picture bride era" of American Shinshū.[1] The Immigration Act of 1924, which ended immigration from Asia entirely, combined with alien land laws and other racially exclusionary tactics, curtailed the growth of the community while at the same time set the stage for intergenerational change in the coming decades. As Azuma has argued, by the 1920s, Issei had begun to develop a sense of collective identity that cut across class lines and was not wholly invested in the nationalistic rhetoric espoused on the other side of the Pacific. "Instead, what bound diverse groups of Issei was their shared experience of being a racial Other in America, which revealed the futility of the modernist belief that the Japanese should be able to become honorary whites through acculturation."[2] In the exclusion era following 1924, Issei leaders increasingly became focused on their children, the Nisei, and how they would simultaneously navigate a racially exclusionist America while maintaining and developing the Japanese community. This question became phrased as *the Nisei problem*, "which ranged from questions of marriage to employment, and from education to the racial inferiority complex."[3] Azuma writes that solutions to the problem included, on the one hand, creating socioeconomic opportunities for Nisei to advance themselves and take over the already robust agricultural industry that Japanese immigrants had developed, and, on the other, educational programs to "mold the Nisei mind." Such programs were intended to instill in Nisei a sense of racial identity based on the concept of *Nippon seishin* or Japanese spirit. These educational programs were often part of or the sole reason for Japanese-language schools, which, as Asato and others have shown, were sites of controversy within and beyond the Japanese community.

Whereas Issei may have had specific goals in mind when thinking about how to educate their children, here I am concerned with the questions: what did Nisei think about this "problem," and what role did Buddhism play in its solution? In looking at the Nisei problem and related discourses in both the pre- and immediate postwar volumes of the *Bussei*, I argue that the Nisei are involved in a specific racial project, in Omi and Winant's use of the term, one that overlapped with but was distinct from their Issei parents' conceptualization of being "Japanese

The Making of American Buddhism. Scott A. Mitchell, Oxford University Press. © Oxford University Press 2023.
DOI: 10.1093/oso/9780197641569.003.0004

in America."[4] More specifically, I am concerned here with how Buddhism functions within this racial project of forming a Japanese American identity both in response to and as a balm for the effects of racial trauma. I complicate the notion that the "big event" of incarceration was solely responsible for this racial trauma and, instead, note the current of white supremacy and racial and religious othering (intersected with normative gender roles and expectations) that began long before the camps and continued well after.

This chapter begins in the prewar period and discusses the Nisei problem from the point of view of the Nisei themselves. Solutions to the "problem" invariably include Buddhism, which acts not only as a balm to racial trauma but also as a bridge between Japan and America, between East and West. In the postwar era, as discussed in the second section of the chapter, the bridge discourse displaces the Nisei problem and is joined by the rhetoric of "contribution"—that is, what are Japanese Americans *contributing* to American society? This discourse is invariably bound up with larger midcentury and quintessentially American discourses about self-determination that evoke what will, eventually, be used as part of the "model minority" stereotype. However, I argue that here in the early 1950s, Japanese American Buddhists are not making the claim that they are a "good minority" or a better minority than other marginalized persons; they are simply claiming to *be* American. What's more, their claim to an Americanness is based, in part, on their simultaneous claim to be Buddhist. In fact, Nisei make the claim that the "problem" is America itself, that Buddhism is the solution to this problem, and that in bringing Buddhism to America they simultaneously make America more Buddhist and themselves more American. Finally, in the concluding section, which anticipates the following chapters, I reflect on the gendered nature of the "Nisei problem" and the labor that was involved in the making of American Buddhism.

The "Nisei Problem"

Following his incarceration at Tule Lake, Tamotsu Shibutani (1920–2004) earned his doctorate at the University of Chicago and went on to become a successful sociologist and teacher at the University of California.[5] In 1941, however, he was by his own admission just a "college student," one incapable of fully understanding the complexity of social and economic problems facing the Nisei.[6] Contemporary readers would likely disagree with Shibutani's self-assessment; he submitted two essays to the *Bussei* that year that not only addressed the Nisei problem from his own individual point of view but also offered a deft historical and sociological analysis. Indeed, the essays seem to be shorter versions of what would become a heavily researched thirty-five-page report submitted to his economics professor.[7] His spring 1941 *Bussei* contribution, "Retreat from Shangri-la," begins:

> Of late, the pipe dreams of paradise indulged in by many have been shattered by the impact of the cold, uncompromising touch of reality, a state of existence inconsistent with our hopes, ideals, and ambitions. Instead of our wished-for haven, we find widespread demoralization, economic dependency to an appalling extent, a rising rate of crime, delinquency and immorality, and increasing personality maladjustments.[8]

This "state of existence inconsistent with our hopes, ideals, and ambitions" is, of course, the Nisei problem. In his fall 1941 essay, "A Preface to Reflection," Shibutani is more explicit in naming the "complications facing the Nisei" as "the external inter-racial difficulties, and . . . the internal problems within the Nisei group."[9] These problems lead inexorably to the demoralization, "economic dependency," and rising crime rate mentioned in his essays. Shibutani draws a direct link between the lack of access to social and economic opportunities and the many young Nisei who feel demoralized and turn to drinking, gambling, and "frequenting the houses of ill-fame." This concern with immorality and crime reflects in many ways how the Nisei problem was first articulated by Issei more than a decade earlier, often in response to incidents of crime. Perhaps the most extreme example was the 1928 murder of a white man by a Nisei in Honolulu, which led Issei leaders and writers to fear that the bad actions of one or two Nisei would tarnish the reputation of the Japanese community as a whole and further hinder any hope of racial advancement. Increasingly, Issei blamed Nisei delinquency on a lack of moral education and a failure to properly instill Japanese values in their children. Thus, *Nippon seishin* became a regular part of Japanese-language school curricula, and so it is perhaps not surprising that we would see parallels in the writing of Nisei educated with this curriculum. Not only does Shibutani's work evoke a concern about Nisei delinquency, but in the 1939 volume we find the essay "You Are on Trial," the very title evoking a sense of being constantly judged. The essay is straightforward in its assertion that Nisei are "in the public eye" and therefore it is essential that they remain faultless, that they contribute positively to society.[10]

Whereas Azuma's analysis of the Nisei problem is told from the point of view of Issei and the "trans-National" concerns of empire-building during the interwar period, here I am more concerned with how this "problem" was understood by Nisei, how they articulated their own location as racial and religious others, and what coping strategies or solutions they employed. Or, as Shibutani puts it in "Shangri-la," "one of the characteristic frailties of human nature is to find a culprit for all things undesirable," and Nisei generally blame the problem

on "racial intolerance, the narrow-mindedness of the immigrants, the stupidity of our leaders, and even upon the fragility of the Nisei themselves."[11] In
"Preface," Shibutani presents a far more astute analysis of the problem, laying
out the historical circumstances by which Japanese immigrants first arrived in
California as cheap agricultural labor. Once they began to demand better pay
and working conditions, white owners simply replaced them with successive
waves of "Filipinos, Mexicans, and 'Okies' "; consequently, the "Nisei find themselves today in the midst of an anti-Oriental heritage." What's more, "the present
crisis in the Pacific has aroused the suspicion of many in regard to the loyalty of
the American-born Japanese." His analysis reveals not only a deep awareness of
the causes and complications of racial and labor history in California but also a
sensitivity to the deleterious effects of racial and religious exclusion, effects that
cannot be simply dismissed as "moral failings" or an inability to live up to an
essentialized "Japanese spirit." As we will see in what follows, the Nisei here are
expressing a type of melancholy associated with racial trauma.

This melancholy is particularly strong in "Shangri-la," where Shibutani asks,
"What can we do about [the Nisei problem]?" His answers are ambivalent at best.
While at first suggesting that Nisei cooperate with political and religious leaders
to better their situation, he also acknowledges that there are many who will simply
give up hope, adopt a "melancholy outlook and [relapse] into a world of illusions
and dreams." In response, Shibutani says, "Let us place before ourselves one all-
important query: *What do we want out of life?*"[12] His answer to this question at
first seems to be "happiness," but it quickly takes a turn into the type of defeatism
he has argued against when he suggests that most "normal" people will fail to
achieve their goals, that the Nisei should instead "set goals within the reach of
our capacities, and then work earnestly to achieve our humble ends." Shibutani's
"Preface" is less overtly pessimistic or filled with melancholy as its intent is to
simply "clarify the nature of the difficulties that beset us" rather than attempting
to offer any specific solutions to the Nisei problem. Again, these difficulties
are related to racial exclusion, which inevitably prohibits full assimilation into
American society. And when racial and religious exclusion are combined with a
general lack of social organization among Nisei or with Nisei men's inability to
find wives, the decline to immorality and "personality maladjustments" seems
not only expected but inevitable.

The Nisei problem, whether used by Issei to describe their children or deployed
by Nisei themselves, is set within the context of prewar anti-Japanese and anti-
Buddhist sentiment in California and across the western United States, a topic
well covered by others.[13] As but a few examples: There was no path to citizenship
open to Japanese immigrants. Despite cases in which Japanese immigrants sued
the government to be included in the category of "white persons" eligible for naturalization, the U.S. Supreme Court repeatedly restricted citizenship to whites,

formerly enslaved Black persons, and their descendants, thus codifying the category of whiteness itself. In California and elsewhere, laws were passed to prohibit "aliens ineligible for citizenship" to own property, a move that was in direct response to the competitive threat Issei farmers posed to white-owned agricultural industry. Immigration laws restricted the movement of Japanese and Asians generally into the country, beginning first with laws targeting women and later with the wholesale exclusion of Asian immigration beginning in 1924. Japanese-language schools were regularly under attack as barriers to assimilation, with the assumption that a conflated Buddhism/Shintoism ("Mikadoism," as mentioned in the introduction) was promoting "Emperor worship" and disloyalty to America. This, in turn, led the U.S. government to begin surveillance of Japanese community organizations and leaders, with special scrutiny given to Buddhist priests and temples. In the years leading up to the Pacific War, Buddhist priests were labeled as most likely to be disloyal and were the first persons arrested in the hours after the attack on Pearl Harbor. The cumulative effect of these policies reinforces what Lowe describes as "the contradictions of immigrant marginality" in the United States, which requires Asian labor while repeatedly marginalizing Asians as unassimilable.[14] We should take it as a given that the Nisei Buddhists would have *problems*, and that they would be suffering from what is now widely recognized as racial trauma.[15]

Trauma studies has emerged in recent decades as a rich site for interrogating the ways specific events or cultural processes create and reinforce trauma at both the individual and collective levels. Racial or cultural trauma can be understood as both discursive and physical/psychological. As a discourse, cultural trauma may refer "to more abstract and mediated notions of collective identity, including religious and national identity," often in relation to "an invasive and overwhelming event that is believed to undermine or overwhelm one or several essential ingredients of a culture."[16] This is certainly one way that the Japanese American community has understood the camp experience, which remains "the mournful reference point from which these Americans describe changes in their communities, their personal lives, their aspirations."[17] The camp experience is traumatic in part because it cannot be cognitively assimilated and so becomes a missed memory—in Caroline Chung Simpson's terms, an "absent presence."[18] For Emily Roxworthy, the camp experience was "spectacularized"— that is, internees were on public display and asked to participate in their own victimization—which contributes to the traumatizing effects of the experience.[19] For our present purposes, however, two issues need to be brought to the fore. First, trauma is not merely discursive; it has physical, psychological, and multigenerational effects. Donna Nagata, Jacqueline Kim, and Kaidi Wu, for example, highlight the avoidance, detachment, and strategies of silence within the Japanese American community that are indicative of post-traumatic stress disorder and persist into the Sansei and even Yonsei (fourth) generations. This might manifest as a type of "melancholia," to use Anne Anlin Cheng's term.[20] Second, as we can see in these examples from the *Bussei*, it is not simply the camp experience that produces melancholy, that is the cause of trauma; it is ongoing anti-Japanese and anti-Buddhist animus that predates the war and continues well after.[21] As Natalie Avalos notes in regard to the historical trauma experienced by Indigenous peoples, whereas trauma may be caused by a "big event" (like World War II incarceration), "it can also develop as a result of a set of events, such as acts of genocide, in concert with structural violence."[22] Indeed, incarceration was traumatic, a "big event" that left a "mournful scar" on the community, but it was not the first trauma endured by Nisei Buddhists nor was it the last. This ongoing racial trauma experienced by Nisei is a bodily one, as Sharon Suh reminds us. In writing about her experience as an Asian American woman existing in a body indelibly marked as "other" in a white patriarchal society, she points out how "many of us have felt constricted or limited in how we self-express in the wrong time and place and our ability to choose how, when, where, and why we move our bodies has been compromised. The compromise made by our bodies to ac-commodate whiteness by growing smaller, less threatening, less confrontational is also a survival tactic, one that has the further effect of also reinforcing the he-gemony of whiteness which insists on an unequal distribution of power."[23]

One of the more striking features of the Nisei problem rhetoric in the *Bussei* is the extent to which the problem is individualized and pathologized. Whereas Shibutani's "Shangri-la" is filled with melancholy, he and other writers are clear that the Nisei simply need to "work hard" to overcome the problem. Again, Shibutani's aforementioned statement that Nisei "must . . . set goals within the reach of our capacities, and then work earnestly to achieve our humble ends" is an expression of this individualized effort needed to overcome racial exclusion. (Interestingly, immediately following Shibutani's essay is a quote by Henry Ward Beecher that begins, "It is not work that kills men; it is worry.")[24] Similarly, in the 1939 "You Are on Trial" essay, the author argues that a Buddhist "must strive to better himself continuously to benefit both he and society."[25] Such sentiments re-flect a fairly normative American-style self-determination rhetoric while having the effect of drawing one's attention away from the causes of systemic racism and discrimination and toward the responsibility of the individual to be a good cit-izen. Moreover, layered atop this call to hard work and self-determination, this individualism, is the awareness of the emotional and psychological effects of discrimination—the melancholy—oft referred to in the *Bussei* as "personality maladjustments."

Two essays by James Sakoda from 1941 demonstrate this tendency to pa-thologize Nisei and their problems. Sakoda, a psychology major at UC Berkeley, does some dream analysis for a friend, "Dick Kobayashi," in his essay "Betrayed: Ps[y]choanalysis of a Nisei."[26] "Dick Kobayashi is a queer mixture of introversion and extroversion," Sakoda writes. "While he was in college he seemed so sociable, especially with Caucasians, but now he rarely smiles, except in a cynical sort of way. It seems the same dream has been bothering him off and on for some time." In the dream, Dick finds himself on the bottom of the sea, possibly as a hermit crab, and he's unable to swim freely like the fish around him, which eventually turn on him and try to eat him. Sakoda thinks Dick is repressing something, and details Dick's life in and recently out of college. In college, he was distant from other Nisei, preferring the company of whites, calling other Nisei "damned Japs," and saying that they needed to be "more American." Once out of college, however, he is unable to get a job, "hindered by his shelly burden of Oriental characteristics." He ends up getting a job through a family friend at a Japanese laundry; thus, despite his attempts at Americanization, his upward social mobility remains limited, and he must rely on the Japanese immigrant community he'd spent so much time disparaging. In Sakoda's analysis, the fish trying to eat him represent Dick's feelings of betrayal by white Americans, and his Japanese American identity is represented by the "burden on his back," the hermit crab shell keeping him from swimming freely. "He must have clung desperately to the thought that America wouldn't let him down and that he wouldn't depend on the Japs." Sakoda thus performs an interesting bit of dream interpretation in this piece and deftly (if somewhat heavy-handedly) connects the dream metaphor to larger social and economic issues facing Nisei (e.g., Dick "having to crawl on the bottom on the socio-economic sea, instead of swimming as free as the fish"). He also draws out the complex relationships playing out in the Japanese American community more broadly, such as Dick's sentiment that Japanese should be "more American."

Sakoda offers no solution to Dick's problem. And in this, it is worth pairing his essay with another maritime-themed essay from the fall 1941 volume, "All This & Discrimination 2" by George Yasukochi, a parable about a "typical Nisei" named Aloysius Yoshizabukuro who, lost at sea, discusses his plight with "Old Man Rationalization."[27] Aloysius, it seems, has "developed a strong allergy to the bugaboo Discrimination." After he delivers a "searing indictment against Society-at-Large on the charge of discrimination," Old Man Rationalization suggests that there's nothing to be done about it. "Discrimination, prejudice and minority are not terms peculiar only to racial matters. . . . You'll find [other minority groups are] faced with this necessity of making adjustments, even though conformity is, in many cases, out of the question." He goes on, "We may then tentatively conclude that as long as Nisei retain their identity as a race, we shall always find some degree of racial presence present, both on your own choice and regardless of choice, to your own advantage as well as to your disadvantage." Before sinking back into the sea, Old Man Rationalization states: "One thing is certain. You will get nowhere by 'bitching' in self-pity." It would seem that there is nothing to be done about racial discrimination; whether or not you have a strong Japanese ethnic identity or try to be more American seems to make little difference. The moral of Yasukochi's parable appears to be a metaphorical throwing up of the hands in resignation and defeat—*shigatakanai*.[28]

However, in Sakoda's second piece, "Nisei Personality Adjustment," he does offer a solution. The essay opens:

> Have you noticed the following behavior in your fellow Nisei? He likes to keep to himself and shuts up like a clam when approached by a stranger. He is extremely conscious of being a Japanese. He is cliquish and is jealous of the success of other Niseis. He blames Isseis and Kibeis for his woes. He is confused; he feels insecure. All of these are signs of a disturbed personality.[29]

Sakoda goes on to suggest that the cause of the of the "disturbed personality" is, on the one hand, "discrimination from Caucasians and criticisms from Isseis." That is, the Nisei problem is a bicultural and intergenerational conflict caused by "being expected to act in two different ways by Isseis and Caucasians; our wanting to be 100 per cent American and being rejected." One can read in the opening of this essay the complex of competing desires within Nisei—the expectations from their parents to embody the "Japanese spirit," the desire to be fully American, and the knowledge that white America will not accept them. For all these reasons, "most of us are afraid of becoming failures." Sakoda goes on to note that a "criticism of Niseis is that they complain about their plight, but do very little about it." He suggests that Nisei should do something about their situation, but it is important to keep in mind what the "problem in a need of a solution" is for Sakoda. The problem is not racial discrimination but the "disturbed personality" *caused* by racial discrimination. Evoking Suh's article quoted above, the disturbed personality is a form of trauma, one caused by Nisei's being indelibly marked as "other" and excluded from normative white Christian American society. Whereas one might argue that the solution to this problem would be to dismantle systems of oppression and white supremacy, Sakoda offers instead coping strategies. How might Nisei deal with their "disturbed personality" caused by racism? How might Nisei attend to the trauma of white supremacy? For Sakoda, the solution or coping strategy is twofold: first, join a group; second, lose yourself.

"It is important," he writes, "that those of us who are lonesome and bewildered seek the protection of some sympathetic group. We should find a group well-suited to our nature, possessing ideals and attitudes similar to ours." Becoming part of a movement, "a group well-suited to our nature," finding a suitable role in the group "and being active in that capacity" is the precursor to losing oneself. Sakoda here makes the case that Nisei should move beyond a self-centered view of the problem. Rather than seeing discrimination as something unique to Nisei (recall Old Man Rationalization's advice), the Nisei problem is actually "a part of the greater American problem." And "if we could lose ourselves in a movement or interest that absorbed all of our energies, we would have little time left to devote to our petty selves." For Sakoda, then, the problem is not racism per se but the psychological effects of racism on individual Nisei. The solutions to this problem are therefore to find comfort and solidarity in a group of like-minded people which can work toward a larger, common purpose; in this, one lets go of individual grievances and no longer has the time to "brood," worry constantly, or, presumably, suffer from the fear and anxiety that characterize the Nisei personality maladjustment.

Of course, Sakoda is not suggesting that one join just any group—one should join the "Buddhist movement." His reference to Buddhism here is in passing but underscored by the sentiment that everyone should have a "philosophy of life" to free themselves from worry. Other prewar Nisei writers are more explicit about the value of Buddhism both in terms of the Nisei problem as well as for America writ large. In his fall 1941 piece "Buddhist and Why," Tad Tani is unequivocal: "I am a Buddhist because I am an American of Japanese ancestry."

> As an American, it is my duty to contribute something to the culture of the United States. We Americans are like a huge symphony—an orchestra of cultures—and each nationality and group adding their bit to make a real composite culture of these United States harmonious. I can add to the culture of America by introducing the best things in the culture and philosophy of Japan. As a Buddhist this comes naturally to me, for by studying the Buddhism of Japan one learns the very history and civilization and spirit of Japan. . . .
>
> As an American Buddhist we are capable of understanding Japanese philosophy and Bushido. We learn to appreciate things of Japan and of the Japanese ways of thinking. It is our duty as Americans to introduce all the marvels and cultures of the East. We are the bridges between the East and West. We can better interpret Japanese actions by having a glimpse into their souls and the background which molds their character. We can and will add our bit and influence to the artistry and culture of these United States.[30]

Though he does not make reference to the Nisei problem as such, Tani anticipates a postwar rhetoric of Buddhism-as-contribution. Following his declaration that he is a Buddhist because of his Japanese ancestry, he provides a short history of Japan that foregrounds (problematically) Buddhism's role as a civilizing force.[31] Indeed, Tani's argument is that without Buddhism, and more specifically without Shōtoku Taishi's promotion of Buddhism, Japan would have remained in a state of "semi-barbarism." There is a subtle implication here that America itself is in a less-than-idealized state, suggesting that it is not the "Nisei problem" that needs fixing but America itself. To equate American culture with a symphony orchestra while at the same time claiming that Buddhism civilizes and that Nisei will add to the orchestra and thereby make it harmonious is to suggest that the current American orchestra is, in a sense, out of tune. As a Nisei Buddhist, Tani can contribute the very thing that America needs—Buddhism, which is what allowed the Japanese nation to grow and flourish. Nisei, as American Buddhists, are in an idealized location for this transmission of Buddhism owing to their bicultural status, their ability to know and understand "naturally" the "soul" of Japan while simultaneously being American.

Whereas Japanese-language school curricula and Issei leaders may have desired to instill in their children a "Japanese spirit" or a generalized sense of morality, for these Nisei writers it is Buddhism specifically that is needed to solve the Nisei problem. As we saw in Sakoda's piece, the Buddhist community serves the important function of being a site for solidarity and healing; by being surrounded by like-minded persons who are experiencing the trauma of racism, Nisei can assuage their sense of anxiety, their fear of failure, and their feeling of betrayal by the systems of white supremacy. But Buddhism serves other functions as well. For Sakoda, joining the Buddhist movement provides one with the opportunity to "[interpret the] cultures of the East and the West"; in this, he evokes the bicultural or liminal space in which Nisei find themselves between Japan and the United States. This translocative position is repeated in Tani's piece when he speaks of being a bridge between East and West. Thus, the Buddhist community serves as a safe haven while, simultaneously, Buddhism acts as way to cross this divide between cultures. Finally, in addition to being a bridge, it is also an offering; it is what Nisei will contribute to American culture as Americans. And it is this theme of Buddhism's dual aspects of bridge and offering that will be carried froward and amplified in the postwar *Bussei*.

Making America Buddhist

There was no solution to the "Nisei problem" in the prewar years; in fact, things only got worse. Within hours of the bombing of Pearl Harbor, Japanese Buddhist leaders were being arrested, first in Hawai'i and quickly thereafter on the West Coast. Curfews were enacted limiting the movement of Japanese Americans. And in February 1942 President Roosevelt signed Executive Order 9066, which effectively allowed the West Coast to be declared a "military zone" and set the stage for "evacuation." By March, the wholesale removal of all persons of Japanese descent had begun—including American citizens, including women and children, including orphaned babies—on the pretext that they represented a threat to national security.[32]

The final prewar issue of the *Berkeley Bussei* was published in the spring of 1942. In an editorial foreword, George (Jobo) Nakamura wrote:

> We have undertaken a task of editing the "Berkeley Bussei," the record of Berkeley YBA activities in the most significant year of our lives—with the sincere desire of producing a publication worthy of the effort the organization has strived for its place in American democracy and to which we rededicate this book. . . . We will be asked to leave our home very soon. We do not want to leave. We want to stay. Yet we know that our petty grievances are so small when a serious realization of a gigantic task our country is brought close to us. We are glad to be able to do even a little to ease her burden.[33]

A detailed history of the profound injustice of the camps is beyond the scope of this book, needs to be told and retold, and has been done expertly and with care and precision by Kashima, Williams, and others.[34] It is worth pausing here, in the early months of 1942, to hear the voices of these young American Buddhists who can see the world changing, the world falling apart around them, before we continue to the postwar years. In pausing here on the words of Nakamura, it is worth drawing our attention to the lament—"We do not want to leave"—juxtaposed with the notion that this lament is but a "petty grievance." As discussed in the last section, these are expressions of trauma. These are the laments of persons denied their basic rights as citizens and resigned to their fate.

And yet, while dismissing the lament as a petty grievance, Nakamura dedicates this volume of the *Bussei* to democracy itself. On the eve of evacuation, on the eve of illegal incarceration in the camps, Nakamura subtly aligns the Bussei movement with the core American ideal of democracy. Even as their rights as citizens are being denied them, the Nisei affirm their position as both Americans and Buddhists. Or, as YBA president Jim Sugihara put it in the same 1942 volume: "As loyal Americans and followers of the Buddhist faith we know that we have but one course to traverse, that being to serve our country in whatever way she may ordain simultaneously guided by the Teachings of the Buddha."[35]

We find one example of this service to country in Yukio Kawamoto (1919–2019). Kawamoto was born in Berkeley; his family was active in the Berkeley Buddhist Temple community, and his mother taught at the Japanese-language school. He was in his final semester at UC Berkeley in 1942 when he was drafted into the Army. Originally, he was sent to the Presidio in Monterey for basic training, an experience he wrote about via a series of short letters to his mother and father published in the *Bussei*. His final letter offers two prescient observations: "All the nihonjin, including myself, were interviewed by the lieutenant today. I figure, therefore that we will be sent in the not too distant future. . . . I read the evening newspaper after the dinner tonight. It looks as if evacuation is becoming a reality, isn't it? Please take care of yourselves and don't worry." He was indeed "sent" somewhere, specifically Camp Robinson in Arkansas to complete basic training. His bilingual upbringing led to his eventual service as a translator in the 37th Infantry Division, and he was deployed to the South Pacific for most of the war where he interrogated Japanese prisoners and translated intercepted communications. Meanwhile, his parents were "evacuated" to the War Relocation Authority camp in Topaz, Utah. Kawamoto was released from active duty before the war's end specifically to help his family resettle in Berkeley in 1945.[36]

Meanwhile, the Imamuras had also returned to Berkeley. The Imamura family was first relocated to the Tulare Assembly Center in central California before being incarcerated in the Gila River War Relocation Center in Arizona. Unlike other ministers, Imamura was not separated from his family, and almost immediately he began holding Buddhist services at both Tulare and Gila River.[37] In March 1945 the Imamuras were released from camp and, at the request of Julius Goldwater, went to Los Angeles where they helped run a hostel at the Senshin Buddhist Temple, near the Watts neighborhood, to resettle other Japanese Americans returning from the camps. There were a number of other Berkeley Temple members at Senshin, and after a year in Los Angeles, the family returned to Berkeley where the situation was much the same. The temple had been used as a storage facility for internees' belongings; families lived in the cramped spaces of the dormitories, and the Imamuras did their best to help the community resettle. The community, suffering economically due to incarceration, could not afford to pay Imamura a large enough salary to support his growing family. He worked briefly as a janitor at a nearby apartment building. A connection to Robert Lowie, however, led to a better job at the UC Berkeley anthropology museum.[38] By 1947, "everything began to take on a semblance of normalcy. Temple members returned . . . the Women's Dorm was reopened. The Imamuras moved out of the one room and into the little house in the back. And the Jichiryo was again filled with eleven energetic male students."[39] With the return of normalcy came the Bussei movement and the publication of the *Berkeley Bussei*. The inaugural edition of the now-annual publication was released in January 1950 and recounted the activities of the previous year.[40]

Yukio Kawamoto was "asked to contribute an article," and so penned "Outlook on American Buddhism." It is worth quoting a significant portion of this piece to fully grasp not only Kawamoto's sense of being both American and Buddhist but also how Buddhism, in effect, *defines* his Americanness. Kawamoto begins his essay by reflecting on how the question of the "future of Buddhism in America" seems to be on everyone's mind, and various ideas have been offered since the end of the war. He also notes the general consternation in the community about finances, about making sure the organization can support itself—issues, he says, that are certainly important and deserving of consideration. But, he writes, none of this gets to the "fundamental issues" facing the Japanese American Buddhist community. The real question is "Why am I a Buddhist?"

> Yes, why are we? Because our parents were, no more no less? Because we've been going to church since a little child and it's kind of "grown-into" us? Or is it because our "group" goes to the Buddhist church so I am a Buddhist? Is it because we believe in Buddhism because we know or feel (truthfully) that it is the religion that best satisfies our needs of a religion? . . .
> . . . [W]e must go a step further. [For] Buddhism to prevail at all [it] must contribute more than just personal satisfaction to the individual follower. As a group matter it must contribute something more than the existing religions already here. Otherwise it wouldn't have justification for its introduction and existence. If it can offer no more than the already existing religions is there a truthful justification to continue it? It would merely be prolonging an eventual end with a great deal of sacrifice involved in the interim prolongation. It would be just a retardation on the completion of the integration and assimilation of the Japanese group into American life. In short, why make ourselves even more "different" when there is no real reason to? Or to put it another way, our conviction of our faith in Buddhism must be so strong, so firm, so overwhelmingly positive that it can justify our being "different."
> Now this business of being "different." Being in the minority is no disgrace in itself. Anyone who's read at all knows how the Christians at one time were very much in the minority and persecuted terribly. It soon becomes obvious too that no amount of official persecution, governmental authority could stamp out a movement wherein the followers were firmly convinced of their faith. This is it. An overwhelming conviction in our faith is necessary for the survival of the Buddhist movement in America. Or to put it more positively, with a solid nucleus of firm followers of our faith, we can overcome any and all obstacles that may come our way.[41]

Kawamoto ends his essay by declaring that a firm foundation in the faith is necessary to promote Buddhism in America, and such a project is necessary not just for Buddhists but for Buddhism to make any meaningful contribution to American culture.

I call our attention to this essay because it is a stirring rallying cry, an unapologetic defense of Buddhist Americans' right to be Buddhist, to be different. This plea is made, in part, by reference to the dominant religion—Christianity—which is framed as also having once been a persecuted minority religion. Christianity's success in spite of persecution is then used to bolster Kawamoto's claim that a religion whose followers are firmly convinced of their faith can overcome any obstacle. Without naming either the "official persecution" (surveillance followed by incarceration) or the "governmental authority" (the United States) acting against his own religious tradition, given the context of this piece and Kawamoto's personal history, the subtext is clear—Japanese American Buddhist have been singularly persecuted by the U.S. government, but such persecution cannot stop persons so "firmly convinced of their faith." Kawamoto further invokes the discourse of assimilation, the desire on the part of his fellow Nisei to both become fully and be fully accepted as American. This impulse to assimilate led some to convert to Christianity—in Kashiwagi's father's estimation, to try to be both Christian and white.[42] In the calculus of assimilation, being Christian would be easier than the double difference of being Japanese *and* Buddhist. But Kawamoto rejects this as well. Rather than abandoning their faith, he argues, Japanese Americans need to embrace their religion even more strongly, for in claiming a strong Buddhist identity they will be able to integrate into American society *as Buddhists*. Finally, note that this is not simply an argument for the "integration and assimilation of the Japanese group into American life"; it is also an argument that Buddhism is something that Japanese Americans can *contribute* to American society.

In the prewar *Bussei* we find the rhetoric of the "Nisei problem," an intractable problem whose roots lie in the racial and religious othering of Japanese American Buddhists. Whereas a resigned acceptance to the inevitability of discrimination is persistent, so is Buddhism as at least a partial solution to the problem. The support and solidarity one finds within a community or a movement (specifically the Bussei movement) combined with the moral conditioning that comes with religious faith may not solve the problem of racial or religious discrimination, but perhaps it will lessen the psychological harm. After camp, direct references to the "Nisei problem" drop from the *Bussei* and in their place one finds references to bridges, contributions, and Buddhism's import not just for the Nisei but for America itself. As we saw in Tani's 1941 piece, Nisei "are the bridges between the East and West." The metaphor of bridge is repeated and phrased in a variety of ways and becomes stronger in the postwar *Bussei*. But the message is essentially the same: as bicultural persons who intuitively understand both Japanese and American culture, Nisei are in the ideal position to transmit the dharma to the West. For example, in "Asian Studies," a report on the establishment of the American Academy of Asian Studies in San Francisco, the anonymous author recounts a talk in which Alan Watts says that when the Western world "realizes and understands the philosophy of Buddhism, it will find spiritual peace."[43] Watts goes on to claim that "it is the Nisei Buddhists who hold the key to this realization, or in his terms, 'treasure box.'" The author concludes the report by asking, "We, the Niseis, may have the key to open the box of treasures, but do we know that we have it?"

More than being a metaphorical link across the Pacific, Buddhism is something that Nisei are being called to introduce or contribute to American society.
Again, Tani invokes this same language with the claim that what he has to contribute to America are "the best things in the culture and philosophy of Japan,"
and implies that in so doing Nisei will make the American symphony of cultures
all the more harmonious. In discussing the cover illustration of the 1952 *Bussei*—
a line drawing of a Japanese pagoda and the United States Capitol (Figure 3.1)—
the editors remark on the "present turmoil" of international strife and conflict;
they have chosen this cover as "a symbol of the need for a better understanding of
two different cultures—a mutual understanding of the East and the West . . . And
perhaps, with cooperative effort and understanding of these two cultures, we
may someday realize a harmonious and tranquil society of men."[44] They go on to
link the study of Buddhism directly to this end. In addition to Buddhism being a
necessary component of peacemaking and the betterment of American society,
there is also an exhortation that Nisei need to work hard to bring this to realization. The author of the "Asian Studies" piece suggests as much in his question/
challenge: "Do we know that we have it?" The editors of the 1952 volume are
more straightforward and forceful in their editorial "A Time for Action." They
make the claim that the Berkeley community is the ideal location for Buddhist
education in the United States owing to the prevalence of college students, "the
community and church leaders of tomorrow," who come from all over the West
Coast and will thus spread their education (and presumably Buddhism) far and
wide upon graduation. They implore the reader to see "the necessity for a student center here in Berkeley, the necessity for *immediate* action on *your* part if
the coming generations are to have that necessary ingredient of life provided by
Buddhist teachings."[45] The repeated calls to hard work might be taken as part and
parcel of a quintessentially American discourse of self-determination. That is,
one might rightly assume that Nisei Buddhists are simply making the quotidian
argument of their (white) American peers that all one needs to do is work hard to
achieve the success owed any hardworking American.

As something of an aside, I feel it important to note that this self-determination
rhetoric in the *Bussei* may be mistaken by some as a type of "model minority"
discourse. It is not. To understand how the *Bussei*'s rhetoric of hard work differs,
let us recall that the "model minority" stereotype was first invoked by William
Petersen via a *New York Times* article in 1966, "Success Story, Japanese-American
Style."[46] Not only did Petersen's piece essentialize Japanese Americans into a racial caricature, but its intent was comparative in nature—to demonstrate how,
through hard work and self-determination, a racial minority could lift itself up
within systems of white supremacy, hence absolving whiteness of any responsibility to reform racist institutions. The comparison to other minority groups
begins in the essay's opening paragraph: "Like the Negroes, the Japanese have

Figure 3.1 Cover of the 1952 *Berkeley Bussei*.

been the object of color prejudice. Like the Jews, they have been feared and hated as hyper efficient competitors." And having declared that "we barely know how to repair the damage that the slave traders started," Petersen gets to his point: that "[by] any criterion of good citizenship that we choose, the Japanese Americans are better than any other group in our society, including native-born whites."[47] On the one hand, Petersen claims this success is the result of education and strict parenting; on the other, he makes essentialist claims about the wide gulf between Japanese and American culture, which has forced Nisei and Sansei to be particularly good at navigating cultural difference. These claims may or may not be worth interrogating, but that is not the problem with "Success Story." The problem is the context within which these claims are made. Petersen highlights the strong community support Nisei and Sansei have (their strict upbringing) without mentioning one of the reasons for this community support; as we saw earlier, Issei parents strictly monitored Nisei behavior and attempted to "mold the Nisei mind" out of a fear of white backlash should their children run afoul of the law. In other words, Petersen overlooks the white supremacist context in which these cultural practices emerged. Further, his depiction of Nisei and Sansei "success" and lack of "trouble-making" is always made in comparison to other minority groups, reinforcing the suggestion that as long as the community works hard, they can overcome racial oppression, which in turn reinforces the argument that minority problems are caused not by systemic racism but by individual moral failings. Petersen's argument in essence does what Claire Jean Kim labels "racial triangulation," whereby Japanese Americans are rendered better than Blacks but still different from whites and therefore their "model minority" status is undercut by their remaining perpetual foreigners.[48] As David Palumbo-Liu argues, "The model minority myth reifies Asian American identity and deploys this reification programmatically against other groups, mapping out specific positionings of minorities within the U.S. political economy."[49] Generally, in the *Bussei* one does not find the type of "racial triangulation" endemic to Petersen's "Success Story." Nisei are not arguing that they are "better minorities" than other minorities; indeed, they are not claiming to be *good minorities*. Rather, they are claiming to be *good Americans*.

One of the things that made Nisei good Americans was their service to country, as demonstrated by Yukio Kawamoto, who not only served in the Army during the war but worked for the U.S. State Department in the decades following. As Williams notes in *American Sutra*, military service was certainly a site of tension within the Japanese American community, but it was also rhetorically deployed as part of a larger strategy for their acceptance as Americans. For example, noting a funeral service at Manzanar by Shinjō Nagatomi, Williams remarks that the Shin Buddhist priest connected the soldiers' service in the military to "a Japanese warrior spirit" and "affirmed that the nisei soldiers' sacrifice would earn a place for those of Japanese descent in America."[50] More than this, Nisei Buddhists' wartime service, as Williams argues, helped to secure the rights of religious freedom for Japanese Americans. The issue of Buddhist chaplains, mentioned in the previous chapter, was bound up with existing military policy that recognized only Catholicism, Protestantism, and Judaism as legitimate religions and had no formal mechanism for recognizing the deaths of Buddhist soldiers, who were buried in Christian graves. In the waning years of the war and the immediate postwar years, Nisei Buddhists' service forced the military to recognize Buddhism, and fallen Buddhist soldiers were given proper burials and memorials.[51] Of course, despite these gains, racial and religious discrimination persisted (as evidenced by Father Murphy's appeal); nevertheless, the Nisei wartime experience, both inside and outside the camps, created "the possibility of being both fully Buddhist and fully American."[52]

In calling our attention to the ways in which Nisei Buddhists argued for the need to work hard, the ways in which they served their country during the war, and the ways in which Buddhism was deployed in this regard, it is also important to call our attention to the fact that Buddhism was not just of value for the Japanese American community—it was also something to be given to American society at large. Simply put, the *Bussei* argues that Buddhism is something America *needs*.

If we return to the anonymous "Asian Studies" article, recall that Watts's claim is both that Nisei hold the key to the "treasure box" of the buddhadharma and that Buddhist philosophy will bring peace to the West. Similarly, in the 1952 volume, Kanmo Imamura recounts a community meeting held to discuss raising funds to build a new temple and educational center. In attendance that evening was D. T. Suzuki, who, according to Imamura, "spoke with earnestness to the effect that it is on the shoulders of the Nisei and Sansei, the inheritors of both Eastern and Western cultures, to bring the true Buddhism to the West and help enrich the American way of life."[53] Moreover, in a Japanese-language article in the same volume, Imamura elaborates Suzuki's position that there is a great deal of interest among white Americans in Buddhism. However, without some sort of intermediary (e.g., Nisei American Buddhists) who understands the cultures of both the East and West, the process of transmitting Buddhism to America will be difficult if not impossible.[54] In his 1953 essay "Panorama," Imamura uses the bridge metaphor once again in arguing that "[if] Buddhism is to become the envoy of hope for peace, the bridge of East-West that our parents have started must be completed."[55] Thus, he is arguing, all at once, that Buddhism is a pacifying force, America needs pacification, the Issei started this process but it remains incomplete, and the Nisei must take up the charge. These examples demonstrate the persistent assumption that something is wrong with America— that America has a problem, not the Nisei—and the solution is Buddhism. As discussed in the previous chapter, this is fairly standard modernist rhetoric (e.g., the modern world is lacking; Buddhism fills that lack). What is of relevance here is the twofold step of, first, identifying not just *what* will fill the lack but *who* and, second, asserting that this fulfillment will fundamentally change both Japanese Americans and America itself. That is, first the *Bussei* posits that there is something wrong with America (or the modern world)—that it is teetering on the brink of war, that people are disaffected and morally adrift. Buddhism is put forth as the solution to this problem, a pacifistic, moral, and civilizing force. And Nisei cast themselves as being in the ideal position to contribute Buddhism to America. The logic of this claim of Nisei being ideal bridges between East and West rests on the fact that *Nisei are already American*. When Nisei authors speak of the "youth today" who are bereft or without moral guidance and in need of Buddhism's positive influence, the youth in question are not merely "Japanese Americans" but "Americans," with the latter including the former. And thus we get to the second step: if Nisei are in need of Buddhism, by implication they, too, are lacking something, something that Buddhism will supply. If they are as firmly convinced in their faith as Kawamoto implores them to be, they will become fully Buddhist while remaining fully American. In effect, this firm embrace of a dual Buddhist and American identity makes America itself more Buddhist. America can no longer claim an exclusive white Christian identity, as it must contend with the reality of Asian Buddhist Americans. The Nisei contribution of Buddhism to America is made possible both via their "translation" of Buddhist or Japanese culture—the "bridging of East and West"—and via their own location in and identity as Americans. In this way, the contribution of Buddhism to America is both modern (Buddhism fixes the failures of modernity) and simultaneously Nisei.

The bridge metaphor is not merely an image of Asians crossing the Pacific and settling in America; it is also an image of how Buddhism itself will become part of and transform America. To recall Tani's "Buddhist and Why," and to mix our metaphors, if America is an orchestra of cultures, let us suppose then that each instrument represents a different culture. If a new culture/instrument is added, the music changes. The orchestra is no longer playing the symphony it was before the bridge was crossed.

Bridges connect. In the real world, bridges are part of larger infrastructural projects, transportation and communication networks, not mere metaphorical crossings. And in the following chapter we will trace out some of the in-fact networks and connections made by Buddhists across the Pacific that created the conditions for the in-fact contribution of Buddhism to American society and culture. Making Buddhism possible required work; it required the labor of the Japanese American community. And just as the Nisei problem is gendered in the *Bussei*, so too is labor.

"A Whirl with the Girls"

In addition to philosophical and religious essays, most *Bussei* volumes immediately before and after the war include "Sports" and "Features" sections, which report on basketball games and YBA events, provide lists of YBA members and residents of the dorms, and print gossip columns that describe the lives and activities of the young Buddhists living in Berkeley. One column, from the 1952 volume, is titled "A Whirl with the Girls: Never a Dorm Moment." In it, Marge Kataoka describes life in the girls' dorm:

> One thing that can be said about the Girls' Dorm is that there is never a dull moment. Interest in world affairs is demonstrated by our morning battle for the Chronicle [the local San Francisco newspaper]—King Aroo, crossword puzzle, and the horoscope. No one could possibly doubt our concern over becoming good cooks after he tasted one of the dinner we prepare for the gourmands next door [at the boys' dorm]. . . . We are also concerned about the cultured game called bridge. Since our hand was broken up by the departure of Rosie and Betty, we are forced to regress into the uncouth stage of gin rummy.[56]

Azuma has argued that while the early Japanese immigrant population was diverse, including both wealthy entrepreneurs and the urban elite as well as migrant laborers and rural farmers, once they were in the United States and subject to racial discrimination class differences were flattened so as to become virtually meaningless. For women in this equation, their role became the maintenance of an "ideal domesticity commensurate with the middle-class white model" while their husbands engaged in work outside the home.[57] These gender dynamics played out in Nisei educational programs, which, as we saw earlier, were focused on raising well-behaved and morally upright Japanese American citizens. Nisei girls were expected to become paragons of gentleness, tranquility, and chastity.[58] Moreover, as discussed earlier, when defining the "Nisei problem" themselves, Nisei often did so in part by discussing men's inability to find suitable wives. This way of framing the problem obviously speaks to the intended audience of such pieces and necessarily foregrounds the experiences of heterosexual men. And when reading Kataoka's essay here, it is hard not to feel, if nothing else, *disappointed*. "A Whirl with the Girls" perpetuates this idealized domesticity and gives us little to balance out the perspective of the men. While claiming to be interested in "world affairs," when the women get the newspaper they go straight for comics, crosswords, and horoscopes, not the world news section. To make matters worse, they apparently are charged with cooking dinner for the boys next door, who, it is implied, complain about the quality of their cooking. Given the context of this piece written in the early 1950s and the gender dynamics of Nisei educational programs, perhaps it should not be surprising that we find in the *Bussei* a repetition of gender stereotypes; we might simply dismiss this type of writing as "of its time," despite the disappointment of not being able to clearly hear the voices of Nisei women.

However, I am not content in my disappointment. Fortunately, columns such as "A Whirl with the Girls" are not the only women's voices we have in the *Bussei*. Whereas a generous estimate of the number of women-authored pieces in the *Bussei* hovers at around 12 percent, women were nevertheless contributors.[59] As we saw in the previous chapters, Jane Imamura and Kimi Hisatsune contributed sophisticated articulations of Shin Buddhist modernism, and beyond writing essays for the *Bussei*, they were active leaders in the community. In fact, in the early 1950s, Hisatsune was not only a frequent contributor to but also one of the editors of the *Bussei*. And in addition to discussing Buddhist modernism, some of her work gestures toward the Nisei problem. Writing under her maiden name, Yonemura, in 1951 in words as urgent and forceful as those of the men mentioned earlier in this chapter, she states: "Living in this atmosphere of insecurity, our youths are either turning to a steadying faith in an existing religion to seek meaning in an otherwise meaningless existence, or throwing overboard all moral and spiritual values to seek gratification in a devil-may-care fashion. . . . [I]t is the duty of each Bussei to reevaluate the teachings of the Buddha and come to realize the necessity for the preservation of ethical values to save the world from the shackles of misguided domination."[60] It is worth noting that this was the editorial message for the 1951 volume and that Yonemura was, along with Taitetsu Unno, one of that volume's editors. Other women both pre- and postwar, such as Hisako Kuroiwa and Lily Matsuura, also served as editors of the *Bussei* or in other capacities to make possible the publication and the study groups—not to mention the temple choir and children's educational programs.

It is certainly worth our efforts to count bylines and acknowledge that a generous estimate of 12 percent hardly comes close to gender parity—indeed, it's not even in the same universe as gender parity. Representation matters. It matters that women's voices were not centered in the *Bussei* as the men's were; it matters that the "Nisei problem" was defined, in part, as men being unable to find wives because that framing obscures and ignores how the problem was experienced by women.[61] Perhaps they, too, were concerned about marriage. Did they have difficulty finding suitable marriage partners? Did they care about marriage at all? Were they concerned about racial inequality? Did they suffer from personality maladjustments like "Dick Kobayashi"? Were they frustrated by their exclusion from white-centric spaces or thwarted in their attempts at upward social mobility? Did they work? Were they able to find jobs?[62] Were they frustrated by the expectation that they were responsible for feeding their male classmates? On these questions, the *Bussei* is mute.[63] And so representation matters.

It also matters who is doing the actual labor, and this is as important as representation-by-byline. As will be discussed in more detail in the following chapters, the *Bussei* as publishing project made possible the promotion and promulgation of a particular version of Buddhist modernism. Such projects were the result of sustained effort and the labor of persons, something often obscured by the results of that labor. When someone picks up the *Bussei*, they read the words of Taitetsu Unno or Alan Watts, but they likely do not know who *typed* those words, who made possible the printing of those words on paper. Some volumes of the *Bussei* make known the typists and others who did the behind-the-scenes work, and often these persons were women (Figure 3.2).[64] This division of labor, of course, replicates midcentury gender norms, with women serving as secretaries and typists, labor that is obscured by the bylines of more famous and more widely recognized men.

Of course, one reason the men are more widely recognized is precisely that theirs are the names on the bylines. This is yet one more reason representation matters. Achieving gender parity in bylines is a worthwhile project. And it should be encouraged alongside another project: a revaluation of how we value labor itself.[65]

Lisa Sloniowski begins her "Affective Labor, Resistance, and the Academic Librarian" with a discussion of Marx and the distinctions between productive, unproductive, and immaterial labor. Unproductive labor, for classical Marxists, was considered housework and childcare, labor that did not produce surplus value and thus existed outside capitalist systems. "Marxist feminists and feminist socialists sought to correct Marxist views by pointing to the importance of unpaid reproductive and domestic labor in capitalist societies."[66] This body of work forces us to rethink how the domestic sphere interacts and relates to the public. Whereas the public becomes the domain of men and is valued in its relationship to producing surplus value for capitalist systems, the domestic is feminized and devalued as unproductive. However, rather than viewing unproductive labor as such, feminist scholarship has noted that such labor is a necessary component of capitalist systems and, indeed, of society itself. Unproductive labor, such as emotional or affective labor, creates and reinforces social cohesion and is deployed in support of traditionally defined productive labor. Sloniowski aptly describes the situation and its gendered dynamics through her own experience as a university reference librarian. She writes how she is often called upon to emotionally support colleagues, faculty members, and students, leaving her drained at the end of the day and feeling as though she has accomplished nothing. This experience is in contrast to that of male colleagues, who are often tasked with immaterial labor, labor focused on problem-solving or quantifiable and recognizable tasks such as data entry. More generally, librarianship has historically been considered women's work and is often undervalued within the university setting despite its central importance. "The work of librarians in supporting faculty research, teaching information-literacy skills to students, and building and maintaining collections is undervalued, as evidenced by the low profile that librarians have on most campuses and the ways in which the operational budgets of libraries

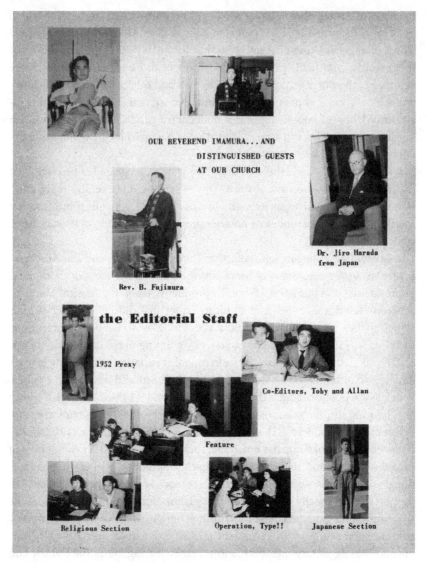

Figure 3.2 Photo montage from the 1952 *Berkeley Bussei* including images of editorial staff, typists, and contributors.

are continually under siege."[67] I trust that the reader intuitively understands this argument: universities cannot function without a library. Libraries provide innumerable services and benefits to the campus, and many of these services are "unproductive" from a classical Marxian perspective. And yet faculty and students would be unable to conduct teaching and research without them. There is an inherent relationship between productive and affective labor. However, in part precisely because it is "women's work," affective labor is devalued, undervalued, or ignored altogether in favor of productive labor. For this reason I want to avoid focusing solely on a list of bylines as the means by which we value the contribution of women Nisei Buddhists in the making of American Buddhism. Their intellectual and written contributions are of immense importance, to be sure; so too are their contributions as typists, copyeditors, mothers, caregivers, chefs, and even gin rummy players. Without this labor, no *Bussei* would have been published and the words of Unno or Watts would never have seen the light of day. Indeed, neither would the book in your hands.

Again, as Azuma says, it may be that Nisei Buddhists here are replicating an ideal domesticity based on white middle-class norms. However, I want to guard against replicating uncritically a Western feminist approach that would claim Nisei women as merely subjugated or passive victims. Drawing on the work of Amy Borovoy, I call attention to the fact that in European and North American contexts, we have created a series of devaluing dichotomies.[68] The dichotomy between productive and unproductive work discussed above is linked to the dichotomy between public and private and the Victorian-era concern to "protect" the home (the domain of women) from the deleterious effects of capitalism and the market. Productive labor, moreover, is often equated with "paid work" and is valued both economically (as surplus value) and morally because "paid work" is contrasted not with "unpaid work" (reproductive or affective labor) but with "unnecessary" work—hobbies, individual or purely selfish pursuits. To the extent that the domestic is rendered unproductive and simultaneously feminized, women are trapped in a double bind. If they find value or satisfaction in the domestic (or even in personal hobbies), they are not being productive members of society and are thus devalued. If they leave the domestic sphere for the male-dominated public sphere, they are abandoning their proper role as caregivers.[69]

In response to this complex of binaries and false equivalencies, Borovoy turns to the "Japanese housewife problem" and notes how, according to the logics of North American feminist theory, Japanese women who find meaning in the home must have a sort of "false consciousness." To the contrary, she details the historical construction of the ideal Japanese home in the modern period and draws on ethnographic studies to demonstrate the very different relationships between the public and private in the Japanese context. Whereas in the Euro-American context, the Victorian-era concern to "protect the home" created a sharp divide between the political and the domestic, this was not the case in post-Meiji Japan where the state actively promoted the home generally as a microcosm of the nation. In this way, housewives became public figures in themselves and the very ideas of the political and the domestic could expand beyond the boundaries we might expect in the American context. In her ethnographic case studies, Borovoy is able to detail the nuanced ways in which Japanese housewives have agency and find meaning in their work. Moreover, she draws attention to late twentieth-century Japanese feminists who "have resisted celebrating 'work for money' as the sine qua non of women's liberation."[70] When equality is defined solely as women seeking men's roles in the "public," "women become doubly exploited" by capitalism and patriarchy. Consequently, the true feminist goal for thinkers such as Ueno Chizuko will never be attained without men's full participation in the home—that is, without the "feminization of men."[71]

From one point of view, Jane Imamura was herself a housewife. She was largely responsible for taking care of the home, as her husband worked a day job at UC Berkeley's anthropology museum and a night and weekend job as a temple minister. However, to call Imamura a housewife is not at all accurate; in her memoir she refers to herself explicitly as a *bōmori*. "The role of the bomori is difficult to define," Imamura writes. "Of course, she supports and complements the work of her husband. Yet, her own work is demanding, often difficult, requiring flexibility, discretion, and creativity, all in the spirit of *Dana*, pure giving."[72] The specific work of the *bōmori*, for Imamura, included being on site at the temple every day to receive visitors; generally assuming the role of office manager, including handling the mail and bookkeeping; "public relations" in the form of hosting guests and being a representative of the temple and community; and playing the role of chauffeur, picking up and dropping off guests and visitors at the airport and elsewhere. Additionally, she was the mother of four children, ran the Berkeley Temple's choir, and served as housemother for the dorms. *Bōmori* literally means "temple guardian" (not wife), and this list of duties in Imamura's memoir points to the range of activities temple wives may be expected to perform, both "domestic" and "religious."[73] In her groundbreaking ethnographic study of *bōmori* in contemporary Japan, Jessica Starling highlights the limitations of this binary. "As domestic religious professionals, temple wives' experiences directly challenge conceptual boundaries such as public/private, outside/inside, professional/domestic and sacred/profane."[74] In their study of the aesthetics of food in the Japanese Buddhist context, Kolata and Gillson further collapse the dichotomy between the religious and the domestic by noting how women deploy "food literacy" to make connections and facilitate a sense of Buddhist belonging. This is not incidental to Buddhist practice or merely "social" but rendered as a Buddhist practice itself in the form of acts of *dāna* or charity or in the maintenance of dietary rules such as vegetarianism. "Food-related labor is not just domestic labor, it is meritorious. It represents small projects whereby women forge connections and experience the values and meanings of Buddhist practice. Through food literacy, women teach, learn, and practice the meanings and ways of doing Buddhism."[75] In the case of the *bōmori*, whereas she may be expected to attend to "domestic" work such as childcare, she is also expected to care for the temple—the "Buddha's home"—and be on hand for parishioners who may call upon the temple at any and all hours. Visitors to the temple may be seeking religious or ritual services as well as pastoral care, roles *bōmori* may be expected to fill. This overlap between the religious and the domestic happens, in part, because temple priests and their families often reside at the temple, as the Imamuras did in Berkeley in the 1950s. Thus, we find a collapsing of rhetorical spaces, a collapsing of the dichotomies between the gendered labor associated with the public and that associated with the private.

Starling argues that when attempting to understand Buddhism, our usual focus in Buddhist studies is on the altar—the priest chanting a sutra. Even though this focus may be on a ritual, it is still textual. Whatever meaning may be derived from that ritual, it is related to the text being chanted. Starling challenges us to "widen our focus" beyond the priest to see the whole of the temple community, the Buddha's home. "I suggest that domesticity—which often coincides with feminized space and feminized labor but is not necessarily spatially demarcated—is one of the less noticeable yet crucial modes in which religion is performed."[76] Whereas the circumstances are different (I do not mean to suggest a simplistic equivalency between the twenty-first-century Japanese women in Starling's study and the mid-twentieth-century American women in mine), the fact that Imamura claims for herself the role of *bōmori* is significant. Imamura was in many ways an equal partner with her husband in the development of the Berkeley Buddhist Temple. In addition to her responsibilities as wife and mother, she also ran a music program, started a choir, taught for the dharma school, supported the study programs, was chiefly if not solely responsible for one of the temple's most enduring fundraisers, and hosted Jack Kerouac, Gary Snyder, Alan Watts, and others in her home.[77] The boundaries of what we take for granted as "religious activities" are expanded beyond the confines of the temple conceived as a public space and into the realm of the domestic. As we will see in the following chapters, domestic religious activities in the homes of Japanese American women were an essential part of the making of American Buddhism.

The labor associated with *bōmori* may be read as affective, immaterial, emotional, nonproductive, or reproductive; regardless, it is *necessary*. This labor is a part of the religious infrastructure built by Nisei Buddhists, which made possible the flow and spread of religious ideas, persons, and practices. The very possibility of American Buddhism is contingent upon the domestic, upon acts of hospitality—in short, upon the labor of women. And we fail to see this labor not merely because it is outside the temple proper; we fail to see it because we do not value it.

Over the following chapters we will discuss these and many other acts of labor and love that made possible the spread of Buddhism in America, that made possible American Buddhism.

4

A House for Our Hopes

"We need to think beyond the nation," Arjun Appadurai writes in *Modernity at Large*. Of central concern in his work is the "imagination as social practice"—the ways in which persons understand themselves as members of imagined communities, communities that transcend the geopolitical borders of modern nation-states.[1] These imagined communities are made possible and connected via Appadurai's now well-known five *scapes*—ethnoscape, mediascape, technoscape, financescape, and ideoscape—which both allow for the development of cultural practices and identities and transcend geopolitical boundaries. Whereas Appadurai's work focuses on developments at the end of the twentieth century, much of his theoretical framework applies to the late nineteenth. Surely, Jōdo Shinshū immigrants to the United States, as suggested by Linda Learman, can be located in both the ethnoscapes and mediascapes of the turn of the twentieth century.[2] That is, they were persons on the move and, in publishing magazines directed at white converts and sympathizers, exploited the dominant mediascape of the day. In short, they were missionaries; not unlike Christian missionaries, they took on "the roles of scholar, civilizer, and converter to the truth" of Buddhism, as we saw in Chapter 1.[3] The missionary work of Issei immigrants was taken up by their Nisei children but within a new context and under the logics of a specific racial project in the United States, as we saw in the previous chapter. Nevertheless, whether before or after the Pacific War, American Shin Buddhists have long drawn upon transnational networks to spread the dharma and, as a result, create a shared imaginary, one that transcends the local. As we will see in this chapter, this labor results in the creation of religious infrastructure—that is, the local yet translocally connected communities, institutions, and networks that allow both for the movement of peoples and spread of ideas and for the creation of an imagined community of modern Shin Buddhists.

This chapter begins with a discussion of a different twentieth-century Buddhist periodical, *The Pacific World*, as a way to discuss broader world-systems and networks that made possible religious and cultural exchange. The very presence of Shin Buddhist missionaries in the Americas at the turn of the twentieth century directs our attention to what Tweed has called the Meiji-Victorian Pacific World, a vast transoceanic field of exchange made possible, in part, by America's interests in the Pacific following centuries of westward expansion.[4]

The Making of American Buddhism. Scott A. Mitchell, Oxford University Press. © Oxford University Press 2023. DOI: 10.1093/oso/9780197641569.003.0005

By tapping into vertical networks such as global economic systems, Buddhists are able to move about this transoceanic field and establish horizontal networks between Buddhist communities in specific locales. The Berkeley Buddhist Temple becomes one node within a larger network of Buddhist exchange. Projects such as the BCA Study Center and the *Berkeley Bussei* itself allow for the emergence of local Buddhist identities; but because they are bound up with global networks, local identities participate in the emergence of translocal imaginaries—the pan-Pacific Buddhist world.[5]

Building on our discussion of affective, emotional, and domestic labor in the previous chapter, here we will focus on how such labor not only built the Berkeley Buddhist Temple community but fed into the pan-Pacific Buddhist world. Nisei Buddhists from Berkeley traversed this world, drew insight and inspiration from Asian Buddhist reformers and modernizers, and viewed America and themselves from the perspective of Allied-occupied Japan. In this viewing, America was reaffirmed as the ideal location for the growth of the dharma and the future of the Bussei movement. In the creation of local community and translocal networks, other things became possible. The Study Center, publications, translation projects, and symposia were a draw for other Buddhists beyond the Jōdo Shinshū and Japanese American communities. And this work supported the efforts of better-known popularizers such as D. T. Suzuki. This chapter closes with a reflection on Suzuki's connections to the American Shin Buddhist community and how these connections were an invaluable part of his success in popularizing Zen in the 1950s and beyond.

The Pacific World

The editorial for the inaugural 1925 volume of *The Pacific World* reads, in part, "It is the mission and life of this magazine to promote unity in society and to aid in bringing about a better understanding among people. . . . We will devote ourselves in earnest effort to acquaint the Orient with the best of the Occident, and vice versa. By exchanging the thoughts of the East and the West, do we hope to accomplish our purpose. Our materials are collected from diverse sources in order to present the thoughts of one people to another people." Anticipating the language of Nisei-as-bridges, the editors go on to state that *The Pacific World* is published by university students "born and raised in the Orient but educated in this country"—that is, Japanese studying in American universities, who "have both these lands in our hearts, and we will strive to bring them together for the benefit of both."[6] This short magazine, perhaps thirty pages not including advertisements from its sponsors, did indeed draw from diverse sources covering religion, economics, and politics. An essay on Japanese poetry is followed by an overview of trade relations between the United States and Japan. There is a six-page essay titled "Extra-Curricular Activity at the University of California" that includes panoramic photos of Cal football games, new buildings around campus, and architectural drawings of the new Japanese Students Club. Following the editorial are a series of letters expressing support and admiration for this new publication from, among others, the president of the University of California and the mayor of Berkeley.

The editorial was almost certainly written by Yehan Numata (1897–1994). Numata was born into a Jōdo Shinshū temple family in Hiroshima Prefecture. As the third-born son, he was not obligated to take over the temple from his father; nevertheless, many in his devout family recommended he become a priest.[7] The family was unable to afford to send all their children to school, and so at nineteen he made his way to the United States and, eventually, Berkeley where he earned an advanced degree in engineering. As a Shin Buddhist, Numata was well known to the Berkeley Temple community, though his time in Berkeley predated the opening of the temple's dorm Jichiryo.[8] Instead, he lived at the only housing available to Japanese students at the time, the aforementioned Japanese Students Club, on the north side of campus. In the early twentieth century, North Berkeley was sparsely populated, but an influx of residents following the 1906 San Francisco earthquake led to rapid development. Notable Bay Area architects such as Bernard Maybeck and Julia Morgan designed and built Arts and Crafts–style homes and "Berkeley brown-shingles" in the hills north of campus, houses that were mostly destroyed in a fire that devastated the neighborhood in 1923.[9] It was this same fire that destroyed the Japanese Students Club. In response, Numata—then just twenty-six years old—successfully raised more than $30,000 to rebuild the club.[10]

It was around this same time that Numata decided to begin publishing *The Pacific World* in collaboration with fellow students from both UC Berkeley and Stanford University. Even though the magazine's inaugural volume contained a diversity of essays, very few of which had anything to do with Buddhism directly, Buddhism was the magazine's inspiration. During a speech at Sensoji Temple in Tokyo in 1975 wherein Numata reflected on his life and accomplishments, he related a story of how, after arriving in America, he was diagnosed with tuberculosis. Near death, he recited the *nenbutsu* daily, and he credited this practice with his recovery. "At the time it occurred to me that I could introduce this wonderful Buddhism to the American people. . . . However, the anti-Japanese sentiment was growing stronger and it was almost impossible to teach Buddhism directly. So at first, I tried to introduce Oriental culture in general."[11] As we have seen in earlier chapters, California laws prohibiting property ownership by "aliens ineligible for citizenship," passed in 1913 and strengthened in 1920, targeted the Japanese immigrant community. The Immigration Act of 1924 effectively barred all immigration from Asia. California agricultural, business, and political leaders were threatened by the successes of the Issei in white-dominated fields, and Americans generally were becoming increasingly concerned about Japanese colonial expansion in the Pacific. It is no wonder, then, that the young Numata felt he needed to propagate Buddhism indirectly via "Oriental culture." Despite these overtly religious sentiments expressed in 1975, it is of course likely that in 1925 Numata was just as concerned with political matters as religious ones; these two impulses are not mutually exclusive, after all. For example, in the January 1926 volume of *The Pacific World*, the head priest of Honganji published an essay, "Mahayana Buddhism and Japanese Civilization," which was as concerned with explicating a Mahāyāna understanding of nirvana as it was with promoting peace between the United States and Japan.[12]

Numata and his collaborators were plagued with funding problems, and by 1928 *The Pacific World* ceased publication.[13] By 1930, Numata had returned to Japan, where he worked for a time as a civil servant before starting his own company, the Mitutoyo Corporation, which, to put it mildly, became incredibly successful. Profits from this company would eventually be used to establish the Society for the Promotion of Buddhism (Bukkyō Dendō Kyōkai) in 1965, a story for a later time. Here, and remaining in the 1920s and 1930s, we can read Numata's early life history—his travels from Hiroshima to Berkeley, his establishment of a religious/political magazine, his explicit desire to promote (Shin) Buddhism to Americans—as part of an emergent pan-Pacific network of Buddhist exchange. A growing body of literature over the last several decades has focused on theorizing the transnational, the global, diasporas, and the movements of persons and ideas within such networks of exchange and global imaginaries. And, increasingly, scholars of religion have begun to follow the flows, to borrow a phrase, of specifically religious actors, artifacts, and ideas. This chapter seeks to locate the *Bussei* and Japanese American Shin Buddhists within one such network, what Michael Masatsugu has called the *pan-Pacific Buddhist world*.

In his comprehensive study *Buddhism and Ireland*, Laurence Cox relies on world-systems theory—especially "world-empires" and "world-economies"—to trace the movement of Buddhist ideas, texts, and artifacts from Asia to Ireland as far back as the Roman Empire. As a world-empire, the Romans created a vast network of exchange and infrastructure that connected the remote island of Ireland on the far edges of Eurasia with Buddhism's homeland thousands of kilometers away. "As one world-system broke down and another developed, new circuits of exchange developed," and world-empires would eventually be replaced by the world-economy of global capitalism.[14] Such structures allow for movement, bringing, for example, the Barlaam and Josaphat story (the Christian adaptation of the historical Buddha's life story) to Ireland in 1600.[15] And in the modern period, the British Empire and capitalist networks allowed for movement from

Ireland, as in the case of U Dhammaloka.[16] Born, possibly, as Laurence Carroll in the 1850s, as a young man Dhammaloka left his native Ireland and made his way across the Atlantic, the United States, and the Pacific before finding himself in Burma, becoming ordained, and then spending his later years defending Buddhism against British colonialists, Christian missionaries, and alcoholics. Dhammaloka's travels, like other Irish encounters with Buddhism of the time, were made possible in part due to economic and colonial networks. Dhammaloka got odd jobs aboard ships crossing the Atlantic and jumped trains to cross the American continent, and Cox notes that this movement reflects a different kind of engagement between Europeans and Buddhism than the more visible "Orientalist civil servants and universities," an exchange indelibly marked by class.[17]

This Irish-born Theravada monk has a surprising connection to the present study. Thomas Tweed opens his essay "Tracing Modernity's Flows" with a discussion of a three-page pamphlet, discovered in an archive, that is attributed to U Dhammaloka and includes a *gāthā* and a selection from the *Gospel of Buddha*. The pamphlet and the song, Tweed argues, were almost certainly used by members of the Dharma Sangha of Buddha in San Francisco, the group of white converts supported by the early Shin community discussed in Chapter 1. Given the ambiguity that surrounds Dhammaloka's life, it is difficult to know what direct connection he may have had with the Shin community in California. Though "without further evidence we cannot say if [the *gāthā*] ever actually was sung," the pamphlet certainly hints at a musical practice performed by white converts in the early years of the twentieth century.[18] This should not be surprising; the early Shin community was not only a place for immigrants to practice the religion of their homeland but, simultaneously, an attractor for a wide variety of spiritual seekers—some more idiosyncratic than others (e.g., Swami Mazzinianananda). Whereas much scholarship has focused on the textual transmission of Buddhism to the West, and even Tweed admits that his earlier work suggests that white converts and sympathizers were more interested in *reading* about Buddhism than *doing* Buddhism at this early stage, it should not surprise us that some practices are simply hidden to us by the passage of time, practices that were lived and embodied and not necessarily written down except in obscure pamphlets now hidden in archives. However important this recovery of a forgotten practice is, more germane to our present purpose is that this pamphlet and these points of contact represent the early Shin missionary success at, to put it bluntly, converting the heathen Christians in America.

Recall that the priests dispatched to San Francisco in 1899 almost immediately established not only an umbrella organization to support Issei Buddhists' activities along the West Coast but also a *mission*. This signals that Shin Buddhist priests were as interested in supporting their fellow immigrants' religious and spiritual needs as they were in spreading the dharma to white Americans. And in the interwar period, these efforts were beginning to pay off in more substantive ways than the chance encounters with Irish monks or charlatan swamis. The best evidence of this comes from the ordination of white priests. For most of North American Shin Buddhist history prior to World War II, priests serving in American temples were sent from Japan, where they had been ordained, educated, and trained as both ritual experts and dharma teachers.[19] Indeed, for most of the twentieth century, the only way for a priest to be recognized and authorized to serve in an American Shin temple was to travel to Kyoto for formal ordination at Honganji. However, there have been exceptions to this norm, and during the 1920s and 1930s at least eight white converts were ordained by BMNA bishop Kenju Masuyama. Perhaps two of the best-known ordinands were Julius Goldwater and Gladys Pratt, discussed in earlier chapters. According to Michihiro Ama, "It was unclear how the Nishi Honganji classified their status."[20] That is, *tokudo* (ordination) is generally only given by the Honganji in Kyoto; once a priest is ordained, they may receive other forms of training or certification allowing them to become a temple head priest or a dharma teacher or to work in specific contexts—for example, as a *kaikyōshi* (overseas dharma teacher) outside Japan. Masuyama may have given *tokudo* to these white converts; it is unlikely they received any other certification from him. Moreover, regardless of whether or not Masuyama felt these ordinations were legitimate, the Honganji authorities would have had a different opinion—if they knew about them at all. In reviewing official BCA records, however, it is clear that many of these American-ordained priests subsequently went to Japan for ordination at Honganji or were otherwise officially recognized.[21] However, to my mind, the question of institutional recognition or legitimacy is not the only question worth asking. Regardless of their "official" status, these persons often had some stature within their communities, and the fact of their ordination—even if never legitimated by the Honganji— points to the missionizing impulse within the Shin community, the desire to spread the dharma beyond the confines of the Japanese immigrant group.

Moreover, it is important to draw our attention to questions of *choice*. As Ama notes in his discussion of Pratt, she was not a woman of means who could have afforded a trip to Japan. So when she desired to learn about Buddhism, her only recourse was to seek out the nearest Buddhist community in the Pacific Northwest, where she lived—and that community happened to be Jōdo Shinshū. Japanese immigrants had already come to America, had already established temples, had already begun the process of building religious infrastructure; because of this infrastructure, when some white sympathizers wanted to learn more about or practice Buddhism, this was the tradition they met. This is not to suggest that their affiliation with the Shin community was merely by happenstance or insincere. Whereas some early white converts and sympathizers drifted away from the tradition after a period of time, others maintained a lifelong af-filiation.[22] What's more, as we saw in the case of Dhammaloka, these affiliations represent a different stream of transmission than the more elite forms of trans-mission via colonial networks or Orientalist scholarship. For those without the means to travel in the Himalayas or to study in Japanese Zen monasteries, local connections with living Buddhist traditions were their only means of sustaining a Buddhist practice. I propose that, rather than dismissing these connections and practices as inauthentic or illegitimate due to lack of orthodox recognition, we view them as constitutive of a larger social imaginary, as generative of a common "Buddhist world."

To understand this process of world creation, so to speak, let us return to Tweed for a moment. In his aforementioned essay, he makes use of the phrase "the Meiji-Victorian Pacific world"—a phrase Tweed does not necessarily define but suggests represents a "vast transoceanic cultural space" in which "modernity emerged from the crossing of cultural currents."[23] The term is used as something of a corrective to prior scholarship on transnational religion, religious history, and modernity, a scholarship that Tweed sees as in need of new models, with "dif-ferent temporal and geographical referents," in order to "more adequately attend to the spatial dynamics of religions in modernity."[24] On this point I am in agree-ment. At the same time, the "temporal" referents of both "Meiji" and "Victorian" feel wanting. Whereas the hyphenated joining of Japan and America in this way helpfully directs our attention to a sort of shared transnational culture, the Meiji and Victorian eras do not, in reality, so neatly overlap.[25] Further, they pre-date by several decades the subjects in the present study, who lived during the Taishō and Shōwa eras in Japan and the interwar period in the United States. At the same time, naming conventions that rely on either dynastic conventions or scholar-produced epochs or eras can be problematic, as they may reinforce rhetorics of rupture or discontinuity. That is, if we assume that once the emperor passes and a new one is enthroned we are now in a new era, we may overlook the continuities between the old era and the new. As we saw in the previous chapter, whereas the camp experience was undeniably a radical and traumatic "big event" in Japanese American history, one that serves as a useful benchmark ("prewar," "after camp"), there was also a fair amount of continuity in terms of both external factors (anti-Japanese racism) and internal development (education and propa-gation projects).[26]

Nevertheless, the main thrust of Tweed's argument is that we benefit by conceptualizing a "transoceanic cultural space" such as the Pacific world.[27] Such a conceptualization allows us to see shared cultural practices, different and often competing and conflicting lines of influence, and the complexity of religious modernity. "*Modernity* in the circum-Pacific region," Tweed writes, "should be understood as the converging of plural ways of being human," and "a defining feature of modernity was not secularity but pluralism. To be shaped by modernity in the Pacific . . . was to be carried along by a stream of multiple, often competing, cultural practices, some of which were secularist and some of which appealed to" religion.[28] If we bracket religion for a moment, and seek inspiration in Takashi Fujitani, it seems to me that the "cultural practices" most operative in the interwar Pacific world centered around nationalism and the move from "vulgar racism" to "polite racism." Fujitani defines vulgar racism as that which was actively exclusionary, inhumane, and "relatively unconcerned about the health and well-being of marginalized people" who were considered ineligible for assimilation into the nationalist/racial majority. The objects of such racism in the Japanese Empire were colonial subjects (e.g., Koreans), and in the United States they were nonwhites (e.g., Japanese Americans). As the two nations moved closer to war, this discourse shifted to a "polite racism," a version of nationalism that was inclusionary and admitted the possibility of assimilation into the racial majority while maintaining the inherent "otherness" of the racial minority. Crucially, such an inclusionary nationalism requires the regulation of marginalized subjects, who "participate at least to some extent in their own regulation."[29] This set of nationalist and racial discourses, I would argue, is far more important to understanding the early history of American Buddhism than the cultural referents invoked by "Meiji" and "Victorian." As we saw in Chapter 3, systemic racism was the underlying cause of the "Nisei problem," and Buddhism served as one solution. And as we saw in Chapter 1, whereas the early Shin community may have engaged with charlatan swamis as part of a larger missionary project, when these engagements brought unwanted attention to the community, ties were severed. This unwanted attention is best understood within the larger context of America's relationship to Asia and its engagements in the Pacific.

According to David Palumbo-Liu, American history can be told in large part by this relationship. In the nineteenth century, Manifest Destiny discourses turned America's gaze ever westward. Once the "frontier" of western North America was crossed (in other words, once the Indigenous peoples there were colonized, displaced, and slaughtered), the logics of Western civilizational expanse necessitated another crossing, an oceanic one. And thus we see the beginnings of America's long economic involvement in the Pacific: from the opening of Japan to "the purchase of Alaska in 1867, the staging of a *coup d'état* in Hawai'i in 1893, . . . seizing control of Philippines, and the final annexation of Hawai'i. Between 1913 and 1929, U.S.-Pacific trade increased nearly four hundred percent."[30] Of course, the irony is that this oceanic crossing not only allowed for westward expansion and the movement of persons across the Pacific but also was made possible by Asian laborers; it was Chinese immigrants who had built the transcontinental railroad, after all, allowing America to connect both coasts and set its gaze across the Pacific. As America expanded its influence across the ocean, a contradiction arose, to use Lisa Lowe's term, that placed Asians both within and outside the U.S. nation-state. The necessity of Chinese immigrant labor and simultaneous exclusion from citizenship, Japanese Americans conscripted to fight Hitler's army while their families were illegally interned during that same war, and Filipino immigrants already impacted by American colonialism before making the journey across the Pacific attest to the ways in which the contradictions of immigration, colonization, and nationalism "express distinct yet continuous formations in the genealogy of the racialization of Asian Americans."[31] The movement from East to West—or West to East, depending on one's point of view—already implicated Asia and required Asian labor while disavowing Asians' place as Americans.

From a world-systems point of view, we might conceptualize such crossings as transnational or global—or, to use Arif Dirlik's term, the *ecumene*. Dirlik suggests "historical ecumene" not only as a corrective to the nation-state (which is implied in the term "transnational") as the basic unit of analysis but also to decenter the primacy of European or Western culture. Ecumenes are understood to be "areas of intense and sustained cultural interaction," and a spatial metaphor gesturing toward commonality and difference.[32] Using the idea of a "Confucian or Neo-Confucian Eastern Asia" as an example, Dirlik points out that when Japan, Korea, and Vietnam adopted Confucian values or models of statecraft, they did so not to "become Chinese." After all, Confucius himself wasn't Chinese but rather a Zhou Dynasty sage who represented a longer tradition of methods of statecraft that these other cultural locations could draw from in creating their own specific cultural and social realities. Thus while one can still speak of a broader set of cultural similarities that may fall under the umbrella of "Confucianism," local variation emerges simultaneously. In applying the concept of the ecumene to global history, "the important issue [is] the foregrounding of commonalities as well as differences, and recognizing a multiplicity of spatialities within a common space marked not by firm boundaries but by the intensity and concentration of interactions, which themselves are subject to historical fluctuations."[33] Crucially, it is not that there is a single ecumene in which historical actors participate or are subject to; rather, there is a multiplicity of ecumenes.

Michael Masatsugu uses the concept of the ecumene to great effect in his study of the postwar pan-Pacific Buddhist world, finding it "useful for thinking about the transnational religious networks in which Japanese Americans participated, and the particular contours and dynamics that shaped an emerging global Buddhist perspective shared by Japanese American and Asian Buddhists."[34] In 1950, the inaugural meeting of the World Fellowship of Buddhists (WFB) was held in Sri Lanka, an event attended by delegates from nearly thirty countries, including Nisei Buddhists from the United States. The WFB grew out of political movements as Buddhist-majority countries gained independence from colonial rule following World War II. The initial constitution of the WFB was explicit regarding the need to promote Buddhist values and world peace while also seeking to overcome differences between Buddhist lineages and sects. Certainly, such movements were motivated by decolonization as well as in response to communist movements across Asia.[35] However, like Dirlik's conceptualization of a "Confucian Eastern Asia," the WFB and other movements allowed for the emergence of a translocal and shared cultural sphere, an ecumene, in which Buddhists were able to share insights, resources, and perspectives for mutual benefit in locally specific ways. Thus, the WFB created religious infrastructure in the form of networks of regional centers across South and East Asia that supported local programs and events as well as facilitating connections between local centers and Buddhists traveling throughout the network. Two Nisei Buddhists, Sunao Miyabara and Teumika Maneki, were among the delegates at the first WFB meeting, and the Buddhist Churches of America regularly sent delegates to subsequent meetings and reported on their activities in such publications as the *Berkeley Bussei*. "Contact with Asian Buddhists," writes Masatsugu, "and subsequent participation in the Buddhist world emerged at a critical moment when Japanese Americans were reconstructing individual and community identities that had been thoroughly disrupted by the Second World War."[36] Moreover, "a global Buddhist perspective provided an important alternative to ethno-national identity, a source of inspiration for addressing racial and religious discrimination and marginalization in the United States, and an alternative perspective from which to view the Cold War policies of the United States and Soviet Union."[37]

Here I do not intend to restate research already done expertly by Masatsugu. Suffice it to say that his work well traces out the movement of Nisei across the Pacific in the 1950s and beyond, using much of the same material under study here. Indeed, several figures we've already met—Unno, Fukada, Takemoto, Matsuura, and so on—were founding members of the WFB or deeply engaged with its work. What I would like to call our attention to here is how these connections created networks of exchange or religious infrastructure that, in turn, made possible American Buddhism.

By religious infrastructure, I mean simply the vertically and horizontally networked individuals, communities, and institutions that connect disparate locations and allow for the dissemination of shared resources, cultures, and identities. In this definition, I am drawing on the ethnographic work of Omar McRoberts.[38] Horizontal networks are easy enough to recognize; they are the in-community connections religious institutions and persons make that allow them to share information, ideas, and practices across space and over time. The Berkeley Buddhist Temple, for example, can be seen as one node within a larger network of local Shin Buddhist temples that are connected both because of their proximity to one another and through umbrella organizations such as the Buddhist Churches of America or regional Young Buddhist Associations. Such organizations are also connected to international organizations such as Honganji and the WFB. Collectively, these networks allow for the movement of persons and practices locally, across the state, across the nation, and ultimately across the Pacific. But religious infrastructure does not exist separate from other networks, both political and economic. Religious organizations must register with local and state governments, and religious groups regularly seek funding from nonreligious sources or exploit larger economic systems to raise funds. These types of engagement are examples of vertical networking. Taken as a whole, this is religious infrastructure. Just as premodern empires built roads and maritime trade routes that allowed for the spread of religions across vast geographical spaces, modern infrastructure—railroads, steamships, and jet planes; the telegraph, telephone, and internet; books and magazines; and so forth—have allowed for Buddhism's spread into and from the United States. What I would call our attention to here is the agency of religious actors in creating specifically religious networks in tandem with or on top of other networks.

Numata's desire to introduce Buddhism to the American people in the 1920s was made possible by the preexisting infrastructure of magazine publishing and distribution as well as international trade and local financing. *The Pacific World* was sponsored by and contained numerous ads from local banks and trading companies that had connections to Japan. This type of vertical networking allowed for the magazine to be viable, at least for a time. The existence of the magazine, in turn, allowed for the publication of essays and articles about Buddhism that were consumed by American audiences. This horizontal networking allowed for the very possibility of the head priest of one Japan's largest temples to publish his thoughts on Mahāyāna Buddhism to be read by interested Americans.

As Bryan Lowe notes in his study of premodern Japanese road-building, roads (infrastructure) lead to mobility and connections, but roads also create "in-between spaces" of risk and isolation.[39] If nothing else, once we are on the road, our perspectives shift. I turn our attention now to the view of America from the vantage point of Nisei Buddhists abroad.

"A Time for Action"

George (Jobo) Nakamura was a frequent contributor to the *Berkeley Bussei* both before and after the war. During his incarceration at Tule Lake, he was one of the editors of the short-lived *Tulean Dispatch*, a newspaper highly censored by camp authorities. After the war, Nakamura worked for a variety of newspapers such as the San Francisco Bay Area–based *Hokubei Mainichi* and contributed stories to other Japanese American publications such as the Los Angeles–based *Rafu Shimpo* and the Japanese American Citizens League's *Pacific Citizen.* He also contributed articles to national magazines. In a 1954 story for *Holiday,* for example, Nakamura wrote about his trip to Japan to reunite with his mother and sisters, who had left the United States before the war. The tone of the article "is one of nostalgic loss and loneliness," reflecting Nakamura's "ambivalence about his life in the United States" after witnessing the destruction and postwar poverty in Japan and failing to convince his family there to leave.[40] A similar ambivalence can be seen in a pair of essays in the *Bussei* revealing the "in-between" nature of Nisei sojourns around the pan-Pacific Buddhist world.

Nakamura opens his 1953 "Nisei and Japan" by noting that his time there "was a rich, rewarding experience" in part because he was "a Nisei experiencing for the first time the interminable depth and wealth of my cultural heritage." "Of course," he continues, "many, many Nisei have preceded me in visiting Post-war Japan."[41] Indeed, between 1945 and 1952, nearly ten thousand Nisei worked in occupied Japan, and many thousands of them were trained by the U.S. government as translators and linguists. Nisei linguists were recruited en masse on the assumption that, as ethnic Japanese, they would have a natural understanding of Japanese culture and language, which of course was not necessarily true. Nevertheless, as "cultural brokers" between the United States and Japan, Nisei linguists were expected to support the occupation force's agenda of bringing "civilization" to the Japanese people and, again, serve as "bridges" between East and West. This complex of racial discourses at times led to conflict, with reports of Nisei both acting in exemplary ways and taking advantage of their privileged status in Japan or behaving cruelly toward Japanese nationals.[42] These tensions lie just beneath the surface in Nakamura's essay when he writes that Nisei in Japan are "in an unique position to appreciate not only the surface beauty of Japan but its inside as well." Further, "those [Nisei] who have made good impressions have gained a strong rapport with the [Japanese] people, more so probably than a Caucasian American could. The Japanese unerringly believe that Nisei can understand his feelings more readily 'because you are a Japanese,' as they would put it as though to infer that the Japanese seishin (spirit) is innate with the race. 'Yappari Nihonjin da ka ra!' "[43] He goes on to say that while nothing would make a Nisei feel more American than a trip to Japan, going so far as to quote Roosevelt's claim that "Americanism is not a matter of ancestry," a "Nisei will not gain anything by rejecting his racial heritage in the anxiety to become 150 per cent 'Americanized.' "[44] In the end, Nakamura's essay reaffirms the role of Nisei as bridges, bringing peace and understanding between Japan and the United States, suggesting that they remain in some sense naturally Japanese (*da ka ra*).

This naturalness, however, is undermined by Nakamura's 1954 *Bussei* article, "Reflection on a Visit to Japan." Nakamura opens this piece by noting that when a

Nisei writes about Japan, his "description and sentiments are usually as detached as they can possibly be from himself as a person of Japanese heritage." He goes on to say that "there has been no Lafcadio Hearn among Nisei writers." It is unclear what Nakamura means by this sentiment, whether he admires Hearn's writing or not, but it prefaces a lament that many Nisei writers "poke fun at the customs and rituals" of Japan. Nakamura places blame for this attitude on the fact that, as expressed in the previous essay, being in Japan makes Nisei aware of just how American they are. Nevertheless, after some time in Japan, Nisei become more aware of their "racial and cultural heritage . . . how can [a Nisei] deny his own racial heritage any more than an Italian American or a Swedish American?" And yet, after making this claim of racial affinity, Nakamura offers the following observation:

> We have yet to hear a single Nisei who has visited Japan since the war or has worked with the Occupation Forces tell us that he didn't enjoy his sojourn over there. However, none has given me a concrete reason why he liked his stay.
>
> While we were in Tokyo two summers ago, we asked several of them for an answer. . . . One said, although he would have liked to remain in Japan a little longer, he felt that he had to go back soon. "Why?" I asked. He had no family or job in America to return to.
>
> "Well," he replied, "I guess it's because I'm an American citizen. I belong back there." It was as good as any we supposed.[45]

Despite the essentialist assumption that Nisei possess an innate "Japanese spirit," and despite the sense of superiority some Nisei felt owing to their privileged status as Americans in occupied Japan, Nakamura nevertheless ends his essay with a caution: the Japanese can spot a Nisei tourist a mile away by his "behaviors, attitudes, gestures, facial expressions," and clothes, suggesting that perhaps the Japanese spirit is not so innate after all. At the end of the day for Nakamura, America is where Nisei "belong."

The ambivalence of this "in-between" space, the ambivalence of being Japanese American in Japan, is also read in explicitly religious terms within the pages of the *Bussei*. Not all postwar Nisei in Japan were there as part of the occupation forces or as tourists. Many were there to study Buddhism with the explicit intention of bringing Buddhism back to America.

Writing about her experiences in Kyoto in 1955, Kaye Fujii notes: "We all came with the understanding that Japan was without luxuries. We were ready to endure hardships; yet, once here, we found life much more difficult than we had anticipated."[46] Difficulty arose from the general state of despair Japan found itself in following the war, destruction from Allied bombing campaigns, language barriers, limited financial support, and so on. Nevertheless, Fujii is convinced that the "future of the Nisei, in America and Japan, is a great one," and that Nisei "came to this country with the dream of studying and understanding Buddhism so that we may carry this knowledge back to the United States in one form or another."[47]

One of Fujii's fellow students in Kyoto was Art Takemoto, who had been instrumental in helping the Imamuras establish post-camp hostels at both the Senshin and Berkeley temples. In a pair of essays in 1952 and 1953 Takemoto was quite clear on his opinion of Buddhism in Japan and its promise in America. Takemoto writes, in tones that will be immediately familiar to ethnographers of contemporary Japanese religion, that Japanese Buddhism is in decline.[48] "Today in Japan," he writes, "particularly in the rural areas, Buddhism which once flourished is now facing a dilemma."[49] The war has worsened temple finances, priests and the laity are often at odds, and the younger generation is drifting away. The solution, for Takemoto, is to go back to the teachings of Shinran, "who made Buddhism a moving, dynamic force in the lives of the masses."[50] By contrast, America is presented as a place of possibility, as the ideal location for Buddhism's future flourishing, precisely because of Nisei Buddhists. Takemoto admits that American Buddhists have their own problems, that younger people (presumably Nisei) are at odds with or do not always agree with existing leaders (presumably Issei). Nevertheless, in another essay he states plainly that "propagation of Buddhism must come from America. My impressions [from Japan] make me appreciate greater the activities of the American Buddhist. If we had the surroundings of Japan and the activities of the American Bussei, we'd have a good combination."[51]

"Through their participation in WFB conferences and cultural exchange programmes," writes Masatsugu, "and as part of an emerging post-war global Buddhist print culture, Japanese Americans both contributed to and gained insight, solace, and inspiration from an emerging global Buddhist perspective."[52] In addition to providing both a sense of belonging to pan-Asian Buddhist communities and an alternative to Cold War–era discourses, participation in the Buddhist world gave Nisei Buddhists a sense of belonging and confidence in their identity as American Buddhists. Moreover, as we see in Fujii and Takemoto's writings here, their experiences traversing the pan-Pacific Buddhist world provided different perspectives on the realities of Japan and promise of America. The United States became an idealized field for spreading the dharma. In some ways, this rhetoric mimics an earlier generation of missionary activity, as we have discussed in previous chapters. But it is important to recall that in the postwar era, both the landscape of this idealized field and the players in it had changed. Whereas Issei ministers dispatched from Japan to the Americas had laid the foundations of Jōdo Shinshū in the West via the establishment of the Buddhist Mission of North America and its associated temples, their Nisei children were now charged with assuming leadership of the community. It was during the internment that the BMNA was officially transformed into the Buddhist Churches of America, with new articles of incorporation and a new board of directors, all of whom were American citizens.[53] Thus, in the postwar period it was no longer just Japanese missionaries journeying to America but also American Buddhists returning home from Japan and assuming greater responsibility for building on the foundation laid by the previous generation.

In the pages of the *Bussei*, then, it is no surprise that we find article after article discussing the need for new leadership within the North American Shin community. Especially in the early 1950s, these essays make it clear that Nisei recognized the need for their generation to take active leadership roles and foster Buddhism's growth in America. Taitetsu Unno, for example, reflected on the "lack of dynamic leadership" within the BCA in his 1951 essay "Faced with a Dilemma." Whereas his essay hints at widespread criticism of BCA leadership as generally disorganized, underfinanced, and unable to introduce Buddhism to the West "on a truly solid basis," Unno is also clear that Nisei should "have sympathy and understanding," as "nothing can be perfect in this world of imperfections."[54] Indeed, such criticisms and future-oriented perspectives did not come at the expense of or reject the previous generation but were self-consciously linked to that foundational work. The editorial for the 1950 volume, for example, states that "the Bussei have cried for the Americanization of Buddhism, called for English-speaking ministers, and asked for materials on Buddhist fundamentals. The emphasis is on the future." And yet, the editors go on, "as we look into 1950 and the future, let us look back into the past and learn from the triumphs and defeats of the Issei. . . . As we provide ample scholarships for the future ministers, let us not forget the aging Issei priesthood."[55] Education and the training of the next generation of ministers quickly becomes the focus in the 1950s, as the author of the article "A Time for Action" makes clear: "Because the Isseis who have so long made possible the existence of the Church are now passing on; it is now time for the Nisei and Sansei to carry on the work. . . . The success of our mission can be assured only if there are an adequate number of qualified individuals who can serve as leaders."[56] The Berkeley Temple became a hub of educational and training programs in part because of its proximity to the University of California and preexisting connections to Shin Buddhist networks such as the California Young Buddhist Association. The "Time for Action" article goes so far as to list a handful of well-known Buddhist leaders who had spent time in Berkeley. At times, this call to action was linked explicitly to larger social issues on the assumption that Buddhism is naturally beneficial or good for the world—again, a common modernist trope. Writing in the 1951 volume, for example, Sei Shohara discusses how the world is on the brink of a "third world war." The essay is not necessarily a call for peace but does suggest that Buddhism can address serious issues such as death and the meaning of life. "It is the duty of the Y.B.A.," Shohara writes, "to foster more serious thinking along these lines. The Bussei can no longer afford to remain indifferent to these problems besetting the world-at-large. There is too much at stake."[57] Contributors to the *Bussei* routinely detail the modern and positive aspects of Buddhism and its value and utility for American society and world peace, and they call on Nisei Buddhists to foster and grow the tradition in the United States.

Such exhortations for active engagement had concrete results. In 1948, Enryo Shigefuji (1886–1958) became BCA bishop and, according to official histories, recognized the importance of propagating Buddhism in English.[58] In the waning months of 1949 he oversaw a series of study classes that would eventually develop into the official BCA Buddhist Study Center housed at the Berkeley Temple. A short note in the 1950 *Bussei* states plainly that "November 11 [1949] was a memorable day for many Buddhists, for it was on this day that the first meeting of the Study Group" was held in Berkeley.[59] Whereas undoubtedly official support from the BCA and Bishop Shigefuji was central to the establishment of the group, in her memoirs Jane Imamura notes that "there was as yet no financial foundation" and that the group was "nurtured by the members of the Berkeley Buddhist Temple . . . Today, when even ideals are measured in dollar signs, the thought of initiating important projects without a budget would surely raise eyebrows." But following the disruptions of the camps, the Berkeley Temple members were left "with only our ideals and bare hands."[60] Despite the *Bussei*'s reference to the bishop's support, the first meetings of the study group were not very well funded and, in fact, were conducted in the living room of Shinobu Matsuura's home. Like her daughter Jane, Matsuura describes herself as a *bōmori* in her own memoirs; even though her husband had already passed and she was not living on temple grounds, the religious activities of the Berkeley Temple extended to her home.

The study group was eventually endorsed by the BCA and renamed the BCA Study Center. A 1955 report on the center's activities, almost certainly penned by Kanmo Imamura, covers not only the study classes but also related YBA and temple activities, including the publication of the *Bussei*, maintenance of a temple library, the dormitory, the music program, and hosting "visiting dignitaries and students from Japan, Ceylon, Cambodia, Burma, Thailand," and so on. A note at the bottom of the report states that the center has been operating on "the voluntary help of the staff and members" as well as an "annual grant of $200 from the BCA."[61] These limited funds and the voluntary labor of temple members, however, had a large impact. In his Japanese-language report in the 1953 *Bussei*, for example, Imamura lists among the activities of the YBA and Study Center numerous classes for both high school and college students; sutra translation projects; the publication of the *Bussei* itself; the dissemination of *gāthās* and

Buddhist music; and propagation of the dharma generally. Imamura comments that the participants in the group and the classes change frequently in part because students graduate, but when they leave, they take their experiences and the dharma with them.[62] The aforementioned study classes included the Advanced Study Group, as it was called in a short note in the 1952 *Bussei*, and which was presided over by Imamura and Hitoshi Tsufura. Topics ranged from Jōdo Shinshū to "Buddhism and Art," "Buddhist Poems (Contemporary)," Yogācāra, and the *Heart Sutra*. Guest speakers for these courses included, among others, Alan Watts and Saburo Hasegawa from the Academy of Asian Studies. And students included many of the authors discussed in this and previous chapters such as Kimi Hisatsune (also credited as the secretary of the first meetings), as well as Vanita Meyer, Hiroshi Kashiwagi, and Robert Jackson. The 1955 report is a bit ambiguous as to who were the students and who were the teachers; Gary Snyder, for example, seems to be the one leading the conversation on contemporary Buddhist poems. Also listed is Alex Wayman (1921–2004), responsible for a course on Yogācāra; at the time, Wayman was a graduate student at Berkeley and would later go on to a successful career in academic Buddhist studies. Thus, regardless of the initially limited funding and virtually all-volunteer labor needed to support the nascent BCA Study Center, the *Bussei's* prediction that it would be a "significant step forward for American Buddhism" and "have far-reaching consequences" may not have been far off the mark.[63]

The enthusiasm and interest in studying Buddhism led, in 1952, to the first "Buddhist seminar" at the Berkeley Temple. The seminar was a three-day conference attended by some 250 persons and was dedicated to "imparting greater and wider familiarity of Buddhism" to the public.[64] Presentations and lectures were delivered by many Shin priests from across California and the West Coast, but also by local and international scholars, including Haridas Chaudhuri, Alan Watts, Tokan Tada, and Ferdinand Lessing. The seminar draws our attention to the networked connections running through Berkeley in the 1950s to other academic centers such as the American Academy of Asian Studies. The *Bussei* makes regular reference to the academy in the early 1950s, members of the temple often attended lectures on Buddhism and Asian philosophy at the nascent school, and Watts became a frequent figure at the temple, delivering the occasional lecture and even dharma talk.[65] Watts was also a frequent contributor to the *Bussei*; a half dozen of his essays were published between 1952 and 1960 on topics ranging from American Buddhism to Daoism to religion and psychology. In addition to Watts and connections to the Academy of Asian Studies, the *Bussei* also published articles by Hajime Nakamura, at the time on the faculty of Tokyo University and a visiting professor of Indian philosophy at Stanford University from 1951 to 1952. Thus, these study classes and symposia were not merely ingroup projects limited to the education and training of Shin priests but were outward-facing with the intention of increasing awareness of Buddhism among the general public and made possible by new and existing networks of Buddhist exchange across the western United States and the Pacific. "To Rev. Imamura," writes Jane Imamura in her memoir, "these classes were like a potter's wheel helping to shape the sangha in America. Following the way of Nembutsu without walls or boundaries, beyond sectarian distinctions, he oversaw the development of the Study Center. Although he was a man of few words, his path was clear."[66]

The growing success of these programs, and in particular the BCA Study Center, was the impetus for a major redevelopment of the Berkeley Temple.[67] Kanmo Imamura opens his 1952 essay "A House for Our Hopes" with the following: "The urgent need for a Buddhist Center in Berkeley need not be repeated at this time."[68] The small wood-shingled building and adjacent dorm were home both to a thriving Buddhist community and to its minister, his family of six, and a dozen college students. Reflecting on this time in her memoir, Jane Imamura recalls that "lack of space became a major problem. With much of the property occupied by the dormitories, the only space available for services, meetings, classes, printing, choir practices, socials, not to mention the many weddings and funerals, was the small and modest main religious hall."[69] So the community began planning for a major renovation and rebuilding of the temple. The project was not without controversy. Imamura's 1952 essay describes a late-night meeting held at the old temple to discuss the project, "attended by an unprecedented large and serious crowd." And Jane's memoir mentions that the project "was not entirely smooth sailing." While neither speaks to the specific cause of controversy, like most controversies, it was probably money. Even though the community had grown considerably in the immediate post-camp years, the economic impact of that experience was surely still being felt. Kanmo Imamura, recall, was not being paid as a full-time minister and had to take a second job at the anthropology museum at UC Berkeley. Despite the challenges and heated conversations, a major fundraising campaign was initiated and eventually supported by the BCA national leadership, which recognized the "urgent need" for new leadership and Berkeley as an ideal location for future educational programs. "Being in the proximity of the University of California," the editors of the 1955 *Bussei* write, "the Berkeley Buddhist Church has long attracted university students from all parts of the country. It is with the intent of providing adequate facility to train the many students of Buddhist faith that the new construction was undertaken."[70]

Construction began in late 1954. The brown-shingled building was moved to the back of the lot and wholly remodeled. The Jichiryo dorm was demolished, and a new temple and social hall were built.[71] The building was designed by local architects Harry and George Nakahara, who designed many midcentury modern homes in and around Berkeley (Figure 4.1). The building is indeed in classic midcentury modern style, with exposed wood beams, straight lines, and

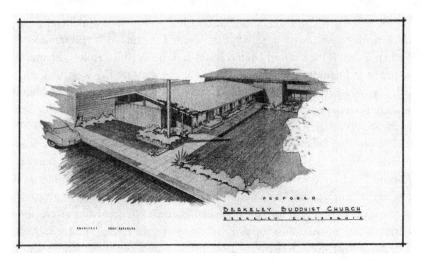

Figure 4.1 Architectural plans for the new Berkeley Buddhist Temple printed in the 1954 *Berkeley Bussei*.

cement walls. Perhaps most striking of all is the temple's main hall or *hondō*. The *hondō* in most Jōdo Shinshū temples, both in Japan and United States, is often elaborately decorated with large lanterns hanging from the ceiling and as often murals and lacquered wood carvings around the room. The main seating area in the *hondō* is separated from the main altar or *naijin* in several ways; typically, the *naijin* is raised and usually enclosed by sliding doors or folding screens. Very often, the floor of the entire *hondō* (but in the United States usually just the *naijin*) will be made of tatami. Dominating the space will be the *gohonzon* or main image of the Buddha (or sometimes a hanging scroll with the *nenbutsu*). The *gohonzon* itself is also usually enclosed within an ornate and decorated structure called the *kuden*. Flanking the *kuden* will be images of Shinran on the right and Rennyo on the left; if the temple's *naijin* is large enough, one might also find images of Shōtoku Taishi and the so-called Seven Masters of the Jōdo Shinshū tradition.[72] By contrast, the Berkeley Buddhist Temple's *hondō* is decidedly simple, even austere. There are no large, ornate lanterns or murals. While the *naijin* is elevated from the floor of the main seating area, it is mostly open, separated only by a pair of planter boxes. There is a single shelf affixed to the unadorned wood of the back wall, and on this shelf stands a statue of Amida Buddha. A photo of this statue is used as the cover image of the 1957 *Bussei*. The inside front cover states: "Amida Buddha, carved over 600 years ago in the Kamakura period. Gift of Joen Ashikaga of Kyoto, Japan. The arrival of the image in America was celebrated officially at the Buddhist Churches of America Study Center—Berkeley Buddhist Church Dedication Ceremony on July 10, 1956"

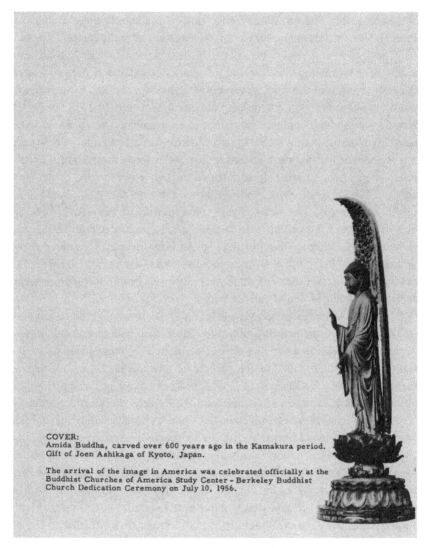

COVER:
Amida Buddha, carved over 600 years ago in the Kamakura period.
Gift of Joen Ashikaga of Kyoto, Japan.

The arrival of the image in America was celebrated officially at the
Buddhist Churches of America Study Center - Berkeley Buddhist
Church Dedication Ceremony on July 10, 1956.

Figure 4.2 Inside front cover of the 1957 *Berkeley Bussei* announcing the dedication
of the new temple and installation of the Amida image.

(Figure 4.2). This simple statement belies a rather more interesting story, one that
by all rights belongs to Shinobu Matsuura (1896–1984).[73]

Joen Ashikaga was a Jōdo Shinshū priest who was partly responsible for
arranging Shinobu Matsuura's marriage to her husband, Issei, who in the early
1900s was a Shin minister in the small California farming town of Guadalupe,
where their daughter Jane would be born. The couple were separated for most

of the war, as Rev. Matsuura was arrested almost immediately after the attack on Pearl Harbor. Shortly after their return to Guadalupe after the camps, he passed away, and Shinobu moved to Berkeley to be near her daughter and her growing family. An active member of the Buddhist community, Matsuura not only hosted the early sessions of the study group but was also a participant at meetings of the WFB and international Buddhist Women's Association. In 1955, she was in Hawai'i visiting her daughter Mary and newest grandchild when she received word from Kanmo Imamura that the new Berkeley Buddhist Temple would need a new *gohonzon* for the altar. He asked her to travel to Japan in search of an appropriate image. Imamura had already written to Hajime Nakamura, Tokan Tada, and Joen Ashikaga, who were awaiting Matsuura's arrival and willing to assist her search. Matsuura traveled first to Kyoto and went to Nishi Honganji, where she met with the *monshu* and his wife, "who expressed their special interest in the activities at the Berkeley Buddhist Temple." Ashikaga escorted her around Kyoto on her search. "Being the ancient capital that it was," she would later write her in memoir, "wherever we went, there were numerous beautiful Buddha images. I was struck by the profound and noble heritage of this country."[74]

Eventually, Ashikaga invited Matsuura to his recently established community on Ikuta Island in the Seto Inland Sea in Hiroshima Prefecture. Ashikaga and his followers had built a thriving community there as a refuge from the Pacific war. It was here that Matsuura first encountered the image of Amida. During a memorial for Shōtoku Taishi in the Hall of Peace, Ashikaga revealed that he was gifting the Amida image to Matsuura and the Berkeley Buddhist community. "[His followers] were at first saddened. But when they realized that this Buddha, so dear to them, would soon extend joy to people in America, they became elated."[75] A farewell ceremony was held in Kyoto, attended by the former bishop Masuyama. Ashikaga noted that when Buddhism left India to China, and then from China to other places, the image of the Buddha was always accompanied by the sutras, and so he included a copy of the three Pure Land sutras along with the Amida statue. And thus the Buddha image was wrapped in white silk and carried by Matsuura across the Pacific along with the sutras and a scroll of Rennyo's calligraphy of the *nenbutsu*. In 1956, a dedication ceremony was held to install the image in the *naijin* of the new Berkeley Buddhist Temple, and Rennyo's scroll was hung at the Study Center for some decades following.[76]

This is the "house for our hopes" built by the Imamuras, by Shinobu Matsuura, by the Japanese American Shin Buddhist community. Building this house made things possible and connected Berkeley to larger transnational networks. The Study Center and the activities of the Young Buddhist Association, the academic symposia and the *Berkeley Bussei* reached far beyond the temple itself while simultaneously drawing in people such as the West Coast counterculture figures who would popularize Buddhism in the back half of the twentieth century.

It is worth pausing for a moment to reflect on the story of the Amida statue's journey to America and Jane Imamura's assessment of her husband, mentioned earlier: "Following the way of Nembutsu without walls or boundaries, beyond sectarian distinctions . . . [Imamura's] path was clear."[77] As we have discussed previously, scholarship on North American Shin Buddhist history has tended to foreground the second clause ("beyond sectarian distinctions") while skipping over the first ("the way of Nembutsu"). The Berkeley Temple, with an image of Amida as the sole icon on its altar, is a Jōdo Shinshū Buddhist temple, one that has had long-standing and deep connections beyond that sectarian identity. As we will see in the next chapter, this "house for our hopes" made things possible— namely, it made American Buddhism possible. And while men like D. T. Suzuki, Alan Watts, Jack Kerouac, and those who would come later made Buddhism palatable to mainstream white America, it is incumbent upon us to pause, recognize that this future history was not at all a foregone conclusion in the years immediately after World War II, and note that the later popularity of American Buddhism has obscured its origin story, rooted in the Japanese American Jōdo Shinshū tradition.

D. T. Suzuki and the Shin Buddhist Connection

Among the "unprecedented large and serious crowd" described in Imamura's "A House for Our Hopes" was the "great D. Suzuki." As mentioned in the previous chapter, D. T. Suzuki was at this community meeting and spoke to the effect that it was on the shoulders of Nisei and Sansei to bring Buddhism to America. Suzuki, it goes without saying, has been the subject of no small amount of scholarship. His connection to Jōdo Shinshū, often framed in terms of his mother's faith, is well known, as are his activities in America more generally. More recently, Richard Jaffe has done excellent work uncovering the connection Suzuki had to American philanthropic organizations, and it is this type of networked connection I wish to highlight here.[78]

Charles Richard Crane was the heir to the Crane Company, a manufacturer of valves, elevators, and plumbing fixtures. Rather than taking on his family's business, he sold his shares to his younger brother and used his fortune to pursue a variety of intellectual and philanthropic causes, including an abiding interest in Russian studies. Having served the Wilson administration as the U.S. minister to China in 1920–1921, Crane became interested in East Asia as well. In 1930 he was introduced to Suzuki by Kenneth Saunders, who had taught at the Pacific School of Religion in Berkeley and elsewhere. Impressed with Suzuki, Crane offered to support him among other Japanese intellectuals to give lectures at Columbia University and Union Theological Seminary. In 1935 and 1936,

Suzuki's travels not only in the United States but also in Europe were funded in large part by Charles Crane. According to Jaffe, the subject of these lectures appears to be an early version of what would become one of Suzuki's best-known works, *Zen Buddhism and its Influence on Japanese Culture*, which Suzuki dedicated to his benefactor upon its publication.

This connection to Charles Crane no doubt helped Suzuki make a connection to his nephew Cornelius Crane. Like his uncle, the younger Crane was adventurous and curious about the world, but it appears he learned of Suzuki not through his uncle but through his first wife's therapist. At some point in 1950 or 1951 when Suzuki was in New York, she arranged a dinner party to meet him, and this sparked Crane's interest in Zen Buddhism and his support for Suzuki's work. Suzuki was in New York on a Rockefeller Foundation–funded lectureship at Union Theological Seminary, and Crane began funding him to give lectures at Columbia University. Through 1956, when Suzuki was fielding offers to teach at several universities in both New York and California, Crane continued to support him financially, and once his employment at Columbia ended in 1957, Crane helped to finance the Zen Studies Society. As Jaffe says, "For almost three-quarters of a century, Suzuki's work in the United States, Europe, and, in the last decade of his life, Japan, was sustained to a substantial degree by U.S. industrial wealth," and "U.S. philanthropy thus played a crucial role in the globalization of Japanese Zen."[79] On this point I do not disagree. I would only add that American Shin Buddhists *also* played a crucial role in the globalization of Japanese Buddhism.

In his discussion of Cornelius Crane's establishment of the Zen Studies Society, Jaffe mentions that a Japanese American lawyer, George Yamaoka (1903–1981), was one of the original directors of the organization. Yamaoka's role was clearly legal and financial in nature, helping to ensure that Crane's money was being directed to a charitable nonprofit for tax purposes, and for many years afterward he acted as a go-between Suzuki and his wealthy American benefactors. Yamaoka was born in Seattle, Washington, earned his law degree at Georgetown, and became the first Japanese American admitted to the New York State Bar Association in 1931. He worked for various international concerns, brokering legal and trade deals between the United States and Japan up until the outbreak of war. As he lived in New York, he was not incarcerated, though most of his family were; later, he helped them and other Japanese Americans resettle on the East Coast. Yamaoka was also asked to participate in the Tokyo War Crimes Tribunal as a defense attorney for Japanese war crimes suspects, and afterward he went on to have a successful law career representing several major Japanese corporations in the United States. Prior to all this, in 1938 he assisted Rev. Hozen Seki (1903–1991) in purchasing a building for the recently established New York Buddhist Church.[80] Seki had originally been assigned to a Los Angeles temple in 1930 but like many missionaries of the day had grander plans to spread the dharma in America. Before founding the New York church, he had also established a temple in Arizona, and following his incarceration during the war he worked to found the American Buddhist Academy at the New York temple in 1948.[81] Whereas Suzuki's interest in Jōdo Shinshū is often linked to his mother, he was also a regular at the New York Buddhist Church. When a statue of Shinran—a statue that had survived the atomic bomb at Hiroshima—was installed in front of the church in 1955, Suzuki was there to deliver an address.[82] He regularly gave talks at the church and its associated American Buddhist Academy, including a series of lectures in 1958 that were eventually compiled into the book *Shin Buddhism* and published twelve years later. Carrying on the theme we covered in Chapter 1 regarding Japanese modernists' claims that Buddhism reached its full potential in Japan, Suzuki's opening lines in this volume are: "The Pure Land school of teaching was originated in China, but it accomplished its full development in the Shin school of Pure Land Teaching. The Shin school is the culmination of Pure Land thought, and that took place in Japan."[83]

Perhaps more well-known than George Yamaoka, Suzuki's postwar success in America was also made possible by Mihoko Okamura (b. 1934). The Okamura family was incarcerated at Manzanar during the war and relocated to New York afterward. The father, Frank, was hired by the Brooklyn Botanic Garden to repair its Japanese garden, which had been vandalized during the war. In doing so, he began a long and prolific career as a noted bonsai expert.[84] The family often rented out a room in their Upper West Side brownstone to visitors from Japan, including D. T. Suzuki. Even before Suzuki lived with the Okamuras, however, Mihoko had already begun serving as his secretary and personal assistant, a role she played from 1953 until his death in 1966. "By all accounts, Okamura is recognized as Suzuki's primary caretaker in his later years, looking after his administrative and personal needs and freeing the preoccupied scholar from these everyday concerns."[85] Jane Iwamura, in her groundbreaking study of Asian representation in American media, *Virtual Orientalism*, notes that media representations during the 1950s and 1960s consistently portrayed Suzuki as "the model of a venerable Eastern sage—wise, noble, aged, and mysteriously foreign."[86] His image was widely circulated in magazines such as *Time*, *Newsweek*, the *New Yorker*, and, notably, fashion magazines, where he was most often photographed in traditional Japanese attire even though he usually wore a sports coat and slacks. This image of Suzuki (and by extension Buddhism), Iwamura argues, was as important to Zen's popularization in America as Suzuki's work or publications. That is, it was precisely his image as an Oriental fantasy that attracted white American interest that helped to inaugurate the Zen boom of the 1950s and 1960s.

At the same time, media representations of Japanese American Buddhists were ambiguous at best. Mihoko Okamura, for example, is included in a 1957 profile of Suzuki published in the *New Yorker*, where she is presented as simultaneously exotic and domestic. Okamura is described as speaking English as well as "any American college girl"; the reporter compares her physical features and mannerisms to a geisha, but then quickly dismisses such comparisons as "purely romantic" before reassuring the reader that Okamura is "an American girl with ideas of her own, as well as a sound knowledge of typing and shorthand."[87] Iwamura shows that such a description limits Okamura's role to that of Suzuki's inferior assistant rather than his peer. That subordinate role is extended to the entire Okamura family as well; the *New Yorker* reporter remarks that Suzuki is staying at their home, that the father is a gardener, and that the mother makes Suzuki's "favorite Japanese dishes," comments that locate them squarely in the realm of the domestic, in stark contrast to the intellectual, scholarly, and Orientalized role in which Suzuki is cast. Finally, the reporter notes that the Okamuras aren't Zen Buddhists themselves, but does not mention the Buddhist sect to which they belonged (Jōdo Shinshū). Such renderings do a lot of discursive work. By labeling Okamura "an American girl," she is separated from the exotic and foreign Suzuki and therefore portrayed as not his equal, not equally responsible for bringing Zen to America. But by reaffirming her "otherness," her "almond eyes and porcelain complexion," and her ability to speak clear English, she is rendered not fully American either. And by relegating the entire family to the role of caretakers and domestics, their labor is feminized as "women's work" and thus devalued. In other words, while remaining not really American, they are also too American and not effectively contributing to this newfound fascination with Zen Buddhism brought to the United States by the exotic Asian other, D. T. Suzuki. In the American media imagination, "Japanese Americans are allowed to serve as able caretakers providing a comfortable environment for more authentic Buddhist representatives from Asia."[88]

As will be discussed in more detail in the following chapter, Okamura is often elided in standard histories of American Buddhism, a background figure obscured by the presence of Suzuki (which, incidentally, can also be said of Suzuki's wife, Beatrice, who helped translate his work in the interwar period). "In the narrative of the Oriental Monk, the character of the Japanese American will always be relegated to the supporting cast *if* she appears at all."[89] In this way, the relationship between Suzuki and Okamura is a synecdoche for white (mis) understandings of Buddhism and Japanese Americans. Attracted to the unfamiliar and the exotic, we are drawn to the idiosyncratic yet familiar approach to religion offered by the likes of Suzuki and other "Oriental Monk" figures while never quite knowing what to do with the familiar, the already American Buddhism of Okamura, the Imamuras, and other Asian American Buddhists already present. As an Oriental Monk figure, Suzuki is charged with bringing Asian wisdom to the West. He will be in need of an heir, and that heir, as we will see later, will be Alan Watts. In this way the transmission of Buddhism from Asian missionary to white convert bypasses the Asian Americans who facilitated the connection.

Suzuki was not just *among* the large crowd described by Kanmo Imamura back in 1952; Suzuki was a well-known and frequent figure in American Shin Buddhist circles more generally. Again, he frequently gave lectures at the American Buddhist Academy in New York, and he was among the speakers at the Berkeley Temple's 1952 symposium alongside Alan Watts and others. In fact, it was likely Jane Imamura who picked up Suzuki from the airport and brought him to Berkeley in the first place.[90] As mentioned in the previous chapter and according to her memoir, this was but one of many duties expected of a *bōmori*. "Public relations was her domain, which meant hosting the abundant guests, including chauffeuring them to and from the airport. Those were pre-freeway days when the stop-and-go traffic to the San Francisco airport meant almost a day's trip. Mari [the Imamuras' youngest daughter] would often accompany me in the baby seat."[91] Suzuki would not have been able to accomplish what he did in the postwar period without the financial support of the Cranes or the Rockefeller Foundation. But it was the Imamuras who picked him up from the airport. This may seem a trivial act, a small contribution to a much larger life. But anyone who has landed in an airport after a very long flight to a country where you have but a slim grasp on the local language knows the feeling of gratitude at having a local there to meet you. And let us return briefly to the Upper West Side brownstone and Mrs. Okamura's cooking. Such acts of hospitality create safe spaces that can be of profound emotional or affective value.[92] The comfort and familiarity of one's "favorite Japanese dishes" is no small act; despite the adulation Suzuki may have been receiving from the *New Yorker*, he was still a foreigner, a person of color, in 1950s America.[93] We need to humanize Suzuki the man and recognize the value of even these small acts of hospitality.[94] This often unacknowledged labor is no less valuable than the more easily recognized (monetary) value of charitable contributions. In other words, when Japanese American Buddhists are rendered merely as "able caretakers," their contributions are devalued because they are representative of affective, immaterial, or unproductive labor—women's work. However, without this labor, Suzuki would have been stranded at the airport, would have no safe haven in 1950s New York.

As mentioned in this book's introduction, I would invite the reader to speculate, to imagine a history that could have been—to ask, *what if?* Even if he had a pocketful of cash from the Cranes, how long would Suzuki have survived in the United States without the support of the Imamuras or the Okamuras? Perhaps his story would be more akin to that of Nyogen Senzaki. In Rudiger Busto's "reconstructed Asian American version" of Senzaki's early life in the United States, we are reminded that after the young immigrant was unable to either find work or establish himself as a Zen teacher, he met his (and Suzuki's) teacher Shaku Sōen in Golden Gate Park in 1905. There Sōen famously said, "Just face the great city and see whether it conquers you or you conquer it."[95] Then followed decades of Senzaki looking for work up and down California, letting his hair grow out to avoid anti-Japanese discrimination, occasionally raising enough money to rent a hall to lead discussions on Zen or practice meditation—what he euphemistically called his "floating zendo"—and ultimately being one of the more than 120,000 Japanese and Japanese Americans incarcerated during World War II. Whereas hagiographies by his disciples and later white converts would cast these stories as "skillful means," Busto's retelling of his life reminds us that he was also a Japanese immigrant and that these innovations were as much about economic necessity as they were religion.[96] Here, I argue that in the absence of the religious infra-structure built by Japanese American Buddhists, D. T. Suzuki's fate in the 1950s might have been much the same. Unlike his dharma-brother Senzaki, Suzuki was buoyed by the Nisei Buddhist community, who attended his lectures and considered themselves among his students. And Nisei Buddhists picked him up from the airport (Imamura), gave him a place to stay (the Okamuras), facilitated financial transactions (Yamaoka), and attended to his personal affairs (Mihoko Okamura). This labor—the labor of Japanese Americans and women—made things possible. And in the following chapter, we will discuss that what became possible was American Buddhism.

5

Where the Heart Belongs

The final piece of the final volume of the *Bussei* is a short, untitled prose poem by Jack Kerouac recounting his meeting with D. T. Suzuki. In familiar Kerouac style—long, run-on sentences often connecting disparate ideas—he begins by noting that he rang the door three times before Suzuki answered. Kerouac mentions Suzuki's long eyelashes, that he has grown old and hard of hearing. Suzuki prepares for Kerouac and his two friends green tea, "very thick and soupy" and served in "cracked old soupbowls of some sort." He asks the scholar, "Why did Bodhidharma come from the West?" but receives no reply. The piece ends almost like a koan. Kerouac proclaims, "I would like to spend the rest of my life with you"; Suzuki "held up his finger and said 'Sometime.' "[1]

Coming at the end of the decade and the beginning of the next, this piece sets the tone perfectly for what would come—the Zen boom. As we've seen over the previous chapters, Kerouac's meeting with Suzuki was made possible, in part, by religious infrastructure created and maintained by the Japanese American Jōdo Shinshū community. This infrastructure supported and published the work of men like Kerouac, Snyder, and Suzuki, who in turn brought Buddhism to the attention of white American audiences. However, far more influential in the 1950s than Kerouac alone was the West Coast countercultural movement generally and, in particular, Alan Watts. As Iwamura has argued, in the American media imagination of the 1950s Suzuki played the role of the Asian sage or "Oriental monk" bringing Eastern wisdom and enlightenment to the West; however, the success of this project hinges on the transmission of Buddhism to a Western figure. Alan Watts thus plays the role of Suzuki's heir apparent, and we begin this chapter with a discussion of his success as a popularizer of Asian philosophy and religion. Here, I do not merely recount Watts's publications, radio broadcasts, and public lectures by which he was able to popularize Buddhism; following on Iwamura's *Virtual Orientalism*, I discuss how Watts's life and work was presented and represented to the public. First, I note how these representations obscure and often ignore his connections to the Shin Buddhist community; second, I argue that this presentation of Watts's life and work represents the construction of a *genre*.

In this chapter I play with the idea of genre and argue that the religious infrastructure built by Japanese American Buddhists made possible the genre of "American Buddhism." Building off my discussion of Watts and the ways in

The Making of American Buddhism. Scott A. Mitchell, Oxford University Press. © Oxford University Press 2023.
DOI: 10.1093/oso/9780197641569.003.0006

which his work has been framed and represented, I return our attention to the *Bussei* and ask in what way the poems and literature contained therein are representative of a genre of Buddhist art or literature. Through the presentation, representation, and repetition of particular works of art as essentially *Buddhist*, I argue that genre boundaries are formed, maintained, and indeed canonized. In short, we come to *know* what makes something (and someone) Buddhist by its repeated representation and inclusion in said category. Further, I argue that religious categories are formed by similar processes of repetition and inclusion. The genre of religion known as American Buddhism has come to be known by its association with figures such as Suzuki, Watts, and later converts and, as a result, its origins in the American Jōdo Shinshū community have become obscured.

Fundamentally, in what follows I am less interested in constructing a historical narrative or in tracing out connections between specific historical actors. Rather, I am interested in reading across disciplinary boundaries and thinking through the processes that enable the emergence of academic categories and literary genres. Such processes bring the world into being, to borrow a phrase from David Graeber; they reflect both our values and what is valued, and they authenticate religion, art, and persons. Above all, it is with persons I am most concerned: who is included in our categories and who is left unnamed or rendered invisible by these evaluative and authentication projects?

Beat Zen, Square Shin

Alan Watts (1915–1973) had been in the United States since the late 1930s, having married the daughter of Ruth Fuller Everett Sasaki, whose wealth helped support the early Zen community in New York. Her daughter's marriage to Watts was short-lived, and they were separated by the time of his move to San Francisco in 1951. It is unclear from available materials exactly when or how Watts was introduced to the Imamuras, but—given his association with the founders of the American Academy of Asian Studies and the Fuller-Sasakis—he ran in similar circles, so to speak. Because he was part of the networks and connections discussed in the previous chapter, it was probably inevitable that he would become acquainted with the Jōdo Shinshū community in the San Francisco Bay Area. Regardless of how the connection was made, he became a regular fixture at the Berkeley Buddhist Temple and maintained a relationship with the Imamura family for the remaining two decades of his life. This relationship is recounted in family stories, memories of his frequent lectures at the temple, letters, and his publications in the *Bussei*.[2] This was also the moment at which Watts became the leading proponent of Zen in the mainstream American press.

Jane Iwamura convincingly argues that in the late 1950s, American popular media "had selected Alan Watts as Suzuki's heir apparent."[3] Whereas Suzuki had brought Zen to America's attention, it was Watts who made it palatable. In 1958, the *Chicago Review* dedicated itself to Zen and its increasingly popular image in the United States with essays by Suzuki, Jack Kerouac, and Philip Whalen, among others; the issue's first essay was Watts's "Beat Zen, Square Zen, and Zen." In this essay, Watts decries "beat" and "square" Zen as "either a revolt from the culture and social order [beat] or a new form of stuffiness and respectability [square]."[4] It is clear that "beat" refers to the Beat Generation writers such as Kerouac, who were revolting against normative American values, and "square" represents the Japanese Zen Buddhist establishment with its hierarchy and rigid discipline. The merits of this argument are beside the point; Iwamura notes that in the immediate aftermath of the *Chicago Review* volume, Watts's essay was quoted, reprinted, commented on, and lauded by journalists and essayists in a range of publications, from the *New York Times Book Review* to *Time* magazine. Whereas not everyone who commented on the essay necessarily understood his point, the attention elevated Watts's reputation considerably and in a way that was distinct from the Beats'. Kerouac's work, for example, was being taken less seriously by critics, and his novels, including *The Dharma Bums* and later *Big Sur*, were reviewed poorly.[5] This dismissal was in part due to the very rebellion that the Beats were articulating, one that rejected normative middle-class white American values, often via heavy drinking and drug use. To the contrary, while still embracing the exotic "other" of Eastern spirituality, Watts was more acceptable. In 1960, *Life* magazine ran a pictorial of Watts wherein he was described as the "chief exponent" of Zen in America and "its most lucid interpreter."[6] Iwamura argues that whereas Suzuki's appeal was his exotic appearance, Watts's appeal was the opposite. Whereas Suzuki was always photographed in Japanese robes to highlight his "otherness" and usually alone (save for his cats), Watts was presented in rather conservative Western clothing and often with his family. Zen had become domesticated. Thus, whereas Suzuki is portrayed as the exotic missionary bringing Zen to the West, the Beats are dismissed as a challenge to normative American values, and Japanese Americans are becoming increasingly invisible, Watts embodies a nonthreatening religiosity easily accepted by white American audiences. "Watts fit the conventional standards of the time in terms of educational background, class standing, lifestyle, and image. Unlike the Beats, he posed no offense to a popular audience. . . . [He] emerged as Suzuki's most perfect pupil, his most appropriate heir."[7] This lineage transmission, however, completely bypassed the Japanese American Jōdo Shinshū community, which, as discussed in the previous chapter, supported and enabled these connections and transmissions.

It is worth pausing here and reflecting on the curious way that Watts has be-come associated exclusively with Zen but not Jōdo Shinshū while at the same time clearly having connections to the Shin community. What is the source of this disconnect? His first published piece in the *Bussei* gives us some hints as to his complex relationship with the tradition. While on the one hand he was clearly on good terms with the Imamuras, his "Program for Buddhism in America" (1952) disparages precisely the type of Buddhism the Imamuras prac-ticed. His essay begins with a rather meandering conversation about different types of "wisdom" (religious, philosophical, and scientific), the ways in which Buddhism does or does not fit into these categories, and Buddhism's poten-tial for all that ails the West. Watts claims that Japanese American Buddhists have an opportunity to make an enormous contribution to the West; however, there is a problem. Watts sets up a dichotomy between what he calls "temple Buddhism" and "ashram Buddhism," the former representing a way to pay re-spect to ancestors, the Buddha, and other deities and the latter representing "informal schools for the study and practice of Buddhist teachings."[8] Whereas temple Buddhism is "wonderful," Watts says, it must not get in the way of ashram Buddhism, which he claims was what the Buddha himself and his initial disciples practiced. Watts then goes on to outline the "program" alluded to in the essay's title to make Buddhism more widely known in the West. This program consists mainly of reading Buddhist books (a list is provided) and making the services at temples "a real Buddhist affair" and not a mere imitation of a Christian worship service (a sample schedule is provided).[9] The dismissive attitude toward how Japanese American communities were practicing their religion and comparisons to Christianity were, according to Masatsugu, "a source of anxiety" for Nisei, who worried that their practice was inauthentic and that practical similarities to Christian churches threatened the vitality of the Buddhist movement in America.[10]

In an essay originally published in 1941 and reprinted posthumously in 2003, "The Problem of Faith and Works in Buddhism," Watts addresses Jōdo Shinshū directly and at length.[11] The essay opens with a reference to the Pali canon and the fairly routine appeal-to-tradition fallacy to authenticate Watts's claims, his first one being that the core of Buddhist philosophy is "self-help." That is, one's salvation is attained by one's own effort, which is contrary to the Christian con-cept of grace. Therefore, at first glance, one might assume that "faith and works" have no place in Buddhism. Not so, says Watts, who then discusses at length the Mahāyāna approach, which includes the possibility of salvation by faith. The essay meanders about before making the claim that "in modern China and Japan, by far the most popular form of Buddhism is a way of salvation by faith."[12] Watts appears to be making a type of psychology-of-religion argument when he states that this impulse toward faith is a "pure concession to unregenerate human nature, which demands supernatural beings to achieve what men are too lazy and too frightened to achieve for themselves."[13] In other words, the very notion of faith (and by extension Christian grace) is rendered as character flaw; it is only those who are too lazy to bother trying who need rely on faith. He goes on to discuss at length the origins of Pure Land Buddhism in Japan and, despite this earlier suggestion that Pure Land Buddhists are lazy, presents a fairly sympathetic and fair treatment of the tradition—no doubt in part because he relies almost exclusively on the work of D. T. Suzuki. In fact, in noting the superficial similarities between the Christian conceptualization of grace and Amida's promise of rebirth in the pure land, Watts relies on Suzuki's work to argue that Shin Buddhism represents the deepest experiences of Mahāyāna Buddhism as represented by the *Lankavatara Sutra* and Rinzai Zen teachers.[14] This is a move he will repeat for the remainder of the essay; time and again he explains Shin teachings by way of reference to Zen koans and Suzuki's writings. In short, Watts uses Zen Buddhist teachings to legitimate Shin Buddhist ones. And lest we forget the true purpose of this path, he reminds us that Shinran tried the arduous path of "self-help," failed, and then relied on faith. Thus, even though Watts is at turns sympathetic to the Shin tradition and clearly well versed in some of its more nuanced teachings, his presentation of the tradition nevertheless relegates it to the path of those too lazy to help themselves while authenticating or rationalizing Pure Land practice by reference to Zen rather than on its own terms.

Regardless of how we might interpret Watts's essays or his personal feelings or relationship to the Shin Buddhist community, we must acknowledge that there is a way in which his writing has been contextualized that reproduces his status as a "chief exponent" of Zen in America. Consider, for example, that the above essay was published in a collection titled *Become What You Are* by Shambhala Publications in 2003. Promotional copy on the book's cover describes Watts as an "interpreter of Eastern thought" without mentioning which strands of thought he is interpreting. Discursively, this can be read as a perennialist move whereby the distinctiveness of diverse religious and spiritual traditions is flattened or obscured.[15] And yet, despite his association with a generic "Eastern thought," Watts is simultaneously associated with a specific sectarian form of Buddhism— Zen. In his biography on the official website of his estate, his connections to Zen are mentioned repeatedly, as are his broadcasts for the Berkeley radio station KPFA, but his connections to other forms of Buddhism such as Jōdo Shinshū and the Shin Buddhist community in Berkeley are absent.[16] Whereas the list of Watts's publications is fairly comprehensive, including both academic journal articles and popular magazine articles, his half-dozen articles published in the *Bussei* are not included. Watts is given an entry in *The Princeton Dictionary of Buddhism* and described as playing "a leading role in popularizing Buddhism and Zen."[17] Retrospectives are regularly published about Watts in Buddhist magazines such as *Lion's Roar* or *Tricycle*, and therein he is described solely in terms of his Zen connections and never in connection with the Berkeley Shin community.[18] Scholarly accounts, which often focus more on what Watts got wrong than on his biography, fall into a similar trap of overlooking his connections to the Imamuras and Jōdo Shinshū more generally.[19] David Smith, for example, recounts Watts's move to California and his connection to the San Francisco literary scene, Beat writers, Gary Snyder, and the various Buddhist teachers he associated with, including Shunryu Suzuki and "Lama Govinda in Berkeley"—but no mention of the Imamuras.[20] Iwamura rightly notes that though Watts becomes the heir apparent to Suzuki, it is not through individual choice, either his own or others'. She writes that in the early days of American Zen "there were a number of teachers and a multitude of pupils." Put another way, there were multiple lines of transmission. "However, it is often difficult to capture such complexity and relay it to a popular audience."[21] Thus, out of this complexity emerges the relatively simple story of Zen's transmission from Suzuki to Watts. This story is told and retold, reinforced by repetition and larger discursive processes in media and publications that, over time, render Alan Watts visible and the Imamuras invisible.

One consequence of this public presentation of Zen would be the emergence of American Buddhism itself, a slew of origin stories, and claims to authenticity and lineage. Ellen Pearlman, for example, in the opening of her account of meeting Mihoko Okamura, discusses Allen Ginsberg's death. "An ancestor, a keeper of the flame of knowledge," she writes, "was extinguished, but it wasn't only Allen who had died. It was also the *first wave* of those who had discovered and engraved Buddhism into the New York avant-garde."[22] She notes the deaths of John Cage, Gregory Corso, and other Beat-era artists, and while it is inarguable that these men were responsible for bringing Buddhism into New York's art scene, the language of "discovery" evokes a colonialist understanding of the transmission of knowledge. That is, first converts and so-called pioneers are portrayed as "discovering" the wisdom of Asia, which rhetorically renders them as active agents in the transmission of Buddhism from East to West while eliding the contribution of Asian immigrants and Asian American Buddhists. One finds the language of "firsts" and "pioneers" often in standard histories of Buddhism in the West, as in Stephen Prothero's *The White Buddhist*, wherein Henry Steel Olcott is defined as "the first American of European decent to formally convert to Buddhism."[23] In his *Luminous Passage*, Prebish recounts the history of Zen in America and notes that it was in the 1960s that Zen made the turn from the philosophical to the practical, and that Sōtō Zen specifically "began to appear on the American scene around 1950."[24] I am not sure what Prebish means by the "American scene," but on the following page he writes that Shunryu Suzuki had been assigned to the Sōtō Zen Mission in San Francisco in 1959 and that that temple had been established in 1934. This begs the question: did Zen appear on the "American scene" in the 1950s or the 1930s? This section of Prebish's book relies on the perennially referenced *How the Swans Came to the Lake* by Rick Fields, originally published in 1981. Fields employs the "pioneer" motif often, in reference both to Western Buddhist sympathizers and to Japanese Zen missionaries. Though voluminous and comprehensive, the work pays scant attention to Jōdo Shinshū despite discussing Japanese immigration to both Hawai'i and the mainland, immigrants who were overwhelmingly Shin Buddhist. Fields does mention the Beats' connection to the Berkeley Temple in passing, noting that Snyder, Whalen, and others met regularly with "Reverend Imamura and his wife Jane" and quoting Snyder as saying that there were "a number of really sharp Japanese-American Nisei and Sansei" in the community.[25] Fields's chapter detailing the period between 1905 and 1945 is focused almost exclusively on Zen Buddhist missionary work and the activities of white sympathizers and converts, and his final chapter—focused on the present and future of American Buddhism—does not mention Shin Buddhism at all.

I mention these works, and could add several more popular and scholarly accounts of American Buddhism, not to disparage the authors in question or to critique their work. Rather, I want to draw our attention to a persistent pattern of thought and the emergent discourse about American Buddhism's origins—and the consequence of this discourse. Namely, Jōdo Shinshū Buddhist history in the United States is often elided, relegated to the past, or authenticated via its relationship to white converts. It is telling that scholarly and popular accounts mention Watts's connection to virtually every Buddhist in the mid-twentieth century *except* the Imamuras, despite their long friendship. Similarly, Snyder had a long and close relationship with the Imamuras. He speaks fondly of them in his own writings and maintained a regular correspondence with Jane Imamura until her death.[26] In Fields's account, however, Kanmo Imamura is not even named fully, and Snyder's only reported comment on this relationship is the patronizing reflection that there were many "smart people" within the community. (Why would one assume otherwise?) In Pearlman's account of her encounter with Mihoko Okamura, she notes that when they first spoke, Okamura "picked up the phone, answering in clear, precise English."[27] (Why would one be surprised that an Asian American is speaking precise English?) This comment replicates the 1957 *New Yorker* profile of D. T. Suzuki discussed in the previous chapter wherein Okamura's ability to speak English is highlighted; despite being "an American girl," Okamura is cast in the role of the perpetual foreigner. Pearlman ends her narrative of meeting Okamura by suggesting that she is now one of Suzuki's lineage holders, thus writing herself into the history of transmission.[28] It is this repeated pattern of assuming that the main actors of American Buddhist history are white converts while relegating Asian Americans to supporting roles or reinforcing the "perpetual foreigner" stereotype that obscures the ways in which

Issei and Nisei Buddhists not only were the first pioneers to bring Buddhism to the Americas but also were the first American Buddhists.

Given what we've covered in the previous four chapters, it should be clear that Japanese American Shin Buddhists have been instrumental in the making of American Buddhism. That is, whereas scholarly and popular treatments of American Buddhist history often foreground the accomplishments of white converts or overtly claim that American Buddhism begins with them, it is clear that the origins of American Buddhism are rightfully with Issei and Nisei Buddhists who self-consciously articulated and promoted a version of modern Buddhism that was their contribution to American society as part of a larger project of asserting their right to be fully accepted as Americans. Moreover, whereas the connections between some of the lineage holders of Buddhist modernism are tenuous at best, Nisei Buddhists had direct connection with several of the persons who are routinely credited with (or blamed for) the creation of Buddhist modernism—Watts, Suzuki, Snyder, Kerouac. In some cases, these young converts would not have had direct contact with Buddhism as a living tradition at all were it not for the generosity and hospitality of the Shin Buddhists in Berkeley. This hospitality, this labor, allowed for the emergence of the very category of American Buddhism itself, which, once picked up and propagated by white converts and later generations, has taken on a specific set of meanings and values. In the next section, we will look at the genre of Buddhist art to explore how categories and values are birthed and given meaning.

On Genre

There is very little poetry in the early volumes of the *Bussei*. However, the fall 1941 volume includes a poem titled "Where the Heart Belongs" by Ayako Noguchi.

> Oh, take me to the city,
> And leave me there for a day—
> Let me gaze at the tall buildings,
> And watch me go astray.
> The directions become all jumbled,
> Could this be east or west?
> The sun never sets behind the hills,
> And wearily, I wish for rest.
>
> Oh, take me back to the country,
> Back where the heart belongs—
> There, undisturbed, let me hear again

The familiar woodland songs.
Let me show you the Dipper,
The thrill of the Milky Way—
I need no map, no compass here,
'Tis home, and here I'll stay.[29]

Noguchi's poem juxtaposes urban and rural landscapes. In the city, towering buildings confuse and disorient and ultimately lead to exhaustion. In the still-ness of the country, the poet is reunited with the sounds of nature, the sky is alight with stars, and there is a deep familiarity and connection to the land. It is home. As discussed in previous chapters, Nisei from across California came to Berkeley and the surrounding areas to attend the University of California and other local colleges; many of these young Buddhists had grown up on their Issei parents' farms. It is thus easy to read this poem as a reflection of a young Nisei student far from the familiar comforts of home, awash in the frenetic landscape of a growing city. The nostalgic longing for the familiar sounds of the woods includes an invitation—let me show you the stars, a landscape where no map is needed. Home.

Gary Snyder (b. 1930) is well known for his own connections to the land. Before enrolling in a graduate program at UC Berkeley in the early 1950s, he had already been traveling through the wilderness for most of his young life. Summers were often spent in national park fire lookout towers where he would watch vast landscapes react to the changing light over the course of days, weeks, months.[30] Sometime around 1953, he befriended the Imamuras and began regu-larly attending the Berkeley Buddhist Temple's events and study classes. Snyder's first poem in the *Berkeley Bussei* was published in 1954, and poems appeared in every issue through 1960. Whereas some of these poems evoke a Buddhist theme—such as "Maitreya" (1954) or "Song for a Stone Girl at Sanchi" (1958)—many poems, like Noguchi's, are about the country. Take, for example, "Piute Creek" from the 1956 *Bussei*.

One granite ridge
A tree, would be enough
Or even a rock, a small creek,
A bark-shred in a pool.
Hill beyond hill, folded and twisted
Tough trees crammed
In thin stone fractures
A huge moon on it all, is too much.
The mind wanders. A million
Summers, night air still and the rocks

Warm. Sky over endless mountains.
All the junk that goes with being human
Drops away, hard rock wavers
Even the heavy present seems to fail
This bubble of a heart.
Words and books
Like a small creek off a high ledge
Gone in the dry air.

A clear, attentive mind
Has no meaning but that
Which sees is truly seen.
No one loves rock, yet we are here.
Night chills. A flick
In the moonlight
Slips into Juniper shadow
Back there unseen
Gold proud eyes
Of Cougar or Coyote
Watch me rise and go.[31]

Snyder's connection to Buddhism and his status as Buddhist poet are well established. While enrolled at Reed College in Portland, Oregon, he became interested in Chinese landscape painting. This interest expanded to Japanese and Asian culture more generally and, of course, Buddhism. In Berkeley, he took *sumi-e* (Japanese ink wash painting) courses from Chiura Obata, and he introduced his Reed College roommate, Philip Whalen, to the Imamuras. And it was at this time that he became associated with the San Francisco Renaissance. This West Coast literary movement began in the late 1940s around the same time that, on the East Coast, Kerouac first coined the phrase "Beat Generation." The movements met in the Bay Area in the mid-1950s, with Allen Ginsberg's 1955 reading of his epic poem "Howl" at San Francisco's Six Gallery remaining a quintessential and iconic moment. Snyder is widely credited with bringing Buddhism to the Beat Generation: "Ginsberg, Kerouac, as well as Diane di Prima would follow Snyder's example in their subsequent deep engagement with Buddhism."[32] Snyder also became the inspiration for the character Japhy Ryder in Kerouac's *The Dharma Bums*, a novel that includes many fictionalized accounts of their time in California.[33] Snyder's status as a Buddhist is thus often understood in connection with his and the Beats' literary or artistic output. In their introduction to *The Emergence of Buddhist American Literature*, for example, John Whalen-Bridge and Gary Storhoff explicitly list Snyder as a "Buddhist writer" along with contemporaries such as J. D. Salinger and Allen Ginsberg. But what, precisely, makes Snyder a *Buddhist* writer? Or, put another way, is "Piute Creek" a *Buddhist* poem? For that matter, is Ayako Noguchi a Buddhist writer? Is "Where the Heart Belongs" a Buddhist poem? Why or why not? The answers to these questions are often framed in terms of genre. Here I would like to reflect on how genre categories are defined and maintained, how the maintenance of genre categories includes and excludes, and the consequences of this border mainte-nance on persons and communities. Much as there is a genre of Buddhist art (poetry, literature, film, and so on), one might say that there is a genre of religion known as American Buddhism.

To be clear, there are a great many poems and other literary pieces in the *Bussei* that are explicitly Buddhist, however we might want to define the term. For ex-ample, noted printmaker Will Petersen (1928–1994) contributed the poem "Notes of a Bombu" to the 1958 *Bussei*. As discussed in Chapter 1, *bonbu* refers to the deluded sentient beings who are the object of Amida Buddha's compassion within normative Shin Buddhist thought. Petersen's poem discusses samsara, karma, and the wheel of rebirth. In the 1957 *Bussei*, Judy Mukaida contributed a poem titled "My Journey to Enlightenment" that references the eightfold path. Arguably, Kerouac's encounter with Suzuki with which we opened this chapter is Buddhist inasmuch as it seems to be playing with the idea of koan. And, of course, we would be remiss if we ignored the publication of Hiroshi Kashiwagi's stage play *Kisa Gotami: The Parable of the Mustard Seed* (Figure 5.1). Published in 1957, the play recounts the well-known story of a mother who, so distraught over the death of her child, is believed to have gone mad. Seeking council from the Buddha, he tells her that he can bring the child back to life if she can collect mus-tard seeds from the village, but only from homes where no one has experienced death. Of course, she cannot. In realizing the universality of grief and the im-permanence of life, she enters the first stage of enlightenment. When Kashiwagi produced his play at the Berkeley Buddhist Temple, a young and as yet unknown George Takei played the role of the Buddha.[34]

Apart from these overtly Buddhist pieces, there are many poems in the *Bussei*, such as Snyder's and Noguchi's, that are not explicitly *about* Buddhism. Were one to read Philip Whalen's two contributions, for example, out of context they would not immediately be recognized as Buddhist. The first, "Unfinished, from 3:XII:55" (1957), is a poem about intellectual struggle; whereas one could cer-tainly interpret the poem and its theme of struggling against ignorance from a Buddhist point of view, there is nothing *overtly* Buddhist about it. The second, "Scholiast" (1958), is a series of three haiku-like stanzas describing the natural world. Again, there is nothing overtly Buddhist about the poem. Apart from their publication in a Buddhist magazine, what makes these pieces (and their author) Buddhist?

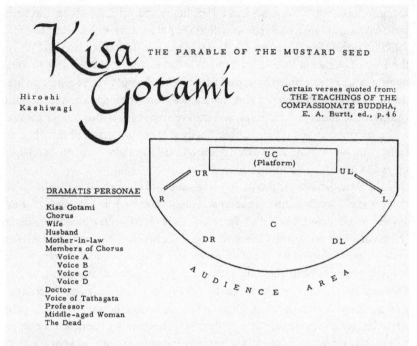

Figure 5.1 Excerpt from *Kisa Gotami: The Parable of the Mustard Seed*, Hiroshi Kashiwagi's stage play published in the 1957 *Berkeley Bussei*.

As I have discussed elsewhere, and building on the work of Kimberly Beek, the genre of Buddhist literature might be said to include works that are either *about* or *of* Buddhism. "Work *about* Buddhism takes Buddhist concepts or themes as a central plot device or as an explicit concern . . . [whereas work] *of* Buddhism might be said to be infused with a Buddhist sentiment or take certain Buddhist understandings for granted" while not explicitly mentioning Buddhism.[35] To say a work of art or literature is *about* Buddhism is straightforward enough—Mukaida's "Journey to Enlightenment," for example. The *of* side of the equation is inherently more subjective. For example, even though not explicitly about Buddhism, one could read the reference to a "clear, attentive mind" from Snyder's "Piute Creek" with a Buddhist lens and reflect on the "mind-as-mirror" metaphor found in some strands of Mahāyāna thought. One could read Whalen's "Scholiast" as a series of haikus, as evoking the bare attention of the natural world with a nondiscriminative mind, or his "Unfinished" as a reflection not on intellectual struggles generally but as a specific lament on ignorance and greed leading to suffering—and that poem's closing line, "Work on that," as an invocation to do Buddhist practice. Thus, one could read much of the poetry in the *Bussei* as either *about* or *of* Buddhism. Beek's definition then helps us move past the question of authorial intent; moreover, it does not rely on the self-identity of the artist. That is, something may be of Buddhism regardless of the author's intention to create "Buddhist art" and regardless of the artist's identity as a Buddhist. To claim that something is *of* Buddhism allows us to include in the genre category not only work that is not explicitly about Buddhism but also work that is not by Buddhists. However, this way of approaching the question of genre opens up the possibility that whether or not something counts as Buddhist is entirely in the eye of the beholder. To take an example from cinema, critics and Buddhists regularly claim that the 1993 film *Groundhog Day* is "Buddhist." The film is the story of a less-than-likable television reporter who relives the same day until he works at bettering himself, and it is often read as an allegory for samsara and the bodhisattva path. Writing in the foreword to *Buddhism in American Cinema*, the film's screenwriter, Danny Rubin, recounts that a friend once commented on the movie by saying, "You probably don't know this, but you're Buddhist." "My friend's observations may or may not have merit," Rubin says. "I once wrote a western about a hanging. Does that make me a cowboy?"[36] In other words, Rubin does not identify as a Buddhist, nor did he write *Groundhog Day* as a Buddhist film, but we can still read it as a Buddhist allegory. It is *of* Buddhism.

It is this "of-ness" that allows *Groundhog Day* to be included in lists of Buddhist films and screened at Buddhist film festivals. And here I would draw our attention to the act of *collection*. John Whalen-Bridge discusses the relationship between film festivals and the genre of Buddhist film, noting that organizers employ specific strategies to determine whether or not a film is sufficiently "Buddhist" for screening at a festival. In discussing the Buddhist Film Foundation and its selection process, Whalen-Bridge notes that many films (including *Groundhog Day*) are "drafted" into or become "implicated" in the genre category of Buddhist film for various reasons, including that they may be used as an allegory for Buddhist themes or ideas. Additionally, some films are included for strategic or financial reasons. Whereas some films screened are explicitly about Buddhism, produced by Buddhists in Buddhist-majority countries, such films may not attract a wide audience. By including major studio films such as *Ghost Dog, Seven Years in Tibet,* or *Groundhog Day*, organizers hope to attract larger audiences and expose them to a wider diversity of films and independent filmmakers. That is why a festival may screen movies that are *about* or *of* Buddhism as well as those produced by Buddhists. In the process of collecting these films, the organizers' motivations are varied, including concerns for identifying obviously or explicitly Buddhist work as well as purely financial concerns; regardless of motivation, however, in the process of collection a genre category emerges. Such a genre does not rely on authorial intent and may disregard the of/about criteria entirely. Let us not dwell on whether or not such a genre is good or bad; instead let us explore the process of how it came to be and how, through collection and repetition, it emerges. One could examine the lists of films regularly screened at Buddhist film festivals or commented on by Buddhist critics (indeed, that is precisely what Whalen-Bridge has done), and whether or not we are able to define the genre, we know which films fit and which films do not.

We can discern a similar process at work in the case of American Buddhist literature. Collections such as *Nixon Under the Bodhi Tree* and *You Are Not Here*—both of which are subtitled *And Other Works of Buddhist Fiction*—bring together short stories that meet the *of* or *about* definition of Buddhist literature, and most authors are self-identified Buddhists. Promotional copy for *You Are Not Here* hints at a definition of the genre when it states that the included stories "dramatize the spirit of Buddhism" but only a few "touch on the Dharma explicitly"; nevertheless, "collectively these stories paint a living portrait of the face of Buddhism."[37] Consequently, the genre of Buddhist literature may include work that is only tangentially about Buddhism (merely "touching" on the dharma) but which in some ways defines Buddhism and Buddhists. Such work is also the subject of scholarly study; as we've seen, often scholars, too, gesture toward genre definitions, as Whalen-Bridge and Storhoff do when they write that something may be considered Buddhist art if it "affirms identity not in terms of a self-existent soul or a chosen people but rather as an impermanent and fully contingent artifact."[38] Again, my concern is not for the definition itself but with the act of collection. Whalen-Bridge and Storhoff's *The Emergence of Buddhist American Literature* is focused almost exclusively on Snyder, Ginsberg, and other countercultural figures, as well as Maxine Hong Kingston, all of whom make an appearance in their other edited volume, *Writing as Enlightenment: Buddhist American Literature into the Twenty-first Century*. Charles Johnson is under study here as well, and his work has similarly been included in anthologies of Buddhist fiction; he also authored the foreword to *Nixon Under the Bodhi Tree*. Thus, without defining the genre of Buddhist literature, this work of collection, of *canonization*, does the definitional work for us. In its simplest sense, a "canon" is merely a collection of privileged texts. Charles Jones points out that this use of the term certainly carries Protestant biases that may not be applicable to non-Christian religions.[39] Nevertheless, this is not the strong argument I am making. Rather, I am making the observation that it is largely through repetition or *tradition* that a collection of texts (and in this case persons) becomes understood as authoritative. In short, over time we come to recognize that *these* texts/films/artworks constitute the genre of Buddhist art and *these others* do not.

Through the processes of repetition and canonization, the genre of Buddhist art emerges. Returning to Jane Iwamura's *Virtual Orientalism*, whether the icon of the Oriental monk takes the form of real persons such D. T. Suzuki or fictionalized characters such as Kwai Chang Caine, we come to "know" them and what they represent via their repeated mediated images. We *know* the Oriental Monk "not only because we understand his views and admire his actions but also because we are deeply—even unconsciously—familiar with what he represents and the role that he plays."[40] And that role is a stand-in for the exotic other, the transmitter of ancient Asian wisdom to the modern West. In the same way that we come to know the icon of the Oriental Monk, we come to know the genre of Buddhist art. The reflexive and even subconscious understanding of what makes something *of* Buddhism is reinforced by repetition, the repetition of certain works of art with the aura of Buddhism that are included in anthologies, screened in festivals, and become the subject of scholarly attention.[41] The boundaries of the genre are solidified by repetition as well as their reference to other genres. We know the genre of American Buddhist literature in part because we know that it is distinct from the genre of Asian American literature. Beek addresses the tension between these genres by bringing into conversation Amy Tan's *The Kitchen God's Wife* and Keith Kachtick's *Hungry Ghost*. Both novels have Buddhist themes and could be read as *of* or *about* Buddhism and/or are written by Buddhists. In paying attention to the critical reception of the novels, however, Beek explains that the Buddhist elements of Tan's novel are glossed over; she speculates that because they were set within the context of Asian cultural practices, reviewers may have taken them for granted or viewed them merely as a representation of Chinese American culture. By contrast, she points out that some reviewers were put off by Kachtick's Buddhist references or suggested that only Buddhists would get the "in jokes."[42] While both novels could fit into the genre definition of Buddhist literature, Beek draws our attention to extratextual sources that define and reinforce the genre categories regardless of the individual author's intentions or even our subjective read of the novels. Institutional structures, publishing houses, scholarly interest, and so forth reinforce the genre categories as distinct, even if overlapping.

In some ways, the work of genre construction and maintenance is merely about the work itself. From this point of view, definitional questions are about films, artwork, poems, or literature. There is no doubt great pedagogical value in, say, showing one's undergraduates a film and reading it allegorically to demonstrate some Buddhist concept. And there's nothing inherently harmful in that. But let us return for a moment to Danny Rubin's friend and their observation: "You probably don't know this, but you're Buddhist." Note that his friend did not call *Groundhog Day* a Buddhist film; they called *Rubin* a Buddhist. So it is important to note that even if we define Buddhist art in such a way as to remove authorial intent or the personal identity of the author, a *relationship* is still forged between the artist and the religion.

For example, Maxine Hong Kingston is included as a subject of study in *The Emergence of American Buddhist Literature* despite being quoted as saying that *The Woman Warrior* is not a "Buddhist book."[43] One can imagine, then that the edited volume is not unlike Rubin's friend, conscripting her into the genre category of Buddhism regardless of her personal identity or motivations for writing the book in the first place. Through repetition, her inclusion in the canon becomes a matter of tradition and she finds herself alongside Charles Johnson, Gary Snyder, Jack Kerouac, and so on. But not Ayako Noguchi.

To be clear, Ayako Noguchi never made a name for herself as a poet; to the best of my knowledge, Noguchi lived out her life never publishing another poem after "Where the Heart Belongs." I doubt anyone would claim that Noguchi should not be included in the genre category of Buddhist literature; equally, no one would claim that one published poem in an obscure journal is enough for inclusion in a canon. But this lack of publication is the point. Whereas we may make subjective decisions that particular artists and writers and their works properly count as Buddhist or not, publishing houses and larger institutional systems also do this work, and to greater effect. We might imagine an alternative reality wherein Noguchi went on to a successful career as a poet; regardless of how she may or may not have self-identified, were her work included in anthologies and scholarly studies alongside Snyder's and Hong Kingston's, her inclusion in the canon would be a matter of course. This is to say that regardless of how any of the individuals discussed here may or may not self-identify, their inclusion in or exclusion from collections, anthologies, and scholarly treatments identifies them regardless. An example by comparison can be seen in the label "Beat Generation." Whereas Kerouac and several of his close companions embraced the term early on, most of his contemporaries flatly rejected it, including Snyder, who considered himself to be part of the West Coast countercultural movement.[44] Other Beat writers, such as William S. Burroughs, loathed the term, and even Kerouac himself rejected it later in his career. Nevertheless, it stuck. These writers are regularly referred to as the Beat Generation regardless of their personal feelings about the moniker. Via repetition and collection in anthologies and ongoing scholarly attention, genres of Beat and Buddhist writing emerge—and we come to know them, understand what they represent and what role they play in American culture. Moreover, to the extent that published anthologies are also commodities, the poems and the poets included therein are valued differently than those not included, a point to which we will return later in this chapter.

As I said, much as there is a genre of Buddhist literature, there is also a genre of religion known as American Buddhism, one that is defined as much by individual practitioners or scholars as it is by larger institutional forces. And it is these larger systems with which I am concerned. Whether it is a network of Buddhist communities, large-scale publishing projects such as *Tricycle: The Buddhist Review* or *Lion's Roar*, university religious studies departments, or academic presses, these systems play a role in creating and maintaining the boundaries of the genre category of American Buddhism. I am not arguing that any one individual is including or excluding other individuals or whole communities; rather, I am calling our attention to the ways in which collective and often unconscious or uncritical decisions are made that reinforce existing patterns that do this boundary maintenance for us. These systems structure our thought and reinforce the boundaries of our categories and lead to the false choices I have sought to reveal in this book—the false choice between American Buddhism and Buddhism in America, between traditional and modern, between general Buddhism and sectarian Buddhism. Such categories ultimately create value for those included while minimizing and rendering invisible those excluded. And yet, it is often the labor of invisibilized persons that in part makes the categories possible.

The question then becomes: now that the genre category of American Buddhism has been created, who is included within its boundaries?

Śrīmālādevī and Pie à la Mode

In 1953, Tokan Tada (1890–1967) was a visiting scholar at the American Academy of Asian Studies, an occasional lecturer at Bay Area universities, and a regular figure at the Berkeley Buddhist Temple. Tada was born into a Jōdo Shinshū temple family in Japan and while a student at Ryukoku University in Kyoto was a part of the Otani expeditions. Then abbot of Nishi Honganji, Kozui Otani was one of several Japanese priests and intellectuals who studied abroad during the Meiji and Taishō eras. This connection gave Tada the opportunity to live in Lhasa for a number of years, befriend the Thirteenth Dalai Lama, and bring a large collection of Tibetan manuscripts back to Japan.[45] Perhaps because of this connection to Tibet, in the *Bussei* he is usually referred to as "Lama Tada," as he was in the 1954 piece "Lama Tada's Contribution."[46] The one-page article describes how twice a week for over a year Tada met with Kanmo and Jane Imamura and Hitoshi Tsufura to work on a pair of translations. The foursome met in "the upper room of the Buddhist Church." The meetings would go late into the night. Tada worked with Tibetan scrolls stretched out over a low table, and slowly and methodically he translated the text line by line, offering explanation or engaging in conversation with the Imamuras and Tsufura, and consulting a Tibetan-Sanskrit-English dictionary. Jane Imamura and Tsufura translated his Japanese into English as best they could. And Kanmo Imamura sat nearby offering his occasional thoughts and feedback. Often members of the Advanced Study Group and Shinobu Matsuura joined the foursome.

The two texts being translated were the *Śrīmālādevī Siṃhanāda Sūtra* and the *Vimalakīrti Nirdeśa Sūtra*. This translation project had apparently begun at the Academy of Asian Studies with Alan Watts; however, "due to language difficulties," the project was moved to the Berkeley Temple. The article says that Tada had chosen these particular sutras because, along with the *Lotus Sutra*, they were the texts upon which Shōtoku Taishi based his own understanding of Mahāyāna Buddhism and subsequently propagated the dharma in seventh-century Japan. For more than a year, the foursome met and worked, sometimes translating as little as a paragraph or as much as a dozen pages in each session. Discussion about the subtle meanings of single words lasted long into the night. And Tada used these as opportunities to give further explanation on the fundamentals of Mahāyāna Buddhism. At last, a week before Tada was set to return to Japan, on October 6, 1953, "for the first time in history, the translations were completed on American soil." The article comments that the translations will need to be edited and revised; however,

> the important thing is that the sutras were explained in their entirety in America. They will some day bear fruit as Lama Tada wished, as Prince Shotoku wished in 600, as King Asoka wished in the third century B.C. and as Lord Buddha himself wished 2500 years ago.[47]

The foursome celebrated their accomplishment with pie à la mode at midnight.

A few observations should be made about this remarkable story. First, note that this translation project took place in the "upper room of the Buddhist Church." Because the Imamura family still resided at the temple, the "upper room" was essentially their living room. As we discussed in Chapter 3, the boundary between home and temple is often blurred in Japanese Buddhist contexts, and it was blurred here in Berkeley as well. The conditions are different, of course; the Imamuras lived at the temple in the early 1950s because they had no other options. However, regardless of the circumstances, Jane Imamura and her mother before her were *bōmori*. And so it should not surprise us that their homes—the domestic space—should be used for a religious purpose, in this case a translation project. Just as Jane's living room here is being used as a translator's office, Shinobu's living room was used for the Study Center. Even though she lived roughly a mile away from the temple, the temple's activities could be said to extend to her domestic space as well.

Second, we need to take note of the choice of sutras. Tokan Tada did not choose the three Pure Land sutras, nor did he choose to translate a work of the sect's founder, Shinran. Because of this, one may mistakenly conclude that this act of translation had little to do with Jōdo Shinshū. But recall our discussion from Chapter 1 of Shinran's elevation of Shōtoku. The pride of place Shōtoku carries within the Shin tradition is clear, and so it should not surprise us that these specific sutras would be chosen for translation. Moreover, note that what they celebrate with pie à la mode is not the translations per se but that the translations were *completed in America*, that the sutras were *explained* in the United States, and that this act will bear fruit. The explicit connection drawn between this act, Shōtoku, Aśoka, and the Buddha himself suggests that the foursome is linking their translations to a longer Buddhist or karmic lineage. In sum, the translation is a deeply religious act—and, I would argue, an explicitly Jōdo Shinshū one at that.

Despite the article's claim that the translations will need to be edited and revised, thus suggesting that the foursome may have had the intention of publishing them, I have found no evidence that their translations were published or distributed in any fashion, with the sole exception of chapter 8 of the *Vimalakīrti*, which was published in the same 1954 edition of the *Bussei*. Publication of course would have been a natural outcome of the translation project. As evidenced by the *Bussei* itself, the Berkeley Temple, many other Shin temples, and the Buddhist Churches of America have over the decades published a great deal of material including translations, songbooks, institutional histories, books by noted priests, and so on. Publication may very well have been one of the intentions of the foursome's meeting twice a week in that upper room of the Berkeley church. But publication seems not to have happened. And given the tone of "Lama Tada's Contribution," publication takes a backseat to the religious aims of the project—planting karmic seeds, ensconcing the foursome within a lineage of Buddhist transmission and propagation stretching back across Asia and to the Buddha himself. The prestige that may come from translation and publication was likely not the point; it was the future growth of the dharma in America.

Buddhologists may be more familiar with another translation of the *Śrīmālādevī Sūtra*, one completed and published by Alex and Hideko Wayman. The Waymans' publication of *The Lion's Roar of Queen Śrīmālā* was begun at the University of Wisconsin in 1962—less than a decade after Tada's and the Imamuras'—but was not completed until the end of the decade and ultimately published in 1974 by Columbia University Press. In that volume's preface, the translators note the importance and popularity of this short sutra across East Asia. "It is surprising that such an influential Buddhist work as the Śrī-Mālā has not yet been translated into a Western language."[48] But of course it had been translated, back in Berkeley, twenty years earlier.

What is also surprising is that in 1953 Alex Wayman was a student at Berkeley and working on Tibetan texts.[49] The essay that immediately follows "Lama Tada's Contribution" in the *Bussei* is "Remarks on Translation of Buddhist Works" by Wayman. Wayman was part of the Advanced Study Group, whose members, recall, occasionally sat in on these translation sessions with Tada, the Imamuras, and Tsufura. Apart from these references to Wayman's participation in the study group and his *Bussei* publication record, I do not have any direct evidence that he was in the "upper room of the Buddhist Church," nor do I have any direct evidence that he knew what Tada was translating or why. However, to the extent that Wayman was, at the time, studying Tibetan, it would have been odd for him to not have met this visiting scholar of Tibetan texts. Whereas in the "Translator's Note" to the Waymans' published translation they are clear about which versions of the text they worked from, the same cannot be said of the Imamuras' and Tada's work. They may have been working from completely different sources. As I have said, I have not located the foursome's translation of the *Śrīmālādevī Sutra* and therefore cannot compare it to the Waymans' translation published two decades later. I am not claiming that the Waymans were duplicitous or engaged in any unethical actions in their own translation project, nor disparaging the curious fact that nowhere in their list of acknowledgments do they hint at any connection to the Berkeley Buddhist Temple or the Imamuras. Rather, I am calling our attention to two different versions of a translated text and two different uses of the word "first." For the Imamuras, the "first" that was important was the mere act of translation, the mere fact of the work being done, and its larger significance as part of a religious tradition connecting the present to the past. For scholars, the "first" that is important is what remains, the physical artifact, the published piece. The Waymans can lay claim to the prestige that comes with first translation precisely because their translation was *published*. It remains, in physical form, an artifact I happened upon in a colleague's office while writing this book.[50]

As mentioned earlier, publications are commodities and therefore have value. And here I would call our attention to the different meanings of "value" and how, to draw on anthropologist David Graeber's work, value brings the world into being. As I have argued elsewhere, the products of scholarly labor—translations such as the Waymans', monographs, published research, public presentations, and so forth—have specific economic value within the knowledge economy of late capitalism.[51] This is one type of value, a specifically monetary one. Graeber draws our attention to the relationship between (monetary) value and *values*;

building on Marx's value theory of labor, he argues that if we understand social worlds not just as collections of persons and things but as a "project of mutual creation," then value becomes a key element in the creation and recreation of our social world. That is, in the process of giving value to specific material objects or in articulating values such as justice, loyalty, or beauty, humans create collective social imaginaries. The processes of creating and pursuing value are creative acts of labor whether in the form of factory wage labor or religious rituals. The worlds created by these acts of labor are often taken for granted, assumed to be true, or understood as the ideologies that predetermine social behavior. "Marx's theory of value was above all a way of asking the following question: assuming that we do collectively make our world, that we collectively remake it daily, then why is it that we somehow end up creating a world that few of us particularly like, most find unjust, and over which no one feels they have any ultimate control?"[52] In referring to the world "few of us particularly like," Graeber is, of course, referring to modern capitalism and its assumption that the pursuit of wealth is to be valued as an end in itself. In this social world, value is inextricably tied to specific types of wage labor, and the only things of value are commodities. The published translation of a sutra exists within this social world; it is a commodity, one that has a specific and literal value (the used copy of the Waymans' translation on my desk has "$10.00" written in pencil on the front page); by extension, the scholar who produces it is also of value or valued as the laborer who brought it into being.

However, there are other forms of labor and other values. As Graeber puts it: "The moment we enter the world where labor is not commoditized, suddenly we begin talking about *values*."[53] And the most recognizable form of noncommoditized labor is, in Marxist language, "reproductive labor"—housework, childcare, and other labor often conducted in the domestic realm. Religious or ritual labor may exist on the margins of capitalist systems or may be engaged in creating alternative social worlds or imaginaries, ones where the pursuit of wealth is not assumed to be the thing of highest value. As discussed in Chapter 3, in the case of the Jōdo Shinshū household, there is considerable overlap between the domestic realm and the religious realm, and this overlap is very often the domain of the *bōmori*. Within this religious home one finds multiple forms of labor, some "reproductive" in the Marxian sense, others purely capitalist, and still others religious—whatever that word might mean. In the case of the Imamuras, in the case of the "upper room of the Buddhist church," the labor of translating the sutras was at the very least religious in nature. It was carried out for the express purpose of explaining the essence of Mahāyāna Buddhism in a new country. The value of this labor was not monetary but expressed in relationship to the project's foundation-building promise. From this first creative act, the dharma would grow. At the same time, this labor overlaps with the domestic. It is happening in the Imamuras' home. And one can imagine who was most likely responsible for serving the celebratory pie à la mode that October night and the values associated with that act of hospitality. (Spoiler: it was most likely Jane.)

Creative acts of labor are generative, bringing into existence shared social realities. Jane Imamura's acts of hospitality and the translation (without publication) of the sutras are generative as well. As we saw in the previous chapter, the creative labor of building and maintaining the Berkeley Temple, the publication of the *Bussei*, the organization of the study groups, and the local and international networks created by Japanese American Jōdo Shinshū Buddhists may be understood collectively as religious infrastructure. This infrastructure is, in turn, possibility-making in that it attends to its own raison d'être (religious services, community support, and so on) while also allowing for other work, other projects, to come into being. In creating a place, a religious home, to support a translation project, the sutras are explained for the first time on American soil. In allowing an eclectic group of poets, artists, scholars, and philosophers to "hang around" the temple, other projects came into being.[54] Symposia created a space for an eccentric philosopher (Watts) to give presentations and lectures to an interested public. The *bōmori* played chauffeur for a traveling scholar (Suzuki), enabling him to attend to his writing without worry. Enthusiastic young converts (Snyder and Whalen) came into contact with practicing Buddhists in the flesh and were encouraged in both their Buddhist and artistic pursuits. And young Nisei artists struggling with their conflicted American identities (Kashiwagi) were supported and found comfort in community. The labor of building the Berkeley Buddhist Temple—both the physical building and the broader community, a place for specifically Jōdo Shinshū activities but also one that actively invited a diversity of persons and perspectives—was generative not just of the community itself but also of the future possibility of Buddhism in America. Religious infrastructure is thus necessary for the spread and popularization of Buddhism in the latter half of the twentieth century.

This popularization can also be read as the creation of a shared social world. As discussed here, through the processes of presentation, representation, and repetition a canon is formed, one that defines the genre category of American Buddhism. This genre category became so taken for granted in form and meaning that in 1991, in her editorial for the second edition of *Tricycle: The Buddhist Review*, Helen Tworkov could state that, so far, Asian Americans "have not figured prominently in the development of something called American Buddhism." In the thirty years since she made this claim, seemingly very little has changed.

The context within which Tworkov made her remark was in response to a "growing number of voices . . . concerned with the shape of American Buddhism, concerned with arbitrating which interpretations seem appropriate for this society and which may be better left behind in Asia."[55] In this discourse, she notes, the most vocal spokespeople had been "almost exclusively, educated members of the white middle class." Had she stopped there, her comment would have been a curious historical anomaly. I suspect I would have brought it up earlier in this chapter as an example of the framing of American Buddhism, not unlike how Alan Watts was set up as the foremost proponent of Zen in America. Unfortunately, Tworkov did not stop there; she followed up this observation with her refrain that Asian American Buddhists had not also been spokespeople. And this comment set off three of decades of debate about the nature and character of American Buddhism within the pages of both Buddhist magazines and academic journals.

Most notable in this regard was Charles Prebish's 1993 article "Two Buddhisms Reconsidered." One could read this essay as little more than a defense of typologies in general, especially for scholars of religion charting the acculturation of Buddhism in its latest cultural contexts. Underlying Prebish's argument, however, are two unvoiced assumptions: first, a presumption that acculturation is a naturally appropriate frame for understanding Buddhist development in America; and, second, that all of this infighting across different Buddhist traditions is necessarily a bad thing. To the first point, uncritical acceptance of acculturation as a frame risks replicating Orientalist concerns for purity as what comes under study is not so much cultural practices in their present contexts as how those practices have diverged from their origins.[56] Moreover, in the American context, such narratives often become subsumed under the larger narrative of the melting pot, whereby, once in America, all cultural difference is reduced to a hegemonic sameness. As we discussed in Chapter 3, some Nisei offer a different metaphor, that of a symphony, and suggest that once they are allowed to join the orchestra, the music necessarily changes. We can no longer assume we are all basically the same once our differences are revealed. Which brings us to the second point: can't we all just get along? Prebish ends his essay by championing ecumenicism as "provid[ing] hope and potential [that the] 'Two Buddhisms in America' [will] coalesce, [and] grow and mature into an 'American Buddhism,' valorizing the notion that, in Helen Tworkov's words, 'There is no one way to be a Buddhist.'"[57]

It might seem counterintuitive for me to argue against this point, to argue against the idealistic notion that we might all get along in our diversity and difference. To be clear, in principle, I don't disagree with the idea. However, this is not the most interesting part of Prebish's essay. The most interesting part begins on the first page, when he states that in his original research he argued that "there had been two *completely distinct lines* of development in American Buddhism."[58] And a few pages later, he reprints selections from a rebuttal to Tworkov's editorial written by Ryo Imamura, the Imamuras' youngest son. In his letter, Imamura states: "It was my American-born parents and their generation who courageously and diligently fostered the growth of American Buddhism" and "who welcomed countless white Americans into our temples, introduced them to the

Dharma, and often assisted them to initiate their own Sanghas when they felt un-comfortable practicing with us."[59]

The logic of the "two Buddhisms" typology rests, as Prebish originally argued, on the assumption that there have been two *distinct* lines of development for American Buddhism—the two streams I discussed in this book's introduction. Imamura's letter complicates this assumption by drawing our attention to, as Masatsugu has shown, the early history of American Buddhism, which was more "fluid" than we usually suppose, marked by "cross-cultural exchanges between ethnic and convert Buddhists."[60] I do not raise this point to criticize Prebish (and he was hardly alone in asserting variations on the "two Buddhisms" theme); I raise this point in the spirit of this book's ongoing project to ask, *what if?* What if, rather than writing an article that argues for the utility of typologies and laments Buddhists' inability to behave nicely toward one another, Prebish had instead argued that the central logic underlying the "two Buddhisms" typology is flawed? Not flawed because of systemic racism, nor because typologies are themselves inherently arbitrary, but flawed because these two streams were not, at least originally, *distinct*.[61] What other types of research might have emerged in the subfield? Instead, for the last thirty years we have been collectively arguing for or against different classificatory systems or making moral claims about individuals, casting a pall over the subfield.[62]

The consequences of this are, to my mind, twofold. First, to the extent that the "two Buddhisms" typology and debate about the typology have persisted, been repeated, been represented fairly or unfairly over and over again, it functions in much the same way as the repetition, collection, and canonization of certain individuals, texts, and artworks that constitute the genres of both Buddhist art and American Buddhism. Much as the mainstream American press could not get enough of D. T. Suzuki and Alan Watts in the 1950s, repeatedly presenting their images to Americans as the faces of Zen, we scholars cannot seem to get enough of this typology and debates about it. And as we continue to argue over it, the typology itself has become a defining feature of American Buddhism, an in-tegral part of its shared social imaginary.[63] "Two Buddhisms" is part of our tradi-tion now, and American Buddhism is simply taken for granted as divided along the racial line of "ethnic" and "white" Buddhists. Second, and more importantly given the subject of this book, the debate works subtly to reinforce the exclusion of Asian American Buddhists from our shared history and scholarly studies. To put it plainly, rather than discussing the content of an Asian American's first-person testimony (Ryo Imamura's letter), we have collectively spent thirty years telling a white woman she was wrong (Helen Tworkov's editorial). This rhetor-ical move foregrounds the white Buddhist perspective and, ironically, reinforces the claim that the spokespeople for American Buddhism are "educated members of the white middle class."

What if? What if we simply stopped having this conversation?[64]

It is worth noting that Ryo Imamura's letter, which Prebish quoted in part, was actually written to the editorial board of *Tricycle* back in 1992. Imamura requested that they publish the letter unedited and in its entirety; the editors declined. Gary Snyder happened to be on the *Tricycle* advisory board at the time; he resigned in protest over that decision. The letter was eventually published in full on the website of the Buddhist Peace Fellowship in 2017. Ryo Imamura had been one of the original founders of the organization, but it took a younger generation of Asian American Buddhist activists to get the whole letter published and presented within the context of a lineage of Asian American Buddhist resistance to exclusion and misrepresentation. Funie Hsu says in her essay introducing the letter that though she does not agree with everything Imamura wrote, "being able to access and read these thoughts from a fellow Asian American raised in the Buddhist tradition makes possible the very opportunity to disagree and be in conversation. It makes community possible, and for Asian American Buddhists, such pan-sectarian, sacred spaces are very much needed."[65]

Given the subject of this book—young Asian American Buddhists at midcentury—it is worth reflecting on more recent scholarship on and advocacy by young American Buddhists. There is an interesting bit of symmetry between one of the contributors to the *Bussei* discussed in this book and one of Chenxing Han's interviewees in her *Be the Refuge: Raising the Voices of Asian American Buddhists*. In her interview with Landon, a young Japanese American Shin Buddhist, Han notes that he "was hardly an enthusiastic youth member of his church. He readily admits he didn't care about Buddhism."[66] During an online symposium in November 2020, Sei Shohara—whom we met in Chapter 2 via his essays on Buddhism and science in the 1950s—was interviewed by a young member of his current BCA community in Southern California. He recalled that when he first enrolled at UC Berkeley in 1948, he thought he was finally getting away from the Buddhist church his parents kept pressuring him to attend.[67] Instead, however, his parents arranged for him to stay with Shinobu Matsuura; as a result, he became active in the Berkeley Temple and, like Landon, developed a "strong base in Buddhism" that has served him to the present.

As a matter of full disclosure, I should note that Chenxing Han was a student of mine, and I oversaw her master's thesis, from which *Be the Refuge* grew.[68] In revising her thesis for publication, Han originally hoped to find an academic or university press. I must admit I am glad that book never materialized; what did is superior. *Be the Refuge* is personal, weaves together the academic and the experiential, and is far more reflective of the reality most of us inhabit—a messy and complicated reality filled with real persons, not mere "subjects" of a detached intellectual project. As I have argued elsewhere, Buddhist studies scholars are implicated in the Buddhist tradition regardless of our personal identification as

162 THE MAKING OF AMERICAN BUDDHISM

Buddhists or not.[69] This relationship calls into question the very possibility of a truly "objective" scholarship. But I would suggest that this is perhaps the wrong question; rather than asking whether or not objective scholarship is possible, let us ask instead why we value it more. Han's work blurs the boundaries of academic disciplines, complicates received theoretical frameworks, and calls into question the assumed superior value that a traditional academic monograph has over the personal, the subjective.

In my reading of Han's work—as well as other scholarly work covered here, the mediated representations of persons and art that co-create the genres of Buddhist literature and American Buddhism, and the messy and complicated realities in which we live—I am once again drawn to the work of Lisa Lowe. In *Immigrant Acts*, Lowe complicates readings of historical documents, legal testimony, and literary works from within the limiting boundaries of academic disciplines. She argues that of equal importance to the contexts within which history is recorded is "the way we read, receive, and disseminate" history. Lowe "seeks to understand Asian American cultural production critically and broadly and to interpret the interconnections between testimony, personal narrative, oral history, literature, film, visual arts, and other cultural forms as sites through which subject, community, and struggle are signified and mediated. While specifying the differences between forms, this understanding of cultural production troubles both the strictly empirical foundations of social science and the universalizing tendencies of aesthetic discourse."[70] Disciplinary framings of our collective past predetermine not only how texts are read but also which texts should be read in the first place. To draw again on Graeber, values bring the world into being, and our field has tended to value some texts and some persons more than others. The field of American Buddhism studies has been preoccupied with locating the "firsts" and the "pioneers." Studies of Buddhist modernism are obsessed with the question of "what happened" and locating the site and cause for the rupture between an idealized traditional past and a corrupted modern present. Pushing back against these disciplinary frames allows us to draw from a wider collection of sources, which in turn reveals a more complex but ultimately more truthful view of American Buddhism's origin story. In this version, rather than foregrounding the work of charismatic missionaries and eccentric converts, we can lift up the invisibilized labor of the Japanese American Jōdo Shinshū Buddhists who made possible American Buddhism.

Conclusion

As All Things Go

"An Illustrious Past; a Promising Future"

In 1954, the Berkeley Buddhist community broke ground on its ambitious building project. Whereas the final design of the new temple building and Study Center did not look exactly like the architectural plans published in the 1954 *Bussei*, the general design was there. As we saw in Chapter 4, the new Berkeley Buddhist Temple, officially dedicated in 1956 with the installation of the Amida statue brought from Japan by Shinobu Matsuura, is a classic example of midcentury modern architecture. The *hondō* is a sparse and open space with exposed wood beams, concrete walls, and a minimalist *naijin*. Whereas the original plans included a larger complex than what was eventually constructed, there remains space for a library, classrooms used by the temple's dharma school, and a large social hall for events, the annual bazaar fundraiser, and of course *ōbon*, which spills out of the temple into Channing Street every summer.

This new construction, however, brought with it a loss. The boys' dorm, Jichiryo, was demolished. An uncredited essay from the 1954 *Bussei* begins: "As all things go, so must the 'Jichiryo.' The wooden building which defied the changes of time and surroundings and displayed so proudly her ornate curlicues and which withstood the enthusiastic slamming doors and bouncing feet, will finally succumb and disintegrate to make way for progress."[1] The essay details memories of past and current residents and visitors to the dorm: the Matsuuras and the Imamuras; Taitetsu Unno and his younger brother Tetsuo; Kimi Yonemura Hisatsune and Hitoshi Tsufura. "Yes [the dorm] will pass on with the names that passed through. And yet, will it all be gone?" the anonymous author asks.

> Certainly as in all else, there lives something eternal within this transiency. This Sangha of living and laughing together, helping one another, cannot be measured by time or place. Every happiness and anxiety born in the old Dorm have left a mark upon time which breathes with this infinity.
>
> It is not with sadness but with warmth that we say "Farewell" to Jichiryo. The next Dorm, wherever and whenever it may come, shall live in the same unchanging Sangha.[2]

The Making of American Buddhism. Scott A. Mitchell, Oxford University Press. © Oxford University Press 2023.
DOI: 10.1093/oso/9780197641569.003.0007

Figure 6.1 "An Illustrious Past," *Berkeley Bussei*, 1954; photo montage of past events held at the Berkeley Temple, including the arrival of Lama Tada, center image middle row.

The construction of the new temple undeniably changed the community, and yet, as the *Bussei* author here reminds us, within this change was the constancy of the sangha itself. Over the ensuing decades, while some educational and propagational programs at the Berkeley Buddhist Temple continued, others came and went, moved to other locations, ceased altogether, or inspired new

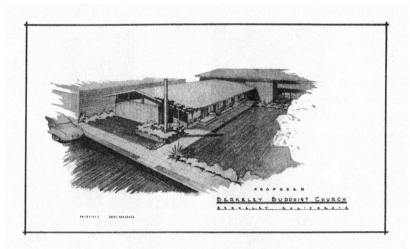

A Promising Future

After 30 years of service, the brown shingled building on 2121 Channing Way will

make room for the new $50,000 structure shown above.

Standing on her record of constant hospitality and ever rising standards, the

Berkeley Buddhist Church will be able to accumulate a sum sufficient to start the

building project on the 1st day of July, 1954.

Within this new building will be transplanted the tradition of the Berkeley YBA:a

warm and inspiring atmosphere conducive to the elevation of active minds and en-

lightened leadership for not only the Buddhist Churches but for our whole social

makeup.

Included in the original plans,but presently postponed for a later project,is the

$20,000 dormitory to some day continue the "living in true Sangha" on a more ade-

quate scale.

Figure 6.2 "A Promising Future," *Berkeley Bussei*, 1954; a one-page summary of the plans to rebuild the temple.

projects elsewhere. For a time in the late 1950s, the Honganji sponsored a BCA Ministerial Training Center in Kyoto, which included a dormitory for American-born students studying Buddhism and preparing for ordination.[3] This project overlapped with the activities in Berkeley to the extent that several students who participated in the BCA Study Center or published in the *Berkeley Bussei* were among those who studied at the Kyoto center. However, by 1959 the Kyoto center was closed and officially moved to the United States—specifically the Berkeley Temple, which once again became the center of Buddhist education for American-born ministerial aspirants.[4]

Nevertheless, the *Bussei* did cease publication in 1960, with a final volume that had considerably fewer essays than poems written by a smaller overall number of authors than previous editions. Why did the *Bussei* come to an end while, at the same time, other temple projects continued? On this question, we can only speculate. Several interrelated factors were likely the cause. First and foremost, it is important to remember that the *Bussei* was always a project of the *Young* Buddhist Association, and the reality is that none of us are young forever. Following the closure of the dorm, even though a new one was opened and there was still a sizable and active YBA at the Berkeley Temple, it is likely that the core group of writers, thinkers, and leaders who initiated the project began to drift away from the temple as they graduated from college, finished graduate programs, married, began careers, and in many cases left the Bay Area altogether. Whereas new members of the group certainly would have replaced those who aged out, they may have simply had other priorities or other interests.

Relatedly, in 1957 the Buddhist Churches of America's headquarters in San Francisco began publishing a monthly newsletter, *The American Buddhist.* Several writers and editors of the *Berkeley Bussei* were involved with this new publication, including Hiroshi Kashiwagi. At least initially, there were many similarities between the two publications. Early editions of *The American Buddhist* include essays on Buddhism and psychology, Buddhist philosophy, editorials taking specific political stances on both local elections and national events, and reviews and reflections on Buddhist literature and art. However, as the official publication of a growing national organization, the newsletter also published news and updates from BCA headquarters, reports from the BCA's annual national council meeting, and so forth. And unlike the *Bussei*, it was a monthly publication. It is likely that the persons who were dividing their time between *The American Buddhist* and the *Bussei* gradually shifted their focus to the former.

On a more speculative note, as the North American Shin Buddhist community entered the 1960s, from such publications as *The American Buddhist* one gets the sense that the community has grown up. The BCA theme for 1963 was "Our Family Worships Daily Before the Family Shrine," and in 1964 it was "Our Family Attends Church Regularly."[5] A related article in the January 1964 edition of *The American Buddhist* defines "the Buddhist family" as "the cradle of all Buddhist values." These include living in the "wisdom and compassion of Amida Buddha," worshiping daily at the home altar, attending and supporting the church, dignity, education, and compassion toward all persons.[6] Arguably, this focus on the family, so to speak, could be read as a larger demographic shift within the community whereby the Nisei generation was generally reaching middle age and enjoying the economic successes of the post–New Deal and Eisenhower era. In other words, American Shin Buddhism had become middle-class. In this new context, whereas one still finds in *The American Buddhist* explicit political positions—such as denouncements of increasing anti-Buddhist violence in Southeast Asia and arguments against discriminative housing laws in California—more broadly it appears that the work Nisei Buddhists did in the immediate postwar years had paid off.[7] Buddhism had become American, and in this way publications such as the *Bussei*, which argued consistently and vocally for the creation of American Buddhism, were simply no longer necessary. The project was a success.

Finally, the role of the Imamuras cannot be overstated. In 1958, for a variety of reasons, the Imamura family moved off the temple grounds into a new home elsewhere in Berkeley. For a time, Kanmo Imamura was in Japan tending to the needs of his ancestral temple in Fukui. Rev. Masami Fujitani became the resident minister. Jane Imamura continued to direct the Berkeley choir; however, she was no longer the *bōmori* and found part-time work at UC Berkeley's Music Department, where she became a well-known figure, creating a sense of community among the faculty and students.[8] Upon his return from Japan, Kanmo Imamura did not return to the ministry but instead went back to the anthropology museum at the university, and, briefly, the family had a bit of rest following seventeen years of leading and growing the Berkeley Buddhist community. Whereas originally Fujitani had been assigned as both the resident minister of the temple and director of the study classes, by 1963 it was clear that these were too many responsibilities for one person. Thus, Kanmo Imamura was once again asked to lead the BCA Study Center. In 1966 the BCA secured the purchase of a new building for the center, which was renamed and incorporated with the State of California as the Institute of Buddhist Studies, the first Buddhist graduate school and seminary in the United States. Imamura oversaw this transition and the Institute until 1967, when he was asked to serve as bishop of the Honpa Hongwanji Mission of Hawai'i, the position his father had held some thirty years earlier. While in Hawai'i, the Imamuras once again dedicated themselves to the growth of the dharma in the West and once again established an educational center, this time in Honolulu. Ryo Imamura became the center's first director. By the mid-1970s, Kanmo's health was declining, the family returned to Berkeley, and he was diagnosed with Parkinson's disease. Kanmo Imamura passed away in 1986, followed by Jane some twenty-five years later. In her later years, their long-time family friend and supporter Hitoshi Tsufura continued to look after Jane at her Berkeley home.

Despite the changes to the community that followed in the wake of the rebuilding project, and despite the comings and goings of various persons who were responsible for producing the *Bussei* and running the study classes, the work of the Berkeley sangha continued. More than that, American Buddhism continued. As we saw in the previous chapter, persons such as Alan Watts and Gary Snyder would become increasingly associated with Buddhism in the later 1950s. Other Japanese Buddhist priests and missionaries such as Shunryu Suzuki would come to America at a time when this rising popularity provided them opportunities to further promote Buddhism beyond the ethnic Japanese community. And following changes to immigration laws in the mid-1960s and as a result of American military involvement in Southeast Asia, by the 1980s America's Buddhist population would grow and diversify in ways the young Nisei traversing the pan-Pacific Buddhist world of the 1950s could have hardly imagined. But we would do well to recall that these encounters, the successes of popularizers and proselytizers, were made possible in part by the labor of a previous generation of American Jōdo Shinshū Buddhists who built networks, communities, and infrastructure—labor that is rarely seen, seldom valued, but necessary for the "promising future" predicted by the *Berkeley Bussei* at midcentury.

The Making of American Buddhist Studies

Having reminded the reader that the Study Center would eventually transform into the Institute of Buddhist Studies—the institute at which I am employed— now is a good time to return to the question of my relationship to this book's subject, first mentioned in the introduction. The reader may be justified in asking if my location as an "insider" to this community compromises my scholarly objectivity. However, in the spirit of this book's project of interrogating unhelpful dichotomies, I want to critique the binaries of insider/outsider or subjective/ objective scholarship. I suggest that my connection to my subject is not at all unique; in some way or another, we are all connected to the Berkeley Buddhist Temple.

In this book, I have argued that Issei missionaries and their Nisei children were responsible for building religious infrastructure. Ensconced within the context of the early twentieth century, this project was necessarily of its time and conducted in relationship to larger cultural and political currents. Modernity played a key role in how these missionaries understood their specific sectarian tradition and its relationship to the broader Buddhist world, as well as the burgeoning field of academic Buddhist studies in Europe and America. Once having crossed the Pacific, in addition to supporting immigrant communities navigating the fractured terrain of American racial politics, they found ways to promote Buddhism not only within the community but to curious outsiders as well. This was to be expected; they were *missionaries* after all. Their children, Nisei American Buddhists, carried on this work, though in their own way and in response to the trauma of religious and racial discrimination before, during, and after the camps. To make claim to an unapologetically American Buddhist identity was not merely a personal choice nor even a communal one—it was to hold America accountable to its ideals of religious and cultural pluralism. These projects, this collective labor, created the religious infrastructure that attracted non-Japanese to the community and helped support the spread and populari-zation of Buddhism into the latter half of the twentieth century. Such labor is possibility-making; it made possible American Buddhism itself. Such labor also made possible academic Buddhist studies. Of course, the academic study of Buddhism predates the publication of the *Berkeley Bussei* by a century or more; after all, "Buddhist Studies is a product of the Enlightenment and European co-lonialism," a project that began with the work of figures such as Eugène Burnouf and other Orientalists located mainly in Europe or colonial Asia, as discussed in this book's introduction.[9] So I am not making the argument that Nisei Buddhists in the United States are responsible for making Buddhist studies possible in the same way that they are for making American Buddhism possible. What I am arguing is that there is a relationship, a series of interconnections and points of contact, between North American Buddhist studies and communities of practice inclusive of the Berkeley Shin Buddhist community of the 1950s.

In his 2020 presidential address, "The Study of Buddhism and the AAR," José Cabezón discusses the history of North American Buddhist Studies through aca-demic publishing as well as participation at the annual meeting of the American Academy of Religion. Whereas "North American buddhologists were instru-mental in founding or expanding Asian language programs in North American Universities in the 1930s and 1940s," Cabezón notes that "the beginnings of North American buddhology really dates to the 1960s."[10] He claims that the flourishing of Buddhist studies at this time was the result, in part, of the Cold War and the U.S. government's funding of area studies programs to study Asian cultures as well as the counterculture more generally, to say nothing of the number of per-sons studying or serving in Japan in the postwar period who became interested in Buddhism as a result. These are certainly important developments for the his-tory of our field. But it is equally important to keep in mind their larger national and transnational contexts, many of which we have covered in the preceding five chapters, namely: the establishment of Buddhist communities of practice by Japanese immigrants and their children in North America; the U.S.-led occu-pation of Japan that allowed not just white Americans but also Nisei American Buddhists to live and work in Asia in the postwar period; the development of pan-Pacific Buddhist networks that further allowed for transnational movement and exchange; and anti-communist Buddhist organizations that were, at times, clandestinely backed by the United States. Budding buddhologists and Nisei American Buddhists both benefited from these connections, networks, and intellectual exchanges, and both groups participated in the emergence of Buddhist studies in North America from the 1950s onward.

As but one example of the connections between the nascent field of North American Buddhist studies and Buddhist networks, I turn to Charles Prebish's autobiography in his "Generations of Buddhist Studies" project. Prebish discusses his first encounters with his mentor, Richard Robinson, in the 1960s, when he was beginning his own academic career. He notes that at the time there were only a handful of graduate programs in the United States focused on Buddhism, and that the University of Wisconsin with Robinson and Harvard with Masatoshi Nagatomi were the centers of North American Buddhist studies. He goes on:

> However, what most people never knew was that the connection between Robinson and Nagatomi went far beyond their students. Both had a deep association with Jōdo Shinshū Buddhism in Southern Alberta, Canada. Masatoshi Nagatomi's father, Shinjo Nagatomi had been the first resident minister of the Raymond Buddhist Church, arriving on 4 June 1930. . . . Shinjo Nagatomi was succeeded by Yutetsu Kawamura in 1934, and Richard Robinson learned some of his very first Buddhist lessons from Reverend Kawamura.[11]

The younger Nagatomi, of course, went on to train generations of Buddhist scholars at Harvard, including Duncan Ryūken Williams (one of my mentors), a connection that inspired Williams's own telling of American Buddhist history in *American Sutra*. Williams uncovered the history of Buddhism in World War II incarceration camps as a result of collecting the personal effects of Nagatomi and finding dharma talks written in the camps by his father.[12] Nagatomi had a long and productive career at Harvard, serving as the university's first professor of Buddhist studies and training a generation of Buddhist studies scholars including Paula Arai, Jan Nattier, and many others. In 2008, the Nagatomi family donated a selection of his personal library to the Institute of Buddhist Studies.

Leslie Kawamura (1935–2011), Yutetsu Kawamura's son, had his own successful academic career. Kawamura earned graduate degrees at both Ryukoku and Kyoto Universities as well as a doctorate at the University of Saskatchewan, studying under Herbert Guenther. His academic specialty was in Yogācāra studies, and he taught at the University of Calgary for over three decades. This long career helped to establish Buddhist studies in Canada more generally, and Kawamura went on to train dozens of students, many of whom contributed to a Festschrift in his honor edited by Sarah Haynes and Michelle Sorensen.[13] Kawamura also spent time in Berkeley studying and teaching for the BCA Study

Center and, later in his career, teaching at the Nyingma Center, where he first met Richard Payne (another of my mentors), then doing his own graduate work.[14] Along with George Bond, Collett Cox, and Charles Prebish, Kawamura was instrumental in establishing the Buddhism Unit at the American Academy of Religion, which remains, to this day, one of the primary academic homes of Buddhist studies scholars. All the while, Kawamura served the Canadian Shin community as a priest in Alberta and, later in his life, as a director of the Living Dharma Centre to promote scholarship on Shin Buddhism.[15]

Taitetsu Unno has also made numerous appearances in this volume. In addition to serving as the *Bussei* editor in 1950 and 1951, he contributed essays and translations to virtually every volume through 1957. During most of this time, Unno was studying at Tokyo University. Upon returning to the United States, he spent forty years teaching, first at the University of Illinois at Urbana-Champaign and then at Smith College, where he served as the Jill Ker Conway Professor of World Religions. At Smith, Unno was one of only a handful of Buddhist studies scholars in the area, and he maintained connections with a range of other scholars while encouraging students, such as Jeff Wilson, to pursue careers in Buddhist studies—as well as his son, Mark Unno, who has had his own successful academic career.[16] Unno was also heavily involved with the American Buddhist Academy at the New York Buddhist Church, teaching classes, and editing the center's publication series which included the republication of D. T. Suzuki's lecture series mentioned in Chapter 4. In addition to his academic career, Unno was a lone source for Shin Buddhist practice in New England; along with his wife, Alice (also an ordained Shin Buddhist minster), they held space for Buddhists in the area at a distance from more established centers and sanghas, created community, performed weddings and funerals, and inspired scholars and practitioners alike.[17]

And of course we would be remiss not to return to Yehan Numata. As discussed in Chapter 4, Numata spent his younger years in Berkeley promoting Buddhism clandestinely via "Oriental culture" in the first iteration of *Pacific World*. After returning to Japan and his business success with the Mitutoyo Corporation, Numata founded Bukkyō Dendō Kyōkai, or the Society for the Promotion of Buddhism, in 1965. Since that time, the BDK/Numata Foundation has funded dozens of professorial chairs, programs, publications, awards, and scholarships, including, among others, professorial chairs or Buddhist studies programs at the University of California campuses at Berkeley and Los Angeles, Harvard University, McGill University, the University of Oxford, and the University of Vienna; the Toshihide Numata Book Award in Buddhism (initiated by Numata's son); fellowships for the study of Buddhism in Japan (funding that has supported untold numbers of scholarly projects); and the continuing publication of *Pacific World*, now in its fourth series and published by the Institute of Buddhist Studies.

Such programs have made possible generations of scholarship and contributed to the spread of academic Buddhist studies in North America and Europe.[18]

As discussed in Chapter 5, Alex Wayman spent time at the Berkeley Temple and was a member of the Advanced Study Group. A host of other scholars from both Japan and America were connected in some way to the Berkeley Temple, giving lectures for the study classes or at symposia, and contributing to the *Bussei*. As we have seen, Tokan Tada, D. T. Suzuki, and Hajime Nakamura all made appearances in this book. Frederic Spiegelberg, professor at Stanford University and one of the founders of the Academy of Asian Studies, taught for the Advanced Study Class, as did Sanskritist Glen Grosjean. Wayman not only was a student but also led some of the classes, as did Gary Snyder. Other students included Dennis Hirota, who would later go on to a successful career as a noted scholar of Shin Buddhism and translator of the *Kyōgyōshinshō*, and Seigen Yamaoka, who would later be one of the Buddhist Churches of America's longest-serving bishops. Such connections and interconnections point to the various ways that the Berkeley Temple and American Shin Buddhists generally have been engaged with, if not directly supported, academic Buddhist studies for at least a century. And, of course, we cannot overlook Alan Watts.

Whereas Watts's scholarly contributions have been dismissed as lacking rigor or for being inaccurate or idiosyncratic, one cannot deny the pull he has even to this day as something of a "gateway drug" to the study of Asian religions and philosophy. As David Smith tells it:

> His books, lectures, and radio broadcasts reached hundreds of thousands. Even some of his harshest detractors acknowledge his role as an awakener or precursor to a spiritual or scholarly engagement with Buddhism. Edward Conze, for example, writing in the 1970s, noted that "most of my American students first became interested in Buddhism through Alan Watts. It is true that they had to unlearn most of what they had learnt. It is equally true that he put out the net that caught them in the first place." Although the current climate of academic opinion makes most readers reluctant to admit that they ever took him seriously, his after-image and influence have been remarkably persistent.[19]

Regardless of how one feels about Watts's work or the quality of his scholarship, he functions as a means by which individuals first encounter Buddhism and are thus inspired to continue their (sometimes more serious) study. We should not be so quick to discount this effect. In the ongoing spirit of this book, once again, let us ask, *what if?* Surely, many of us have had a student (or were once themselves a student) who will admit that their first taste of Buddhism came by way of Alan Watts. What if that connection had never been made? How might the trajectory of that student's life been altered? Where might they find themselves at present? This playful and speculative project of "what if" is not incidental. It is in this act of imaginative play that we see alternative realities and can come to appreciate the full impact of the many lives and many persons who have made the present possible.

In some way, this speculative project is not dissimilar to Donald Lopez's lineage project, discussed in Chapter 2. In his *A Modern Buddhist Bible*, we will recall, Lopez notes that the thirty-one people he has assembled constitute a lineage in two respects: first, they are all basically saying the same thing, and, second, they have some connection to one another. I call this a "speculative" project because these persons are not, in fact, a lineage. That is, none of them saw themselves as members of a lineage any more than the Seven Pure Land Masters as conceived of by Shinran understood themselves as part of a lineage. Rather, it is only after the fact, by a third party, that they are collected in this way as a heuristic to help those in the present understand their relationship to the past. However, lineage construction projects are necessarily authentication projects. That is, one creates a lineage to authenticate some present condition by way of an appeal to the (imagined) past. In claiming that one's teacher received dharma transmission from a lineage of past Zen teachers who trace their transmission back to Bodhidharma and to the Buddha himself, one is authenticating oneself and one's tradition. Similarly, in constructing a lineage of Buddhist moderns, if nothing else Lopez is claiming that these persons are *authentically* modern. And by extension, those not included on the list—Asian Americans generally, American Shin Buddhists specifically—are *not authentically* modern. As detailed in this book, however, the contributors to the *Berkeley Bussei* both were acquainted with many of the figures in Lopez's lineage and presented Buddhism in similarly modern ways. Thus, if scholars are going to engage in lineage construction projects, American Shin Buddhists are rightly included.

To be clear, however, I am not arguing that scholars should engage in lineage construction projects. Rather, I am calling for better metaphors and narratives to describe the shared history of American Buddhism and academic Buddhist studies. Lineages necessarily include and exclude. American Shin Buddhists are excluded from Lopez's lineage; so too are Buddhist studies scholars. As Lopez, Cabezón, and others show, academic Buddhist studies emerged within the context of colonialism, the same source as Buddhist modernism.[20] For this reason the lineage of Buddhist moderns cannot adequately tell the story of American Buddhism's development, nor does it account for academic Buddhist studies' participation in that story. Similarly, the Buddhist modernism paradigm, as Quli calls it, is a limiting narrative, one that relies on a particularly post-Enlightenment rhetoric of rupture and the myth of disenchantment.[21] As discussed in Chapter 2, the lineage of Buddhist moderns is a cast of characters upon whom either praise or blame is laid for making Buddhism modern and/or bringing it to the West.

As Pema McLaughlin has argued, this praise/blame is laid by both scholars and Buddhists alike, as they occupy the same "textual space," hold many of the same assumptions about religion, and deploy modernism normatively to authenticate different forms of Buddhism and Buddhists.[22] In charting the connections between North American Shin Buddhists and North American Buddhist studies, I am calling our attention to the shared history of and ongoing interconnection between communities of practice and scholarship. I make this move not to build a more inclusive lineage but to call into question the opposition of objective and subjective positionalities and to challenge us to think in new and creative ways about our field and shared history. I trust that the reader will recognize their relationship to some of the names, publications, institutions, and places listed here that create a web of connections that confound the insider/outsider dichotomy.

A lineage project, one that authenticates lines of transmission, ordinarily relies on connections between individuals—a teacher passing wisdom on to their student and the student, in turn, passing that wisdom on to their own. Such connections are important, to be sure, but can only tell a part of the story. In addition to a sole teacher, mentor, or advisor, a student is supported by larger networks and webs of connections that make their work possible—friends, colleagues, parents, siblings, children, spouses, lovers, even rivals. It is the sum total of this labor and love that makes things possible. And in the case of the field of Buddhist studies, we may add to the list Buddhism and Buddhists. The generative labor that made possible American Buddhism, as discussed in this book, had consequences not just for the *practice* of Buddhism but for the *academic study* of Buddhism. As scholars, we benefit from the same labor that made possible Buddhism's popularity—the domestic, religious, and affective labor of North American Shin Buddhists.

This labor is generative. It brings the world into being. It is possibility-making. And to be clear, our labor as scholars is also generative. We too bring worlds into being. Indeed, the generative labor of American Buddhists and Buddhist scholars brings *Buddhism* into being, a shared and mutually sustaining project. That is, Buddhists and scholars (co-)create and (co-)recreate Buddhism through collective acts of labor. We have both the ability to change that discourse and a responsibility to the communities with which we share space. Beyond discourses of modernism, postmodernism, or even metamodermism, beyond the authenticating logics of lineage construction projects or unhelpful binaries, what metaphors or heuristics might we employ to describe the messy lived realities of our historical subjects? What metaphors might we employ to describe our own messy lives?

Regardless of how we answer these questions, we must acknowledge the collective debt we owe to the communities and persons we take as the subjects of our studies. Regardless of our personal identities as scholars, practitioners, or scholar-practitioners, we must acknowledge that we are not "outside" the tradition.[23] Whereas it has become passé to suggest that "Buddhism" is a scholarly invention, this way of framing history elides the active participations of Buddhists in its construction. As we continue to do the necessary and import work of critical self-reflection on the history (and future) of our field, when we do historiographies of Buddhist studies such as Cabezón's noted here, let us include practicing Buddhists within that history and self-reflection. The American Jōdo Shinshū Buddhists under study here did not predate academic Buddhist studies, but someone did. Buddhists are the makers not merely of Buddhist modernism but of Buddhist studies itself.

Epilogue: Our Narrative

> Now you were stirred by the moments that came and went because
> you had found a direction, a meaning in life. You felt rich and re-
> sponsible, yet the you that had been so prominent now receded in
> size and importance. You found a measure of peace and you felt
> strangely happy. And how different the world seemed, how full of
> wonder.[1]

This book is the culmination of several years of focused research and several
decades studying American and Jōdo Shinshū Buddhism, but the bulk of the
writing was done in 2020 and 2021. These years are blurred together in my
memory owing to the way the pandemic made time meaningless, each day
resembling the day before. Except, of course, for those days that stood out for
their incredible and at times literal darkness. We recall waking one October
morning to find the sun blacked out by wildfire smoke so thick it never truly
became day. We recall the deaths of a half dozen Asian women in Atlanta,
deaths brushed aside because the white murderer was merely having a "bad
day." We recall the deaths of yet more Black men and women at the hands of
the police, and the cruel absurdity of the former president clearing protesters
with tear gas so that he could stand lamely before a church, holding aloft a
borrowed Bible. We recall not working at all while watching his supporters
storm the Capitol live on C-SPAN. We recall the soaring words of Amanda
Gorman—"For there is always light, / if only we're brave enough to see it /
if only we're brave enough to be it"—and the hope they inspired despite the
fact that 2021 felt like little more than a continuation of 2020, with endless
Zoom meetings, social distancing, and cancelled travel plans; or as Theodor
Adorno might say, the repetitiveness of the continually same today. All the
while plugging away at a book about a history that seemed so removed from
the present.

History, of course, is always in the present, in the process of being told.
History is not just a collection of facts but emerges in the *telling*. As Natalie
Gummer argues, the work of the historian is fundamentally creative work. The
telling of history puts us into relationship with both the past and the future.
We are heirs to collective memories and traditions, narratives that are constitutive of our present space of experience; these, in turn, set the horizon of expectation, provide conceptual parameters for what is possible in the future.

We are living simultaneously in the past-present-future, and "the meaning and value of studying the past is surely its potential for challenging and potentially transforming present assumptions and future possibilities."[2] Gummer draws a connection between the presentation of time in the *Lotus Sutra* and the work of the historian in her discussion of the appearance of the long-dead, but simultaneously still living, Buddha Prabhūtaratna, whose appearance is proof of the sutra's power to effect the future enlightenment of those in the audience. "Is not this image quite illuminating of the writing of history?" she asks. "A history brings the past to life as past, but nonetheless grants it a form of present existence with potential vitality and agency."[3]

During the course of writing this book, our daughter turned ten. She has begun her own imaginative time travels, speculating on what her world will be like when she is an adult and asking us to tell her about what we were like when we were young. In this imaginative space, we realized that (climate willing) she has a good chance of seeing the twenty-second century. Her children certainly will, and through their connection to their grandparents, they will have a direct connection to the twentieth century. And because I cannot stop thinking about the past, I can tell them stories of the nineteenth. The past is in the present in the future.

The Jōdo Shinshū Buddhists at the heart of this book made possible the present. And we, in the now, are collectively making the future.

While the sun was blocked out by wildfires and our daughter attended impromptu Zoom grade school, I plugged away at this book. This book will, in the future, be a part of history. I call our attention to the conditions under which this book came to be because of my awareness that someday it, too, will be an artifact. Future scholars (climate willing) will note this book as part of the early twenty-first-century intellectual milieu. Perhaps someone will find it on their colleague's bookshelf as I happened upon the Waymans' *Śrīmālādevī* translation. Much as we can look back at Yemyō Imamura's *Democracy According to the Buddhist Viewpoint* and consider that he wrote this Shin Buddhist apologetic in the waning days of World War I, consider how this must have influenced his thinking, in the future we can look back at our present scholarship and reflect that it was written during a pandemic and an increasingly precarious global climate. These contexts shape how we think about the world, influence our read of the past, alter the historical narratives we construct. And, simultaneously, this scholarship is shaping the future. We are sowing the seeds for the next generation. Are we brave enough to see it?

Looking to the past, we can see the collective history Buddhists and Buddhist scholars have co-created, the world we have brought into being. Generative acts of labor and love brought the world of Buddhism and the world of Buddhist studies into being. As has been discussed at length in recent years, Buddhist studies—and academia generally—is in a period of crisis and change. The land-scape of higher education is trembling, both from its own weight as well as from an onslaught of forces seeking to undermine it, forces who, in a cynical bid to protect academic freedom from "woke activists," are laying waste to tenure, col-lective bargaining, and making it illegal to even discuss the latest bogeyman in conservatives' crosshairs—*critical race theory* (academic freedom be damned). It is easy to despair. It is easy to lay blame for these maladies at the feet of "the other," our own boogeymen of conservative fascists. And that's true, of course. But it is also true that reality is messy and our problems more complicated. There are forces beyond our control, to be sure, but we are also the makers, the co-creators, of the social worlds we inhabit. We are "rich and responsible," Kashiwagi reminds us (and I assume the "riches" he refers to are not material). We are re-sponsible for the world we have created. And our present actions (and inactions) are creating the future; we are responsible for that, too. We are responsible for creating the world our children will inherit. We are responsible for whether or not my daughter and her children will see the next century.

I referenced Adorno earlier but did not cite him. I will not cite him because this idea actually comes from the work of Melissa Curley and the Japanese anarchists, socialists, and Pure Land ne'er-do-wells under study in her book.[4] I reference her work so that I can invoke utopian thinking. Adorno's quip about the con-tinually same today was a lament that contemporary people had come to find utopian thinking passé. With all our imaginative needs met (or at least placated through television and, now, social media), we have lost our ability to imagine new ways of being. The criticism against utopian thinking is that it is naive, childish, and escapist. It does not deal with the world *as it is*. This is a wrong view. Utopian thinking always begins with the acknowledgment that the world as it is is not ideal. *And then it offers up an alternative*—the world as it should be. Utopian imaginings are at once a critique (deconstruction) and an act of gen-erative play (construction). Or, in the words of Joan Wallach Scott, "The aim of critique is to make things better."[5] In imagining a world that could be, we are free of the constraints of the world as it is. The challenge, of course, is in making this imagined utopia a reality. Is this even possible?

Curley's work—or, that is, her subjects'—suggests that the answer is yes, with limits of course. One of her many insights is the characterization of the early Shin community in Japan as an alternative social reality set against their eve-ryday one. Curley convincingly argues that premodern Shin thinkers consist-ently saw the Pure Land as at once thoroughly other and ever-present. We are done a disservice by assuming that our present distinction between transcend-ence and immanence had any meaning in the past. By conceptualizing the Pure Land as radically other, even utopian, when compared to this world while at the same time claiming that awakening is possible in the present, in this very body,

Buddhist thinkers are able to critique the world as it is and create communities in opposition to the status quo. "Shinshū communities organized in this way actively registered their opposition to a totalizing state system, constituting themselves as sites within which the laws that govern the real world were suspended."[6] This may not have upended the reality of social and political life in premodern Japan; it may not have unseated the ruling class; it was neither perfect nor, really, a utopia. But it was *good enough*. It at least made life easier for Jōdo Shinshū followers; it at least made a safe haven within an otherwise totalizing and totally oppressive reality.

The undercurrent of this book has been the persistent question *what if?* This is a question not just of the past but of the present and of the future. What if we deployed utopian thinking in our own lives? What if we tried to create our own micro-utopias? How might that change our day-to-day reality? What kind of future might we create? Even in our limited capacities within our academic departments or on editorial boards or in professional organizations—what if we behaved more humanely? What if we put into place policies and practices that reflected not the world as it is but the world as it should be? Even if only in our citation practices.

We need not do it alone. The building of a utopia is collective labor. Kashiwagi's narrative begins with a reflection on his youth, growing up in a central California farming town, negotiating his "Nisei" and "American" identities, which seemed wholly incommensurable. He rejects his "old man's religion," and even though he doesn't mention it in the *Bussei*, he has rejected his U.S. citizenship as well. But, after the war, he "picked up the broken pieces and began to rebuild." It is here that his narrative takes the abrupt shift to the second person. It is not "Kashiwagi" who picked up the pieces, but "you." It is not "Kashiwagi" who found a way to be American, to be thoroughly of Japanese culture, who "found a direction, a meaning in life"—it is "you." However, the "you that had been so prominent now receded in size and importance." Kashiwagi is using the second person not to speak to his audience but rather to draw them in, to move us away from individuality and to the collective. The individual is no longer at the center of the narrative. It is the community, the collective "we," that is responsible for this rebuilding. And in Kashiwagi's case, we know this collective includes both his Nisei Buddhist community and the support of civil rights attorney Wayne Collins. At Tule Lake, Kashiwagi and thousands of other Nisei gave up their U.S. citizenship; following the war, Collins sued the government, arguing that these renunciations were made under duress and thus were unconstitutional. Though the case dragged on until 1959, they eventually won, and the U.S. government restored full citizenship to Kashiwagi and nearly five thousand other Nisei Americans. In his memoir, Kashiwagi writes that in 1971 he sent Collins a letter thanking him "for all he did for me in restoring me as an American, making possible the life I enjoyed now. He sent me a letter in response that reveals so much of the character of this great man who as the agent of democracy worked hard and long to right the wrong that we had suffered. I value this letter more than anything I have."[7]

We are not mended by going it alone. We right the wrongs together. Such collective acts of generative labor will not be perfect. They may include the idiosyncrasies of Alan Watts. They will occasionally overlook the affective labor of Jane Imamura. They will, at times, fail utterly. But try we must. In the end, ask yourself: what if? Would not an imperfect and messy utopia be better than the world as it is?

Notes

Prologue: Kashiwagi's Narrative

1. Hiroshi Kashiwagi, "A Narrative," *Berkeley Bussei*, 1956, 38.
2. Hiroshi Kashiwagi, *Swimming in the American: A Memoir and Selected Writings* (San Mateo, CA: Asian American Curriculum Project, 2005), 33.
3. In 1943, the War Department and War Relocation Agency distributed a questionnaire to determine the loyalty and "Americanness" of Japanese American citizens illegally incarcerated in the camps. The questionnaire was then used as the basis for where to send those who were deemed "disloyal" or troublemakers.
4. Kashiwagi, "A Narrative," 39.
5. Kashiwagi, *Swimming in the American*, 176–178.
6. Kashiwagi, "A Narrative," 39.
7. Duncan Ryūken Williams, *American Sutra: A Story of Faith and Freedom in the Second World War* (Cambridge, MA: Harvard University Press, 2019), 11–13.

Introduction

1. "Harmony in Sangha," *Berkeley Bussei*, Spring 1941, n.p.
2. "Credit Lines," *Berkeley Bussei*, Spring 1941, n.p. Julius Goldwater (1908–2001), cousin of Arizona senator Barry Goldwater, was formally introduced to Buddhism in Hawai'i by Ernest Hunt and Yemyō Imamura. Here, "Credit Lines" describes Goldwater as the head of the "Buddhist Brotherhood," but he was also an ordained Jōdo Shinshū priest who served at a Los Angeles Shin temple for many years. Whereas he had a falling-out with the community in the postwar years, in 1941 the editors of the *Bussei* write that Goldwater "has done more than his share in spreading the faith of Buddhism among Caucasians. We are indeed fortunate to have such a prominent leader contribute his article to our Berkeley Bussei."
3. Julius Goldwater, "Our Future," *Berkeley Bussei*, Spring 1941, n.p.
4. See Wendy Cadge, *Heartwood: The First Generation of Theravada Buddhism in America* (Chicago: University of Chicago Press, 2005), 30. In discussing the development of convert/white American Theravada communities, Cadge notes Sharon Salzberg's reflection on the early days of the insight meditation movement: "The questions the teachers concerned themselves with in the early years . . . were about what it meant to take the Buddhist tradition, steeped in the imagery and metaphor of Asia, to try and find its unchanging essence, and then to express that essence in the imagery of a new time and place."

5. For more on "Mikadoism" as pretext for anti-Japanese animus, see Noriko Asato, *Teaching Mikadoism: The Attack on Japanese Language Schools in Hawaii, California, and Washington, 1919–1927* (Honolulu: University of Hawai'i Press, 2006); and Noriko Asato, "The Japanese Language School Controversy in Hawaii," in *Issei Buddhism in the Americas*, ed. Duncan Ryūken Williams and Tomoe Moriya (Urbana: University of Illinois Press, 2010), 45–64.

6. The term "Asian American" was not coined until the 1960s, and thus the Nisei authors under study here would not have self-identified as such. I use the term anachronistically here to draw our attention to the fact that "Nisei" was a marker of racial identity as much as it was a generational term.

7. See Lori Pierce, Paul Spickard, and David Yoo, "Japanese and Korean Migrations: Buddhist and Christian Communities in America, 1885–1945," in *Immigration and Religion in America: Comparative and Historical Perspectives*, ed. Richard D. Alba, Albert J. Raboteau, and Josh DeWind (New York: New York University Press, 2009), 106–134.

8. Kanmo Imamura, "A House for Our Hopes," *Berkeley Bussei*, 1952, n.p.

9. Kenneth K. Tanaka, "Issues of Ethnicity in the Buddhist Churches of America," in *American Buddhism: Methods and Findings in Recent Scholarship*, ed. Duncan Ryūken Williams and Christopher S. Queen (Richmond, Surrey: Curzon, 1999), 3–19. Whereas Tanaka, here, attempts to "clear up some points concerning the common perception of the BCA as, at best, a paradigmatic ethnic Buddhist institution and, at worst, an 'ethnic fortress,'" his essay nevertheless foregrounds ethnicity and, when uncritically used by other scholars, reinforces the essentializing trope that American Shin Buddhism is nothing more than a Japanese form of Buddhism in America. See also Jeff Wilson, "Pennies in the Pure Land: Practicing the Dharma, Hanging Out, and Raising Funds for the Oldest Buddhist Temple Outside Asia," *Journal of Global Buddhism* 23, no. 1 (2022): 63–78.

10. Senryō Asai and Dunan Ryūken Williams, "Japanese American Zen Temples: Cultural Identity and Economics," in *American Buddhism: Methods and Findings in Recent Scholarship*, ed. Duncan Ryūken Williams and Christopher S. Queen, Curzon Critical Studies in Buddhism (Richmond, Surrey: Curzon, 1999), 20–35.

11. The reader will note that whereas Nisei were making overtures to white Americans (explicit calls to propagate the dharma to "Caucasians"), other nonwhite and non-Japanese Americans are notably absent from the *Bussei*. Apart from some passing references, which will be discussed in Chapter 3, the *Bussei* does not mention Black Americans, other Asian Americans, or Latinx Americans at all. I cannot explain this absence. It is particularly difficult to account for given research on Black-Asian connections before the war and Japanese Americans' active participation in the civil rights movement after (e.g., Yuri Kochiyama). All of this, of course, is the subject of a different book, and here we can only speculate as to the reasons for this absence in this one particular Nisei publication. See Adeana McNicholl, "The 'Black Buddhism Plan': Buddhism, Race, and Empire in the Early Twentieth Century," *Religion and American Culture* 31 (2021): 332–378; and Diane Carol Fujino, *Heartbeat of*

Struggle: The Revolutionary Life of Yuri Kochiyama (Minneapolis: University of Minnesota Press, 2005).

12. Jane Imamura, "Gathas in the West," *Berkeley Bussei*, 1952, 20.

13. Michael K. Masatsugu, "'Bonded by Reverence Toward the Buddha': Asian Decolonization, Japanese Americans, and the Making of the Buddhist World, 1947–1965," *Journal of Global History* 8 (2013): 142–164.

14. *Jichiryo* (自治療) simply means "dormitory," specifically one managed by its residents.

15. The genre of "Bussei journals" was widespread at this time; most local YBA groups produced some form of regular publication with or without "Bussei" in the title, many of which survive to the present in library or temple archives. And many of the authors covered in this book would have written for and/or read the Bussei journals from other temples. The Oakland-produced *Bussei Life*, for example, has many overlaps with the *Berkeley Bussei*. It is no doubt due to the active efforts of Kanmo Imamura to promote the *Berkeley Bussei* in the postwar period, as well as the contributions from now better-known (largely white) figures, that the Berkeley publication became more prominent and widely distributed as compared to other publications.

16. Despite being hastily produced and only half the size of the other volumes, the spring 1942 edition of the *Bussei* is of surprising quality and contains some valuable information about Nisei as they departed Berkeley for the camps or, in some cases, service in the U.S. military. Many of the YBA leaders were involved in camp publication projects, some of which carried titles that were some version of *Bussei*, and many of which were under the direct supervision of camp authorities. For more on wartime publications, see Takeya Mizuno, "Censorship in a Different Name: Press 'Supervision' in Wartime Japanese American Camps 1942–1943," *Journalism and Mass Communication Quarterly* 88, no. 1 (2011): 121–141; see also "Newspapers in Camp," *Densho Encyclopedia*, accessed December 2, 2021, https://encyclopedia.densho.org/Newspapers_in_camp/.

17. I have been unable to locate an extant 1959 volume and suspect that no *Bussei* was published that year.

18. Whereas not the longest issue, the 1957 *Bussei* is notable for the quality of writing and diversity of pieces. Included are dense articles on psychology and religion by Alan Watts and F. D. Lessing, a stage play by Hiroshi Kashiwagi, poetry by Gary Snyder and Philip Whalen, translations by Alex Wayman and Taitetsu Unno, and art and design by Will Petersen. The issue was featured in the Buddhist Churches of America's then-official publication, *The American Buddhist*, wherein the editor notes that the *Bussei* is "now being distributed to readers all over the world" and that it "exceeds all previous issues both in content and form" (Hiroshi Kashiwagi, "Magazine Review: 1957 Berkeley Bussei Exceeds Previous Editions," *The American Buddhist*, August 1, 1957).

19. This collection of five document boxes includes letters to Jane Imamura from D. T. Suzuki, Jack Kerouac, Tokan Tada, Alan Watts, and others; dharma talk notes and draft essays by both Kanmo and Jane Imamura; audio and video tapes; various ephemera from the Imamuras' time in both Berkeley and Hawai'i; photographs; and

Buddhist music scores, among other items. Also included are copies of letters by (and sometimes replies to) Kanmo Imamura to various organizations and individuals seeking funding for the *Berkeley Bussei* specifically or the Study Center generally. These letters attest to his active and ongoing efforts to both support his local community and make Buddhism better-known to Americans generally. I am deeply grateful to the Imamura family for gifting these items to the Institute of Buddhist Studies and to Rev. Dr. David Matsumoto for making them available for this project.

20. See Thomas Tweed, "Theory and Method in the Study of Buddhism: Toward a Translocative Analysis," in *Buddhism Beyond Borders*, ed. Scott A. Mitchell and Natalie E. F. Quli (Albany: State University of New York Press, 2015), 3–20.

21. Duncan Ryûken Williams, "At Ease in Between: The Middle Position of a Scholar-Practitioner," *Journal of Global Buddhism* 9 (2008): 155–163.

22. In what follows I use the terms "Jōdo Shinshū," "Shinshū," and "Shin" interchangeably, and unless otherwise noted, I am generally referring to the Nishi Honganji branch of Jōdo Shinshū.

23. I too am guilty of perpetuating this narrative. Despite my best intentions in *Buddhism in America* to present the interrelationships between different Buddhist groups by using Tweed's translocative analysis (convergence and divergence), I must be honest about how my own telling of American Buddhist history began with European colonialists, followed by nineteenth-century Chinese and Japanese immigrants, and culminated in post-1965 diversification. Thus, my own work falls under the following critique. See Scott A. Mitchell, *Buddhism in America: Global Religion, Local Contexts* (London: Bloomsbury Academic, 2016); and Thomas A. Tweed, *Crossing and Dwelling: A Theory of Religion* (Cambridge, MA: Harvard University Press, 2008).

24. Richard H. Robinson and Willard L. Johnson, *The Buddhist Religion: A Historical Introduction*, 3rd ed. (Belmont, CA: Wadsworth, 1997), 299.

25. See Joseph Cheah, "US Buddhist Traditions," in *The Oxford Handbook of Contemporary Buddhism*, ed. Michael K. Jerryson (New York: Oxford University Press, 2017), 316–331. Cheah's account of Buddhism in the United States explicitly links current trends with the tradition's Orientalist and colonialist past; nevertheless, the essay still follows this basic framework, opening with an account of colonial history somewhat detached from the simultaneous activity and participation of Asian and Asian American Buddhists.

26. Charles S. Prebish and Damien Keown, *Introducing Buddhism*, 2nd ed. (London: Routledge, 2010), 210.

27. C. J. Wakefield, in the 1952 volume of the *Bussei*, writes cryptically: "Somewhere in California (according to old Chinese records) there are trees which were planted by visiting Buddhist monks in 1300 A.D" (C. J. Wakefield, "Trees," *Berkeley Bussei*, 1952, 9). This curious aside—with no references, no details, no corroborating evidence—surely is insufficient for supporting the widely refuted theories of pre-Columbian Chinese exploration of the Americas. The point here is not to give credence to theories with no evidence but to note the work our historical narratives do. For five centuries, the historical narrative of "Columbus the explorer and discoverer of the New World" has elided the devastating impact of European colonization of

the Americas and indigenous genocide; more recently, it has acted as a proxy for a vaguely defined "Italian American pride." Counternarratives do the important and necessary work of challenging our uncritical acceptance of shared histories and what they reveal or obscure. Thus, again, the point here is not to argue for the Chinese as the rightful discoverers of America but to ask what our history would look like if told from the point of view of the West Coast moving east (e.g., from the East), rather than the East Coast moving west (e.g., from the West).

28. Arthur Nishimura, "The Buddhist Mission of North America 1898–1942: Religion and Its Social Function in an Ethnic Community," in *North American Buddhists in Social Context*, ed. Paul David Numrich (Boston: Brill, 2008), 91.

29. Michihiro Ama, *Immigrants to the Pure Land: The Modernization, Acculturation, and Globalization of Shin Buddhism* (Honolulu: University of Hawai'i Press, 2011).

30. For summaries, as well as the limitations, of the "two Buddhisms" typology, see Chenxing Han, "Diverse Practices and Flexible Beliefs Among Young Adult Asian American Buddhists," *Journal of Global Buddhism* 18 (2017): 1–24; and Wakoh Shannon Hickey, "Two Buddhisms, Three Buddhisms, and Racism," in *Buddhism Beyond Borders*, ed. Scott A. Mitchell and Natalie E. F. Quli (Albany: State University of New York Press, 2015), 35–56.

31. Moreover, in framing the history of American Buddhism as a false binary between white and Asian Buddhists, other Buddhists of color are completely excluded from this history, one of the main limitations of the "two Buddhisms" typology. Regrettably, this book will not be able to fill this lacuna, as I have found little to no engagement with Black or Latinx Buddhists in the material under study.

32. Michael K. Masatsugu, "'Beyond This World of Transiency and Impermanence': Japanese Americans, Dharma Bums, and the Making of American Buddhism During the Early Cold War Years," *Pacific Historical Review* 77, no. 3 (2008): 427.

33. Ama, *Immigrants to the Pure Land*, 39.

34. For a discussion of the problematic and often unexamined "imperialist nostalgia" in Buddhist studies, see Natalie E. Quli, "Western Self, Asian Other: Modernity, Authenticity, and Nostalgia for 'Tradition' in Buddhist Studies," *Journal of Buddhist Ethics* 16 (2009): 1–38.

35. Robinson and Johnson in *The Buddhist Religion* very clearly link colonial and Orientalist projects to modern Buddhology. Similarly, Charles Prebish, in his discussion of "scholar-practitioners" in modern Buddhist studies, notes how the "intellectual forebears" of American scholars were primarily interested in textual studies and philology. To the extent that Prebish, here, is primarily interested in discussing scholars who are *also* practicing Buddhists, the work implicitly connects contemporary self-identified scholar-practitioners with the textual/translation tradition that runs through the colonial period and elides any connection to communities of practice. Charles Prebish, "The Academic Study of Buddhism in America: A Silent Sangha," in *American Buddhism: Methods and Findings in Recent Scholarship*, ed. Dunan Ryûken Williams and Christopher S. Queen (New York: Curzon, 1999), 183–214.

36. Stephen Prothero, "Introduction," in *Big Sky Mind: Buddhism and the Beat Generation*, ed. Carole Tonkinson (New York: Riverhead Books, 1995), 2.

37. Ibid., 3.

38. As will be discussed in Chapters 4 and 5, and as discussed by Michael Masatsugu, Kanmo and Jane Imamura forged close friendships with Jack Kerouac, Gary Snyder, Alan Watts, and others within the West Coast countercultural movement. See Michael K. Masatsugu, "Reorienting the Pure Land: Japanese Americans, the Beats, and the Making of American Buddhism, 1941–1966," PhD diss., University of California, Irvine, 2004.

39. See Ama, *Immigrants to the Pure Land*, 70–81; Michihiro Ama, "'First White Buddhist Priestess': A Case Study of Sunya Gladys Pratt at the Tacoma Buddhist Temple," in *Buddhism Beyond Borders*, ed. Scott A. Mitchell and Natalie E. F. Quli (Albany: State University of New York Press, 2015), 59–74; and Thomas A. Tweed, "Tracing Modernity's Flows: Buddhist Currents in the Pacific World," *The Eastern Buddhist* 43, nos. 1–2 (2012): 35–56.

40. Tetsuden Kashima, *Buddhism in America: The Social Organization of an Ethnic Religious Organization* (Westport, CT: Greenwood Press, 1977); Donald R. Tuck, *Buddhist Churches of America: Jodo Shinshu* (Lewiston, NY: E. Mellen Press, 1987).

41. Jane Iwamura, "Altared States: Exploring the Legacy of Japanese American Butsudan Practice," *Pacific World: Journal of the Institute of Buddhist Studies* 3, no. 5 (Fall 2003): 275–291; Tetsuden Kashima, "The Buddhist Churches of America: Challenges for Change in the Twenty-First Century," in *Shin Buddhism: Historical, Textual, and Interpretive Studies*, ed. Richard K. Payne (Berkeley: Numata Center for Buddhist Translation and Research, 2007), 321–340; Scott A. Mitchell, "Locally Translocal American Shin Buddhism," *Pacific World: Journal of the Institute of Buddhist Studies* 3, no. 12 (2010): 109–126; Scott A. Mitchell, "The Ritual Use of Music in US Jōdo Shinshū Buddhist Communities," *Contemporary Buddhism* 15, no. 2 (2014): 1–17; Anne C. Spencer, "Diversification in the Buddhist Churches of America: Demographic Trends and Their Implications for the Future Study of US Buddhist Groups," *Journal of Global Buddhism* 15 (2014): 35–61; Karma Lekshe Tsomo, "Japanese Buddhist Women in Hawai'i: Waves of Change," *Pacific World: Journal of the Institute of Buddhist Studies* 4, no. 3 (2022): 25–51. Jeff Wilson, "'All Beings Are Equally Embraced by Amida Buddha': Jodo Shinshu Buddhism and Same-Sex Marriage in the United States," *Journal of Global Buddhism* 13 (2012): 31–59; Jeff Wilson, *Dixie Dharma: Inside a Buddhist Temple in the American South* (Chapel Hill: University of North Carolina Press, 2012) (an ethnographic case study of a temple that, while originally founded by Shin Buddhists, is now a trans-sectarian Buddhist center); Patricia Kanaya Usuki, *Currents of Change: American Buddhist Women Speak Out on Jodo Shinshu*, IBS Monograph Series (Berkeley, CA: Institute of Buddhist Studies, 2007).

42. Richard Hughes Seager, *Buddhism in America* (New York: Columbia University Press, 1999), 51ff.; Mitchell, "Locally Translocal," 109–110.

43. See Charles S. Prebish, *Luminous Passage: The Practice and Study of Buddhism in America* (Berkeley: University of California Press, 1999), 242ff.

44. Joseph Cheah, *Race and Religion in American Buddhism: White Supremacy and Immigrant Adaptation* (New York: Oxford University Press, 2011).

45. For examples of scholarship focused on Asian American religions and Buddhism, see Jane Iwamura and Paul Spickard, eds., *Revealing the Sacred in Asian and Pacific America* (New York: Routledge, 2002); Sharon A. Suh, *Being Buddhist in a Christian World: Gender and Community in a Korean American Temple* (Seattle: University of Washington Press, 2004); and Duncan Ryūken Williams and Tomoe Moriya, eds., *Issei Buddhism in the Americas* (Urbana: University of Illinois Press, 2010), among many other titles. This work may be contrasted with such work as James William Coleman's *The New Buddhism: The Western Transformation of an Ancient Tradition* (New York: Oxford University Press, 2001) which treats white converts as rescuing a pure form of Buddhism from immigrant traditionalism. The trope of the "pioneer" is well-trodden, as in a recent edited volume by Brian Bocking et al., *A Buddhist Crossroads: Pioneer Western Buddhists and Asian Networks 1860–1960* (London: Routledge, 2020). The colonial implications of the pioneer figure (a lone figure venturing into unexplored lands that are, in fact, already populated by indigenous peoples) is a subject for a different book.

46. Masatsugu, "Beyond this World," 427.

47. Pyong Gap Min, "Introduction," in *Religions in Asian America: Building Faith Communities*, ed. Pyong Gap Min and Jung Ha Kim (Walnut Creek, CA: AltaMira Press, 1992), 6.

48. "Acknowledgments," in *Revealing the Sacred in Asian and Pacific America*, ed. Jane Iwamura and Paul Spickard (New York: Routledge, 2002), xi–xii.

49. Rudiger V. Busto, "Disorienting Subjects: Reclaiming Pacific Islander/Asian American Religions," in *Revealing the Sacred in Asian and Pacific America*, ed. Jane Iwamura and Paul Spickard (New York: Routledge, 2002), 24.

50. Ian F. Haney López, "White by Law," in *Critical Race Theory: The Cutting Edge*, ed. Richard Delgado and Jean Stefancic, 3rd ed. (Philadelphia: Temple University Press, 2013), 780 (emphasis in original).

51. David Yoo, *Growing Up Nisei: Race, Generation, and Culture Among Japanese Americans of California, 1924–49* (Urbana: University of Illinois Press, 2000), 40.

52. Kashima, *Buddhism in America*; Duncan Ryūken Williams, *American Sutra: A Story of Faith and Freedom in the Second World War* (Cambridge, MA: Harvard University Press, 2019).

53. Takashi Fujitani, *Race for Empire: Koreans as Japanese and Japanese as Americans During World War II* (Berkeley: University of California Press, 2013), 7.

54. Jolyon Baraka Thomas, *Faking Liberties: Religious Freedom in American-Occupied Japan* (Chicago: University of Chicago Press, 2019).

55. Eiichiro Azuma, *Between Two Empires: Race, History, and Transnationalism in Japanese America* (New York: Oxford University Press, 2005), 6.

56. Ibid.

57. Ibid.

58. Masatsugu, "Bonded by Reverence," 145.

59. Arif Dirlik, "Performing the World: Reality and Representation in the Making of World Histor(ies)," *GHI Bulletin* 37 (2005): 21–22.

60. Lisa Lowe, "Heterogeneity, Hybridity, Multiplicity: Marking Asian American Differences," in *Literary Theory: An Anthology*, ed. Julie Rivkin and Michael Ryan, 2nd ed. (Maiden, MA: Blackwell, 2004), 10–34.

61. Tweed, "Theory and Method in the Study of Buddhism"; cf. Tweed, "Tracing Modernity's Flows."

62. Lisa Lowe, *Immigrant Acts: On Asian American Cultural Politics* (Durham, NC: Duke University Press, 1996), 157.

63. For ways in which larger geopolitical and economic forces impact cultural flows, see Manuel A. Vásquez, "The Limits of the Hydrodynamics of Religion," *Journal of the American Academy of Religion* 77, no. 2 (2009): 434–445.

64. Michael Omi and Howard Winant, *Racial Formation in the United States*, 3rd ed. (New York: Routledge, 2014), 125 (emphasis in original).

65. Ibid.

66. See Williams, *America Sutra*, esp. 2–4, 258, as well as his discussion of Japanese American Buddhist military service, 149–182.

67. Cheah, *Race and Religion in American Buddhism*, 4.

68. See Ann Gleig, "Undoing Whiteness in American Buddhist Modernism: Critical, Collective, and Contextual Turns," in *Buddhism and Whiteness: Critical Reflections*, ed. George Yancy and Emily McRae (Lanham, MD: Lexington Books, 2019), 21–42.

69. Galen Amstutz, "Missing Hongan-Ji in Japanese Studies," *Japanese Journal of Religious Studies* 23, no. 1–2 (1996): 155–178.

70. As but a few examples, see Jason Ānanda Josephson, "When Buddhism Became a 'Religion': Religion and Superstition in the Writings of Inoue Enryō," *Japanese Journal of Religious Studies* 33, no. 1 (2006): 143–168; Victoria R. Montrose, "Making the Modern Priest: The Ōtani Denomination's Proto-University and Debates About Clerical Education in the Early Meiji," in *Methods in Buddhist Studies: Essays in Honor of Richard K. Payne*, ed. Scott A. Mitchell and Natalie Fisk Quli (London: Bloomsbury Press, 2019), 39–53; Melissa Anne-Marie Curley, *Pure Land, Real World: Modern Buddhism, Japanese Leftists, and the Utopian Imagination* (Honolulu: University of Hawai'i Press, 2017); and Orion Klautau and Hans Martin Krämer, eds., *Buddhism and Modernity: Sources from Nineteenth-Century Japan* (Honolulu: University of Hawai'i Press, 2021). All of this is excellent scholarship, and it is worth noting that Issei Shin missionaries to the United States occupied the same cultural, religious, and political worlds as the figures under study in these works. However, scholars working on American Buddhism have generally foregrounded processes of cultural adaptation or acculturation. Comparable studies of American Shin Buddhist modernism are few and far between.

71. See Eiichiro Azuma, "The Making of a Japanese American Race, and Why Are There 'Immigrants' in Postwar Nikkei History and Community? The Problems of Generation, Region, and Citizenship in Japanese America," in *Trans-Pacific Japanese American Studies: Conversations on Race and Racializations*, ed. Yasuko Takezawa and Gary Okihiro (Honolulu: University of Hawai'i Press, 2017), 257–287, wherein

he discusses how the privileging of the first wave of Japanese immigration and the West Coast in scholarship has led to the erasure of other Japanese American, Nikkei, and Shin Issei experiences. Similarly, Jeff Wilson, in "Regionalism Within North American Buddhism," in *Buddhism Beyond Borders*, ed. Scott A. Mitchell and Natalie E. F. Quli (Albany: State University of New York Press, 2015), 21–33, notes that the vast majority of studies on American Shin Buddhism are based on research conducted in California and the West Coast. I am particularly sensitive to this critique here, given the focus of the present study on Berkeley. It is a fair critique of the field, and it is not my intention to make generalized claims about North American Shinshū based on the limited experiences of this one case study. At the same time, it is one of my claims that networks and flows of culture matter and have an impact. The Buddhist Churches of America is a national-level small village with connections running throughout and beyond California. If anything, it is my hope that this one study inspires scores more.

72. Tomoe Moriya, "'Americanization' and 'Tradition' in Issei and Nisei Buddhist Publications," in *Issei Buddhism in the Americas*, ed. Duncan Ryūken Williams and Tomoe Moriya (Urbana: University of Illinois Press, 2010), 126.

73. See Kashima, *Buddhism in America*, esp. 57ff.

74. Anecdotally, I have heard from Japanese colleagues that the term "Bussei" (佛青) took on overtly political meanings in Japan in the 1960s, in particular as part of anti-war rhetoric on Japanese university campuses. I have seen no evidence of this usage in the *Bussei*, though, given the transpacific crossings noted in this book, I would be curious about such connections and influences.

75. Debating the internal diversity of "white people" as a class would only serve to center white perspectives, a project I am simply not interested in, especially in a book whose intention is to center the voices of Asian Americans.

Chapter 1

1. "On Nirvana," *Berkeley Bussei*, 1952, 6, 23.

2. Amitābha ("limitless light") is sometimes referred to as Amitāyus ("limitless life"), both names being derived from the Sanskrit *amita*, or "limitless." Indeed, in early Chinese translations of Pure Land texts, his name is just this—"limitless"—and thus both names can be used for the same Buddha. However, in some traditions, especially Tibetan and tantric traditions, the two Buddhas are distinct both iconographically and ritually. See Jan Nattier, "The Names of Amitabha/Amitayus in Early Chinese Buddhist Translations (1)," *Annual Report of the International Research Institute for Advanced Buddhology* 9 (2006): 183–199.

3. See Hisao Inagaki and Harold Stewart, *The Three Pure Land Sutras*, BDK English Tripitaka, 12-II, III, IV (Berkeley, CA: Numata Center for Buddhist Translation and Research, 1995).

4. As but one example of the interplay of Pure Land and other forms of Buddhist thought and practice, see Jennifer Lynn Eichman, *A Late Sixteenth-Century Chinese Buddhist*

Fellowship: Spiritual Ambitions, Intellectual Debates, and Epistolary Connections (Leiden: Brill, 2016), a study of the Ming-era monk Lianchi Zhuhong and his debates with other Buddhist and Confucian scholars concerning the place of buddhaname recitation.

5. For but one example of the scope of Pure Land thought and practice across Buddhist Asia, see Georgios T. Halkias and Richard K. Payne, *Pure Lands in Asian Texts and Contexts: An Anthology* (Honolulu: University of Hawai'i Press, 2019). For the nonexistence of a discrete Pure Land school in China, see Robert H. Sharf, "On Pure Land Buddhism and Ch'an/Pure Land Syncretism in Medieval China," *T'oung Pao* (2nd ser.) 88, fasc. 4–5 (2002): 282–331.

6. See Eichman, *A Late Sixteenth-Century Chinese Buddhist Fellowship*; Daniel A. Getz, "Shenghang's Pure Conduct Society and the Chinese Pure Land Patriarchate," in *Approaching the Land of Bliss: Religious Praxis in the Cult of Amitābha*, ed. Richard K. Payne and Kenneth K. Tanaka, Kuroda Institute Studies in East Asian Buddhism no. 17 (Honolulu: University of Hawai'i Press, 2004), 52–76; Jacqueline I. Stone, "By the Power of One's Last Nenbutsu: Deathbed Practices in Early Modern Japan," in *Approaching the Land of Bliss: Religious Praxis in the Cult of Amitābha*, ed. Richard K. Payne and Kenneth K. Tanaka, Kuroda Institute Studies in East Asian Buddhism no. 17 (Honolulu: University of Hawai'i Press, 2004), 77–119.

7. It is important to note that though these schools have been categorized as esoteric, it would be a mistake to assume that exoteric practices—including Pure Land practices—were absent, as the recent work of Aaron Proffitt makes clear. Aaron Proffitt, "Taking the Vajrayana to Sukhāvatī," in *Methods in Buddhist Studies: Essays in Honor of Richard K. Payne*, ed. Scott A. Mitchell and Natalie Fisk Quli (London: Bloomsbury Press, 2019), 54–64.

8. This is not to uncritically reproduce the now antiquated "Kamakura new Buddhism" narrative; it is simply to note the sequence of historical events whereby specific movements, traditions, cults, lineages, and so forth were established during the Kamakura period and, several centuries later, came to dominate both the Buddhist landscape of Japan and scholarship on Japanese Buddhism. See Richard K. Payne, ed., *Re-Visioning "Kamakura" Buddhism* (Honolulu: University of Hawai'i Press, 1998), as well as the 1996 special issue of the *Japanese Journal of Religious Studies* (vol. 23, nos. 3–4) dedicated to the work of Kuroda Toshio.

9. The term *nenbutsu* is a common transliteration, but it is most commonly pronounced "nembutsu," with an "m" sound. Here, I will follow the academic convention of using the standard Romanization of 念仏 (ねんぶつ) .

10. S. N. Pratt, "What Did Lord Buddha Teach?," *Berkeley Bussei*, Fall 1939, n.p.

11. It is worth noting that this project of spreading the dharma beyond the Japanese community was certainly not a universally supported one. Whereas this propagational stance was clearly important to the Imamuras and others discussed in this volume, there were others within the community that sought to preserve its Japanese "purity." These internal and at time conflicting projects are the subject for an altogether different book.

12. Michihiro Ama, "'First White Buddhist Priestess': A Case Study of Sunya Gladys Pratt at the Tacoma Buddhist Temple," in *Buddhism Beyond Borders*, ed. Scott A. Mitchell and Natalie E. F. Quli (Albany: State University of New York Press, 2015), 66ff.

13. Jacqueline Stone, "Seeking Enlightenment in the Last Age: Mappō Thought in Kamakura Buddhism," *The Eastern Buddhist* (n.s.) 18, no. 1 (1985): 28–56.

14. Kimi Hisatsune, "Shinshu in a Changing World," *Berkeley Bussei*, 1955, 25.

15. Kimi Hisatsune, "The Problem of Faith," *Berkeley Bussei*, 1953, 6–7, emphasis in original.

16. The editorial committee of the Jōdo Shinshū Hongwanji-ha's 1997 *The Collected Works of Shinran* ultimately decided to leave *shinjin* untranslated, as it was in the first edition of that same committee's translation of the *Tannishō* two years prior. However, the second edition decided to translate *shinjin* as "'entrusting heart,' the heart that Amida transfers directly to the practicer who realizes the truth of Amida's Vow of compassion." Hisao Inagaki, ed., *A Record in Lament of Divergences: A Translation of Tannishō*, 2nd ed. (Kyoto: Hongwanji International Center, 2005), vii. See also *The Collected Works of Shinran*, ed. Dennis Hirota, Shin Buddhism Translation Series (Kyoto: Jōdo Shinshū Hongwangji-ha, 1997).

17. S. N. Pratt, "Buddhism in Daily Life," *Berkeley Bussei*, 1950, 6, 16.

18. Manabu Fukuda, "Let Us Gasshō," *Berkeley Bussei*, Spring 1940, n.p.

19. See Michihiro Ama, "Shinran as 'Other': Revisiting Kurata Hyakuzō's *The Priest and His Disciples*," *Japanese Journal of Religious Studies* 43, no. 2 (2016): 253–274. and Scott A. Mitchell, "The Stories We Tell: The Study and Practice of Jōdo Shinshū Buddhism," *Pacific World: Journal of the Institute of Buddhist Studies* 3, no. 19 (2017): 81–97.

20. Toshio Yamagata, "Buddhism in the Home," *Berkeley Bussei*, Fall 1939, n.p.

21. The Second World Buddhist Conference, held in Tokyo in 1952, was organized by the World Fellowship of Buddhists, based originally in Sri Lanka. Nisei connections to this organization are discussed in Chapter 4 and in more detail in Michael K. Masatsugu, "'Bonded by Reverence Toward the Buddha': Asian Decolonization, Japanese Americans, and the Making of the Buddhist World, 1947–1965," *Journal of Global History* 8 (2013): 142–164.

22. Taitetsu Unno, "A Life of Naturalness," *Berkeley Bussei*, 1954, 15.

23. Ibid., 17. Unno's use of the word "naturalness" here is almost certainly a reference to *jinen hōni* (自然法爾), a term referring to the "the ultimate reality of Buddhism . . . or things-as-they-are" which, in Shinran's writing, is the ultimate cause of *shinjin*. A person of *shinjin*, thus, lives in this state of ultimate reality, free from the discriminative thinking of ordinary existence and experiencing the world as it is, spontaneously and naturally. See *The Collected Works of Shinran*, II:191–192.

24. James C. Dobbins, *Jōdo Shinshū: Shin Buddhism in Medieval Japan* (Honolulu: University of Hawai'i Press, 2002), 23–24.

25. The position of *monshu* (門主, keeper of the gate) was established by Shinran's youngest daughter, Kakushinni. As overseer of Shinran's shrine in Kyoto, Kakushinni inherited the future site of the Honganji when her husband died. She installed a direct descendent to oversee the site, her son Kakue, thus beginning a patrilineal line of succession that continues to the present.

26. For a discussion of Rennyo's life and work, as well as a translation of his letters, see Minor Rogers and Ann Rogers, *Rennyo: The Second Founder of Shin Buddhism: With a Translation of His Letters*, Nanzan Studies in Asian Religions vol. 3 (Berkeley, CA: Asian Humanities Press, 1991).

27. H. T. Terakawa, "Sayings of Rennyo-Shonin," *Berkeley Bussei*, Fall 1939, n.p.

28. In 1868, the first year of the Meiji era, 150 Japanese emigrated to Hawai'i. Even though the Japanese government explicitly prohibited immigration to Hawai'i for the next two decades, and the official introduction of Shin Buddhism is dated to 1889, Ichido Kikukawa's research suggests that Shin priests were actively promoting Buddhism during the 1870s and 1880s, albeit without official recognition. Ichido Kikukawa, "Unofficial Envoy: Shin Ministers Who Went to Hawaii Prior to the Hongwanji's Mission," paper presented at the International Association of Shin Buddhist Studies Biennial Meeting, Taipei, May 25, 2019.

29. See Noriko Asato, *Teaching Mikadoism: The Attack on Japanese Language Schools in Hawaii, California, and Washington, 1919–1927* (Honolulu: University of Hawai'i Press, 2006); Tomoe Moriya, *Amerika bukkyō no tanjō: Nijisseiki shotō ni okeru nikkei shūkyō no bunka hen'yō* [アメリカ仏教の誕生: 二〇世紀初頭における日系宗教の文化変容 / 守屋友江著; Birth of American Buddhism: Acculturation of Japanese religions in the early twentieth century] (Tokyo: Gendai shiryō shuppan, 2001); and Lori Pierce, "Constructing American Buddhisms: Discourse of Race and Religion in Territorial Hawai'I," PhD diss., University of Hawai'i, 2000.

30. Tetsuden Kashima, *Buddhism in America: The Social Organization of an Ethnic Religious Organization* (Westport, CT: Greenwood Press, 1977), 15. Nishi Honganji (西本願寺), literally "Western Temple of the Original Vow," is often transliterated Hongwanji; however, I will be following the standard academic transliteration, without the "w."

31. Jessica Starling, *Guardians of the Buddha's Home: Domestic Religion in Contemporary Jōdo Shinshū* (Honolulu: University of Hawai'i Press, 2019), 37; see also Dobbins, *Jōdo Shinshū*, 64ff.

32. The BMNA and later the BCA oversaw the Canadian temples on and off before and after the war, until the 1960s. For more details on the relationship between these organizations, see Jeff Wilson, "What Is Canadian About Canadian Buddhism?," *Religion Compass* 5, no. 9 (2011): 536–548.

33. Initially, the head of the BMNA held the position of *kantoku* (director). In 1918, the position was elevated to that of *sochō* (総長), which roughly approximates the position within the larger Honganji religious hierarchy. For a discussion on how Japanese titles were rendered into English, see later in this chapter as well as Arthur Nishimura, "The Buddhist Mission of North America 1898–1942: Religion and Its Social Function in an Ethnic Community," in *North American Buddhists in Social Context*, ed. Paul David Numrich (Boston: Brill, 2008), 96.

34. Berkeley Buddhist Temple, *A Century of Gratitude and Joy: 1911–2011* (Berkeley, CA: Berkeley Buddhist Temple, 2014), 22.

35. Kashima, *Buddhism in America*, 21ff.

36. *Kaikyōshi* (開教使) is a rank signifying a priest's ability to teach the dharma outside Japan; thus, perhaps the best translation of the term would be "missionary." Even

American-born ministers who lead BCA temples are expected to have *kaikyōshi* status. See Scott A. Mitchell, "Locally Translocal American Shin Buddhism," *Pacific World: Journal of the Institute of Buddhist Studies* 3, no. 12 (2010): 118. See Kashima, *Buddhism in America*, 41, 70–72 for a discussion on how Japanese terms were debated and translated over the first half of the twentieth century.

37. San Francisco *Chronicle*, September 13, 1899.

38. Richard M. Jaffe, *Seeking Śākyamuni: South Asia in the Formation of Modern Japanese Buddhism* (Chicago: University of Chicago Press, 2019), 6.

39. Lori Pierce, "Buddhist Modernism in English-Language Buddhist Periodicals," in *Issei Buddhism in the Americas*, edited by Duncan Ryûken Williams and Tomoe Moriya (Urbana: University of Illinois Press, 2010), 93; see also Judith Snodgrass, *Presenting Japanese Buddhism to the West: Orientalism, Occidentalism, and the Columbian Exposition* (Chapel Hill: University of North Carolina Press, 2003).

40. Victoria R. Montrose, "Making the Modern Priest: The Ōtani Denomination's Proto-University and Debates About Clerical Education in the Early Meiji," in *Methods in Buddhist Studies: Essays in Honor of Richard K. Payne*, ed. Scott A. Mitchell and Natalie Fisk Quli (London: Bloomsbury Press, 2019), 39–53.

41. Buddhist Churches of America, *Buddhist Churches of America: A Legacy of the First 100 Years* (San Francisco: Buddhist Churches of America, 1998), 53. This official record of the BCA lists the ordination and educational background of all *kaikyōshi* ministers who have served since Sonoda and Nishijima. I am grateful to Victoria Montrose for helping me identify some of the more obscure and short-lived Buddhist universities listed therein.

42. Michihiro Ama, *Immigrants to the Pure Land: The Modernization, Acculturation, and Globalization of Shin Buddhism* (Honolulu: University of Hawai'i Press, 2011), 38–39.

43. Ama, "First White Buddhist Priestess," 66. See Paul David Numrich, *Old Wisdom in the New World: Americanization in Two Immigrant Theravada Buddhist Temples* (Knoxville: University of Tennessee Press, 1996), 63–79, for a discussion of his "parallel congregations" thesis and how different groups of Buddhists with fundamentally different views and practices may coexist within a single community.

44. I am grateful to Jeff Wilson for this observation.

45. Jaffe, *Seeking Śākyamuni*, 32.

46. Pierce, "Buddhist Modernism in English-Language Buddhist Periodicals," 89.

47. Thomas A. Tweed, *The American Encounter with Buddhism, 1844–1912: Victorian Culture and the Limits of Dissent* (Bloomington: Indiana University Press, 1992), 31.

48. Thomas A. Tweed, "Tracing Modernity's Flows: Buddhist Currents in the Pacific World," *The Eastern Buddhist* 43, nos. 1–2 (2012): 35–56.

49. Wakoh Shannon Hickey, "Swedenborg: A Modern Buddha?," *Pacific World: Journal of the Institute of Buddhist Studies* (3rd ser.), no. 10 (2008): 106.

50. Ibid., 108.

51. For the limitations and failings of perennialism, especially in regards to comparative religious studies generally and Jōdo Shinshū specifically, see Richard K. Payne, "How Not to Talk About Pure Land Buddhism: A Critique of Huston Smith's (Mis)

Representations," in *Path of No Path: Contemporary Studies on Pure Land Buddhism Honoring Roger Corless*, ed. Richard K. Payne (Berkeley: Numata Center for Buddhist Translation and Research, 2009), 147–172.

52. Judith Snodgrass, "Buddha No Fukin: The Deployment of Paul Carus' Gospel of Buddha in Meiji Japan," *Japanese Journal of Religious Studies* 25 (1998): 319–344.

53. Devin Zuber, "The Buddha of the North: Swedenborg and Transpacific Zen," *Religion and the Arts* 14, nos. 1–2 (2010): 17.

54. Philip Deslippe, "Bunko Bishop: Swami Mazzinianda, the Udana Karana Order, and the Buddhist Mission of North America," *Japanese Religions* 44, nos. 1–2 (2021): 33–63.

55. There is no record of Mazzinianda in the official BCA histories.

56. Deslippe, "Bunko Bishop," 43.

57. Pierce, "Buddhist Modernism in English-Language Buddhist Periodicals," 92 (emphasis in original).

58. Ibid.

59. Ryan Anningson, "Theories of the Self, Race, and Essentialization in Buddhism in the United States During the 'Yellow Peril,' 1899–1957," PhD diss., Wilfrid Laurier University, 2017, 244.

60. Michihiro Ama, "The Imamura Families and the Making of American Buddhism," in *Oxford Encyclopedia of Buddhism* (New York: Oxford University Press, 2019), 1–18; Noriko Asato, "The Japanese Language School Controversy in Hawaii," in *Issei Buddhism in the Americas*, ed. Duncan Ryūken Williams and Tomoe Moriya (Urbana: University of Illinois Press, 2010), 45–64; Tomoe Moriya, *Yemyo Imamura: Pioneer American Buddhist* (Honolulu: Buddhist Study Center Press, 2000); Moriya, *Amerika bukkyō no tanjō*.

61. Jolyon Baraka Thomas, *Faking Liberties: Religious Freedom in American-Occupied Japan* (Chicago: University of Chicago Press, 2019), 92.

62. Ibid., 90.

63. Tomoe Moriya, "'Americanization' and 'Tradition' in Issei and Nisei Buddhist Publications," in *Issei Buddhism in the Americas*, ed. Duncan Ryūken Williams and Tomoe Moriya (Urbana: University of Illinois Press, 2010), 124.

64. Yemyō Imamura, *Democracy According to the Buddhist Viewpoint* (Honolulu: Publishing Bureau of Hongwanji Mission, 1918).

65. Ibid., 8.

66. This, I presume, is one of the "patently false" claims Jolyon Thomas refers to in his analysis of Imamura's piece. Though I tend to agree that no matter how one wants to define "democracy" it would be difficult to read the monastic sangha as an inherently democratic institution, it may be worth our effort to think through what, exactly, is meant by democracy during the early twentieth century on either side of the Pacific. Arguably, for thinkers such as Imamura, democracy referred not to a system of governance per se but to the dissolution of class- or caste-based hierarchies and the possibility for equality among persons within specific social institutions. Perhaps, therefore, Imamura judges the sangha as democratic because it admits all persons

regardless of class (even though, once admitted, monastics are subject to different hierarchies). My thanks to Jeff Wilson for thinking through these questions.

67. Y. Imamura, *Democracy*, 11.

68. Ibid., 15.

69. Presumably authored by Shinran's disciple Yuienbō, the *Tannishō* is a short text meant to clarify misinterpretations that were promulgated after Shinran's death. As such, it is a provocative and even radical text, one that Rennyo believed should not be read by those who were not "karmically prepared" to grasp its significance (Dobbins, *Jōdo Shinshū*, 69). In the thirteenth chapter, Shinran seems to suggest a type of karmic fatalism whereby all of our actions are bound by past karma disallowing freedom of choice. See Inagaki, ed., *A Record in Lament of Divergences*.

70. Y. Imamura, *Democracy*, 22.

71. Ibid., 29.

72. Rennyo is noted as having made a distinction between "imperial law" and the buddhadharma, a distinction that over time developed into the specific "two truths" theory of *shinzoku nitai* (真俗二諦), whereby Shin followers were compelled to outwardly follow the rules of the state while inwardly following the buddhadharma. See Minor L. Rogers and Ann T. Rogers, "The Honganji: Guardian of the State (1868–1945)," *Japanese Journal of Religious Studies* 71, no. 1 (1990): 3–28; Melissa Anne-Marie Curley, *Pure Land, Real World: Modern Buddhism, Japanese Leftists, and the Utopian Imagination* (Honolulu: University of Hawai'i Press, 2017).

73. Curley, *Pure Land, Real World*, 32.

74. Ibid., 51.

75. Moriya, " 'Americanization' and 'Tradition,' " 124 (emphasis in original).

76. Y. Imamura, *Democracy*, 3.

77. Ibid., 10.

78. Robert H. Sharf, "The Zen of Japanese Nationalism," in *Curators of the Buddha: The Study of Buddhism Under Colonialism*, ed. Donald S. Lopez (Chicago: University of Chicago Press, 1995), 128 (emphasis in original).

79. Ibid., 129.

80. Ama, "The Imamura Families."

81. Anningson, "Theories of the Self, Race, and Essentialization," 244.

82. Ibid.

83. Kanmo Imamura, "Oneness," *Berkeley Bussei*, 1951, 6.

84. Ama, "Imamura Families," 11.

85. K. Imamura, "Oneness."

86. Galen Amstutz, *Interpreting Amida: History and Orientalism in the Study of Pure Land Buddhism* (Albany: State University of New York Press, 1997), x.

87. Aaron Proffitt, *Esoteric Pure Land Buddhism* (Honolulu: University of Hawai'i Press, 2023), 13.

88. Amstutz, *Interpreting Amida*, x. See also Galen Amstutz, "Missing Hongan-Ji in Japanese Studies," *Japanese Journal of Religious Studies* 23, no. 1–2 (1996): 155–178; Galen Amstutz, "Limited Engagements: Revisiting the Non-Encounter Between

American Buddhism and the Shin Tradition," *Journal of Global Buddhism* 3 (2002): 1–35.

89. Pierce, "Buddhist Modernism in English-Language Buddhist Periodicals," 105. I share Pierce's sentiment that this absence of engagement with Shin Buddhist ideas is disappointing and puzzling; however, what I find more puzzling is her expectation that such engagement should include the *Lotus Sutra*. Whereas the *Lotus Sutra* was almost certainly an important part of the Buddhist background within which Shinran would have been trained on Mt. Hiei, it is not a regularly cited text in the Shin tradition, which generally makes more reference to the standard "Three Pure Land Sutras," Shinran's and Rennyo's writings, or even the *Nirvana Sutra*. This expectation that one should see references to the *Lotus Sutra* in Shin Buddhist writing is part of the issue I am attempting to draw our attention to here—namely, the expectation that Shin Buddhism looks a certain way and the resultant disappointment when reality does not meet said expectations.

90. Ama, "First White Buddhist Priestess," 64.

91. I am once more grateful to Jeff Wilson for this observation.

92. Talal Asad, "The Idea of an Anthropology of Islam," *Qui Parle* 17, no. 2 (2009): 20.

93. Ibid.

94. For a discussion of the Indian-styled Hawai'i Shin Buddhist temple, as well as similar temples built in Japan and its East Asian colonies in the earlier twentieth century, see Ama, *Immigrants to the Pure Land*, 100–107; Jaffe, *Seeking Śākyamuni*, 173–189.

95. James C. Dobbins, *Behold the Buddha: Religious Meanings of Japanese Buddhist Icons* (Honolulu: University of Hawai'i Press, 2020), 99–102.

96. I admit that the composition of this image also strongly evokes the flag of the Japanese Imperial Army, the Kyokujitsu-ki, an image that would have been familiar to this unnamed artist. If this was the artist's intent, then this cover is an even bolder choice than the subtle conflation of Amida and the Statue of Liberty. Again, the point is not to make a strong argument for or against one interpretation; rather, speculation is the point—to ask, and leave unanswered, the question "What if?"

Chapter 2

1. Kimi Hisatsune, "The Problem of Faith," *Berkeley Bussei*, 1953, 6.

2. David L. McMahan, *The Making of Buddhist Modernism* (New York: Oxford University Press, 2008).

3. Richard H. Robinson and Willard L. Johnson, *The Buddhist Religion: A Historical Introduction*, 3rd ed. (Belmont, CA: Wadsworth, 1997), 297ff.

4. Stephen Batchelor, *The Awakening of the West: The Encounter of Buddhism and Western Culture* (Berkeley, CA: Parallax Press, 1994).

5. Natalie Fisk Quli, "A Brief Critical Appraisal of the Buddhist Modernism Paradigm," in *The Routledge Handbook of Buddhist-Christian Studies*, ed. Carol S. Anderson and Thomas Cattoi (London and New York: Routledge, 2023), 353–63.

6. David L. McMahan, "Buddhism and Multiple Modernities," in *Buddhism Beyond Borders*, ed. Scott A. Mitchell and Natalie E. F. Quli (Albany: State University of New York Press, 2015), 181–195; Natalie E. F. Quli and Scott A. Mitchell, "Buddhist Modernism as Narrative: A Comparative Study of Jodo Shinshu and Zen," in *Buddhism Beyond Borders*, ed. Scott A. Mitchell and Natalie E. F. Quli (Albany: State University of New York Press, 2015), 197–215; Scott A. Mitchell, *Buddhism in America: Global Religion, Local Contexts* (London: Bloomsbury Academic, 2016), 233–240; Natalie Quli, "Multiple Buddhist Modernisms: Jhāna in Convert Theravāda," *Pacific World: Journal of the Institute of Buddhist Studies* 10, no. 1 (2008): 225–249.

7. McMahan, *The Making of Buddhist Modernism*, 64.

8. Hisatsune, "The Problem of Faith."

9. Marilyn Ivy, "Modernity," in *Critical Terms for the Study of Buddhism*, ed. Donald S. Lopez (Chicago: University of Chicago Press, 2005), 314.

10. McMahan, *The Making of Buddhist Modernism*, 63.

11. Jeff Wilson, *Mindful America: The Mutual Transformation of Buddhist Meditation and American Culture* (New York: Oxford University Press, 2014), 162–169.

12. For a discussion of the problematic nature of the rhetoric of rupture in academic Buddhist studies, see Richard K. Payne, "Afterword: Buddhism Beyond Borders: Beyond the Rhetorics of Rupture," in *Buddhism Beyond Borders*, ed. Scott A. Mitchell and Natalie E. F. Quli (Albany: State University of New York Press, 2015), 217–239.

13. Jason Ānanda Josephson, *The Invention of Religion in Japan* (Chicago: University of Chicago Press, 2012), 19.

14. James Edward Ketelaar, *Of Heretics and Martyrs in Meiji Japan: Buddhism and Its Persecution* (Princeton, NJ: Princeton University Press, 1990).

15. Melissa Anne-Marie Curley, *Pure Land, Real World: Modern Buddhism, Japanese Leftists, and the Utopian Imagination* (Honolulu: University of Hawai'i Press, 2017), 56.

16. Ibid., 57.

17. Jason Ānanda Josephson, "When Buddhism Became a 'Religion': Religion and Superstition in the Writings of Inoue Enryō," *Japanese Journal of Religious Studies* 33, no. 1 (2006): 149.

18. For a discussion of the development of modern sectarian Buddhist universities and their distinctiveness from their imperial counterparts, see Victoria R. Montrose, "Making the Modern Priest: The Ōtani Denomination's Proto-University and Debates About Clerical Education in the Early Meiji," in *Methods in Buddhist Studies: Essays in Honor of Richard K. Payne*, ed. Scott A. Mitchell and Natalie Fisk Quli (London: Bloomsbury Press, 2019), 39–53.

19. Robert H. Sharf, "The Zen of Japanese Nationalism," in *Curators of the Buddha: The Study of Buddhism Under Colonialism*, ed. Donald S. Lopez (Chicago: University of Chicago Press, 1995), 136.

20. Takashi Fujitani, *Race for Empire: Koreans as Japanese and Japanese as Americans During World War II* (Berkeley: University of California Press, 2013).

21. Eiichiro Azuma, *Between Two Empires: Race, History, and Transnationalism in Japanese America* (New York: Oxford University Press, 2005), 91ff.

22. Donald S. Lopez, *Curators of the Buddha: The Study of Buddhism Under Colonialism* (Chicago: University of Chicago Press, 1995), 1.

23. Tomoko Masuzawa, *The Invention of World Religions, or, How European Universalism Was Preserved in the Language of Pluralism* (Chicago: University of Chicago Press, 2005), 125; cf. Philip C. Almond, *The British Discovery of Buddhism* (Cambridge: Cambridge University Press, 1988); Richard King, *Orientalism and Religion Post-Colonial Theory, India and "the Mystic East"* (London: Routledge, 1999).

24. Charles Prebish, "The Academic Study of Buddhism in America: A Silent Sangha," in *American Buddhism: Methods and Findings in Recent Scholarship*, ed. Dunan Ryûken Williams and Christopher S. Queen (New York: Curzon, 1999), 183–214.

25. Lopez, *Curators of the Buddha*, 2.

26. Richard K Payne, ed., *Secularizing Buddhism: New Perspectives on a Dynamic Tradition* (Boulder, CO: Shambhala, 2021), 10.

27. Natalie E. Quli, "Western Self, Asian Other: Modernity, Authenticity, and Nostalgia for 'Tradition' in Buddhist Studies," *Journal of Buddhist Ethics* 16 (2009): 1–38.

28. Payne, "Afterword," 218.

29. Masuzawa, *The Invention of World Religions*, 127.

30. Quli, "Western Self, Asian Other," 3.

31. Payne, "Afterword," 217.

32. As but one recent example of this tendency, in the introduction to his *Why I Am Not a Buddhist* (New Haven, CT: Yale University Press, 2020), Evan Thompson sets up a dichotomy between modern and traditional Buddhism, finding the former "philosophically unsound" and the latter equated with "monasteries" where he was asked to chant in Asian languages and encountered "anti-intellectualism, sanctimoniousness, naïve reverence, and downright fetishism" (9). Whereas in this deployment of the traditional/modern binary neither side is presented in a particularly positive light, the conflation of anti-intellectualism et al. with non-English-speaking Buddhists is particularly problematic.

33. Vira Dharmawara, "Discourse on the Dharma," *Berkeley Bussei*, 1956, 5.

34. McMahan, *The Making of Buddhist Modernism*, 248.

35. "Religious Section: Introduction," *Berkeley Bussei*, 1951, 5. While this introduction is uncredited, the editors of the 1951 religious section were Taitetsu (Ty) Unno and Kimi Yonemura (Hisatsune) and were thus most likely responsible for this introduction.

36. McMahan, *The Making of Buddhist Modernism*, 43.

37. Ibid., 63.

38. Sei Shohara, "Science and Buddhism," *Berkeley Bussei*, 1955, 23–24.

39. And, not for nothing, we can see here how such projects as Robert Wright's *Why Buddhism Is True* (New York: Simon & Schuster, 2017) are playing catch-up with Nisei writers making the same argument seventy years earlier.

40. Kosho Otani, "Buddhism and Life," *Berkeley Bussei*, 1956, 23; Otani is listed in the contributors section of this volume as "Lord Abbot of Nishi Hongwanji Church"—in other words, the *monshu* of Nishi Honganji in Kyoto, Japan. Otani made numerous

tours to the United States in the postwar period and was an adamant supporter of the North American Shin community.

41. Tokan Tada, "Religious Education," *Berkeley Bussei*, 1953, 7.
42. Tad Tani, "Buddhist and Why," *Berkeley Bussei*, Fall 1941, n.p.
43. Ibid.
44. Azuma, *Between Two Empires*, 129–131.
45. "仏教徒はいつも偏見を持たない真理のもとに人類みんなの発展をねが ふ世界人である." Kanmo Imamura, "仏教徒は世界人なり [Buddhists are cosmopolitan]," *Berkeley Bussei*, Fall 1941, n.p. My thanks to Ichido Kikukawa for his assistance with this essay; any errors in translation are my own.
46. Hajime Nakamura, "The Humanitarian Tendancy of the Japanese," *Berkeley Bussei*, 1955, 4.
47. Sharf, "The Zen of Japanese Nationalism."
48. Nakamura, "The Humanitarian Tendancy of the Japanese," 6.
49. Gene Wood, "Buddhism and Modern Life," *Berkeley Bussei*, Fall 1940, n.p.
50. McMahan, *The Making of Buddhist Modernism*, 8.
51. C. F. Wakefield, "A Rational Teaching," *Berkeley Bussei*, 1950, 10–11.
52. Sei Shohara, "A Layman's Point of View," *Berkeley Bussei*, 1952, 14, 23.
53. Duncan Ryūken Williams, *American Sutra: A Story of Faith and Freedom in the Second World War* (Cambridge, MA: Harvard University Press, 2019), 229ff.
54. "Father Murphy's Appeal to the Nisei," *Berkeley Bussei*, 1952, 24.
55. Ibid.
56. The editors of the 1952 Bussei were Allan Asakawa and Hitoshi Tsufura, with Lily Matsuura (Jane Imamura's sister) serving as associate editor and Sei Shohara as editor of the "religious section." As editor of the section that included Father Murphy's appeal, Shohara almost certainly was the author of this rebuttal.
57. "Father Murphy's Appeal to the Nisei," 27.
58. Williams, *American Sutra*, 210–11.
59. "Father Murphy's Appeal to the Nisei" (emphasis in original).
60. Kimi Hisatsune, "Shinshu in a Changing World," *Berkeley Bussei*, 1955, 25.
61. McMahan, *The Making of Buddhist Modernism*, 46.
62. Ibid., 52ff.
63. Wood, "Buddhism and Modern Life," 6.
64. R. P. Jackson, "A New Outlook," *Berkeley Bussei*, 1954, 22.
65. Scott A. Mitchell, "Sunday Morning Songs," *The Pure Land* (n.s.) 22 (December 2006): 127–138; Scott A. Mitchell, "The Ritual Use of Music in US Jōdo Shinshū Buddhist Communities," *Contemporary Buddhism* 15, no. 2 (2014): 1–17.
66. Keiko Wells, "Shin Buddhist Song Lyrics Sung in the United States: Their History and Expressed Buddhist Images (1), 1898–1939," *Tokyo Daigaku Taiheiyō* 2 (2002): 75–99; Keiko Wells, "Shin Buddhist Song Lyrics Sung in the United States: Their History and Expressed Buddhist Images (2), 1936–2001," *Tokyo Daigaku Taiheiyō* 3 (2003): 41–64.
67. Berkeley Buddhist Temple, *A Century of Gratitude and Joy: 1911–2011* (Berkeley, CA: Berkeley Buddhist Temple, 2014), 36; "The Enduring Buddhist Legacy of Jane Imamura," *Wheel of Dharma* 43, no. 10 (2021).

68. Jane Imamura, "Gathas in the West," *Berkeley Bussei*, 1952, 20.

69. Ibid.

70. Ibid. (emphasis added).

71. Hisatsune, "Shinshu in a Changing World," 25.

72. Hisatsune, "The Problem of Faith," 6 (emphasis in original).

73. Ibid.

74. Ibid. (emphasis added).

75. Hiroshi Kashiwagi, "A Narrative," *Berkeley Bussei*, 1956, 38–39.

76. McMahan, "Buddhism and Multiple Modernities," 183.

77. Quli, "Multiple Buddhist Modernisms," 241–242.

78. Donald S. Lopez, *A Modern Buddhist Bible: Essential Readings from East and West* (Boston: Beacon Press, 2002), x.

79. The term "Protestant Buddhism" was originally developed to describe the specific responses to colonialism within Sri Lanka. *Shin bukkyō*, or "new Buddhism," refers to changes to Buddhist institutions in Japan during the modernization project of the Meiji period.

80. Quli, "Western Self, Asian Other."

81. Martin Baumann, "Protective Amulets and Awareness Techniques, or How to Make Sense of Buddhism in the West," in *Westward Dharma: Buddhism Beyond Asia*, ed. Charles S. Prebish and Martin Baumann (Berkeley: University of California Press, 2002), 56–57.

82. Victor Sōgen Hori, "How Do We Study Buddhism in Canada?," in *Wild Geese: Buddhism in Canada*, ed. John S. Harding, Victor Sōgen Hori, and Alexander Soucy (Montreal: McGill-Queen's University Press, 2010), 18.

83. Ibid., 19; see also Wakoh Shannon Hickey, "Two Buddhisms, Three Buddhisms, and Racism," in *Buddhism Beyond Borders*, ed. Scott A. Mitchell and Natalie E. F. Quli (Albany: State University of New York Press, 2015), 35–56.

84. Hori, "How Do We Study Buddhism in Canada?," 19.

85. Roger Jackson, "Buddhist Scholar Roger Jackson on Rebirth," *Tricycle: The Buddhist Review*, March 14, 2022, https://tricycle.org/trikedaily/roger-jackson-rebirth/.

86. To be fair to Jackson's argument, most of these persons transcend these categories, strategically discussing rebirth in different ways in different contexts; moreover, not all the traditionalists are Asian nor are all the modernists white.

87. Quli, "Western Self, Asian Other," 28.

88. Michihiro Ama, "The Imamura Families and the Making of American Buddhism," in Oxford Encyclopedia of Buddhism (New York: Oxford University Press, 2019), 11.

89. As quoted in Jeff Wilson, *Dixie Dharma: Inside a Buddhist Temple in the American South* (Chapel Hill: University of North Carolina Press, 2012), 75.

90. Lopez, *A Modern Buddhist Bible*, xxxix.

91. Lopez, *A Modern Buddhist Bible*, xl (emphasis added).

92. Wilson argues, rightly, that this short answer is not sufficient—that simplistic readings of Pure Land Buddhism and lack of exposure to modern Shin Buddhists and traditions are just as responsible for this exclusion (Wilson, *Dixie Dharma*, 79–80). Whereas I do not disagree, I also want to challenge the reader to sit with the

feeling of discomfort that arises with the term "racism," which I am using here in its systemic sense. That is, I am not accusing any individual scholars of holding racist views; rather, I want to call our attention to habits of thought that locate the proper subjects of our studies in particular locations and in particular human bodies. Without careful and deliberate interrogation of these habits of thought, we merely replicate the "immediately known" aspects of the traditional/modern binary. Thus, this challenge is meant pedagogically, as both challenge and invitation to the reader to identify the source of their discomfort. See also Sharon A. Suh, "'We Interrupt Your Regularly Scheduled Programming to Bring You This Very Important Public Service Announcement . . .': aka Buddhism as Usual in the Academy," in *Buddhism and Whiteness: Critical Reflections*, ed. George Yancy and Emily McRae (Lanham, MD: Lexington Books, 2019), 1–20.

Chapter 3

1. Tetsuden Kashima, *Buddhism in America: The Social Organization of an Ethnic Religious Organization* (Westport, CT: Greenwood Press, 1977), 21ff.
2. Eiichiro Azuma, *Between Two Empires: Race, History, and Transnationalism in Japanese America* (New York: Oxford University Press, 2005), 62.
3. Ibid., 112.
4. Michael Omi and Howard Winant, *Racial Formation in the United States*, 3rd ed. (New York: Routledge, 2014), 125; Azuma, *Between Two Empires*, 61ff.
5. See "Tamotsu Shibutani," *Densho Encyclopedia*, accessed December 3, 2021, https://encyclopedia.densho.org/Tamotsu_Shibutani/. While incarcerated at Tule Lake, Shibutani worked under Dorothy Thomas on the Japanese American Evacuation and Resettlement Study. After the war, encouraged by Thomas and her husband as well as connections he had made with other Nisei researchers, Shibutani began doctoral studies at the University of Chicago.
6. Tamotsu Shibutani, "A Preface to Reflection," *Berkeley Bussei*, Fall 1941, n.p.
7. Tamotsu Shibutani, "A Racial Minority Population in California," research paper, University of California, Berkeley, 1941, https://oac.cdlib.org/ark:/28722/bk001376n59/?brand=oac4
8. Tamotsu Shibutani, "Retreat from Shangri-La," *Berkeley Bussei*, Spring 1941, n.p.
9. Shibutani, "Preface."
10. James Sugihara, "You Are on Trial," *Berkeley Bussei*, Fall 1939, n.p.
11. In the term paper version of these essays, the phrase "the stupidity of our leaders" is rendered "the stupidity of Nisei leaders," suggesting that Shibutani is frustrated with his generational peers rather than Issei leadership. Shibutani, "Racial Minority," 33.
12. Shibutani, "Shangri-la" (emphasis in original).
13. Cf. Noriko Asato, *Teaching Mikadoism: The Attack on Japanese Language Schools in Hawaii, California, and Washington, 1919–1927* (Honolulu: University of Hawai'i Press, 2006); Kashima, *Buddhism in America*; Duncan Ryūken Williams, *American Sutra: A Story of Faith and Freedom in the Second World War* (Cambridge,

MA: Harvard University Press, 2019); David Yoo, *Growing Up Nisei: Race, Generation, and Culture Among Japanese Americans of California, 1924–49* (Urbana: University of Illinois Press, 2000).

14. Caroline Chung Simpson, *An Absent Presence: Japanese Americans in Postwar American Culture, 1945–1960* (Durham, NC: Duke University Press, 2001), 19; cf. Lisa Lowe, *Immigrant Acts: On Asian American Cultural Politics* (Durham, NC: Duke University Press, 1996), 9.

15. As always, it is our students who are our best teachers. I am indebted to Todd Tsuchiya's work on American Buddhist taiko, which brought to my attention much of the scholarship in what follows.

16. Ron Eyerman, "Social Theory and Trauma," *Acta Sociologica* 56, no. 1 (2013): 43; cf. Neil Smelser, "Psychological Trauma and Cultural Trauma," in *Cultural Trauma and Collective Identity*, ed. Jeffrey C Alexander (Berkeley: University of California Press, 2010), 31–59.

17. Donna K. Nagata, Jacqueline H. J. Kim, and Kaidi Wu, "The Japanese American Wartime Incarceration: Examing the Scope of Racial Trauma," *American Psychologist* 74, no. 1 (2019): 37.

18. Simpson, *An Absent Presence*; cf. Cathy Caruth, *Trauma: Explorations in Memory* (Baltimore: Johns Hopkins University Press, 1996).

19. Emily Roxworthy, *The Spectacle of Japanese American Trauma: Racial Performativity and World War II* (Honolulu: University of Hawai'i Press, 2008).

20. See ibid., 11.

21. On November 1, 2020, the West Los Angeles Buddhist Temple—a Shin Buddhist temple affiliated with the Buddhist Churches of America—hosted an online event featuring young Buddhists interviewing members of the "Silent Generation," including Noriko Matsumoto, Sei Shohara (whom we met in the previous chapter), and Ted Tanaka. All three spoke of their experiences as young people, the difficulties they experienced, and how Buddhism supported them. Tanaka in particular mentioned the ongoing discrimination against Japanese Americans in the postwar years, segregated public schools, and the positive role the Buddhist community played during these difficult years.

22. Natalie Avalos, "What Does It Mean to Heal from Historical Trauma?," *AMA Journal of Ethics* 23, no. 6 (2021): 494. Avalos's work here is specific to the experiences of Indigenous and First Nations persons in North America. I am neither comparing nor equating the experiences of Indigenous persons with the wartime incarceration of Japanese Americans. Such comparisons or equations would be essentializing and reductive. Rather, I want to draw our attention away from the "big event" of incarceration to the ongoing trauma of racism. See also Roxworthy, *Spectacle of Japanese American Trauma*, 2.

23. Sharon A. Suh, "'We Interrupt Your Regularly Scheduled Programming to Bring You This Very Important Public Service Announcement . . .': aka Buddhism as Usual in the Academy," in *Buddhism and Whiteness: Critical Reflections*, ed. George Yancy and Emily McRae (Lanham, MD: Lexington Books, 2019), 12.

24. In many volumes of the *Bussei* immediately before and after the war one finds quotes such as these. Most often the quotes are from well-known American or European historical figures or thinkers. In this case, Henry Ward Beecher was an American abolitionist and brother of Harriet Beecher Stowe, author of *Uncle Tom's Cabin*.

25. Sugihara, "You Are on Trial."

26. James Sakoda, "Betrayed: Ps[y]choanalysis of a Nisei," *Berkeley Bussei*, Spring 1941, n.p.

27. George Yasukochi, "All This & Discrimination 2," *Berkeley Bussei*, Fall 1941, n.p.

28. *Shigatakanai*—literally "it can't be helped" (though I would humbly offer that "eh, what're ya gonna do?" would be more accurate)—has often been used as a cultural shorthand for a sort of Japanese fatalism that allowed the community to suffer through incarceration without putting up any resistance. Roxworthy and others, myself included, reject this simplistic essentialism and its deployment in "model minority" discourses. See Roxworthy, *Spectacle of Japanese American Trauma*.

29. James Sakoda, "Nisei Personality Adjustment," *Berkeley Bussei*, Fall 1941, n.p.

30. Tad Tani, "Buddhist and Why," *Berkeley Bussei*, Fall 1941, n.p.

31. See the discussion of Tani's article in Chapter 2.

32. See Tetsuden Kashima, *Judgment Without Trial: Japanese American Imprisonment During World War II* (Seattle: University of Washington Press, 2011), 132–134; Williams, *American Sutra*, 68–77.

33. George Jobo Nakamura, "Foreword," *Berkeley Bussei*, Spring 1942, n.p.

34. Kashima, *Judgment Without Trial*; Williams, *American Sutra*.

35. Jim Sugihara, "A Message," *Berkeley Bussei*, Spring 1942, n.p.

36. See Yukio Kawamoto and Calvin Ninomiya, "Yukio Kawamoto Collection," Veterans History Project, American Folklife Center, Library of Congress, accessed October 15, 2021, https://memory.loc.gov/diglib/vhp/story/loc.natlib.afc2001001.07420/; Tom Jackman, "Springfield WWII Vets Receive Congressional Gold Medal," *Washington Post*, December 7, 2011.

37. Jane Michiko Imamura, *Kaikyo: Opening the Dharma: Memoirs of a Buddhist Priest's Wife in America* (Honolulu: Buddhist Study Center Press, 1998), 13–20.

38. Ibid., 30.

39. Ibid., 31.

40. Whereas several writers and editors who worked on the *Berkeley Bussei*, such as George Nakamura and Hiroshi Kashiwagi, worked on camp newsletters and magazines, and whereas several of these had some version of "Bussei" in their titles, the *Berkeley Bussei* as such ceased publication during the war. Camp publications are the subject of a different book, of course, owing to their unique context and the fact that many of them were highly circumscribed and/or explicitly censored by the War Department. See Stan Yogi, "Literature in Camp," *Densho Encyclopedia*, accessed October 15, 2021, https://encyclopedia.densho.org/Literature_in_camp/; Takeya Mizuno, "Censorship in a Different Name: Press 'Supervision' in Wartime Japanese American Camps 1942-1943," *Journalism and Mass Communication Quarterly* 88, no. 1 (2011): 121–141.

41. Yukio Kawamoto, "Outlook on American Buddhism," *Berkeley Bussei*, 1950, 8, 15.

42. Hiroshi Kashiwagi, "A Narrative," *Berkeley Bussei*, 1956, 38–39.

43. "Asian Studies," *Berkeley Bussei*, 1953, 32. In the 1960s, the American Academy of Asian Studies would transform into the California Institute of Asian Studies, which began to have more of a focus on integral and counseling psychology. In the 1980s, the school officially changed its name to the California Institute of Integral Studies, became accredited, and began offering graduate degrees in religion, psychology, and related fields.

44. "Foreword," *Berkeley Bussei*, 1952, n.p.

45. "A Time for Action," *Berkeley Bussei*, 1952, 22 (emphasis in original).

46. William Petersen, "Success Story, Japanese-American Style," *New York Times*, January 9, 1966.

47. A good first step to repairing the damage of the slave trade would, of course, be reparations.

48. Claire Jean Kim, "The Racial Triangulation of Asian Americans," *Politics and Society* 27, no. 1 (1999): 105–138.

49. David Palumbo-Liu, *Asian/American Historical Crossings of a Racial Frontier* (Stanford, CA: Stanford University Press, 1999), 174.

50. Williams, *American Sutra*, 219.

51. Ibid., 225.

52. Ibid., 258.

53. Kanmo Imamura, "A House for Our Hopes," *Berkeley Bussei*, 1952, n.p.

54. Kanmo Imamura, "再びブヂストセンタ建設について" [Once again, on the re-construction of the Buddhist Center], *Berkeley Bussei*, 1952, n.p.

55. Kanmo Imamura, "Panorama," *Berkeley Bussei*, 1953, 1.

56. Marge Kataoka, "A Whirl with the Girls: Never a Dorm Moment," *Berkeley Bussei*, 1952, 33–34.

57. Azuma, *Between Two Empires*, 7.

58. Ibid., 126.

59. An accurate ratio of female to male authors is difficult to gauge; many articles are either anonymous, written by "the editors" (in volumes with multiple editors), or are uncredited reports of basketball tournaments or member lists. Some authors only have a first initial amended to their names or it is otherwise difficult to determine the sex of the writer. By my rough estimates, there are about 115 individual authors across the entire print run of the *Bussei*, and only 14 are women.

60. Kimi Yonemura, "Editorial," *Berkeley Bussei*, 1951, n.p.

61. The gendered definition of the Nisei problem also ignores how it was experienced by gay men, who are similarly absent from the *Bussei*.

62. Simpson (*An Absent Presence*, 116) notes that the ideal of a single-paycheck nuclear family household we collectively remember about the 1950s belies the fact that women, especially nonwhite women, continued to work outside the home in the postwar period, and also began to earn less than their male peers for the same labor. Incidentally, Jane Imamura did not work outside the home until after Kanmo retired, when she took up a position in the music department at UC Berkeley. (Conversation with Hiro Imamura David, August 30, 2021.)

63. To understand how contemporary American Shin women may understand their experiences in relationship both to men and to their religion, see Patricia Kanaya Usuki, *Currents of Change: American Buddhist Women Speak Out on Jodo Shinshu*, IBS Monograph Series (Berkeley, CA: Institute of Buddhist Studies, 2007), 59–75.

64. For example, the 1951 *Bussei* lists Ty (Taitetsu) Unno and Kimi Yonemura as religious editors; Margaret Kataoka as circulation manager; and Rosie Morimoto, Toshi Unno, and Jean Kamiyama as typists, among other support staff. Many of these same names appear in other early 1950s *Bussei*. Later in the decade, unfortunately, the *Bussei* began only printing the names of contributors and did not name support staff.

65. I cannot overstate the debt of gratitude I owe to Gwendolyn Gillson, Paulina Kolata, and Jessica Starling for helping me think through the issues discussed in the remainder of this chapter. Their willingness to include me in an ongoing discussion of gender, labor, and religion, provide copious notes and reading lists, and offer insightful questions and observations was invaluable. Whereas any faults in my analysis are my own, I am buoyed by the brilliance of these scholars.

66. Lisa Sloniowski, "Affective Labor, Resistance, and the Academic Librarian," *Library Trends* 64, no. 4 (2016): 648.

67. Ibid., 649.

68. Amy Borovoy, "Not 'A Doll's House': Public Uses of Domesticity in Japan," *U.S.-Japan Women's Journal: English Supplement* 20/21 (2001): 83–124.

69. Ibid., 92–93.

70. Ibid., 114.

71. Ibid.

72. J. Imamura, *Kaikyo*, 43.

73. For a discussion of the term *bōmori* (坊守) see Jessica Starling, *Guardians of the Buddha's Home: Domestic Religion in Contemporary Jōdo Shinshū* (Honolulu: University of Hawai'i Press, 2019), 36.

74. Ibid., 13.

75. Paulina Kolata and Gwendolyn Gillson, "Feasting with Buddhist Women: Food Literacy in Religious Belonging," *Numen* 68, nos. 5–6 (2021): 589.

76. Starling, *Guardians of the Buddha's Home*, 155.

77. In 1949, the Berkeley Temple hosted its first fundraising event, the Satsuki Bazaar. Jane Imamura mentions this in passing in her memoir, and the temple's centennial commemoration book mentions that she was responsible for coming up with the bazaar's name, *satsuki* referring to the fifth month (J. Imamura, *Kaikyo*, 45; Berkeley Buddhist Temple, *A Century of Gratitude and Joy: 1911–2011* [Berkeley, CA: Berkeley Buddhist Temple, 2014], 42.). However, unofficial histories and memories suggest that Jane did more than name the event; she may have been wholly responsible for conceiving the idea in the first place. At the time, this was not without some controversy, as such an explicit fundraising event may have been perceived as beyond the scope of a "religious organization." Regardless, the temple has hosted a Satsuki Bazaar every May since 1949 (recently modified due to COVID but continuing regardless), and the idea was replicated in several other Shin Buddhist communities as an important way to augment temple revenue beyond membership dues. For more on the economic activities of American Shin Buddhist temples, see Jeff Wilson, "Pennies in the

Pure Land: Practicing the Dharma, Hanging Out, and Raising Funds for the Oldest Buddhist Temple Outside Asia," *Journal of Global Buddhism* 23, no. 1 (2022): 63–78.

Chapter 4

1. Arjun Appadurai, *Modernity at Large: Cultural Dimensions of Globalization* (Minneapolis: University of Minnesota Press, 1996), 158, 31.
2. Linda Learman, *Buddhist Missionaries in the Era of Globalization*, Topics in Contemporary Buddhism (Honolulu: University of Hawai'i Press, 2005), 12.
3. Ibid, 3.
4. Thomas A. Tweed, "Tracing Modernity's Flows: Buddhist Currents in the Pacific World," *The Eastern Buddhist* 43, nos. 1–2 (2012): 35–56.
5. Michael K. Masatsugu, "'Bonded by Reverence Toward the Buddha': Asian Decolonization, Japanese Americans, and the Making of the Buddhist World, 1947–1965," *Journal of Global History* 8 (2013): 142–164.
6. Yehan Numata, "Editorial," *The Pacific World* 1, no. 1 (1925): 24.
7. Buddhist temples in Japan typically are patrilineal organizations, with the eldest son of the temple priest expected to assume his father's responsibilities. This has been the norm in the Shin Buddhist tradition going back almost to Shinran himself and has been adapted to other Buddhist traditions as well. Whereas more recently other forms of temple succession and religious authority are possible, in the early twentieth century custom would not have demanded Numata take over his father's temple.
8. The Berkeley Temple's centennial commemorative book (Berkeley Buddhist Temple, *A Century of Gratitude and Joy: 1911–2011* [Berkeley, CA: Berkeley Buddhist Temple, 2014]) dedicates a half-page insert to Numata noting his time in Berkeley, the fire that destroyed the Japanese student dormitory, and his connections to the Berkeley community.
9. Coby McDonald, "September 17, 1923: The Day That Berkeley Burned," Cal Alumni Association, accessed October 29, 2022, https://alumni.berkeley.edu/california-magazine/spring-2019/september-17-1923-day-berkeley-burned; "CJAAA History," accessed October 29, 2021, https://web.archive.org/web/20150206023146/http://cjaaa.org/history.html.
10. It's worth noting this phenomenal feat—that a twenty-six-year-old graduate student was able to raise, in today's dollars, nearly half a million dollars from a small minority community that was, at the time, being actively persecuted, surveilled, and discriminated against, in part by disallowing the rights of citizenship, property ownership, and housing.
11. "Rev. Dr. Yehan Numata," Society for the Promotion of Buddhism, accessed October 29, 2021, http://www.bdk.or.jp/english/about/numata.html.
12. Sonyu Otani, "Mahayana Buddhism and Japanese Civilization," *The Pacific World* 2, no. 1 (1926): 3, 24–26.
13. In the 1980s, the Institute of Buddhist Studies, with support from the Numata Foundation, revived *The Pacific World* as an academic journal. The journal has

recently entered its fourth series as an open-access, peer-reviewed annual publication. As a member of the faculty of the Institute of Buddhist Studies, I serve on the journal's editorial board. See https://pwj.shin-ibs.edu for more information.

14. Laurence Cox, *Buddhism and Ireland: From the Celts to the Counter-Culture and Beyond* (Sheffield, UK: Equinox, 2013), 48.

15. Ibid., 63.

16. Ibid., 248–254; see also Laurence Cox, "Rethinking Early Western Buddhists: Beachcombers, 'Going Native' and Dissident Orientalism," *Contemporary Buddhism* 14, no. 1 (2013): 116–133.

17. Cox, *Buddhism and Ireland,* 254.

18. Tweed, "Tracing Modernity's Flows," 36–37.

19. As discussed in Chapter 1, whereas being a *kaikyōshi* priest, or "overseas dharma speaker," is generally expected for those wishing to lead a temple, not all ministers hold this rank.

20. Michihiro Ama, *Immigrants to the Pure Land: The Modernization, Acculturation, and Globalization of Shin Buddhism* (Honolulu: University of Hawai'i Press, 2011), 74.

21. As but a few examples: Goldwater received some form of *tokudo* (ordination) in Hawai'i from Yemyō Imamura as well as in Los Angeles and Kyoto, though he was never "officially" recognized by Honganji as an overseas minister. Alex White, ordained in San Francisco, eventually went to Japan to receive both *tokudo* and *kaikyōshi*; however, his wife, Violet, who was also ordained by Masuyama, did not go to Japan. Richard Prosser received *tokudo* in Japan in 1936 after being ordained in San Francisco. Even though she was never ordained in Kyoto, Pratt served the Tacoma Buddhist Church until her death and was allowed to serve as resident minister by the BCA despite not being "authorized" by the Honganji. And even though Frank Udale only received *tokudo* ordination in San Francisco, he was asked to "conduct services for non-Japanese" at the San Francisco church during World War II while its Japanese members were incarcerated (Buddhist Churches of America, *Buddhist Churches of America: A Legacy of the First 100 Years* [San Francisco: Buddhist Churches of America, 1998], 178). This last example is perhaps most telling, as it suggests both that Udale was trusted enough to watch over the temple in the absence of more "authorized" leadership and that there were apparently enough non-Japanese members of the community at this time to justify a minister-in-residence.

22. Ernest and Dorothy Hunt, for example, had a strong relationship with Yemyō Imamura in Hawai'i but would eventually develop different views on a number of issues, leading to their drifting away from the Hawai'ian Shinshū community. (See Ama, *Immigrants to the Pure Land,* 70–73.) Goldwater similarly had a falling-out with the Shin community after the war (Michihiro Ama, "'First White Buddhist Priestess': A Case Study of Sunya Gladys Pratt at the Tacoma Buddhist Temple," in *Buddhism Beyond Borders,* ed. Scott A. Mitchell and Natalie E. F. Quli [Albany: State University of New York Press, 2015], 69). It is beyond the scope of this book but worth noting that there has been a history, not often well documented and very rarely analyzed in scholarly literature, of white Shin Buddhist converts being elevated by the community as examples of Shin Buddhist cosmopolitanism, only to be later driven

out of the community due to more conservative elements within the community. In other words, whereas the Imamuras were committed to an inclusive Buddhist community, it would be wrong to suggest that their vision was universally shared by all American Shin Buddhists.

23. Tweed, "Tracing Modernity's Flows," 41.

24. Ibid., 53.

25. The Meiji Era is usually dated 1868–1912, whereas the Victorian is slightly earlier and more than twenty years longer at 1837–1901.

26. I am grateful to Jessica Main and Jeff Schroeder for helping me think through the periodization of Japanese history.

27. And certainly this conceptualization is a nice homage to the original *Pacific World*, established by Yehan Numata.

28. Tweed, "Tracing Modernity's Flows," 41 (emphasis in original).

29. Takashi Fujitani, *Race for Empire: Koreans as Japanese and Japanese as Americans During World War II* (Berkeley: University of California Press, 2013), 25.

30. David Palumbo-Liu, *Asian/American Historical Crossings of a Racial Frontier* (Stanford, CA: Stanford University Press, 1999), 340; cf. Laurie Maffly-Kipp, "Eastward Ho! American Religion from the Perspective of the Pacific Rim," in *Retelling U.S. Religious History*, ed. Thomas A. Tweed (Berkeley: University of California Press, 1997), 127–148.

31. Lisa Lowe, *Immigrant Acts: On Asian American Cultural Politics* (Durham, NC: Duke University Press, 1996), 8; cf. Caroline Chung Simpson, *An Absent Presence: Japanese Americans in Postwar American Culture, 1945–1960* (Durham, NC: Duke University Press, 2001), 20.

32. Arif Dirlik, "Performing the World: Reality and Representation in the Making of World Histor(ies)," *GHI Bulletin* 37 (2005): 25n23.

33. Ibid., 21.

34. Masatsugu, "Bonded by Reverence," 145.

35. It is beyond the scope of this book to fully unpack the complex postwar and Cold War–era politics and connections between Asian and U.S. Buddhists and government or covert organizations. Harrington's research, for example, documents the connections between the Asia Foundation, the CIA, Asian Buddhist organizations, and American Buddhist studies scholars. Similarly, Ritzinger documents these connections via the life and work of Holmes Welch. And Ford traces out connections between Buddhists in Japan and Thailand before the war and postwar U.S. engagements in Southeast Asia. These subjects are clearly deserving of more attention than we have space for here, but suffice to say merely using the nation-state as a level of analysis or foregrounding the agency of American interest without taking into consideration the post-colonial agency of Asian Buddhists overlooks the complexity and nuance of global Buddhist history in the second half of the twentieth century. Laura Harrington, "The Greatest Movie Never Made: The Life of the Buddha as Cold War Politics," *Religion and American Culture* 30, no. 3 (2020): 397–425; Justin Ritzinger, "Tinker, Tailor, Scholar, Spy: Holmes Welch, Buddhism, and the Cold War,"

Journal of Global Buddhism 22, no. 2 (2021): 421–441; Eugene Ford, *Cold War Monks. Buddhism and America's Secret Strategy in Southeast Asia* (New Haven, CT: Yale University Press, 2018).

36. Masatsugu, "Bonded by Reverence," 157.

37. Ibid.

38. Omar M. McRoberts, *Streets of Glory: Church and Community in a Black Urban Neighborhood* (Chicago: University of Chicago Press, 2005).

39. Bryan D. Lowe, "Roads, State, and Religion in Japanese Antiquity," *History of Religions* 59, no. 4 (2020): 274–303.

40. Edward Tang, "From Internment to Containment: Cold War Imaginings of Japanese Americans in *Go for Broke*," *Columbia Journal of American Studies* 9 (2009): 84–112.

41. Jobo Nakamura, "Nisei and Japan," *Berkeley Bussei*, 1953, 30–31.

42. Eiichiro Azuma, "Brokering Race, Culture, and Citizenship: Japanese Americans in Occupied Japan and Postwar National Inclusion," *Journal of American-East Asian Relations* 16, no. 3 (2009): 183–211; cf. Tamotsu Shibutani, *The Derelicts of Company K: A Sociological Study of Demoralization.* (Berkeley: University of California Press, 1978).

43. Nakamura, "Nisei and Japan," 30. *Yappari Nihonjin da ka ra* roughly translates here as "After all, you're Japanese."

44. Nakamura, "Nisei and Japan," 30. Nakamura appears to be paraphrasing Franklin Roosevelt here rather than directly quoting his comments upon the activation of the 442nd, the segregated Japanese American unit deployed to Europe in 1943. Regardless of the accuracy of this quote, the sentiment would surely not have been lost on his Nisei readers.

45. Jobo Nakamura, "Reflections on a Visit to Japan," *Berkeley Bussei*, 1954, 24.

46. Kaye Fujii, "From Kyoto," *Berkeley Bussei*, 1955, 29.

47. Ibid.

48. For the problematic nature of the "scholarly, journalistic, and clerical narratives of Japanese Buddhist decline," see Jolyon Baraka Thomas, "The Buddhist Virtues of Raging Lust and Crass Materialism in Contemporary Japan," *Material Religion* 11, no. 4 (2015): 485–506.

49. Art Takemoto, "Dilemma," *Berkeley Bussei*, 1953, 12.

50. Ibid.

51. Art Takemoto, "From Art Takemoto," *Berkeley Bussei*, 1952, 17.

52. Masatsugu, "Bonded by Reverence," 158.

53. Tetsuden Kashima, *Buddhism in America: The Social Organization of an Ethnic Religious Organization* (Westport, CT: Greenwood Press, 1977), 59–61; Buddhist Churches of America, *Buddhist Churches of America: 75 Year History 1899–1974* (Chicago: Nobart, 1974), 65.

54. Taitetsu Unno, "Faced with a Dilemma," *Berkeley Bussei*, 1951, 16.

55. "Editorial," *Berkeley Bussei*, 1950, n.p.; the editors of the 1950 volume included Kimi Hisatsune (writing under her maiden name, Yonemura), Allan Asakawa, and Art Iwata.

56. "A Time for Action," *Berkeley Bussei*, 1952, 21–22. While this article is uncredited, it was likely written by the volume's editors, who include Allan Asakawa, Hitoshi Tsufura, Lily Matsuura, Sei Shohara, and Rickey Ito.

57. Sei Shohara, "The Crisis," *Berkeley Bussei*, 1951, 15.

58. Buddhist Churches of America, *A Legacy of the First 100 Years*, vii.

59. "Buddhist Study Group," *Berkeley Bussei*, 1950, 7. According to this short note, the first session of the study group was held on November 11; this was followed by a second meeting on December 9. However, according to Jane Imamura's memoir, the first session was on October 29. Jane Michiko Imamura, *Kaikyo: Opening the Dharma: Memoirs of a Buddhist Priest's Wife in America* (Honolulu: Buddhist Study Center Press, 1998), 32.

60. J. Imamura, *Kaikyo*, 32–33.

61. Berkeley Buddhist Church, BCA Study Center, *1955 Report*.

62. Kanmo Imamura, " 「バークレー佛青」の新刊に寄せて" [For the publication of the Berkeley Bussei], *Berkeley Bussei*, 1953, 1 (Japanese section).

63. "Buddhist Study Group," 7.

64. Hitoshi Tsufura, "Buddhist Seminar," *Berkeley Bussei*, 1953, 28.

65. Among the ephemera in the Imamura archive held by the Institute of Buddhist Studies is a letter to Jane Imamura from Alan Watts regarding an invitation to deliver a talk at the Berkeley Buddhist Temple. See also Michael K. Masatsugu, "Reorienting the Pure Land: Japanese Americans, the Beats, and the Making of American Buddhism, 1941–1966," PhD diss., University of California, Irvine, 2004.

66. J. Imamura, *Kaikyo*, 39–40.

67. Buddhist Churches of America, *A Legacy of the First 100 Years*, 25.

68. Kanmo Imamura, "A House for Our Hopes," *Bussei*, 1952, n.p.

69. J. Imamura, *Kaikyo*, 57.

70. Untitled, *Berkeley Bussei*, 1955, 30.

71. J. Imamura, *Kaikyo*, 58; Berkeley Buddhist Temple, *A Century of Gratitude and Joy*, 35–36, 100. A new dorm was opened as part of the renovation.

72. Shinran singled out seven Buddhist thinkers and philosophers as the "patriarchs" of the Pure Land tradition: Nagarjuna, Vasubandhu, Tan-luan, Dao-cho, Shandao, Genshin, and Honen.

73. See Shinobu Matsuura, *Higan: Compassionate Vow; Selected Writings of Shinobu Matsuura* (Berkeley: Berkeley Study Center, 1986), 134–147; cf J. Imamura, *Kaikyo*, 59–64.

74. Matsuura, *Higan*, 137.

75. Ibid., 140.

76. Following the incorporation of the Study Center as the Institute of Buddhist Studies, the scroll was entrusted to the Institute as the school changed locations across Berkeley. Kenneth Tanaka, former dean of the Institute and scholar of Pure Land Buddhism, had the scroll authenticated in Kyoto by a Rennyo specialist, and today it hangs in the president's office at the Institute. Personal communication with David Matsumoto, May 27, 2022.

77. J. Imamura, *Kaikyo*, 39–40.

78. Richard M. Jaffe, "D.T. Suzuki and the Two Cranes: American Philanthropy and Suzuki's Global Agenda," in *Beyond Zen: D. T. Suzuki and the Modern Transformation of Buddhism*, ed. John Breen, Sueki Fumihiko, and Shōji Yamada (University of Hawaii Press, 2022), 133–55. I wish to thank Richard Jaffe for sharing an early draft of this work with me and for his kindness as I conducted research on this project.

79. Ibid, 151.

80. Personal communication, Hoshina Seki, October 29, 2021; see also Greg Robinson, "George Yamaoka for the Defense: The Story of a Transnational Nisei Lawyer and Businessman," Discover Nikkei, accessed October 29, 2021, http://www.discovernik kei.org/en/journal/2019/12/12/george-yamaoka/.

81. In 2000, the American Buddhist Academy changed its name to the American Buddhist Study Center. See https://www.ambuddhist.org/about.

82. Daisetz Teitaro Suzuki, "The Spirit of Shinran Shōnin," in *Selected Works of D. T. Suzuki*, ed. James C Dobbins and Richard M Jaffe (Berkeley: University of California Press, 2015), 2:236–240. See also Michael Haederle, "Profile: The New York Buddhist Church," Lion's Roar, accessed October 29, 2021, https://www.lionsroar.com/profile-the-new-york-buddhist-church/.

83. Daisetz Teitaro Suzuki, *Shin Buddhism* (London: George Allen & Unwin, 1970), 13. Largely thanks to Brian Nagata of Bukkyō Dendō Kyōkai, this book was republished by Shambhala Publications and edited by Taitetsu Unno. See Daisetz Teitaro Suzuki, *Buddha of Infinite Light: The Teachings of Shin Buddhism, the Japanese Way of Wisdom & Compassion* (Boston: Shambhala, 2002).

84. Stuart Lavietes, "Frank Okamura, Bonsai Expert, Is Dead at 94," *New York Times*, January 14, 2006, https://www.nytimes.com/2006/01/14/nyregion/frank-okamura-bonsai-expert-is-dead-at-94.html.

85. Jane Iwamura, *Virtual Orientalism: Asian Religions and American Popular Culture* (New York: Oxford University Press, 2010), 58.

86. Ibid., 26.

87. Quoted in ibid., 58.

88. Ibid., 60

89. Ibid. (emphasis in original).

90. Jane Imamura includes a photograph in her memoir (*Kaikyo*, 55) captioned "Greeting Dr. D. T. Suzuki at the airport." In it, Suzuki is surrounded by a number of people, both Japanese American and white, but none are named. Neither Jane nor Kanmo appears to be in the picture, and the photo is not dated. So it is difficult to know when this picture was taken or who was meeting Suzuki at the airport. However, given her role, generally, of *bōmori* and chauffeur, it is likely that Jane took this photograph herself.

91. J. Imamura, *Kaikyo*, 44.

92. In reflecting on the biographical film *A Zen Life: D. T. Suzuki*, feminist theorist and cultural critic bell hooks notes: "Throughout the film, we witness the role women play in his life, almost always in the background yet always working to help create a sustainable environment for Suzuki to live and work. It is impossible to watch this film and not want to know more about Mihoko Okamura." (bell hooks, "10 Leading

Thinkers Choose Their Favorite Buddhist Films," *Lion's Roar*, accessed January 6, 2022, https://www.lionsroar.com/top-ten-buddhist-films/.)

93. I am grateful to Daijaku Kinst for this observation.

94. As mentioned in the previous chapter, Kolata and Gillson note that acts of hospitality can also serve as Buddhist practice; being a good host can be understood as enacting the bodhisattva virtue of generosity. Paulina Kolata and Gwendolyn Gillson, "Feasting with Buddhist Women: Food Literacy in Religious Belonging," *Numen* 68, nos. 5–6 (2021): 583.

95. Quoted in Rudiger V. Busto, "Disorienting Subjects: Reclaiming Pacific Islander/ Asian American Religions," in *Revealing the Sacred in Asian and Pacific America*, ed. Jane Iwamura and Paul Spickard (New York: Routledge, 2002), 16.

96. Busto, "Disorienting Subjects," 20–21.

Chapter 5

1. Jack Kerouac, untitled essay in *Berkeley Bussei*, 1960, n.p.; Jane Iwamura, in *Virtual Orientalism: Asian Religions and American Popular Culture* (New York: Oxford University Press, 2010), 173n55, discusses the different versions of this piece and how it has maintained a life of its own separate from its publication in the *Berkeley Bussei*.

2. Jane Michiko Imamura, *Kaikyo: Opening the Dharma: Memoirs of a Buddhist Priest's Wife in America* (Honolulu: Buddhist Study Center Press, 1998), 33, 37–41; Hiro Imamura David, personal communication with the author, August 30, 2021.

3. Iwamura, *Virtual Orientalism*, 47.

4. Quoted in ibid., 43; cf. Alan Watts, "Beat Zen, Square Zen, and Zen," *Chicago Review* 12, no. 2 (1958): 3–11.

5. Iwamura, *Virtual Orientalism*, 47; for a more recent analysis of Kerouac's work and its Buddhist elements, see Sarah F. Haynes, "Sad Paradise: Jack Kerouac's Nostalgic Buddhism," *Religions* 10, no. 4 (2019): 1–11.

6. Iwamura, *Virtual Orientalism*, 48.

7. Ibid., 50.

8. Alan Watts, "A Program for Buddhism in America," *Berkeley Bussei*, 1952, 19.

9. Unsurprisingly, the list of authors is a list of men, and, with the exception of D. T. Suzuki, white men. Interestingly, the service schedule Watts suggests is not that far off from how most BCA temples today organize their services. Watts's schedule opens with chanting, continues with reading the sutras, silent meditation, a dharma talk (in Japanese), singing, and instruction in English, and closes with more chanting. This order of events does not seem uniquely Buddhist and, in practice, could easily be considered just as "Protestant" as whatever type of service Watts was objecting to in the early 1950s.

10. Michael K. Masatsugu, "'Beyond This World of Transiency and Impermanence': Japanese Americans, Dharma Bums, and the Making of American Buddhism During the Early Cold War Years," *Pacific Historical Review* 77, no. 3 (2008): 447.

11. Alan Watts, "The Problem of Faith and Works in Buddhism," *Review of Religion* 5, no. 4 (1941): 387–402; cf. Alan Watts, "The Problem of Faith and Works in Buddhism," in *Become What You Are* (Boston: Shambhala, 2003), 97–120.

12. Watts, "The Problem of Faith and Works," 2003, 102.

13. Ibid.

14. Ibid, 109.

15. For a discussion of perennialism, see Richard K. Payne, "How Not to Talk About Pure Land Buddhism: A Critique of Huston Smith's (Mis)Representations," in *Path of No Path: Contemporary Studies on Pure Land Buddhism Honoring Roger Corless*, ed. Richard K. Payne (Berkeley: Numata Center for Buddhist Translation and Research, 2009), 147–172.

16. See "Articles," Alan Watts Organization, accessed November 5, 2021, https://alanwatts.org/articles/.

17. Robert E. Buswell and Donald S. Lopez, eds., *The Princeton Dictionary of Buddhism* (Princeton, NJ: Princeton University Press, 2017), 992. As an aside, and to further reinforce how habits of thought perpetuate our understanding of history, whereas Watts, Snyder, Kerouac, and many other countercultural and Beat figures are given entries in the *Dictionary*, there are no entries for Taitetsu Unno, the Imamuras, the Buddhist Churches of America, or even Yehan Numata (though the Numata Foundation is mentioned in the acknowledgments as a funder of the publication).

18. David Chadwick, "Celebrating the Life and Teachings of Alan Watts," *Lion's Roar*, November 16, 2020, https://www.lionsroar.com/celebrating-alan-watts/; David Guy, "Alan Watts Reconsidered," *Tricycle: The Buddhist Review*, Fall 1994, https://tricycle.org/magazine/alan-watts-reconsidered/. The anonymous Twitter account @EngagedPureLand would call this an example of "Pure Land Deficiency Syndrome," whereby persons with clear and documented connections to Jōdo Shinshū either contemporarily or historically are framed in such a way as to minimize or erase these connections. See, for example: https://threadreaderapp.com/thread/142038788577 4163978.html (accessed November 5, 2021).

19. For a summary of scholarship on Watts, see Scott A. Mitchell, "Buddhism and the Beats," in *Oxford Bibliographies in Buddhism*, ed. Richard K. Payne (New York: Oxford University Press, 2013).

20. David L. Smith, "The Authenticity of Alan Watts," in *American Buddhism as a Way of Life*, ed. Gary Storhoff and John Whalen-Bridge (Albany: State University of New York Press, 2010), 13–38.

21. Iwamura, *Virtual Orientalism*, 51.

22. Ellen Pearlman, "My Lunch with Mihoko," in *American Buddhism as a Way of Life*, ed. Gary Storhoff and John Whalen-Bridge (Albany: State University of New York Press, 2010), 57 (emphasis added).

23. Stephen R. Prothero, *The White Buddhist: The Asian Odyssey of Henry Steel Olcott* (Bloomington: Indiana University Press, 1996), ix.

24. Charles S. Prebish, *Luminous Passage: The Practice and Study of Buddhism in America* (Berkeley: University of California Press, 1999), 15.

25. Rick Fields, *How the Swans Came to the Lake: A Narrative History of Buddhism in America* (Boulder, CO: Shambhala, 1981), 214–215.

26. Gary Snyder, *Mountains and Rivers Without End* (New York: Counterpoint, 1996), 154; Michael K. Masatsugu, "Reorienting the Pure Land: Japanese Americans, the Beats, and the Making of American Buddhism, 1941–1966," PhD diss., University of California, Irvine, 2004; Jeff Wilson, personal communication with the author, July 14, 2021.

27. Pearlman, "My Lunch with Mihoko," 59.

28. Ibid., 66.

29. Ayako Noguchi, "Where the Heart Belongs," *Berkeley Bussei*, Fall 1941, n.p., used by permission.

30. Snyder, *Mountains and Rivers Without End*, 154.

31. Gary Snyder, "Piute Creek," *Berkeley Bussei*, 1956, 7. This poem was included in a 1965 collection and has been reprinted by permission. Gary Snyder, "Piute Creek," from *Riprap and Cold Mountain Poems*. Copyright 1965 by Gary Snyder. Reprinted with the permission of The Permissions Company, LLC on behalf of Counterpoint, counterpointpress.com.

32. Gary Snyder and David Stephen Calonne, *Conversations with Gary Snyder* (Jackson: University Press of Mississippi, 2017), x.

33. For a discussion of Kerouac's *The Dharma Bums*, see Miriam Levering, "Jack Kerouac in Berkeley: Reading *The Dharma Bums* as the Work of a Buddhist Writer," *Pacific World: Journal of the Institute of Buddhist Studies* 3, no. 6 (Fall 2004): 7–26.

34. J. Imamura, *Kaikyo*, 65–66. Family history tells that it was Jane Imamura who encouraged Takei to become an actor; thus, one could argue that both American Buddhism as we know it today and the *Star Trek* fictional universe are what they are because of Japanese American Shin Buddhists. See Chenxing Han, *Be the Refuge: Raising the Voices of Asian American Buddhists* (Berkeley, CA: North Atlantic Books, 2021), 57.

35. Scott A. Mitchell, *Buddhism in America: Global Religion, Local Contexts* (London: Bloomsbury Academic, 2016), 182; cf. Kimberly Beek, "About vs. Of," *Buddhist Fiction Blog*, March 1, 2013.

36. John Whalen-Bridge and Gary Storhoff, *Buddhism and American Cinema* (Albany: State University of New York Press, 2014), ix.

37. This reference to the "face" of Buddhism calls to mind the work of Aaron Lee, the "Angry Asian Buddhist," who regularly tracked the number of Asian Americans represented in such collections, revealing how often this "face" was white. See http://www.angryasianbuddhist.com/tag/asian-meter/.

38. John Whalen-Bridge and Gary Storhoff, *The Emergence of Buddhist American Literature* (Albany: State University of New York Press, 2009), 3.

39. Charles B. Jones, "Is a *Dazang Jing* a Canon? On the Nature of Chinese Buddhist Textual Anthologies," in *Methods in Buddhist Studies: Essays in Honor of Richard K. Payne*, ed. Scott A. Mitchell and Natalie Fisk Quli (London: Bloomsbury Press, 2019), 130–132.

40. Iwamura, *Virtual Orientalism*, 6.

41. Trine Brox, "The Aura of Buddhist Material Objects in the Age of Mass-Production," *Journal of Global Buddhism* 20 (2019): 105–125. Brox complicates a simplistic understanding of "aura" as simply a distinctive air or quality characteristic of an object in her study of how objects' interactions with both their manufacturers and their users creates and reinforces aura (or not).

42. Kimberly Beek, "Telling Tales Out of School: The Fiction of Buddhism," in *Buddhism Beyond Borders*, ed. Scott A. Mitchell and Natalie E. F. Quli (Albany: State University of New York Press, 2015), 138.

43. John Whalen-Bridge, "Buddhism, the Chinese Religion, and the Ceremony of Writing: An Interview with Maxine Hong Kingston," in *The Emergence of Buddhist American Literature*, ed. Gary Storhoff and John Whalen-Bridge (Albany: State University of New York Press, 2009), 182.

44. Jeff Wilson, personal communication with the author, July 14, 2021.

45. Richard M. Jaffe, *Seeking Śākyamuni: South Asia in the Formation of Modern Japanese Buddhism* (Chicago: University of Chicago Press, 2019), 76–77; J. Imamura, *Kaikyo*, 37–8.

46. "Lama Tada's Contribution," *Berkeley Bussei*, 1954, 3. It is also possible that Tada was initiated into a tantric lineage during his time in Tibet.

47. Ibid.

48. Alex Wayman and Hideko Wayman, *The Lion's Roar of Queen Śrīmālā: a Buddhist Scripture on the Tathāgatagarbha Theory* (New York: Columbia University Press, 1974), xi.

49. Hideko, who came to the United States from Japan in the early 1950s, was also studying at UC Berkeley at the time; it is likely that she met Alex at the Berkeley Buddhist Temple.

50. My thanks to Richard Payne loaning me a copy of this book.

51. Scott A. Mitchell, "Drawing Blood: At the Intersection of Knowledge Economies and Buddhist Economies," in *Buddhism Under Capitalism*, ed. Richard K. Payne and Fabio Rambelli (London: Bloomsbury Academic, 2023), 169–83.

52. David Graeber, "It Is Value That Brings Universes into Being," *Hau: Journal of Ethnographic Theory* 3, no. 2 (2013): 219–24, 222; I am extraordinarily grateful to Jessica Starling for bringing this essay to my attention.

53. Ibid., 224 (emphasis in original).

54. J. Imamura, *Kaikyo*, 38.

55. Helen Tworkov, "Many Is More," *Tricycle: The Buddhist Review*, Winter 1991, https://tricycle.org/magazine/many-more/.

56. The logic of acculturation can be used in authentication discourses whereby acculturated practices are denigrated as corrupted, hybridized, or bastardized versions of some authentic or pure cultural practice. In this way, contemporary religious practices are devalued as inauthentic as per the logics of "imperialist nostalgia." See Natalie E. Quli, "Western Self, Asian Other: Modernity, Authenticity, and Nostalgia for 'Tradition' in Buddhist Studies," *Journal of Buddhist Ethics* 16 (2009): 1–38; Margaret J. Kartomi, "The Processes and Results of Musical Culture Contact: A Discussion of Terminology and Concepts," *Ethnomusicology* 25, no.

2 (1981): 227–249; Scott A. Mitchell, "The Ritual Use of Music in US Jōdo Shinshū Buddhist Communities," *Contemporary Buddhism* 15, no. 2 (2014): 2–3.

57. Charles S. Prebish, "Two Buddhisms Reconsidered," *Buddhist Studies Review* 10, no. 2 (1993): 206.

58. Ibid., 187 (emphasis added).

59. Ibid., 190. For the full letter, see Funie Hsu, "Lineage of Resistance: When Asian American Buddhists Confront White Supremacy," *Buddhist Peace Fellowship* (blog), 2017, https://web.archive.org/web/20180423171052/https://buddhistpeacefellows hip.org/lineage-of-resistance; c.f., Han, *Be The Refuge*, 21–24.

60. Masatsugu, "Beyond This World of Transiency and Impermanence," 427.

61. To be clear, the typology does perpetuate racist assumptions and, generally speaking, most academic classificatory systems are pretty arbitrary.

62. Jan Nattier, "Who Is a Buddhist? Charting the Landscape of Buddhist America," in *The Faces of Buddhism in America*, ed. Charles S. Prebish and Kenneth Tanaka (Berkeley: University of California Press, 1998), 183–195; Wakoh Shannon Hickey, "Two Buddhisms, Three Buddhisms, and Racism," *Journal of Global Buddhism* 11 (2010): 1–25; Paul David Numrich, "Two Buddhisms Further Considered," *Contemporary Buddhism* 4, no. 1 (2003): 55–78. Despite the fact that none of these authors make any claims about individuals being racist or prejudiced, that hasn't stopped some from taking their criticisms about structural racism person-ally, resulting in what Gleig and Artinger have called "white backlash." (See Ann Gleig and Brenna Grace Artinger, "The #BuddhistCultureWars: BuddhaBros, Alt-Right Dharma, and Snowflake Sanghas," *Journal of Global Buddhism* 22, no. 1 (2021): 19–48.)

63. As an anecdotal example of the way this typology has been inscribed institutionally into the subfield, during peer review of my own scholarship I have been asked by anonymous reviewers to comment on the "two Buddhisms" trope even when the sub-ject of the work has little or nothing to do with the typology.

64. To be clear, I am not saying we should stop discussing typologies or "cancel" any par-ticular line of academic research. I am merely drawing our attention to the fact that there is no reason to continue researching topics that have run their course. This is a choice. If a scholarly community reaches consensus on an idea, there is no external force compelling one to continue debating and discussing the idea. We choose to do so; therefore, we can choose not to and to turn our attention to other research topics.

65. Hsu, "Lineage of Resistance."

66. Chenxing Han, *Be the Refuge: Raising the Voices of Asian American Buddhists* (Berkeley, CA: North Atlantic Books, 2021), 41.

67. Webinar hosted by the West Los Angeles Buddhist Temple, "Millennials Interviewing Nisei," November 1, 2020; Sei Shohara, personal communication with author, November 2, 2021.

68. Chenxing Han, "Engaging the Invisible Majority: Conversations with Young Adult Asian American Buddhists," MA thesis, Graduate Theological Union, Berkeley, CA, 2014.

69. Mitchell, "Drawing Blood."

70. Lisa Lowe, *Immigrant Acts: On Asian American Cultural Politics* (Durham, NC: Duke University Press, 1996), 157.

Conclusion

1. "Jichiryo," *Berkeley Bussei*, 1954, 27.
2. Ibid., 28.
3. "BCA Ministerial Training Center in Full Swing," *The American Buddhist* 1, no. 5 (1957): 3.
4. "Ministerial Training Center in Kyoto to Be Transferred to the United States," *The American Buddhist* 2, no. 11 (1958): 3.
5. Buddhist Churches of America, *Buddhist Churches of America: 75 Year History 1899–1974* (Chicago: Nobart, 1974), 95.
6. "The Buddhist Family," *The American Buddhist* 8, no. 1 (1964): 1, 4.
7. Some examples include "Just Demands for Religious Freedom in South Vietnam" (June 1963); "BCA Objects to 'Buddha' Film Colossal" (June 1963); "BCA Protests Brutality Towards Buddhists" (August 1963); "Delegates Commend President Johnson's Efforts for World Peace" (February 1964); "Prayer in Public Schools—One Buddhist Answer" (May 1964); "BCA Ministers Oppose Proposition 14" (October 1964); and "Proposition 14 Would Legalize Discrimination in Housing" (October 1964).
8. Hiro Imamura David, "The Enduring Buddhist Legacy of Jane Imamura," edited by Jon Kawamoto, *Wheel of Dharma* 43, no. 10 (2021): 1, 5–6; Hiro Imamura David, personal communication with the author, August 30, 2021.
9. José I. Cabezón, "2020 AAR Presidential Address: The Study of Buddhism and the AAR," *Journal of the American Academy of Religion* 89, no. 3 (2021): 793.
10. Ibid., 794.
11. Charles S. Prebish, "Generations of Buddhist Studies: Prebish, Charles S.," H-Buddhism, accessed December 9, 2021, https://networks.h-net.org/node/6060/pages/3571853/prebish-charles-s. Concerns have been raised about the Generations project—namely, that some scholars used the platform to express offensive comments about historically marginalized persons and other issues. See Adeana McNicholl (@AdeanaMcN), "I'm no longer reading @H_Buddhism's 'Generations' project until editorial oversight is applied to stop allowing entries with offensive statements about women and people of colour. This is unacceptable and reflects poorly on our field," Twitter, March 29, 2019, https://twitter.com/AdeanaMcN/status/111166814092 7152128.
12. Duncan Ryûken Williams, *American Sutra: A Story of Faith and Freedom in the Second World War* (Cambridge, MA: Harvard University Press, 2019), 10–14.
13. Sarah F Haynes and Michelle J Sorensen, eds., *Wading into the Stream of Wisdom: Essays Honoring Leslie S. Kawamura* (Berkeley, CA: Institute of Buddhist Studies and BDK America, 2013).

14. Ibid., vii, 297; Jane Michiko Imamura, *Kaikyo: Opening the Dharma: Memoirs of a Buddhist Priest's Wife in America* (Honolulu: Buddhist Study Center Press, 1998), 66.

15. "Living Dharma Centre | Jodo Shinshu Buddhist Temples of Canada," accessed December 9, 2021, https://www.bcc.ca/ldc.html.

16. Jeff Wilson, "Generations of Buddhist Studies: Wilson, Jeff," H-Buddhism, accessed December 9, 2021, https://networks.h-net.org/node/6060/pages/3585289/wilson-jeff.

17. Jeff Wilson, "'All Beings Are Equally Embraced by Amida Buddha': Jodo Shinshu Buddhism and Same-Sex Marriage in the United States," *Journal of Global Buddhism* 13 (2012): 31–59.

18. Mikael Aktor, "Asymmetrical Religious Commitments? Religious Practice, Identity, and Self-Presentation Among Western Scholars of Hinduism and Buddhism," *Numen* 62, nos. 2–3 (2015): 276.

19. David L. Smith, "The Authenticity of Alan Watts," in *American Buddhism as a Way of Life*, ed. Gary Storhoff and John Whalen-Bridge (Albany: State University of New York Press, 2010), 16.

20. Donald S. Lopez, *Curators of the Buddha: The Study of Buddhism Under Colonialism* (Chicago: University of Chicago Press, 1995), 2; Cabezón, "2020 AAR Presidential Address."

21. Natalie Fisk Quli, "A Brief Critical Appraisal of the Buddhist Modernism Paradigm," in *The Routledge Handbook of Buddhist-Christian Studies*, ed. Carol S. Anderson and Thomas Cattoi (London and New York: Routledge, 2023), 353–63; cf. Jason Ānanda Josephson-Storm, *The Myth of Disenchantment: Magic, Modernity, and the Birth of the Human Sciences* (Chicago: University of Chicago Press, 2017).

22. Pema McLaughlin, "Imagining Buddhist Modernism: The Shared Religious Categories of Scholars and American Buddhists," *Religion* 50, no. 4 (2019): 529–5.

23. Scott A. Mitchell, "Drawing Blood: At the Intersection of Knowledge Economies and Buddhist Economies," in *Buddhism Under Capitalism*, ed. Richard K. Payne and Fabio Rambelli (London: Bloomsbury Academic, 2023), 169–83.

Epilogue: Our Narrative

1. Hiroshi Kashiwagi, "A Narrative," *Berkeley Bussei*, 1956, 39.

2. Natalie Gummer, "Sūtra Time," in *The Language of the Sūtras: Essays in Honor of Luis Gómez*, ed. Natalie Gummer (Berkeley, CA: Mangalam Press, 2021), 294; Gummer here is drawing on the work of Reinhart Koselleck, who conceptualized the terms "space of experience" and "horizon of expectation."

3. Ibid., 314.

4. Melissa Anne-Marie Curley, *Pure Land, Real World: Modern Buddhism, Japanese Leftists, and the Utopian Imagination* (Honolulu: University of Hawai'i Press, 2017), 3.

5. As quoted in Gummer, "Sūtra Time," 316.

6. Curley, *Pure Land, Real World*, 30.

7. Hiroshi Kashiwagi, *Swimming in the American: A Memoir and Selected Writings* (San Mateo, CA: Asian American Curriculum Project, 2005), 183.

Select Bibliography

"A Time for Action." *Berkeley Bussei*, 1952, 21–22.

Aktor, Mikael. "Asymmetrical Religious Commitments? Religious Practice, Identity, and Self-Presentation Among Western Scholars of Hinduism and Buddhism." *Numen* 62, nos. 2–3 (2015): 265–300.

Almond, Philip C. *The British Discovery of Buddhism*. Cambridge: Cambridge University Press, 1988.

Ama, Michihiro. "'First White Buddhist Priestess': A Case Study of Sunya Gladys Pratt at the Tacoma Buddhist Temple." In *Buddhism Beyond Borders*, edited by Scott A. Mitchell and Natalie E. F. Quli, 59–74. Albany: State University of New York Press, 2015.

Ama, Michihiro. "The Imamura Families and the Making of American Buddhism." In *Oxford Encyclopedia of Buddhism*, 1–18. New York: Oxford University Press, 2019.

Ama, Michihiro. *Immigrants to the Pure Land: The Modernization, Acculturation, and Globalization of Shin Buddhism*. Honolulu: University of Hawai'i Press, 2011.

Ama, Michihiro. "Shinran as 'Other': Revisiting Kurata Hyakuzō's The Priest and His Disciples." *Japanese Journal of Religious Studies* 43, no. 2 (2016): 253–274.

Amstutz, Galen. *Interpreting Amida: History and Orientalism in the Study of Pure Land Buddhism*. Albany: State University of New York Press, 1997.

Amstutz, Galen. "Limited Engagements: Revisiting the Non-Encounter Between American Buddhism and the Shin Tradition." *Journal of Global Buddhism* 3 (2002): 1–35.

Amstutz, Galen. "Missing Hongan-Ji in Japanese Studies." *Japanese Journal of Religious Studies* 23, nos. 1–2 (1996): 155–178.

Anningson, Ryan. "Theories of the Self, Race, and Essentialization in Buddhism in the United States During the 'Yellow Peril,' 1899–1957." PhD diss., Wilfrid Laurier University, 2017.

Appadurai, Arjun. *Modernity at Large: Cultural Dimensions of Globalization*. Minneapolis: University of Minnesota Press, 1996.

Asad, Talal. "The Idea of an Anthropology of Islam." *Qui Parle* 17, no. 2 (2009): 1–30.

Asai, Senryō, and Duncan Ryūken Williams. "Japanese American Zen Temples: Cultural Identity and Economics." In *American Buddhism: Methods and Findings in Recent Scholarship*, edited by Duncan Ryūken Williams and Christopher S. Queen, 20–35. Curzon Critical Studies in Buddhism. Richmond, Surrey: Curzon, 1999.

Asato, Noriko. "The Japanese Language School Controversy in Hawaii." In *Issei Buddhism in the Americas*, edited by Duncan Ryūken Williams and Tomoe Moriya, 45–64. Urbana: University of Illinois Press, 2010.

Asato, Noriko. *Teaching Mikadoism: The Attack on Japanese Language Schools in Hawaii, California, and Washington, 1919–1927*. Honolulu: University of Hawai'i Press, 2006.

"Asian Studies." *Berkeley Bussei*, 1953, 32.

Avalos, Natalie. "What Does It Mean to Heal from Historical Trauma?" *AMA Journal of Ethics* 23, no. 6 (2021): 494–498.

Azuma, Eiichiro. *Between Two Empires: Race, History, and Transnationalism in Japanese America*. New York: Oxford University Press, 2005.

Azuma, Eiichiro. "Brokering Race, Culture, and Citizenship: Japanese Americans in Occupied Japan and Postwar National Inclusion." *Journal of American-East Asian Relations* 16, no. 3 (2009): 183–211.

Azuma, Eiichiro. "The Making of a Japanese American Race, and Why Are There 'Immigrants' in Postwar Nikkei History and Community? The Problems of Generation, Region, and Citizenship in Japanese America." In *Trans-Pacific Japanese American Studies: Conversations on Race and Racializations*, edited by Yasuko Takezawa and Gary Okihiro, 257–287. Honolulu: University of Hawai'i Press, 2017.

Batchelor, Stephen. *The Awakening of the West: The Encounter of Buddhism and Western Culture*. Berkeley, CA: Parallax Press, 1994.

Baumann, Martin. "Protective Amulets and Awareness Techniques, or How to Make Sense of Buddhism in the West." In *Westward Dharma Buddhism Beyond Asia*, edited by Charles S. Prebish and Martin Baumann, 51–65. Berkeley: University of California Press, 2002.

Beek, Kimberly. "About vs. Of." *Buddhist Fiction Blog*, March 1, 2013.

Beek, Kimberly. "Telling Tales Out of School: The Fiction of Buddhism." In *Buddhism Beyond Borders*, edited by Scott A. Mitchell and Natalie E. F. Quli, 125–142. Albany: State University of New York Press, 2015.

Berkeley Buddhist Temple. *A Century of Gratitude and Joy: 1911–2011*. Berkeley: Berkeley Buddhist Temple, 2014.

Bocking, Brian, Phibul Choompolpaisal, Laurence Cox, and Alicia M. Turner. *A Buddhist Crossroads: Pioneer Western Buddhists and Asian Networks 1860–1960*. London: Routledge, 2020.

Borovoy, Amy. "Not 'A Doll's House': Public Uses of Domesticity in Japan." *U.S.-Japan Women's Journal: English Supplement* 20/21 (2001): 83–124.

Brox, Trine. "The Aura of Buddhist Material Objects in the Age of Mass-Production." *Journal of Global Buddhism* 20 (2019): 105–125.

Buddhist Churches of America. *Buddhist Churches of America: 75 Year History 1899–1974*. Chicago: Nobart, 1974.

Buddhist Churches of America. *Buddhist Churches of America: A Legacy of the First 100 Years*. San Francisco: Buddhist Churches of America, 1998.

"Buddhist Study Group." *Berkeley Bussei*, 1950, 7.

Busto, Rudiger V. "Disorienting Subjects: Reclaiming Pacific Islander/Asian American Religions." In *Revealing the Sacred in Asian and Pacific America*, edited by Jane Iwamura and Paul Spickard, 9–28. New York: Routledge, 2002.

Buswell, Robert E., and Donald S. Lopez, eds. *The Princeton Dictionary of Buddhism*. Princeton, NJ: Princeton University Press, 2017.

Cabezón, José I. "2020 AAR Presidential Address: The Study of Buddhism and the AAR." *Journal of the American Academy of Religion* 89, no. 3 (2021): 793–818.

Cadge, Wendy. *Heartwood: The First Generation of Theravada Buddhism in America*. Chicago: University of Chicago Press, 2005.

Caruth, Cathy. *Trauma: Explorations in Memory*. Baltimore: Johns Hopkins University Press, 1996.

Cheah, Joseph. *Race and Religion in American Buddhism: White Supremacy and Immigrant Adaptation*. New York: Oxford University Press, 2011.

Cheah, Joseph. "US Buddhist Traditions." In *The Oxford Handbook of Contemporary Buddhism*, edited by Michael K. Jerryson, 316–331. New York: Oxford University Press, 2017.

Coleman, James William. *The New Buddhism: The Western Transformation of an Ancient Tradition*. New York: Oxford University Press, 2001.

Cox, Laurence. *Buddhism and Ireland: From the Celts to the Counter-Culture and Beyond.* Sheffield, UK: Equinox, 2013.

Cox, Laurence. "Rethinking Early Western Buddhists: Beachcombers, 'Going Native' and Dissident Orientalism." *Contemporary Buddhism* 14, no. 1 (2013): 116–133.

"Credit Lines." *Berkeley Bussei*, Spring 1941, n.p.

Curley, Melissa Anne-Marie. *Pure Land, Real World: Modern Buddhism, Japanese Leftists, and the Utopian Imagination*. Honolulu: University of Hawai'i Press, 2017.

Deslippe, Philip. "Bunko Bishop: Swami Mazziniananda, the Udana Karana Order, and the Buddhist Mission of North America." *Japanese Religions* 44, nos. 1–2 (2021): 33–63.

Dharmawara, Vira. "Discourse on the Dharma." *Berkeley Bussei*, 1956, 4–6.

Dirlik, Arif. "Performing the World: Reality and Representation in the Making of World Histor(Ies)." *GHI Bulletin* 37 (2005): 9–25.

Dobbins, James C. *Behold the Buddha: Religious Meanings of Japanese Buddhist Icons.* Honolulu: University of Hawai'i Press, 2020.

Dobbins, James C. *Jōdo Shinshū: Shin Buddhism in Medieval Japan*. Honolulu: University of Hawai'i Press, 2002.

"Editorial." *Berkeley Bussei*, 1950, n.p.

Eichman, Jennifer Lynn. *A Late Sixteenth-Century Chinese Buddhist Fellowship: Spiritual Ambitions, Intellectual Debates, and Epistolary Connections*. Leiden: Brill, 2016.

Eyerman, Ron. "Social Theory and Trauma." *Acta Sociologica* 56, no. 1 (2013): 41–53.

Fields, Rick. *How the Swans Came to the Lake: A Narrative History of Buddhism in America*. Boulder, CO: Shambhala, 1981.

Ford, Eugene. *Cold War Monks. Buddhism and America's Secret Strategy in Southeast Asia.* New Haven, CT: Yale University Press, 2018.

"Foreword." *Berkeley Bussei*, 1952, n.p.

Fujii, Kaye. "From Kyoto." *Berkeley Bussei*, 1955, 29.

Fujino, Diane Carol. *Heartbeat of Struggle: The Revolutionary Life of Yuri Kochiyama.* Minneapolis: University of Minnesota Press, 2005.

Fujitani, Takashi. *Race for Empire: Koreans as Japanese and Japanese as Americans During World War II*. Berkeley: University of California Press, 2013.

Fukuda, Manabu. "Let Us Gasshō." *Berkeley Bussei*, Spring 1940, n.p.

Getz, Daniel A. "Shenghang's Pure Conduct Society and the Chinese Pure Land Patriarchate." In *Approaching the Land of Bliss: Religious Praxis in the Cult of Amitābha*, edited by Richard K. Payne and Kenneth K. Tanaka, 52–76. Kuroda Institute Studies in East Asian Buddhism, No. 17. Honolulu: University of Hawai'i Press, 2004.

Gleig, Ann. "Undoing Whiteness in American Buddhist Modernism: Critical, Collective, and Contextual Turns." In *Buddhism and Whiteness: Critical Reflections*, edited by George Yancy and Emily McRae, 21–42. Lanham, MD: Lexington Books, 2019.

Gleig, Ann, and Brenna Grace Artinger. "The #BuddhistCultureWars: BuddhaBros, Alt-Right Dharma, and Snowflake Sanghas." *Journal of Global Buddhism* 22, no. 1 (2021): 19–48.

Goldwater, Julius. "Our Future." *Berkeley Bussei*, Spring 1941, n.p.

Graeber, David. "It Is Value That Brings Universes into Being." *Hau: Journal of Ethnographic Theory* 3, no. 2 (2013): 219–243.

Gummer, Natalie. "Sūtra Time." In *The Language of the Sūtras: Essays in Honor of Luis Gómez*, edited by Natalie Gummer, 293–337. Berkeley, CA: Mangalam Press, 2021.

Halkias, Georgios T., and Richard K. Payne. *Pure Lands in Asian Texts and Contexts: An Anthology*. Honolulu: University of Hawai'i Press, 2019.

Han, Chenxing. *Be the Refuge: Raising the Voices of Asian American Buddhists*. Berkeley, CA: North Atlantic Books, 2021.

Han, Chenxing. "Diverse Practices and Flexible Beliefs Among Young Adult Asian American Buddhists." *Journal of Global Buddhism* 18 (2017): 1–24.

Han, Chenxing. "Engaging the Invisible Majority: Conversations with Young Adult Asian American Buddhists." MA thesis, Graduate Theological Union, 2014.

"Harmony in Sangha." *Berkeley Bussei*, Spring 1941, n.p.

Harrington, Laura. "The Greatest Movie Never Made: The Life of the Buddha as Cold War Politics." *Religion and American Culture* 30, no. 3 (2020): 397–425.

Haynes, Sarah F. "Sad Paradise: Jack Kerouac's Nostalgic Buddhism." *Religions* 10, no. 4 (2019): 1–11.

Haynes, Sarah F., and Michelle J. Sorensen, eds. *Wading into the Stream of Wisdom: Essays Honoring Leslie S. Kawamura*. Berkeley, CA: Institute of Buddhist Studies and BDK America, 2013.

Hickey, Wakoh Shannon. "Swedenborg: A Modern Buddha?" *Pacific World: Journal of the Institute of Buddhist Studies* (3rd ser.) 10 (2008): 101–129.

Hickey, Wakoh Shannon. "Two Buddhisms, Three Buddhisms, and Racism." *Journal of Global Buddhism* 11 (2010): 1–25.

Hickey, Wakoh Shannon. "Two Buddhisms, Three Buddhisms, and Racism." In *Buddhism Beyond Borders*, edited by Scott A. Mitchell and Natalie E. F. Quli, 35–56. Albany: State University of New York Press, 2015.

Hisatsune, Kimi. "The Problem of Faith." *Berkeley Bussei*, 1953, 6–7.

Hisatsune, Kimi. "Shinshu in a Changing World." *Berkeley Bussei*, 1955, 25.

Hori, Victor Sōgen. "How Do We Study Buddhism in Canada?" In *Wild Geese: Buddhism in Canada*, edited by John S. Harding, Victor Sōgen Hori, and Alexander Soucy, 12–38. Montreal: McGill-Queen's University Press, 2010.

Hsu, Funie. "Lineage of Resistance: When Asian American Buddhists Confront White Supremacy." *Buddhist Peace Fellowship* (blog), 2017. https://buddhistpeacefellowship. org/lineage-of-resistance/.

Imamura, Jane. "Gathas in the West." *Berkeley Bussei*, 1952, 20.

Imamura, Jane Michiko. *Kaikyo: Opening the Dharma: Memoirs of a Buddhist Priest's Wife in America*. Honolulu: Buddhist Study Center Press, 1998.

Imamura, Kanmo. "仏教徒は世界人なり" [Buddhists are cosmopolitan]. *Berkeley Bussei*, Fall 1941, n.p.

Imamura, Kanmo. "「バークレー佛青」の新刊に奇せて" [For the publication of the Berkeley Bussei]. *Berkeley Bussei*, 1953, 1 (Japanese section).

Imamura, Kanmo. "A House for Our Hopes." *Berkeley Bussei*, 1952, n.p.

Imamura, Kanmo. "再びブヂストセンタ建設について" [Once again, on the reconstruction of the Buddhist Center]. *Berkeley Bussei*, 1952, n.p.

Imamura, Kanmo. "Oneness." *Berkeley Bussei*, 1951, 6.

Imamura, Kanmo. "Panorama." *Berkeley Bussei*, 1953, 1.

Imamura, Yemyō. *Democracy According to the Buddhist Viewpoint*. Honolulu: Publishing Bureau of Hongwanji Mission, 1918.

Inagaki, Hisao, ed. *A Record in Lament of Divergences: A Translation of Tannishō*. 2nd ed. Kyoto: Hongwanji International Center, 2005.

Inagaki, Hisao, and Harold Stewart. *The Three Pure Land Sutras*. BDK English Tripitaka; 12-II, III, IV. Berkeley, CA: Numata Center for Buddhist Translation and Research, 1995.

Ivy, Marilyn. "Modernity." In *Critical Terms for the Study of Buddhism*, edited by Donald S. Lopez, 311–331. Chicago: University of Chicago Press, 2005.

Iwamura, Jane. "Altared States: Exploring the Legacy of Japanese American Butsudan Practice." *Pacific World: Journal of the Institute of Buddhist Studies* 3, no. 5 (Fall 2003): 275–291.

Iwamura, Jane. *Virtual Orientalism: Asian Religions and American Popular Culture*. New York: Oxford University Press, 2010.

Iwamura, Jane, and Paul Spickard. *Revealing the Sacred in Asian and Pacific America*. New York: Routledge, 2002.

Jackson, R. P. "A New Outlook." *Berkeley Bussei*, 1954, 22–23.

Jaffe, Richard M. *Seeking Śākyamuni: South Asia in the Formation of Modern Japanese Buddhism*. Chicago: University of Chicago Press, 2019.

Jaffe, Richard M. "D.T. Suzuki and the Two Cranes: American Philanthropy and Suzuki's Global Agenda." In *Beyond Zen: D. T. Suzuki and the Modern Transformation of Buddhism*, edited by John Breen, Sueki Fumihiko, and Shōji Yamada, 133–155. University of Hawaii Press, 2022.

Jones, Charles B. "Is a Dazang Jing a Canon? On the Nature of Chinese Buddhist Textual Anthologies." In *Methods in Buddhist Studies: Essays in Honor of Richard K. Payne*, edited by Scott A. Mitchell and Natalie Fisk Quli, 129–143. London: Bloomsbury Press, 2019.

Josephson, Jason Ānanda. *The Invention of Religion in Japan*. Chicago: University of Chicago Press, 2012.

Josephson, Jason Ānanda. "When Buddhism Became a 'Religion': Religion and Superstition in the Writings of Inoue Enryō." *Japanese Journal of Religious Studies* 33, no. 1 (2006): 143–168.

Josephson-Storm, Jason Ānanda. *The Myth of Disenchantment: Magic, Modernity, and the Birth of the Human Sciences*. Chicago: University of Chicago Press, 2017.

Kartomi, Margaret J. "The Processes and Results of Musical Culture Contact: A Discussion of Terminology and Concepts." *Ethnomusicology* 25, no. 2 (1981): 227–249.

Kashima, Tetsuden. *Buddhism in America: The Social Organization of an Ethnic Religious Organization*. Westport, CT: Greenwood Press, 1977.

Kashima, Tetsuden. "The Buddhist Churches of America: Challenges for Change in the Twenty-First Century." In *Shin Buddhism: Historical, Textual, and Interpretive Studies*, edited by Richard K. Payne, 321–340. Berkeley: Numata Center for Buddhist Translation and Research, 2007.

Kashima, Tetsuden. *Judgment Without Trial: Japanese American Imprisonment During World War II*. Seattle: University of Washington Press, 2011.

Kashiwagi, Hiroshi. "Magazine Review: 1957 Berkeley Bussei Exceeds Previous Editions." *The American Buddhist*, August 1, 1957.

Kashiwagi, Hiroshi. "A Narrative." *Berkeley Bussei*, 1956, 38–39.

Kashiwagi, Hiroshi. *Swimming in the American: A Memoir and Selected Writings.* San Mateo, CA: Asian American Curriculum Project, 2005.

Kataoka, Marge. "A Whirl with the Girls: Never a Dorm Moment." *Berkeley Bussei,* 1952, 33–34.

Kawamoto, Yukio. "Outlook on American Buddhism." *Berkeley Bussei,* 1950, 8, 15.

Kawamoto, Yukio, and Calvin Ninomiya. "Yukio Kawamoto Collection." Veterans History Project, American Folklife Center, Library of Congress. Accessed October 15, 2021. https://memory.loc.gov/diglib/vhp/story/loc.natlib.afc2001001.07420/.

Kerouac, Jack. [Untitled article.] *Berkeley Bussei,* 1960, n.p.

Ketelaar, James Edward. *Of Heretics and Martyrs in Meiji Japan: Buddhism and Its Persecution.* Princeton, NJ: Princeton University Press, 1990.

Kikukawa, Ichido. "Unofficial Envoy: Shin Ministers Who Went to Hawaii Prior to the Hongwanji's Mission." Presented at the International Association of Shin Buddhist Studies Biennial Meeting, Taipei, May 25, 2019.

Kim, Claire Jean. "The Racial Triangulation of Asian Americans." *Politics and Society* 27, no. 1 (1999): 105–138.

King, Richard. *Orientalism and Religion Post-Colonial Theory, India and "the Mystic East."* London: Routledge, 1999.

Klautau, Orion, and Hans Martin Krämer, eds. *Buddhism and Modernity: Sources from Nineteenth-Century Japan.* Honolulu: University of Hawai'i Press, 2021.

Kolata, Paulina, and Gwendolyn Gillson. "Feasting with Buddhist Women: Food Literacy in Religious Belonging." *Numen* 68, nos. 5–6 (2021): 567–592.

"Lama Tada's Contribution." *Berkeley Bussei,* 1954, 3.

Learman, Linda. *Buddhist Missionaries in the Era of Globalization.* Topics in Contemporary Buddhism. Honolulu: University of Hawai'i Press, 2005.

Levering, Miriam. "Jack Kerouac in Berkeley: Reading The Dharma Bums as the Work of a Buddhist Writer." *Pacific World: Journal of the Institute of Buddhist Studies* 3, no. 6 (2004): 7–26.

Lopez, Donald S. *Curators of the Buddha: The Study of Buddhism Under Colonialism.* Chicago: University of Chicago Press, 1995.

Lopez, Donald S. *A Modern Buddhist Bible: Essential Readings from East and West.* Boston: Beacon Press, 2002.

López, Ian F. Haney. "White by Law." In *Critical Race Theory: The Cutting Edge,* edited by Richard Delgado and Jean Stefancic, 3rd ed., 775–782. Philadelphia: Temple University Press, 2013.

Lowe, Bryan D. "Roads, State, and Religion in Japanese Antiquity." *History of Religions* 59, no. 4 (2020): 272–303.

Lowe, Lisa. "Heterogeneity, Hybridity, Multiplicity: Marking Asian American Differences." In *Literary Theory: An Anthology,* edited by Julie Rivkin and Michael Ryan, 2nd ed., 1031–1050. Malden, MA: Blackwell, 2004.

Lowe, Lisa. *Immigrant Acts: On Asian American Cultural Politics.* Durham, NC: Duke University Press, 1996.

Maffly-Kipp, Laurie. "Eastward Ho! American Religion from the Perspective of the Pacific Rim." In *Retelling U.S. Religious History,* edited by Thomas A. Tweed, 127–148. Berkeley: University of California Press, 1997.

Masatsugu, Michael K. "'Beyond This World of Transiency and Impermanence': Japanese Americans, Dharma Bums, and the Making of American Buddhism During the Early Cold War Years." *Pacific Historical Review* 77, no. 3 (2008): 423–451.

Masatsugu, Michael K. "'Bonded by Reverence Toward the Buddha': Asian Decolonization, Japanese Americans, and the Making of the Buddhist World, 1947–1965." *Journal of Global History* 8 (2013): 142–164.

Masatsugu, Michael K. "Reorienting the Pure Land: Japanese Americans, the Beats, and the Making of American Buddhism, 1941–1966." PhD diss., University of California, Irvine, 2004.

Masuzawa, Tomoko. *The Invention of World Religions, or, How European Universalism Was Preserved in the Language of Pluralism*. Chicago: University of Chicago Press, 2005.

Matsuura, Shinobu. *Higan: Compassionate Vow; Selected Writings of Shinobu Matsuura*. Berkeley, CA: Berkeley Study Center, 1986.

McLaughlin, Pema. "Imagining Buddhist Modernism: The Shared Religious Categories of Scholars and American Buddhists." *Religion* 50, no. 4 (2019): 529–549.

McMahan, David L. "Buddhism and Multiple Modernities." In *Buddhism Beyond Borders*, edited by Scott A. Mitchell and Natalie E. F. Quli, 181–195. Albany: State University of New York Press, 2015.

McMahan, David L. *The Making of Buddhist Modernism*. New York: Oxford University Press, 2008.

McNicholl, Adeana. "The 'Black Buddhism Plan': Buddhism, Race, and Empire in the Early Twentieth Century." *Religion and American Culture* 31 (2021): 332–378.

McRoberts, Omar M. *Streets of Glory: Church and Community in a Black Urban Neighborhood*. Chicago: University of Chicago Press, 2005.

Min, Pyong Gap. "Introduction." In *Religions in Asian America: Building Faith Communities*, edited by Pyong Gap Min and Jung Ha Kim, 1–14. Walnut Creek, CA: AltaMira Press, 1992.

Mitchell, Scott A. "'Christianity Is for Rubes; Buddhism Is for Actors': U.S. Media Representations of Buddhism in the Wake of the Tiger Woods Scandal." *Journal of Global Buddhism* 13 (2012): 61–79.

Mitchell, Scott A. "Buddhism and the Beats." In *Oxford Bibliographies in Buddhism*, edited by Richard K. Payne. New York: Oxford University Press, 2013. Accessed December 16, 2022. https://www.oxfordbibliographies.com/view/document/obo-9780195393521/obo-9780195393521-0109.xml.

Mitchell, Scott A. *Buddhism in America: Global Religion, Local Contexts*. London: Bloomsbury Academic, 2016.

Mitchell, Scott A. "Drawing Blood: At the Intersection of Knowledge Economies and Buddhist Economies." In *Buddhism Under Capitalism*, edited by Richard K. Payne and Fabio Rambelli, 169–183. London: Bloomsbury Academic, 2023.

Mitchell, Scott A. "Locally Translocal American Shin Buddhism." *Pacific World: Journal of the Institute of Buddhist Studies* 3, no. 12 (2010): 109–126.

Mitchell, Scott A. "The Ritual Use of Music in US Jōdo Shinshū Buddhist Communities." *Contemporary Buddhism* 15, no. 2 (2014): 1–17.

Mitchell, Scott A. "Sunday Morning Songs." *The Pure Land* (n.s.) 22 (2006): 127–138.

Mitchell, Scott A. "The Stories We Tell: The Study and Practice of Jōdo Shinshū Buddhism." *Pacific World: Journal of the Institute of Buddhist Studies* 3, no. 19 (2017): 81–97.

Mizuno, Takeya. "Censorship in a Different Name: Press 'Supervision' in Wartime Japanese American Camps 1942–1943." *Journalism and Mass Communication Quarterly* 88, no. 1 (2011): 121–141.

Montrose, Victoria R. "Making the Modern Priest: The Ōtani Denomination's Proto-University and Debates About Clerical Education in the Early Meiji." In *Methods in*

Buddhist Studies: Essays in Honor of Richard K. Payne, edited by Scott A. Mitchell and Natalie Fisk Quli, 39–53. London: Bloomsbury Press, 2019.

Moriya, Tomoe. "'Americanization' and 'Tradition' in Issei and Nisei Buddhist Publications." In *Issei Buddhism in the Americas*, edited by Duncan Ryûken Williams and Tomoe Moriya, 110–130. Urbana: University of Illinois Press, 2010.

Moriya, Tomoe. *Amerika Bukkyō No Tanjō: Nijisseiki Shotō Ni Okeru Nikkei Shūkyō No Bunka Hen'yō* [アメリカ仏教の誕生: 二〇世紀初頭における日系宗教の文化変容 / 守屋友江著]. Tokyo: Gendai shiryō shuppan, 2001.

Moriya, Tomoe. *Yemyo Imamura: Pioneer American Buddhist*. Honolulu: Buddhist Study Center Press, 2000.

Nagata, Donna K., Jacqueline H. J. Kim, and Kaidi Wu. "The Japanese American Wartime Incarceration: Examining the Scope of Racial Trauma." *American Psychologist* 74, no. 1 (2019): 36–48.

Nakamura, George Jobo. "Foreword." *Berkeley Bussei*, Spring 1942, n.p.

Nakamura, Hajime. "The Humanitarian Tendency of the Japanese." *Berkeley Bussei*, 1955, 4–6.

Nakamura, Jobo. "Nisei and Japan." *Berkeley Bussei*, 1953, 30–31.

Nakamura, Jobo. "Reflections on a Visit to Japan." *Berkeley Bussei*, 1954, 24–25.

Nattier, Jan. "The Names of Amitabha/Amitayus in Early Chinese Buddhist Translations (1)." *Annual Report of the International Research Institute for Advanced Buddhology* 9 (2006): 183–199.

Nattier, Jan. "Who Is a Buddhist? Charting the Landscape of Buddhist America." In *The Faces of Buddhism in America*, edited by Charles S. Prebish and Kenneth Tanaka, 183–195. Berkeley: University of California Press, 1998.

Nishimura, Arthur. "The Buddhist Mission of North America 1898–1942: Religion and Its Social Function in an Ethnic Community." In *North American Buddhists in Social Context*, edited by Paul David Numrich, 87–106. Boston: Brill, 2008.

Noguchi, Ayako. "Where the Heart Belongs." *Berkeley Bussei*, Fall 1941, n.p.

Numata, Yehan. "Editorial." *The Pacific World* 1, no. 1 (1925): 24–25.

Numrich, Paul David. *Old Wisdom in the New World: Americanization in Two Immigrant Theravada Buddhist Temples*. Knoxville: University of Tennessee Press, 1996.

Numrich, Paul David. "Two Buddhisms Further Considered." *Contemporary Buddhism* 4, no. 1 (2003): 55–78.

Omi, Michael, and Howard Winant. *Racial Formation in the United States*. 3rd ed. Routledge: New York, 2014.

Otani, Kosho. "Buddhism and Life." *Berkeley Bussei*, 1956, 23.

Otani, Sonyu. "Mahayana Buddhism and Japanese Civilization." *The Pacific World* 2, no. 1 (1926): 3, 24–26.

Palumbo-Liu, David. *Asian/American: Historical Crossings of a Racial Frontier*. Stanford, CA: Stanford University Press, 1999.

Payne, Richard K. "Afterword: Buddhism Beyond Borders: Beyond the Rhetorics of Rupture." In *Buddhism Beyond Borders*, edited by Scott A. Mitchell and Natalie E. F. Quli, 217–239. Albany: State University of New York Press, 2015.

Payne, Richard K. "How Not to Talk About Pure Land Buddhism: A Critique of Huston Smith's (Mis)Representations." In *Path of No Path: Contemporary Studies on Pure Land Buddhism Honoring Roger Corless*, edited by Richard K. Payne, 147–172. Berkeley: Numata Center for Buddhist Translation and Research, 2009.

Payne, Richard K., ed. *Re-Visioning "Kamakura" Buddhism*. Honolulu: University of Hawai'i Press, 1998.

Payne, Richard K., ed. *Secularizing Buddhism: New Perspectives on a Dynamic Tradition*. Boulder: Shambhala, 2021.

Pearlman, Ellen. "My Lunch with Mihoko." In *American Buddhism as a Way of Life*, edited by Gary Storhoff and John Whalen-Bridge, 57–66. Albany: State University of New York Press, 2010.

Petersen, William. "Success Story, Japanese-American Style." *New York Times*, January 9, 1966. https://www.nytimes.com/1966/01/09/archives/success-story-japaneseameri can-style-success-story-japaneseamerican.html.

Pierce, Lori. "Buddhist Modernism in English-Language Buddhist Periodicals." In *Issei Buddhism in the Americas*, edited by Duncan Ryûken Williams and Tomoe Moriya, 87–109. Urbana: University of Illinois Press, 2010.

Pierce, Lori. "Constructing American Buddhisms: Discourse of Race and Religion in Territorial Hawai'i." PhD diss., University of Hawai'i, 2000.

Pierce, Lori, Paul Spickard, and David Yoo. "Japanese and Korean Migrations: Buddhist and Christian Communities in America, 1885–1945." In *Immigration and Religion in America: Comparative and Historical Perspectives*, edited by Richard D. Alba, Albert J. Raboteau, and Josh DeWind, 106–134. New York: New York University Press, 2009.

Pratt, S. N. "Buddhism in Daily Life." *Berkeley Bussei*, 1950, 6, 16.

Pratt, S. N. "What Did Lord Buddha Teach?" *Berkeley Bussei*, Fall 1939, n.p.

Prebish, Charles S. *Luminous Passage: The Practice and Study of Buddhism in America*. Berkeley: University of California Press, 1999.

Prebish, Charles S. "Two Buddhisms Reconsidered." *Buddhist Studies Review* 10, no. 2 (1993): 187–206.

Prebish, Charles S., and Damien Keown. *Introducing Buddhism*. 2nd ed. London: Routledge, 2010.

Proffitt, Aaron. "Taking the Vajrayana to Sukhāvatī." In *Methods in Buddhist Studies: Essays in Honor of Richard K. Payne*, edited by Scott A. Mitchell and Natalie Fisk Quli, 54–64. London: Bloomsbury Press, 2019.

Proffitt, Aaron. *Esoteric Pure Land Buddhism*. Honolulu: University of Hawai'i Press, 2023.

Prothero, Stephen R. "Introduction." In *Big Sky Mind: Buddhism and the Beat Generation*, edited by Carole Tonkinson, 1–20. New York: Riverhead Books, 1995.

Prothero, Stephen R. *The White Buddhist: The Asian Odyssey of Henry Steel Olcott*. Bloomington: Indiana University Press, 1996.

Quli, Natalie. "Multiple Buddhist Modernisms: Jhāna in Convert Theravāda." *Pacific World: Journal of the Institute of Buddhist Studies* 10, no. 1 (2008): 225–249.

Quli, Natalie E. "Western Self, Asian Other: Modernity, Authenticity, and Nostalgia for 'Tradition' in Buddhist Studies." *Journal of Buddhist Ethics* 16 (2009): 1–38.

Quli, Natalie E. F., and Scott A. Mitchell. "Buddhist Modernism as Narrative: A Comparative Study of Jodo Shinshu and Zen." In *Buddhism Beyond Borders*, edited by Scott A. Mitchell and Natalie E. F. Quli, 197–215. Albany: State University of New York Press, 2015.

Quli, Natalie Fisk. "A Brief Critical Appraisal of the Buddhist Modernism Paradigm." In *The Routledge Handbook of Buddhist-Christian Studies*, edited by Carol S. Anderson and Thomas Cattoi, 353–363. London and New York: Routledge, 2023.

"Religious Section: Introduction." *Berkeley Bussei*, 1951, 5.

Ritzinger, Justin. "Tinker, Tailor, Scholar, Spy: Holmes Welch, Buddhism, and the Cold War." *Journal of Global Buddhism* 22, no. 2 (2021): 421–441.

Robinson, Richard H., and Willard L. Johnson. *The Buddhist Religion: A Historical Introduction.* 3rd ed. Belmont, CA: Wadsworth, 1997.

Rogers, Minor L., and Ann T. Rogers. "The Honganji: Guardian of the State (1868–1945)." *Japanese Journal of Religious Studies* 71, no. 1 (1990): 3–28.

Rogers, Minor, and Ann Rogers. *Rennyo: The Second Founder of Shin Buddhism: With a Translation of His Letters.* Vol. 3. Nanzan Studies in Asian Religions. Berkeley: Asian Humanities Press, 1991.

Roxworthy, Emily. *The Spectacle of Japanese American Trauma: Racial Performativity and World War II.* Honolulu: University of Hawai'i Press, 2008.

Sakoda, James. "Betrayed: Pschoanalysis of a Nisei." *Berkeley Bussei,* Spring 1941, n.p.

Sakoda, James. "Nisei Personality Adjustment." *Berkeley Bussei,* Fall 1941, n.p.

Seager, Richard Hughes. *Buddhism in America.* New York: Columbia University Press, 1999.

Sharf, Robert H. "On Pure Land Buddhism and Ch'an/Pure Land Syncretism in Medieval China." *T'oung Pao* (2nd ser.) 88, fasc. 4/5 (2002): 282–331.

Sharf, Robert H. "The Zen of Japanese Nationalism." In *Curators of the Buddha: The Study of Buddhism Under Colonialism,* edited by Donald S. Lopez, 107–160. Chicago: University of Chicago Press, 1995.

Shibutani, Tamotsu. *The Derelicts of Company K: A Sociological Study of Demoralization.* Berkeley: University of California Press, 1978.

Shibutani, Tamotsu. "A Preface to Reflection." *Berkeley Bussei,* Fall 1941, n.p.

Shibutani, Tamotsu. "Retreat from Shangri-La." *Berkeley Bussei,* Spring 1941, n.p.

Shinran. *The Collected Works of Shinran.* Edited by Dennis Hirota. Shin Buddhism Translation Series. Kyoto: Jōdo Shinshū Hongwangji-ha, 1997.

Shohara, Sei. "The Crisis." *Berkeley Bussei,* 1951, 15, 18.

Shohara, Sei. "Science and Buddhism." *Berkeley Bussei,* 1955, 23–24.

Simpson, Caroline Chung. *An Absent Presence: Japanese Americans in Postwar American Culture, 1945–1960.* Durham, NC: Duke University Press, 2001.

Sloniowski, Lisa. "Affective Labor, Resistance, and the Academic Librarian." *Library Trends* 64, no. 4 (2016): 645–666.

Smelser, Neil. "Psychological Trauma and Cultural Trauma." In *Cultural Trauma and Collective Identity,* edited by Jeffrey C Alexander, 31–59. Berkeley: University of California Press, 2010.

Smith, David L. "The Authenticity of Alan Watts." In *American Buddhism as a Way of Life,* edited by Gary Storhoff and John Whalen-Bridge, 13–38. Albany: State University of New York Press, 2010.

Snodgrass, Judith. "Buddha No Fukin: The Deployment of Paul Carus' Gospel of Buddha in Meiji Japan." *Japanese Journal of Religious Studies* 25 (1998): 319–344.

Snodgrass, Judith. *Presenting Japanese Buddhism to the West: Orientalism, Occidentalism, and the Columbian Exposition.* Chapel Hill: University of North Carolina Press, 2003.

Snyder, Gary. *Mountains and Rivers Without End.* New York: Counterpoint, 1996.

Snyder, Gary, and David Stephen Calonne. *Conversations with Gary Snyder.* Jackson: University Press of Mississippi, 2017.

Spencer, Anne C. "Diversification in the Buddhist Churches of America: Demographic Trends and Their Implications for the Future Study of US Buddhist Groups." *Journal of Global Buddhism* 15 (2014): 35–61.

Starling, Jessica. *Guardians of the Buddha's Home: Domestic Religion in Contemporary Jōdo Shinshū*. Honolulu: University of Hawai'i Press, 2019.

Stone, Jacqueline I. "Seeking Enlightenment in the Last Age: Mappō Thought in Kamakura Buddhism." *The Eastern Buddhist* (n.s.) 18, no. 1 (1985): 28–56.

Stone, Jacqueline I. "By the Power of One's Last Nenbutsu: Deathbed Practices in Early Modern Japan." In *Approaching the Land of Bliss: Religious Praxis in the Cult of Amitābha*, edited by Richard K. Payne and Kenneth K. Tanaka, 77–119. Kuroda Institute Studies in East Asian Buddhism, No. 17. Honolulu: University of Hawai'i Press, 2004.

Sugihara, James. "You Are on Trial." *Berkeley Bussei*, Fall 1939, n.p.

Sugihara, Jim. "A Message." *Berkeley Bussei*, Spring 1942, n.p.

Suh, Sharon A. *Being Buddhist in a Christian World: Gender and Community in a Korean American Temple*. American Ethnic and Cultural Studies. Seattle: University of Washington Press, 2004.

Suh, Sharon A. "'We Interrupt Your Regularly Scheduled Programming to Bring You This Very Important Public Service Announcement': aka Buddhism as Usual in the Academy." In *Buddhism and Whiteness: Critical Reflections*, edited by George Yancy and Emily McRae, 1–20. Lanham, MD: Lexington Books, 2019.

Suzuki, Daisetz Teitaro. *Buddha of Infinite Light: The Teachings of Shin Buddhism, the Japanese Way of Wisdom and Compassion*. Boston: Shambhala, 2002.

Suzuki, Daisetz Teitaro. *Shin Buddhism*. London: George Allen & Unwin, 1970.

Suzuki, Daisetz Teitaro. "The Spirit of Shinran." In *Selected Works of D. T. Suzuki*, edited by James C. Dobbins and Richard M. Jaffe, Vol. 2, 236–240. Berkeley: University of California Press, 2015.

Tada, Tokan. "Religious Education." *Berkeley Bussei*, 1953, 7.

Takemoto, Art. "Dilemma." *Berkeley Bussei*, 1953, 12, 16.

Takemoto, Art. "From Art Takemoto." *Berkeley Bussei*, 1952, 17.

Tanaka, Kenneth K. "Issues of Ethnicity in the Buddhist Churches of America." In *American Buddhism: Methods and Findings in Recent Scholarship*, edited by Duncan Ryûken Williams and Christopher S. Queen, 3–19. Richmond, Surrey: Curzon, 1999.

Tang, Edward. "From Internment to Containment: Cold War Imaginings of Japanese Americans in Go for Broke." *Columbia Journal of American Studies* 9 (2009): 84–112.

Tani, Tad. "Buddhist and Why." *Berkeley Bussei*, Fall 1941, n.p.

Terakawa, H. T. "Sayings of Rennyo-Shonin." *Berkeley Bussei*, Fall 1939, n.p.

Thomas, Jolyon Baraka. "The Buddhist Virtues of Raging Lust and Crass Materialism in Contemporary Japan." *Material Religion* 11, no. 4 (2015): 485–506.

Thomas, Jolyon Baraka. *Faking Liberties: Religious Freedom in American-Occupied Japan*. Chicago: University of Chicago Press, 2019.

Thompson, Evan. *Why I Am Not a Buddhist*. New Haven, CT: Yale University Press, 2020.

Tsufura, Hitoshi. "Buddhist Seminar." *Berkeley Bussei*, 1953, 28.

Tuck, Donald R. *Buddhist Churches of America: Jodo Shinshu*. Lewiston, NY: E. Mellen Press, 1987.

Tweed, Thomas A. *The American Encounter with Buddhism, 1844–1912: Victorian Culture and the Limits of Dissent*. Bloomington: Indiana University Press, 1992.

Tweed, Thomas A. *Crossing and Dwelling: A Theory of Religion*. Cambridge, MA: Harvard University Press, 2008.

Tweed, Thomas A. "Theory and Method in the Study of Buddhism: Toward a Translocative Analysis." In *Buddhism Beyond Borders*, edited by Scott A. Mitchell and Natalie E. F. Quli, 3–20. Albany: State University of New York Press, 2015.

Tweed, Thomas A. "Tracing Modernity's Flows: Buddhist Currents in the Pacific World." *The Eastern Buddhist* 43, nos. 1–2 (2012): 35–56.

Tworkov, Helen. "Many Is More." *Tricycle: The Buddhist Review*, Winter 1991. https://tricy cle.org/magazine/many-more/.

Unno, Taitetsu. "Faced with a Dilemma." *Berkeley Bussei*, 1951, 16–17.

Unno, Taitetsu. "A Life of Naturalness." *Berkeley Bussei*, 1954, 15–17.

[Untitled article.] *Berkeley Bussei*, 1955, 30.

Usuki, Patricia Kanaya. *Currents of Change: American Buddhist Women Speak Out on Jodo Shinshu*. Vol. 2. IBS Monograph Series. Berkeley, CA: Institute of Buddhist Studies, 2007.

Vásquez, Manuel A. "The Limits of the Hydrodynamics of Religion." *Journal of the American Academy of Religion* 77, no. 2 (2009): 434–445.

Wakefield, C. F. "A Rational Teaching." *Berkeley Bussei*, 1950, 10–11.

Wakefield, C. J. "Trees." *Berkeley Bussei*, 1952, 9.

Watts, Alan. "Beat Zen, Square Zen, and Zen." *Chicago Review* 12, no. 2 (1958): 3–11.

Watts, Alan. *Become What You Are*. Boston: Shambhala, 2003.

Watts, Alan. "The Problem of Faith and Works in Buddhism." *Review of Religion* 5, no. 4 (1941): 387–402.

Watts, Alan. "The Problem of Faith and Works in Buddhism." In *Become What You Are*, 97–120. Boston: Shambhala, 2003.

Watts, Alan. "A Program for Buddhism in America." *Berkeley Bussei*, 1952, 11, 19–21.

Wayman, Alex, and Hideko Wayman. *The Lion's Roar of Queen Śrīmālā: A Buddhist Scripture on the Tathāgatagarbha Theory*. New York: Columbia University Press, 1974.

Wells, Keiko. "Shin Buddhist Song Lyrics Sung in the United States: Their History and Expressed Buddhist Images (1), 1898–1939." *Tōkyō Daigaku Taiheiyō* 2 (2002): 75–99.

Wells, Keiko. "Shin Buddhist Song Lyrics Sung in the United States: Their History and Expressed Buddhist Images (2), 1936–2001." *Tōkyō Daigaku Taiheiyō* 3 (2003): 41–64.

Whalen-Bridge, John. "Buddhism, the Chinese Religion, and the Ceremony of Writing: An Interview with Maxine Hong Kingston." In *The Emergence of Buddhist American Literature*, edited by Gary Storhoff and John Whalen-Bridge, 177–187. Albany: State University of New York Press, 2009.

Whalen-Bridge, John, and Gary Storhoff. *Buddhism and American Cinema*. Albany: State University of New York Press, 2014.

Whalen-Bridge, John, and Gary Storhoff. *The Emergence of Buddhist American Literature*. Albany: State University of New York Press, 2009.

Williams, Duncan Ryūken. *American Sutra: A Story of Faith and Freedom in the Second World War*. Cambridge, MA: Harvard University Press, 2019.

Williams, Duncan Ryūken. "At Ease in Between: The Middle Position of a Scholar-Practitioner." *Journal of Global Buddhism* 9 (2008): 155–163.

Williams, Duncan Ryūken, and Tomoe Moriya. *Issei Buddhism in the Americas*. Urbana: University of Illinois Press, 2010.

Wilson, Jeff. "'All Beings Are Equally Embraced by Amida Buddha': Jodo Shinshu Buddhism and Same-Sex Marriage in the United States." *Journal of Global Buddhism* 13 (2012): 31–59.

Wilson, Jeff. *Dixie Dharma: Inside a Buddhist Temple in the American South*. Chapel Hill: University of North Carolina Press, 2012.

Wilson, Jeff. *Mindful America: The Mutual Transformation of Buddhist Meditation and American Culture*. New York: Oxford University Press, 2014.

Wilson, Jeff. "Pennies in the Pure Land: Practicing the Dharma, Hanging Out, and Raising Funds for the Oldest Buddhist Temple Outside Asia," *Journal of Global Buddhism* 23, no. 1 (2022): 63–78.

Wilson, Jeff. "Regionalism Within North American Buddhism." In *Buddhism Beyond Borders*, edited by Scott A. Mitchell and Natalie E. F. Quli, 21–33. Albany: State University of New York Press, 2015.

Wilson, Jeff. "What Is Canadian About Canadian Buddhism?" *Religion Compass* 5, no. 9 (2011): 536–548.

Wood, Gene. "Buddhism and Modern Life." *Berkeley Bussei*, Fall 1940, n.p.

Yamagata, Toshio. "Buddhism in the Home." *Berkeley Bussei*, Fall 1939, n.p.

Yasukochi, George. "All This & Discrimination 2." *Berkeley Bussei*, Fall 1941, n.p.

Yogi, Stan. "Literature in Camp." *Densho Encyclopedia*, n.d. https://encyclopedia.densho.org/Literature_in_camp/.

Yonemura, Kimi. "Editorial." *Berkeley Bussei*, 1951, n.p.

Yoo, David. *Growing Up Nisei: Race, Generation, and Culture Among Japanese Americans of California, 1924–49*. Urbana: University of Illinois Press, 2000.

Zuber, Devin. "The Buddha of the North: Swedenborg and Transpacific Zen." *Religion and the Arts* 14, nos. 1–2 (2010): 1–33.

Index

For the benefit of digital users, indexed terms that span two pages (e.g., 52–53) may, on occasion, appear on only one of those pages.